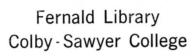

Therapies
for Children

A Handbook
of Effective Treatments
for Problem Behaviors

Charles E. Schaefer
Howard L. Millman

THERAPIES
FOR CHILDREN

 Jossey-Bass Publishers
San Francisco • Washington • London • 1977

THERAPIES FOR CHILDREN
A Handbook of Effective Treatments for Problem Behaviors
by Charles E. Schaefer and Howard L. Millman

Copyright © 1977 by: Jossey-Bass, Inc., Publishers
615 Montgomery Street
San Francisco, California 94111
&
Jossey-Bass Limited
28 Banner Street
London EC1Y 8QE

Library of Congress Catalogue Card Number LC 77-79481

International Standard Book Number ISBN 0-87589-337-6

Manufactured in the United States of America

JACKET DESIGN BY WILLI BAUM

FIRST EDITION

Code 7737

The Jossey-Bass
Behavioral Science Series

Preface

Therapies for Children resulted from our felt need as clinicians, supervisors, and teachers for a practical reference that contained alternative approaches for dealing with frequent childhood behavioral problems. Our search of the literature failed to uncover the type of resource book we wanted—one encompassing specific approaches based on a variety of theoretical positions.

In preparing this handbook, our aim has been to give practitioners both provocative ideas and specific techniques. The wide range of problem behaviors and specific therapeutic approaches covered in this volume may be easily located in the subject index. The article digests represent our attempt to simplify and define often complex, technical language and present useful information in a clear, concise fashion. This presentation, we believe, makes the handbook suitable not only for professionals but also for students and the interested public; for example, parent consumers of therapeutic services might well benefit from knowing available alternatives for children's difficulties.

We have conducted many seminars on child and family therapy for mental health professionals. Frequently, senior clinicians at these seminars seem unaware of clinical practices that have been reported in the last ten years and that are directly relevant to their work with children. Our intent, then, is to provide a source that will maximize therapeutic effectiveness by making it easier to keep abreast of the recent literature on child therapy. Indeed, working on this book immeasurably enhanced our own practices.

We believe that this handbook will be valuable to practitioners in many different areas, including the fields of psychology, social work, counseling, child care, psychiatry, and pediatrics. We also hope that the variety of approaches currently available for the common problems of children will be provocative to those practitioners who adhere to one school of thought and who generally approach childhood problems from that one framework. All readers are encouraged to go to the original sources from which the digests have been abstracted and to read the authors' articles in their entirety; sources for articles are listed at the end of the digests.

Since completing this handbook, we have found it helpful to have copies both in the office and at home. In the office, it provides a quick scan of possible approaches to a specific problem. At home, it can be used to read about innovative techniques and to locate the source of original articles. We trust that other practitioners will find our format and approach as useful as we do.

Permission to digest each article was given by the authors, with the exception of a few cases where the author could not be located. We are grateful for their cooperation. We would also like to thank Daniel Zawel for his help in the early formulation of this book. Finally, Victoria Mc Sweeney provided invaluable assistance during all phases of manuscript development.

Dobbs Ferry, New York   CHARLES E. SCHAEFER
August 1977   HOWARD L. MILLMAN

Contents

xi

Contents

Chapter 2: Habit Disorders   139

Contents

Chapter 3: Antisocial Behaviors   263

The Authors

CHARLES E. SCHAEFER is supervising psychologist at The Children's Village, a residential treatment center for emotionally disturbed children in Dobbs Ferry, New York, and also maintains a private practice for children and their families. In 1967 he received the Ph.D. in clinical psychology from Fordham University, where he remained for another three years conducting research with Anne Anastasi on the identification and development of creative thinking in children and youth.

In addition to numerous psychological tests and articles in professional journals, Charles Schaefer is the author or editor of four books related to children: *Therapeutic Use of Child's Play* (Jason Aronson, 1976); *Developing Creativity in Children* (D.O.K. Publishers, 1973); *Becoming Somebody: Creative Activities for Preschool and Primary Grade Children* (D.O.K. Publishers, 1973); and *Young Voices: An Anthology of Poetry by Children* (Collier-Macmillan, 1971).

Apart from clinical practice, his current professional interest concerns the identification and development of more effective ways for parents and teachers to influence children; that is, better ways for adults to promote the personal and social development of children. His affiliations include the American Orthopsychiatric Association, American Educational Research Association, American Psychological Association, and Psychologists in Private Practice.

Charles Schaefer resides in Yonkers, New York, with his wife Anne and daughter Karine. His avocational pursuits include tennis, swimming, jogging, and reading. He also enjoys writing poetry and painting for his own pleasure.

HOWARD L. MILLMAN received the Ph.D. in clinical psychology from Adelphi University in 1964, after having majored in psychology at the City College of New York. He completed a clinical psychology internship at the Neuropsychiatric Institute at the University of California at Los Angeles, where he first became interested in the effects and treatment of brain dysfunctioning. He later became chief psychologist at the Middlesex County Mental Health Clinic in New Jersey. Currently he is director of Psychological Services and Research at the Children's Village and director of psychology at Psychological and Educational Services of Westchester. He has taught and supervised doctoral psychology students at Rutgers—the State University and at the City College of New York. At present, he teaches courses on interviewing and counseling and group psychodynamics to graduate students at Manhattanville College in Purchase, New York. He is president of the Westchester County Psychological Association and, among other affiliations, is a member of the Council for Exceptional Children and the Division of Psychotherapy of the American Psychological Association.

Howard Millman has published numerous articles in professional journals on psychotherapy, behavior and learning problems in children, brain dysfunction, and research concerning evaluation of programs designed to treat emotionally disturbed children. His training and interest in adolescents and adults resulted in *Goals and Behavior in Psychotherapy and Counseling,* a book widely used in training mental health professionals (with J. T. Huber, Merrill, 1972).

Howard Millman lives in Dobbs Ferry with his wife Judith, a social worker, and his two sons, Jonathan and Joshua. His interests are spending time with friends, meditating, listening to baroque and Indian music, and playing tennis. He is known to frequent wine shops in search of 1961 Bordeaux.

To Anne and Karine Schaefer
and to Judith, Jonathan, and Joshua Millman

Therapies
for Children

A Handbook
of Effective Treatments
for Problem Behaviors

Introduction: Current Trends in Treatment of Children's Behavior Problems

The approach of this book reflects several current trends in child therapy. First, there is a growing emphasis on the prescriptive approach to therapy; that is, given a specific behavior disorder of the child, what specific remedy or therapeutic technique can best be applied? The long-term goal of this approach is to refine therapeutic methods so that one can eventually say what technique is best, given certain child, therapist, and situational variables. Physicians operate in this manner when they write an individualized prescription for a physically sick child. Rather than attempting to force a child into one "all-purpose" therapeutic mold, then, thera-

1

pists are now trying to individualize, to fit the remedies or techniques to the needs of the individual child. Ideally, the prescriptive approach will result in maximum therapeutic effectiveness in the briefest possible time period.

The prescriptive approach has led to a greater interest in the specifics of therapeutic practice, that is, in the concrete application of general principles. Professionals working directly with children want to offer more than a general diagnosis, global approach, or analytical explanation of etiology; they seek to offer a practical approach for alleviating a child's problems. For example, they want to suggest concrete things to do when the child has his next temper tantrum. The state of the art in child therapy has advanced in recent years to the stage that behavior modifiers, nondirective counselors, and others can now give specific "how to's" rather than teaching only process or general goals and principles. Of course, we are far from being an exact science. Clinical judgment and skills based on extensive training and experience are still needed to effectively select and apply the available therapeutic tools and to avoid using them in a standardized or mechanical fashion.

The skillful application of the prescriptive approach involves the development of expertise in a wide variety of therapeutic methods, such as behavioral, cognitive, and dynamic approaches. This means adopting an "eclectic," "pluralistic," or "generalist" position rather than relying on one or two approaches. Concomitant with an increased interest in developing a broad spectrum of clinical skills has been a decreased interest in fostering specialty fields, such as counseling, clinical, and school psychology. Professionals are showing more and more interest in developing clinical skills that cut across disciplines, theories, and specialty fields.[1] Consequently, there seem to be fewer distinctions and more cooperative interplay between the various professional and therapeutic camps.

The thrust toward "prescriptions" or selectively applying different methods reflects the research finding that no one therapeutic approach is equally effective with all types of problems and different types of people. Psychodynamic approaches seem most

---

[1] J. I. Bardon, "The State of the Art (and Science) of School Psychology," *American Psychologist*, 1976, *31*, 785–798.

effective with bright, verbal, highly motivated adults exhibiting neurotic problems, while behavioral techniques have proven particularly successful with phobias and enuresis. A number of disorders, such as delinquent and criminal behaviors, have proven refractory to most forms of intervention.

An eclectic approach to child therapy means using clinical judgment to decide whether to focus on alleviating overt behavior problems; developing cognitive skills; resolving unconscious self-reported or family conflicts; treating organic difficulties; promoting more adaptive, self-enhancing behaviors; or some combination of these objectives. In the past, theoretical biases have led therapists to pursue one of these objectives while, in actuality, other goals may have been equally, or more, important. Clearly, it is important for clinicians to work together and pool their knowledge and skills, because no one discipline has proved sufficient to resolve the complex and diverse behavior disorders exhibited by children.

Freed from the constraints of orthodox adherence to a particular theoretical scheme, clinicians are now *flexibly* applying the methods of diverse approaches. Often the methods that seemed so appealing in theory and proved so successful in laboratory studies turn out to be complete disasters when first applied by the clinician. In the real world, there are simply many more uncontrolled and uncontrollable factors. Thus, the child therapist discovers that the bell-and-pad apparatus does not work because the child either sleeps through the alarm or removes the plug every night before he goes to sleep. Only after more extensive preparations or adaptations does the procedure prove successful in such cases. To be successful in practice, then, clinicians are discovering they need to develop creative problem-solving skills—to become keen observers, flexible thinkers, creative adaptors of methods, and effective collaborators with others, and to become self-confident and persistent in the pursuit of more effective practices.

Recognizing the complex and interrelated nature of human functioning, therapists are frequently combining theories and techniques to effect changes in several dimensions, such as in thoughts, images, and motivation. There seem to be fewer radical behavior therapists or Freudian analysts practicing in an orthodox manner today. Rather, therapists are attempting to integrate methods from such currently popular approaches as social learning theory, general systems theory, and nondirective counseling. Combining methods often increases therapeutic impact by tapping the child's capacity to participate in the experience in a more intense, holistic manner.

In this connection, the psychologist Arnold Lazarus has developed a therapeutic approach—multimodal therapy[2]—that assumes that lasting therapeutic change can only result if the therapist assesses and, where appropriate, alters the following seven different modalities—the behavioral, affective, sensate, imagery, and cognitive modalities—in the context of interpersonal relationships and sometimes, in conjunction with medical professionals, in administering drugs and other medical procedures. Rather than stressing a single panacea, core construct, or critical mode of functioning, the multimodal approach asserts that people experience a multitude of specific problems across the various modalities that can best be treated by a variety of specific techniques. The multimodal approach supplies a framework and rationale for applying technical eclecticism.[3] Rather than generating theory from laboratory knowledge, the multimodal approach organizes inquiry around the problems themselves as experienced in clinical practice. In an inductive, empirical fashion, problems are observed, treatment performed, and judgments made as to what additional approaches and modalities are needed to be effective.

A common finding of psychotherapy research is that little or no generalization of therapeutic success occurs across settings. Thus the progress a child exhibits in the therapist's office frequently dissolves when the child returns to the natural environment. As a result, another emerging trend is for therapists to train significant adults from a child's natural environment to apply therapeutic principles and techniques. Parents, teachers, college students, and others have all been helped to effectively modify children's

[2]A. Lazarus, *Multimodal Behavior Therapy* (New York: Springer, 1976).

[3]Technical eclecticism is discussed in detail by R. L. Woolfolk in his chapter, "The Multimodal Model as a Framework for Decision Making in Psychotherapy," in A. Lazarus, *Multimodal Behavior Therapy* (New York: Springer, 1976).

deviant behaviors that had previously been considered the domain of highly skilled professionals. Typically, these nonprofessionals have little background in psychology and receive relatively little training, so that considerable supervision is required. This trend has important implications for the reduction of treatment costs and the multiplication of therapeutic effectiveness. In a real sense, then, clinicians seem to be actively attempting to "give psychology away" to the general public now in a variety of ways.[4] It is noteworthy that a recent evaluative study[5] found that a training program in which parents were taught to implement a behavioral approach was more effective than conventional treatment strategies employed by a child guidance clinic. The children involved showed less problem behavior after treatment and maintained these gains more over a two-year follow-up period.

In regard to working with parents, there is a greater tendency now for child therapists to see the father's role as particularly important in the socialization of a child. A recent survey of child psychiatrists and psychologists,[6] for example, revealed that half of these therapists reported that they routinely see *both* parents in therapy when a child has a problem. An additional 43 percent of the therapists reported that they generally arrange for some participation by the child's father in the therapeutic process. It seems that both society and child therapists are showing increasing recognition of the impact of *both* parents on a child's psychosocial development.

Another trend is toward preventative and educational models of practice. Rather than waiting until people come seeking help for serious, deeply entrenched problems, child therapists are now reaching out more into the community to teach ways of heading off

[4]B. G. Guerney, Jr. (Ed.), *Psychotherapeutic Agents: New Roles for Non-professionals, Parents, and Teachers* (New York: Holt, Rinehart & Winston, 1969). Also, G. Goodman, *Companionship Therapy* (San Francisco: Jossey-Bass, 1972).

[5]J. D. Barnard, et al. "The Family Training Program: Short- and Long-Term Evaluation." Paper presented at the 84th Annual Convention of the American Psychological Association, Washington, D.C., September 1976.

[6]G. P. Koocher and B. M. Pedulla, "Current Practices in Child Psychotherapy." Paper presented at the 84th Annual Convention of the American Psychological Association, Washington, D.C., September 1976.

or minimizing psychological conflicts. Thus therapists are actively teaching courses on parent effectiveness training, building marital relationships, coping with developmental crises, sex and drug education, assertiveness training, and effective study habits. Psychological growth and inoculation against predictable crises and problems of living are the goals of these efforts. It seems that therapists are broadening their roles and scope so that they are becoming as well versed in ways to promote psychological health and adjustment as in ways to remediate maladjustment. This trend reflects the current emphasis on "outreach" or "community mental health" programs, which seem to comprise at least three basic elements: (1) broadening the client population for whom services are available, (2) providing services in facilities more accessible to clients, and (3) moving away from remedial treatment toward prevention of psychological disorders.[7]

In conclusion, the selection of appropriate treatment techniques is very likely the most crucial of all decisions made by the therapist. It is hoped that this volume will aid such decisions by encouraging an analysis of general complaints into specific components that can be more readily attacked and by helping therapists quickly locate the most effective technique or combination of techniques for relieving a specific behavior disorder. Consistent with an orientation of technical eclecticism, this book stresses the development and refinement of specific, replicable procedures based on clinical practice, rather than emphasizing the role of clinical theory.

Present Handbook as a Reflection of Current Trends. Many of the current trends in child therapy are apparent in this book, particularly the emphasis on practical techniques and eclecticism.

Within the past few decades, a specialized field of child therapy has emerged that contains a significant body of clinical knowledge. Although a number of excellent books are available pertaining to the theoretical and research aspects of psychotherapy, the practice component of child treatment—that is, specific application of clinical knowledge in real-life situations—has received less emphasis. The task of converting theory into practice is both an art and

[7]I. Iscoe and C. D. Spielberger (Eds.), *Community Psychology: Perspectives in Training and Research* (New York: Appleton-Century-Crofts, 1970).

a science, and it is just as important as theoretical formulations and empirical investigations. Because of the large number of variables underlying human behavior, effective clinical practice requires extensive knowledge and development of clinical skills, careful observation and analysis of a problem, creative and flexible application of techniques, and expert clinical judgment based on considerable training and experience.

This book contains a variety of specific practices for dealing with the common behavior problems of children. The focus is on the clinical application of therapeutic principles and techniques to real-life situations. The need for this handbook became most apparent from our experiences in supervising beginning child therapists. While these therapists were generally well-versed in the theories of psychotherapy, they tended to be uncertain when it came to the concrete application of these general theories to the troublesome behavior of children. Our experiences in private practice also convinced us of the need for a comprehensive reference book on child therapy that was oriented more to practice ("how to do it") rather than to theory or research.

Most books on child therapy begin with a broad theoretical orientation and then attempt to relate this theory to specific childhood problems. In contrast, we constructed this book by starting with a list of the common behavior problems of children and then locating specific therapeutic techniques that others have found useful or successful in resolving them. Instead of presenting only one therapeutic technique for a problem, we sought to reflect the current eclectic trend by presenting the reader with at least two or three different approaches to problems. The question we tried to answer was: What do therapists from different orientations actually do and say when working with a child who has a specific problem? By comparing different approaches to a particular disturbance, therapists will be encouraged to become more flexible in their own approaches. The importance of providing alternate approaches is underscored by the growing realization that the field of psychotherapy encompasses a variety of useful treatment practices. It is now apparent that not all approaches or techniques are equally successful in helping children who exhibit a certain type of difficulty.

The number of alternate techniques that this volume offers for particular problems varies considerably, depending on the variety of specific practices reported in the literature. Because some childhood behavior problems have been extensively researched (for example, bedwetting and school phobia), we are able to present a wide number of alternate approaches for these problems. Because of space limitations, we have listed some of these alternate techniques in the annotated bibliographies at the end of each chapter. In general, the practices presented in the bibliographies were judged to be less specific than, or somewhat similar to, the techniques presented in the chapter digests.

The main criteria for selecting practices for this book were *quality* and *specificity*. First, we sought high-quality techniques that are based on sound theoretical and/or research foundations. Thus, we tried to exclude esoteric or highly controversial practices. Second, we looked for specificity—both of technique and of application to a particular disorder. The goal of this approach is to help the practicing clinician locate detailed treatment plans for each of the common childhood disorders. In other words, we want the book to be prescriptive in nature; that is, given a specific problem, what exactly can one do about it? Since a key feature of *learning theory* is its specificity, approaches that systematically apply learning theory principles in an attempt to change maladaptive behavior are over-represented in this book. Included under the learning theory approach are counterconditioning techniques (systematic desensitization, reciprocal inhibition, and other variations of the classical conditioning theme), modeling strategies (use of models who display adaptive behavior to the disturbed child), and operant conditioning (application of positive and/or negative consequences following a child's behavior).

Notwithstanding the larger number of learning theory articles, we sought to provide an eclectic orientation in the book. Accordingly, the reader will find a number of articles based on other major orientations, such as *psychodynamic* and *psychopharmacological* approaches. The essence of psychodynamic therapy is to treat the underlying psychic cause of a problem rather than the overt behavior manifested. The principal forms of dynamic therapy are (1) the child-therapist relationship, (2) working with the family,

(3) spontaneous play with conversation, (4) release and acceptance of fantasy and feelings, and (5) interpretation. Examples of dynamic orientations to child therapy are psychoanalytic, gestalt, family systems, and nondirective play therapy. Psychopharmacological approaches use drugs either to remedy underlying physiological causes of maladaptive behavior or to alter the psychological state of a child in order to facilitate the use of other therapeutic approaches. A basic assumption of this book is that the reader is familiar with both the theoretical and research foundations of the major therapeutic approaches. Basic books by Bergin and Garfield,[8] Patterson,[9] and Meltzoff Kornreich[10] are recommended for those who seek a more detailed understanding of the major system of psychotherapy. See Huber and Millman[11] for a specification of the goals and behavior of various theoretical systems.

An innovative feature of this book is its digest format: The book consists of concise digests or condensations of 133 professional articles. Using a format that presents information in a readily absorbable way, the digests highlight specific therapeutic practices described in the original articles. Each digest begins with a "precis," which is a concise summary of the essential elements in the digest. By eliminating technical research data and lengthy theoretical discussions, the digest format offers the reader more clinically relevant information than would a traditionally structured collection of readings. Accordingly, both professionals and students are provided with a quick, efficient way to locate and evaluate the rapidly growing number of practical techniques in child therapy. In the helping professions, we are witnessing an "information explosion" that requires innovative systems of data storage and retrieval. Most child therapists have an eclectic orientation that presents them with the

[8]A. E. Bergin and S. L. Garfield (Eds.), *Handbook of Psychotherapy and Behavior Change: An Empirical Analysis* (New York: Wiley, 1971).

[9]C. H. Patterson, *Theories of Counseling and Psychotherapy* (New York: Harper & Row, 1966).

[10]J. Meltzoff and M. Kornreich, *Research in Psychotherapy* (New York: Atherton, 1970).

[11]J. T. Huber and H. L. Millman (Eds.), *Goals and Behavior in Psychotherapy and Counseling* (Columbus, Ohio: Merrill, 1972).

Herculean task of keeping current with the latest developments in a wide variety of therapy systems. Hopefully, by facilitating a review of available practices, this book will have heuristic value and lead to creative adaptations and new approaches.

The selections in this handbook have been drawn from a wide number of journals and books, as well as from papers recently presented at scientific and professional meetings. For this reason, very few of our intended readers will have easy access to more than a small sample of these works. By bringing together this widely dispersed material, we hope to enable the reader to quickly identify an appropriate method for a particular childhood problem. Once a promising approach has been located, the therapist should then refer to the original article for a complete description of the technique and its application. In order to judge realistically the efficacy and suitability of a technique, it is essential to read the original article in its entirety. Failure to read an original article before using a technique means that you will be relying on incomplete material taken out of context; this may result in inefficient or harmful clinical practice. In brief, the digests are intended to help you locate the journal articles you need, not substitute for them.

Charles Schaefer and Howard Millman wrote all the digests in this book. In writing the digests, our focus was to give a succinct but clear description of techniques by condensing, paraphrasing, and summarizing the clinical methods employed in the original articles. In the brief commentaries at the end of the digests, we have tried to highlight indications and contraindications for using the techniques rather than to present a critical review. To supplement the digests, an annotated list of additional readings is presented at the end of each section on a behavior disorder to help readers broaden their knowledge of the therapeutic approaches that others have found successful.

A word of caution about the techniques described in this volume. Some of the procedures are based on extensive empirical validation, while others appear promising but were successful with only a limited number of cases. Some of the methods have been rigorously conceived from well-established theories, while others have little (or no) theoretical basis. Obviously, then, a number of the techniques described in this book should be viewed with caution and with full recognition of the need for more extensive and independent replications.

The therapeutic practices presented in this book are organized around the common behavior problems exhibited by children, primarily during the middle childhood years. Thus, each chapter is devoted to techniques for treating one of the six broad types of disturbances typical of this period, namely, neurotic disorders, habit disorders, antisocial behaviors, hyperkinetic behaviors, disturbed relationships with other children, and disturbed relations with parents. A continuing problem for child therapists is the lack of a reliable and valid classification system for childhood disorders. The particular classification system used in this book is based on the factor-analytic research of Alderton.[12, 13] This research was selected for several reasons. First, it is one of the more comprehensive classification systems currently available, including over thirty separate categories of maladaptive behavior, such as fire setting and encopresis. These specific behaviors are further clustered into the six broad categories previously mentioned. Apart from its specificity and comprehensiveness, another feature of this system is the fact that it gives as much weight to disturbed social interactions (such as maladaptive peer, sibling, and parental relationships) as it does to personality problems (such as neurotic behaviors). Other advantages are that it is expressly designed for children and emphasizes concrete, observable behaviors.

The focus of this particular classification system is on parent-reported behavior problems that are of moderate rather than severe intensity. Beyond the scope of this book are behavior problems related to autism, childhood psychosis, mental retardation, psychosomatic disorders, speech (such as stuttering), and overt organic problems, such as focal brain lesions and epilepsy. However, some of the digests and additional readings used pertain to children

[12] H. R. Alderton and B. A. Hoddinott, "The Children's Pathology Index," *Canadian Psychiatric Association Journal*, 1968, *13*, 353–361.

[13] H. R. Alderton, "*The Children's Pathology Index* as a Predictor of Follow-Up Adjustment," *Canadian Psychiatric Association Journal*, 1970, *15*, 289–294.

with these disorders or to somewhat younger or older children than our target population. These articles were included because the techniques employed were deemed applicable to the behavior disorders covered in this book.

To maximize the useability of this handbook, we have included two indexes at the end of the book: author and subject. The *Author Index* lists authors of the original articles as well as authors of all other references cited. In the *Subject Index* we have attempted to provide a comprehensive cross-referencing system to both problems and treatment modes.

1

Neurotic Behaviors

According to Kutash, neuroses "include a large variety of heterogeneous clinical manifestations and syndromes of psychogenic origin, which usually have four elements in common: (1) anxiety, which may be overt and expressed more directly, or covert and hidden, in which case it is controlled unconsciously, in part or full, by psychological defense mechanisms; (2) conflict between unconscious and conscious motivations or between contradictory desires, needs, or drives that are either unresolved or poorly resolved; (3) symptoms that result in unhappiness, inefficiency, problems in interpersonal relationships, or illness; and (4) a character structure or reaction pattern, including character defenses which have become part of the individual's neurotic life-style" (S. B. Kutash, "Psychoneuroses," in B. B. Wolman, Ed., *Handbook of Clinical Psychology,* New York: McGraw-Hill, 1965, p. 949). This broad definition covers the various disorders described in this chapter.

In neuroses, as in other childhood problems, we are using relatively traditional categories; disagreement with the classification system, however, would not preclude a practitioner from appropriately using the therapeutic practices described in this chapter. This chapter covers such neurotic behaviors as nightmares, obsessive-compulsive behavior, hysterical behavior, depression, shy withdrawn behavior, school phobias, childhood fears, and reactions to trauma.

It soon becomes clear to the reader that although successful techniques are clearly described, the *essential* ingredient in successful change of neurotic behaviors is very difficult or impossible to pinpoint. For example, Handler's article (1972) describes a simple, quick, and efficient method that enables a therapist to eliminate disturbing nightmares in children. One might reasonably argue that it is the relationship between child and therapist that is essential, the implosive therapy technique used, both (as Handler claims), or some other unspecified aspect of the process. From a learning theory point of view, another explanation may be even more parsimonious—for example, modeling by the brave, unafraid therapist might be the successful component. Smith and Sharpe (1970) states that implosive therapy alone is a rapid, effective way of treating school phobias, while Hersen (1968) uses both implosive therapy and parental reinforcement. It is clear that the present state of research prevents a definitive answer as to what is most effective in changing neurotic behaviors. Therefore, we do not argue that behavioral approaches are better than psychodynamic approaches to help a child with obsessive-compulsive behavior or a school phobia. We present a variety of practices that other clinicians have found effective in altering specific neurotic behavior of children.

Recently, much public pressure has been placed on the therapist to respect and effectively reach the *client's* goals (see J. T. Huber and H. L. Millman, *Goals and Behavior in Psychotherapy and Coun-*

seling, Columbus, Ohio: Merrill, 1972). When a child displays debilitating obsessive-compulsive behavior or a school phobia that prevents school attendance, the child and/or his parents usually want the quickest possible remedy that will prove effective. It is therefore not sufficient for a therapist to use a favorite approach that does not change the problem behavior or that takes years to be effective. Moreover, a therapist who primarily relies on a relationship orientation, for example, may find methods deriving from other theoretical orientations (such as implosive therapy) extremely helpful in diminishing problem behavior.

Child therapy goals may seem unclear when the child desires to be left alone and the parents and school personnel wish a change to take place in the child. In these cases the adults are the clients who are aided in changing some aspect of the child's behavior (example—return to school). Consumer satisfaction is therefore reached when the clients' goals are attained (the child attends school). In situations where the child perceives himself as unhappy, anxious, or sad, amelioration of his problems (not the adult's wishes) leads to his own satisfaction as a consumer of a service.

It is also a fact that many of the behaviors discussed might diminish over a long period of time, even without intervention. We do say that change must occur in a reasonable and clearly specified period of time. Psychodynamic therapists such as Adams (1973) claim that obsessive children require approximately two years of treatment for basic change. A current trend is for the therapist to negotiate a contract with a family, spelling out goals and a time limit. In this chapter, for example, brief eclectic psychotherapy consisting of a maximum of eight sessions is advocated by Rosenthal and Levine (1971). The movement toward more exact measurement of change, toward satisfying the client's goals, and toward delivery of results within a specified time period has been given impetus by therapists using behavioral approaches.

Arguments continue about "removing" symptoms without changing basic personality and about the possibility of "symptom substitution." The reader will note many of the articles here summarized specifically report that symptom substitution did not occur. For example, school phobias and nightmares once eliminated very often do not return. However, if problem behaviors do return the experience clearly has been that brief intervention (often a reinstitution of the previous method) is successful.

Therapists today need to be familiar with many techniques and be able to use them in a flexible manner. For example, the fearful children (fear of dogs, dark, and going to school) described by Lazarus and Abramovitz (1962) were rapidly desensitized by the use of the anxiety-inhibiting response of "emotional imagery." Another psychotherapist (Kissel, 1972) suggests that desensitization may successfully occur by using the anxiety inhibition that comes from an interpersonal relationship—the fear dissipates because of repeated exposure in the absence of reinforcement. Recent trends in using effective multiple procedures are exemplified by Keat's (1972) treatment of withdrawn behavior by "broad-spectrum behavior therapy," including establishment of a positive relationship, assertive training, behavioral rehearsal, relaxation, motor coordination training, cognitive restructuring, and training the parents as behavioral managers.

Successful reduction of neurotic behaviors is usually a clear goal since the behaviors are problematic to both child and adults around him. The methods described can always take place in the context of an open discussion with the child and his family regarding the "better" way of behaving. The therapist can ask a family if all agree that certain behaviors should be changed. Often, agreement is reached. However, the therapist may state clearly that there are more satisfying alternative ways of feeling and acting. The shy, withdrawn child can be happier and more fun to be with if he feels safer and more able to communicate freely. Traumas to a child can be handled by the child and his family in a relatively calm, effective manner. Neurotic behavior can and should be replaced by adaptable and satisfying behavior.

Nightmares

A nightmare may be defined as a frightening dream accompanied by a feeling of oppression, helplessness, or suffocation that usually awakens the child. An extreme form of nightmare is night terror (pavor nocturnus), after which the child has difficulty reorienting to reality. Nightmares, which are categorized as neurotic behavior, are to be distinguished from other sleep disturbances, which are considered habit disorders. As in any behavioral disorder, a medical evaluation for a possible organic basis is in order. With nightmares, a thorough medical examination is essential to rule out unusual thyroid and electroencephalogram behavior, or other physiological irregularities. (Also see section on Sleep Disturbance*).*

The Use of a Relationship and Implosive Therapy in Ameliorating Nightmares

AUTHOR: Leonard Handler

PRECIS: Diminishing anxiety by having the child imagine bravely confronting fearful situations

INTRODUCTION: This paper presents a case study designed to illustrate the integration of two seemingly diverse approaches: relationship therapy and implosive therapy. The patient, an eleven-year-old boy diagnosed as emotionally disturbed and minimally brain damaged, had been seen by Handler, the therapist, in individual treatment for a year prior to the incident described in the article. During the course of treatment, the boy had often displayed feelings of liking and affection for the therapist.

Although the boy did not mention it himself, his mother complained to Handler that he had been having severe nightmares for about a year and a half. At least two or three times a week, he would wake up in a panic and insist on being comforted in his parents' bed. On close questioning by Handler, the boy admitted having "bad dreams" that scared him: a monster in these dreams chased him and sometimes caught and hurt him.

USE OF IMPLOSIVE IMAGERY: The implosive or confrontation therapy consisted of the following procedure. While holding the boy in his lap, Handler asked him to close his eyes and imagine that the monster was present in the room. The boy was assured that Handler would protect him and help him get rid of the monster. When the child reported visualizing the monster, Handler held him more securely, pounded the metal desk, and yelled repeatedly, "Get out of here, you lousy monster, leave my friend John alone." Later Handler added the following admonition: "Get away and stay away—don't you ever come back or I'm going to get you! You leave my friend John alone." Although the boy reported that the monster was no longer present after these "incantations," Handler again repeated the procedure, alternately demanding "Get away and leave me alone!" as if he was the child, with his own commands and urging the child to join in the pounding and shouting once he had again pictured the monster. Quickly forgetting his initial timidity, the child vigorously participated in this activity. This procedure was repeated for a final time with the room lights turned off. At the completion of this ten- to fifteen-minute rehearsal, Handler once more repeated the directions for "chasing" the monster.

When asked in the next session if he had seen the monster, the boy calmly stated that he had, but that he had "yelled at him" and that the monster soon went away. Handler then spent another five to ten minutes practicing this procedure with the child for the last time. Six months later the boy's mother reported that the nightmares had diminished markedly since this procedure had been initiated and that she had not had any difficulty with the child in this regard since that time.

COMMENTARY: This article illustrates the almost instantaneous effectiveness of a simple fantasy technique once a close relationship has been established with the child. The basic trust and liking that the child had for the therapist in this article was apparently strong enough to help him overcome his fear of imaginary dangers. To fully utilize a therapist's powers of suggestion and persuasion and for expectancy (the Pygmalion effect) to be most influential, a close affectionate bond with the child must be established. Since this article was first written, Handler reports that he used the technique on two other occasions. In each case, the same dramatic behavior change occurred in the child. The use of implosive imagery within a relationship appears quite applicable to other behavior problems, particularly to focused fear, anxiety, or anger. However, Handler employed this technique in a manner that appears to differ from those who use a more dramatic "flooding" technique. (See "Treating a Noise Phobia by Flooding").

SOURCE: Handler, L. "The Amelioration of Nightmares in Children." *Psychotherapy: Theory, Research and Practice,* 1972, *9,* 54–56.

Night Terrors

AUTHOR: Paul R. Keith

PRECIS: Psychotherapy and/or drugs for night terrors (distinguished from anxiety dreams)

INTRODUCTION: Night terrors (*pavor nocturnus*) can dramatically interrupt children's sleep, usually in the first third of a night's sleep. The child begins to show violent bodily activity and physiological activation. Pulse rate nearly doubles, accompanied by rapid irregular breathing, dilated pupils, and often sweating. Crying and screaming usually occur, with a fearful facial expression. The sleeper often speaks in a confused manner and may walk around doing bizarre or nonpurposeful acts. Holding, comforting, or trying to arouse the child does not work. Episodes last up to twenty minutes and may occur several times in one night. There is total amnesia in the morning.

Keith (p. 479) distinguishes night terrors from anxiety dreams (bad dreams, common nightmares), as shown in the following chart.

	Night Terrors	*Anxiety Dreams*
EEG Characteristics	Occurs in Stage 4 sleep with arousal to an awake (alpha) pattern. Seventy percent are in the first non-REM period of the night.	Occurs during REM sleep; no particular time of the night.
Physiological Characteristics	Rapid changes, pulse usually over 108, rapid breathing, intense autonomic activity (sweating, and so forth).	Gradual increase in pulse, usually into 90s; little autonomic activation.
Motility	Great activity (thrashing, sitting up) and often somnambulism.	Lesser movement, no somnambulism, decreased muscle tone.
Verbalizations	Almost always present at onset and usually during episode, may include screaming.	May be present, but subdued.
Mental Content	Single, overwhelming feeling or memory. Elaborate dream in only 10 percent. Violently aggressive, terrifying content.	Elaborate, vivid, longer duration. Less anxiety, more disguised dynamics.

	Night Terrors	*Anxiety Dreams*
Mental State if Awakened	Confused, disoriented, unresponsive, hard to calm, usually amnesic.	Lucid very quickly, can be calmed, clear recall.

THEORIES OF ETIOLOGY: Keith notes that anxiety dreams in children are thought to be caused by repression of intense sexual and aggressive impulses related to oedipal conflicts. Night terrors have been described as "catatonoid reactions," where rising anxiety during sleep is not discharged. The body does not maintain physiological equilibrium. Paralysis of motility occurs followed by an extraordinarily large response. Another theory, says Keith, is that an abnormal pattern of arousal from deep sleep to wakefulness is triggered by a marked lowering of psychological defenses. Abnormally great physiological changes occur, which the person may interpret as anxiety or terror. Finally, Keith notes that elaborate mental content may be a product rather than a cause of physiological changes.

THERAPY: Keith feels that if night terrors are based on normal developmental conflicts, therapy is not necessary. The intensity and frequency of such episodes are mild to moderate and are only of a few months' duration. The frequency of such episodes decreases obviously after onset. In some cases, a clear source of excessive conflict may be identified (for example, when a child is sleeping in the parents' bedroom). Simple intervention can end the problem.

When night terrors are frequent (three to four times a week for months) and do not decrease, Keith believes that serious pathology is indicated. Neurotic daytime symptoms are usually present, and more family problems exist. Psychotherapy for the child and parents is warranted for such situations. Drug therapy may be an additional aid. In one study cited by Keith, children responded well to imipramine and showed no symptom substitution. Some success was also reported with diazepam.

COMMENTARY: This article helps therapists distinguish between night terrors and anxiety dreams. Normal developmental night terrors need not be treated. Drug therapy may be an aid when severe night terrors are identified. Keith does not describe the specifics of psychotherapy, the implication being that traditional psychotherapy is indicated. The consensus of references used by Keith is that oedipal and aggressive fantasies often trigger night terrors. Individual or family therapy might then be employed. Behavioral approaches are not discussed by Keith, but we may add that some therapists might employ desensitization or deconditioning procedures to alleviate night terrors.

SOURCE: Keith, P. R. "Night Terrors: A Review of the Psychology, Neurophysiology, and Therapy." *Journal of Child Psychiatry,* 1975, *14,* 477–489.

Brief Psychotherapy for Nightmares

AUTHORS: Alan J. Rosenthal and Saul V. Levine

PRECIS: Brief psychotherapy, including behavioral observations, reflections of feelings, interpretations, advice giving, and reassurance in treating nightmares

INTRODUCTION: Brief psychotherapy is defined as a maximum of eight hours of patient and/or family contacts within a maximum period of ten calendar weeks. This type of intervention has been widely accepted with adults but has not gained the same recognition with children. Rosenthal and Levine report successful results in a follow-up study of thirty-one children.

THERAPEUTIC METHODS: At the initial interview, the number of sessions to be held is discussed with the child and his family. The therapist explains that the family is to be actively involved in the treatment process. Family members are encouraged to discuss relevant treatment topics while at home, to consciously strive for behavior change in themselves, and to discuss the progress at the next session.

Since there is little time to work with a family, it becomes the responsibility of the therapist to develop a very rapid and well-focused case formulation, accomplished during the initial interview. The therapist develops goals based on this formulation to alleviate the presenting problems as well as to confront the underlying psychopathology. The family is informed of the focus and goals and members' cooperation is enlisted.

Rosenthal and Levine feel that the establishment of a positive working relationship is essential in brief psychotherapy. A cooperative therapeutic alliance must be elicited quickly. They found that positive transference was facilitated by sharing the case formulation and goals with the family.

The issue of ending therapy after a maximum of eight sessions is discussed at the initial session. For many patients, the loss of a love object is part of the therapeutic problem and therefore the ending of therapy is interwoven into many of the sessions as a reality issue as well as being representative of a previous significant loss.

Brief psychotherapy requires a high degree of activity as well as of directiveness. Interventions on the part of the therapist take the form of behavioral observations, reflections, and interpretations as well as of advice giving and reassurance. Additionally, the therapist focuses on the strengths of the child and family and tries to utilize these strengths in overcoming the problem.

CASE STUDY: Carrie was a ten-year-old child who had lived with her natural mother after her parents were divorced when she was four years of age. Her natural father had remarried and Carrie recently started to live with his family after the court ruled that her natural mother was "unfit." Her presenting problem included insomnia, nightmares, and poor peer relations.

The primary treatment goals included helping Carrie to recognize her ambivalence concerning her natural mother, to help foster a more adequate current home adjustment, to develop more effective communication and consistent parenting, and to sensitize the family to Carrie's feelings and their relationship to the presenting problems.

After an initial clinic visit, Carrie was seen for a total of three and a half hours and her parents were seen for an equal amount of time. The therapist actively offered comments and observations directed specifically to help her parents cope with the present problems and those that might arise. The therapist pointed out to Carrie how difficult it was to talk about "very deep feelings" and was generally comforting and supportive. He mentioned that it was very difficult to live in a new household after having lived with her mother for a long period of time. Carrie responded quite positively to his comments. She did not accept all of the suggestions; however, at the end of the eight weeks improvement was noted in her sleeping and in her school performance. However, no significant improvement in peer relations was noted. A one-year follow-up showed improvement in all problems as well as better communication and support from her parents.

COMMENTARY: This study combines varied approaches with specific goal setting in the context of a time limitation. Rosenthal and Levine refer to their own experimental and control groups, reporting success with brief therapy (76 percent showing marked improvement at a one-year follow-up). Other evidence supports their report of the general efficacy of brief psychotherapy (see H. H. Barten and S. S. Barten, eds., *Children and Their Parents in Brief Therapy,* New York: Human Sciences Press, 1972). A rationale for brief therapy is presented and case studies are used as illustrations. It is implied that a knowledgeable, flexible therapist is necessary. As in many case studies, interventions are not specified. For example, we do not know what comments the therapist made to help the parents cope with the present problems and those that might arise. Moreover, the issue of which variables actually make brief therapy successful is not faced: Is specific goal setting the crucial element? Is it the setting of a time limit that mobilizes concentrated effort?

SOURCE: Rosenthal, A. J., and Levine, S. V. "Brief Psychotherapy with Children: Process of Therapy." *American Journal of Psychiatry,* 1971, *128,* 141–146.

Additional Readings

Geer, J. H., and Silverman, I. "Treatment of a Recurrent Nightmare by Behavior Modification Procedures." *Journal of Abnormal Psychology,* 1967, *72,* 188–190.

A twenty-two-year-old male was successfully treated for a recurring nightmare of being threatened by a shadowy figure. While relaxing, he was told to visualize various stages of the nightmare. When visualization produced anxiety, he said "it's only a dream."

Rangell, L. "A Treatment of Nightmares in a Seven-Year-Old Boy." *The Psychoanalytic Study of the Child,* 1950, *5,* 358–390.

Psychoanalytic theory was used by a father to treat his son for nightmares. Guidance was provided by an analyst by mail. Verbatim interaction is presented, with an accompanying explanation. Implications for child rearing are discussed.

Silverman, I., and Geer, J. H. "The Elimination of a Recurrent Nightmare by Desensitization of a Related Phobia." *Behaviour Research and Therapy,* 1968, *6,* 109–111.

A teen-age girl had recurrent nightmares of falling off bridges and was extremely fearful of crossing bridges. Selective desensitization was used to reduce the real fear, resulting in the ability to cross bridges. Without direct treatment, the nightmares ceased.

Obsessive-Compulsive Behavior

To obsess is to be intensely or abnormally preoccupied, often with an un-reasonable idea or feeling. Obsessive doubting or obsessive thinking are frequent. At times, the obsessive thoughts serve to undo "bad" thoughts. Frequently the child is bothered by omnipresent disagreeable thoughts. Compulsiveness is the compelling or irresistible impulse to behave—often, to perform an irrational act. Anxiety results if the behavior (ritual) is not performed. Repetitious or symmetrical (to balance a behavior) acts are frequent. Compulsive behavior often has to do with cleanliness, safety, or superstition.

Dynamic, Here-and-Now, Focused Psychotherapy with Obsessive Children

AUTHOR: Paul L. Adams

PRECIS: Specifies eight psychotherapeutic approaches for obsessive children: "for instance," "here and now," "thou and I," "feelings are in," "honesty pays," "keep it clean," "take the chance," and "at ease"

INTRODUCTION: The natural prognosis for untreated cases of obsession in childhood is considered good if there is underlying depression, but bad if a schizophrenic or psychopathic process exists. Adams presents strategies of psychotherapy that he believes are most effective in working with obsessive children.

Psychotherapy takes from one and one-half to three or more years, averaging one and three-quarter years. Parents are informed that they should anticipate a two-year commitment, a period that may be longer for older children. Adams believes that nondirectiveness, a noncommittal classical psychoanalytic approach, interpreting unconscious symbolic meanings, and offering advice to the obsessive all lead to unnecessarily prolonged therapy. He advocates openness, direct intervention, inviting naturalness, not focusing on symptoms, and assistance in trying out nonobsessive behavior.

Adams considers that a minimum of one session per week is necessary, with three sessions being preferable. He does not see payment or nonpayment as an issue, because he feels that suffering is an adequate motivation for cure. Hospitalization is not recommended, because naturalness can best be achieved in the child's natural setting. Tranquilizing, sedating, or energizing (psychotropic) drugs are not recommended. Adams feels that drugs confuse the issues, distort the treatment relationship, and create interfering dependencies and resistances.

PSYCHOTHERAPEUTIC METHODS: The eight approaches used by Adams are described as follows:

1. *"For instance."* The child's generalized formulations, which block his living, are discouraged. Interest is shown in the child's

discussing real examples of his experiences, not global statements—the child is asked to recall concrete instances of generalities and is told that the therapist is "freeing him up" by helping him to understand what is happening in his life.

2. *"Here and now."* Daily, current life is scrutinized, and the search for origins is discouraged. The search is for interpersonal and intrapsychic contemporary patterns and habits. Focusing on the present helps the child to live a more comfortable daily existence.

3. *"Thou and I."* The out-of-the-ordinary relationship is valued by the therapist. Interactions between child and therapist are seen as an excellent example of the here and now. Adams advocates observations by the therapist of the child at school or play, in family therapy sessions, and in semisocial visits to camp. He notes that it is important to avoid a child's using sessions only as a means of preventing loneliness. A passionate positive transference is not promoted; however, the examined relationship is used as a vehicle for promoting cognitive and emotional growth.

4. *"Feelings are in."* The child's dissociation of affects from his total behavior is discouraged, even though this may make him more anxious at first. His belittling of feelings is seen as a part of his disturbance, and he is encouraged to express feelings. The therapist purposely uses words such as *feel, fear, hate, upset, love,* and *crave* and does not use *think* and *idea.*

5. *"Honesty pays."* The obsessive child is seen as a master of deception. Even when rewarded, telling the truth is not easy for such a child. The therapist uses statements such as "Tell me truthfully what you mean," "Be very frank," and "Speaking very honestly, what are you feeling right now?" to lead the child to making more direct, honest responses.

6. *"Keep it clean."* The child's agonizing verbosity is seen as very unproductive. Adams feels it is better to silence the child than to foster unending obsessive talk. Effective and relevant communication (keep it clean) is encouraged. The therapist restates conversation simply, encourages dialog rather than pronouncements, shows puzzlement at the child's inability to talk and think straight, interrupts compulsive talking, compliments naturalness and directness, asserts his or her own values without hedging, and replays parts of the conversation.

7. *"Take the chance."* The obsessive child needs encouragement, reassurance, and prodding to take risks. For example, a child who scorned feeling and physical movement was urged to ride a bicycle. His wish for perfection was used therapeutically by defining perfection on a bike as getting where one wants to go. Risk taking, such as riding a bike, was frequently encouraged.

8. *"At ease."* Words describing how the child should behave are used by the therapist and the child is directly encouraged also to use them (for example, *at ease, spontaneous, natural, direct, free,* and *letting loose*). The child is cajoled and admonished to try new ways and to be at ease. When a child stresses rugged independence, the therapist expresses amazement that anyone has to be that strong. If orderliness and cleanliness are extolled, the opposite is mildly suggested. Theoretically, Adams assumes that the child felt anxious as a baby and then compulsively propounded his great strength. A balance of real strengths and weaknesses is advocated, with the goal of putting the uptight child at ease.

PLAY AND LARGELY NONVERBAL THERAPY: Without being a ridiculous clown, the therapist shows lightheartedness and good spirits, and serves as a model. Physical play, playing catch with a ball, and taking walks are encouraged; checkers and chess are not permitted. Play with animals, water, clay, dolls, guns, and fingerpaints are considered appropriate. War toys are seen as a means of releasing the rage that drives the obsessive child.

WORK WITH PARENTS: Parents should be seen by another therapist and joint meetings with all parties should be arranged. Even though the parents cannot take back what was done, they can say that they are sorry and initiate changes in current family patterns. Parents are seen as having a deficit in empathy. They do not see things from the child's perspective and do not see him as "being his own man." Frequently they see themselves as exemplary and therefore categorize all the child's defiance as wicked, while conformity is the index of goodness. Parents are helped to change these patterns and to develop higher self-esteem.

TRANSFERENCE AND COUNTERTRANSFERENCE: The therapist does not supplant or compensate for the actual parents. A passionate, distorted attachment to the therapist is not constructive. Negative countertransference is a special difficulty—obsessive children may feel a magical omnipotence and clash with a therapist who has a myth concerning his healing powers. The therapist should avoid feeling like an authoritarian parent, competing with the real parents, and being opposed to the bad child in himself.

ASSESSING CHANGES: Adams uses the following indicators to assess change:

1. *Symptomatic decreases.* Other people can readily see that obsessions, rituals, compulsions, phobias, and ties have decreased. The child feels less plagued by upsetting symptoms.

2. *Behavioral modification.* Gross motor activity becomes more fluid and graceful; play absorbs the entire body and is less stilted; talk is less long-winded or circuitous and more direct and engaged. There is less verbal undoing (shifting from one extreme to the other, such as saying brave when he feels weak) and stuttering. The child smiles more, makes academic progress, and more accurately observes what is going on around him. Thinking is more pragmatic and less literal.

3. *Change in feeling about himself.* A feeling of increased well-being is reported by the child, who also says he feels freer and more natural and spontaneous. He shows more imagination and zest.

4. *Change in ego strengths.* The child feels and shows increased willpower, initiative, and decisiveness and less perplexity and brooding conflict. Child shows improved concentration, communication, and problem solving and perceives himself, others, and situations more accurately.

5. *Changes in superego.* The child's reasoning and feeling about moral issues improves. He develops his own values, is less dependent on the judgment of others, and shuns duplicity and pretense. He can avoid punishment more, because he is more aware of which adults to avoid. Self-criticism and superhuman striving decrease, because he feels less guilty.

6. *Changes in interpersonal relations.* The child develops a broader circle of friends, with whom he feels closer and less guarded and sarcastic. He is also a much better judge of others and engages less in power struggles.

COMMENTARY: The eight psychotherapeutic methods and six areas of assessing changes are clearly spelled out and tailored to working with obsessive children. Most of the points made also appear applicable to many of the other behavior problems covered in this book. The usefulness of this article is that the main problems of working with obsessive children are faced directly and specific approaches are advocated: Obsessive thinking and stilted compulsive behavior are discouraged and a freer more direct approach is encouraged. Learning theorists in this section offer specific approaches to reinforce the appropriate behaving and thinking and diminish the problematic behavior. The behavioral approaches claim similar successes in a lower total number of sessions. We might caution that predicting treatment of at least two years at three times per week could be a self-fulfilling prophecy; it may not need to take that long.

SOURCE: Adams, P. L. "Psychotherapy with Obsessive Children." *International Journal of Child Psychotherapy,* 1973, *2,* 471–491.

A Mother as Therapist for Her Obsessive Child

AUTHOR: Augusta Bonnard

PRECIS: Guiding parents in using psychoanalytic interpretations with an obsessive child

INTRODUCTION: Because there was a long waiting list and the mother was described as free of any marked neurotic disturbance, the mother was used as a "therapeutic intermediary" with her son, Robert, four and a half years old. Robert was very obsessive. His sister, two years younger, showed deviant behavior, screaming continuously and being unendingly provocative. His father (and all of the father's family) showed many pathological characteristics. As therapy progressed, the father became more openly paranoid. The therapist, Bonnard, was open with the mother about her husband's peculiarities and freely commiserated with her.

Robert had lost his sunny disposition shortly after beginning school. He became irritable and complaining. Looking very anxious, he would insist that his parents repeat, "yes, yes, yes," or "no, no, no," endlessly. If they refused, he became very troubled. He began to bite his nails, and became obsessed with clouds. His concern with rain was seen as his fear of wetting himself. He then developed endless hand-washing and fault-finding behavior (his mother was very clean and his father was extraordinarily compulsive). He showed extreme irritability when his endless questions were not answered. He also became fearful of his rights or safety inside his own home.

INTERPRETIVE WORK: Robert's mother was told to answer some of his questions about his origin and to say that he had come from her body via parental seeds. To alleviate his concern about wetting (his sister continuously wet her pants), his mother told him that the "feel" in his penis was a reliable indicator of when it was ready to "rain." Robert used a doll to act out many oedipal and castration fantasies. This doll play was not commented on, because it was seen as a helpful mode of expression. His sister stared and grabbed at his genitals, which frightened him. His mother's explanations of his sister's "exit hole" and the seed-planting analogy helped him understand the difference between girls' and boys' genitals. This understanding led to less fear of castration.

Robert became preoccupied with "bashing" people and with clouds bashing each other. He saw sexual intercourse as a sadistic, violent act. His mother told him that men and women engaged in intercourse by mutual consent, and that women could happily survive the "bashing" of men who were bigger and stronger. After three months of this intermediary therapy by his mother, Robert's obsessional questions and timidity practically ceased. The therapist discussed oedipal concerns with the mother, which helped her feel comfortable at "babying" Robert—having him sit on her lap and holding his hand while in bed in his room.

At one point, Robert shyly admitted that he had always wanted to do naughty and dirty things. He became rude and challenged a bully to a fight and won. Smells preoccupied him and he had to drink copiously to avoid evils that toilet odors might produce in him. After an open discussion with his mother about "using the pot" (the training pot used for his younger sister), he admitted he wanted to use it too, as his sister did. Once he defecated in the pot, took it to the outside toilet to empty, was pleased with his accomplishment, and braver in going outside on a foggy day. He passed through a phase of untidiness and freely expressed aggression.

Robert stopped biting his nails and fingers, and washing his hands, and began to be more open about his death wishes. He expressed concern that his sister might pick up germs from the floor and die. Throughout Robert's reactions, Bonnard offered the mother psychoanalytic explorations and treatment suggestions. For example, his mother was told to tell Robert that death wishes cannot kill anyone. The expression and warding off of specific fears were explained as denial and displacement. The therapist explained that the insensibility of death represented a final castration, in which no more "feel" is possible. (When Robert's mother thus interpreted his contradictory behavior to him, he often called her "my clever little mummy.") His mother praised Robert's diversion of himself from worry (about an operation she had) by intellectual pursuits—copying designs and performing arithmetic. Gradually, his obsessional rituals, demands, and doubts disappeared. The parents, however, continued to have very serious problems.

COMMENTARY: This article describes the work of a psychoanalytically oriented psychiatrist with the mother of an obsessive boy. Bonnard met biweekly with the mother, explaining the meaning of her son's behavior and instructing her as to various responses. The therapist was supportive of the mother and tried to help her understand the father's deviant behavior. Bonnard suggests that this method of working with a "normal" parent should be a method of choice for a variety of childhood neurotic reactions.

SOURCE: Bonnard, A. "The Mother as a Therapist in a Case of Obsessional Neurosis." *The Psychoanalytic Study of the Child,* 1950, 5, 391–408.

Family Therapy and a Behavioral Approach with Obsessive-Compulsive Children

AUTHOR: Stuart Fine

PRECIS: Interrupting and extinguishing compulsive rituals by encouraging the child to freely express anger and getting the family to communicate more freely, solve problems more effectively, and clarify roles

INTRODUCTION: After surveying the literature on obsessive-compulsive behavior in children, Fine concludes that many of the old myths about this disorder have been refuted. These children have not all had difficulty with toilet training nor have they obstinate temperaments, as a rule. Moreover, no increased incidence of sexual assault nor feelings of depersonalization have been found. Children who manifest this disorder tend to show extremely ambivalent feelings toward their parents. The parents, on the other hand, are often social isolates who do not tolerate the open expression of aggressive feelings in the family setting. There is often an emphasis on etiquette and cleanliness in the home.

MULTIMETHOD APPROACH TO TREATMENT: Fine notes that current treatment approaches for this relatively infrequent neurosis tend to be more goal directed, briefer, and more family oriented than in the past. In conjunction with his own brief family therapy approach, Fine recommends to the parents that they extinguish a child's rituals by interrupting him as soon as they occur. Ways of interrupting a child include distraction, cajoling, and gentle physical restraint. Operating on the psychodynamic assumption that these children develop motor rituals and ruminative thoughts because they feel unable to verbalize their feelings, particularly angry feelings, Fine further advises parents to allow the child to freely express his anger and anxiety when his ritual is interrupted. Typically, the child will direct a great deal of hostility at the person who blocks the expression of compulsive behavior.

In family sessions, Fine is quite active in his attempts to facilitate the open communication of feelings and information among family members, to increase their capacity to solve problems rather than just to complain about them, to clarify role functions and child-rearing practices, and to promote the ability of each family member to have some degree of autonomy.

CLINICAL STUDIES OF CHILDHOOD COMPULSIONS: The main part of Fine's article describes the application of Fine's approach to the treatment of two compulsive children. The first case involves an eleven-and-a-half-year-old boy who exhibited a series of rituals at bedtime. If anyone in the family spoke to him after he was in bed, he had to rise and go to the bathroom to urinate. He also tried to get his parents to repeat questions, commands, and statements twice. As part of treatment, family members agreed to refuse to repeat their verbal interactions with the child and agreed to praise him when he responded to their first interaction. The parents also agreed to lock the toilet after he had urinated once. In family sessions, all the members became more verbal and problem centered. In individual sessions, the patient overcame his initial reticence and expressed feelings of resentment toward his mother and his peers. After four months of treatment, Fine reports, there was a marked decrease of the boy's symptoms and the family functioned more as a unit.

In the second case study, a nine-year-old boy displayed a variety of bedtime rituals six weeks prior to the initial interview. He insisted that his pillow be arranged in a certain way and he tried to keep his head raised and off the pillow completely. The boy stated that he had to think of pleasant events lest he die or be changed into a monster. In the morning, he dressed and tied his shoes in a special order. He frequently had to undress and begin again, to be certain that the correct order had taken place. These rituals often made him late for school or else he missed school altogether.

In treatment, the parents agreed that they would take the boy to school even if he was incompletely dressed. The school principal and teacher were advised of this decision and they cooperated fully. When the boy later told the teacher he could not step over the cracks in the school floor, she firmly told him that he would be carried across if he could not manage himself. After an angry outburst, the boy had no more difficulty in school. In the family sessions, the parents became much more open in discussing family problems and expressing feelings of resentment and anger toward each other. During individual sessions, the boy revealed a repressed fear of hospitals and dying, about which he was subsequently able to talk during the family sessions. One year after the family meetings ended, Fine reports, a follow-up questionnaire revealed that the boy's rituals were minimal.

COMMENTARY: In evaluating the success of the treatment approach described in Fine's article, the reader should be aware that, in the two cases cited, the boys were motivated to rid themselves of their rituals and ruminative thoughts. They had expressed guilt feelings about their rituals and were afraid their peers would find out about their peculiar behaviors. A necessary condition for this approach to be effective, then, may be that the symptoms are unacceptable to the child's ego. Also noteworthy is Fine's hypothesis that obsessive-compulsive rituals represent displaced behavior. Ambivalent about openly expressing his anger toward his parents, the child discharges this tension via ritualistic acts. Fine asserts that these rituals are similar to the neutral preening behavior of birds who cannot decide whether to fight or flee from an adversary. Instead, the birds perform neutral rituals, which also are often used in other conflict situations. Where this hypothesis is valid, then, a family therapy approach centering on the open expression of feelings would seem to be the method of choice.

SOURCE: Fine, S. "Family Therapy and a Behavioral Approach to Childhood Obsessive-Compulsive Neurosis." *Archives of General Psychiatry*, 1973, *28*, 695–697.

Mutual Storytelling with a Compulsive Boy

AUTHOR: Richard A. Gardner

PRECIS: After assessing the psychodynamic significance of a child's story, a therapist tells a story promoting more appropriate resolution of conflicts

INTRODUCTION: In Gardner's method, the child first tells a story and then the therapist surmises its psychodynamic meaning and tells his own story. The same characters are used in a similar setting, but healthier adaptations and resolutions of conflicts are introduced. Since the therapist uses the child's own language, there is a good chance of "being heard." Alien psychoanalytic interpretations do not burden the child. The therapist avoids stories involving anxiety-provoking confrontations, which often occur with parents and teachers. Humor and drama enhance the child's interest and pleasure. The method is useful for children who tell stories but who have little interest in analyzing them.

A tape recorder is used and the child's name is written on a label affixed to the tape to be used for the stories. The child is asked to be the guest of honor on a make-believe television program on which stories are to be told. Details of an introduction are specified. Various suggestions are offered both in this article and in Gardner's book *Therapeutic Communication with Children: The Mutual Storytelling Technique* (New York: Science House, 1971).

In story analysis, Gardner notes, two or more figures may represent various facts (often conflicting forces) of a child's personality (for example, a good dog and a bad cat). A hostile father may be represented by bulls; swarms of insects may symbolize unacceptable repressed material. Repressed and projected hostility often lead children to see their parents as more malevolent than they really are. The child's "moral" or "title" of the story assists the therapist in selecting the most significant theme. In the therapist's story, more alternatives are provided and the child can see that he is not enslaved by neurotic patterns.

ANGER INHIBITION PROBLEMS: Gardner presents a detailed exploration and explanation of the origin and significance of inhibiting anger. Anger must be harnessed to deal with frustration and children must not be filled with guilt for the angry feelings they have. Problems around the expression of anger are described as being extremely common in children. The child has many frustrations and resentments, which he cannot overtly express for fear of criticism or restrictions. Since he cannot flee or fight, he maladapts by denial, repression, sublimation, displacement, vicarious release, and projection of blame on others. Dreams and fantasies allowing release of anger are therefore often gratifying. The patient is helped to avoid maladaptive reactions to anger. Gardner feels that symptoms are related to the inappropriate utilization of anger.

Two cases of stuttering and one of disruptive school behavior and poor peer relations are presented. A case of compulsive behavior is selected for description here.

CASE STUDY: For three years, a ten-and-a-half-year-old boy, Charlie, had had a touching compulsion. He feared getting sick or dying if he did not touch certain objects (such as tables, chairs, and walls). He was markedly nonassertive. His parents were very inhibited in expressing their feelings.

After three months in therapy, Charlie told a story about a woman making a trial tape for a television cigarette commercial. (The story is given verbatim in the article.) There was difficulty with the tape (it skipped) and the problem, which was not her fault, eventually led to her being fired. She went to another broadcasting session, but that did not work either. Charlie said the moral was "You shouldn't be in advertising for cigarettes because they're no good and you shouldn't add to it."

Gardner feels that the woman represented Charlie's passivity. She was fired because of the neglect of others. She heard the skipping but did not protest. Like Charlie, she considered criticism of others to be dangerous. The irrational authorities fired the woman rather than the people responsible for the error. Charlie's moral, although true regarding negative effects of cigarettes, avoids the main themes of the story—illogically punitive authority and pathological passivity.

The therapist then told a story in which the woman began to assert herself and to explain that it was not her fault. The point was made by the therapist that the woman should say, "You're firing the wrong person." At the end of the exchange, Charlie was asked what the main lesson was. He said, "Well, if you see an error or something, you should speak up and not let it get through." Even though Charlie liked his own story better, he clearly understood and stated the moral of the therapist's story.

Therapy was terminated after seven months, forty-eight sessions having taken place. The touching compulsion was completely alleviated and Charlie was much more assertive with his friends. His relationships improved and he was no longer scapegoated. Relatively, he was still obsessive and a worrier. Gardner points out that he utilizes the traditional approaches of play therapy, direct discussion, environmental manipulation, and parental counseling along with mutual storytelling.

COMMENTARY: Gardner's article illustrates the use of a specific means of therapeutically communicating with children by mutual storytelling. The case of a boy with compulsive touching was selected to highlight Gardner's technique and theory regarding anger inhibition. Gardner (like many other therapists) has incorporated mutual storytelling in treating almost all of the behavior problems covered in this book. He has devised a board game, *Talking, Feeling and Doing,* to elicit responses, especially from withdrawn, nonverbal children.

SOURCE: Gardner, R. A. "The Mutual Storytelling Technique in the Treatment of Anger Inhibition Problems." *International Journal of Child Psychotherapy,* 1971, *1,* 34–64.

Fantasy Communications with an Obsessive-Compulsive Boy

AUTHOR: Lily H. Gondor

PRECIS: Psychoanalytic interpretations of underlying fearful conflicts in fantasies of obsessive-compulsive children

INTRODUCTION: Gondor notes that the therapist remains an adult with his responses rooted in reality, yet he or she is also an adult who goes with the child into any situation, even into the world of fantasy. A unique situation therefore exists, because the therapist accepts the child and converses in the language of the child's world. Adults have probably seldom taken a serious role in the "make-believe game," so that when the therapist does so, he or she is helping the child feel really understood, perhaps for the first time. For the child, fantasy is a legitimate means of communication that the therapist must understand and use.

CASE STUDY: Peter, six and a half years old, was severely anxious and had various obsessive-compulsive traits—obsessive fears, meticulousness, reaction formations, isolation, sadomasochism, and intellectualization. He was overly conforming, afraid of aggression and injury, and was averse to anything messy or containing germs. Forming relationships was extremely difficult for him. He was afraid of prehistoric animals (although he knew they did not exist anymore), ghosts, skeletons, and goats. Obsessive ruminations about dinosaurs diminished when he played with paper cutouts of a dinosaur family. However, he began to communicate fears of being swallowed, contaminated, and injured. Prior to therapy, Peter had played solitary games. Then Gondor played with him, demonstrated that she was not frightened, and accepted Peter's dual role of victim (the clumsy giant) and attacker (a supermouse called Petey Mouse).

Early in therapy, Peter had no desire for company. His fantasies were lived by himself in an underground house with a secret entrance and a servant robot. As therapy progressed, the fantasies and the relationships with Gondor changed. Peter identified with the supermouse, who conquered giants, beasts, and bandits. Houses were opened by explosions and then made whole again. Fantasies then developed in which one could be hurt by one's own weapons. Bullets that were shot returned: Peter frequently used the term *backfiring* and acted this out in games. Gondor saw this development as fear of retaliation if Peter gave vent to his aggressive feelings. His drawings showed giants contrasted with small, helpless creatures.

Sadomasochism developed in later fantasies, with fear of injury and inflicting injury themes (theoretically seen by the therapist as castration anxiety or feelings of helplessness). Giants (both animals and people) were punished. Their tongues were cut out and noses cut off, and mostly they fell into a bowl of fire or hot oil. While acting this out, Peter asked Gondor if she knew how people were punished in hell. A friend had told him that in hell people who had done bad things were burned or cooked; this thought had bothered him for a long time. He responded very strongly to Gondor's interpretation that he seemed quite concerned about what kind of punishment was awaiting him. At about that time, his anxiety decreased and he was no longer afraid of going to school. He started to play with children, formed closer relationships, became more aggressive, and was less clean at home. In therapy, his games now dealt with real people. His fantasy animals were circus animals that he rode.

In the last session, he drew a picture of a caveman with a pet baby dinosaur. Gondor interprets the story as a communication that a next therapeutic step could be to show Peter that there were no cavemen or dinosaurs that had to be tamed by him. A two year follow-up showed good school progress, many friends, and even leadership in groups.

COMMENTARY: The selected case illustrates the use of fantasies in decreasing obsessive-compulsive difficulties. It is a clear illustration of the psychoanalytic concept of obsessive-compulsive symptoms as symbolic representations of underlying fears and concerns. The focus here is on communicating understandings to the child, and then interpreting the fears in a meaningful way to him. His fantasies are used, in essence, to help him overcome the underlying

fears. In this report, Gondor's approach is reminiscent of the therapeutic use of heroes as models in learning theory procedures, a
technique developed later by behavior therapists.

SOURCE: Gondor, L. H. "Use of Fantasy Communications in Child
Psychotherapy." *American Journal of Psychotherapy,* 1957, *11,*
323–335.

Behavior Therapy with a Compulsive and Phobic Boy

AUTHOR: Michel Hersen

PRECIS: Visualizing and gradually eliminating a hierarchy of anxiety-laden ritualistic behaviors

INTRODUCTION: Hersen believes that compulsions are learned in the presence of intense anxiety. Therefore, compulsions can be extinguished by using visual imagery that evokes intense anxiety. As the anxiety is experienced and nothing bad happens, anxiety to the imagery extinguishes. Generalization of reduced anxiety takes place in the presence of the real-life situation. Hersen further believes that phobias are learned and reinforced by inappropriate parental behavior. Counseling the parents is necessary to change the reinforcement pattern.

CASE STUDY—DAVID: Traditional psychoanalytically oriented therapy had failed to help David, a twelve-year-old boy. David was referred because (1) he complained of painful, burning sensations in his testicles (physiological cause ruled out); (2) he had been missing a great deal of school, because he remained home for several days after frequent viruses (type of school phobia); and (3) he was socially introverted and had few friends. David's mother and grandmother were claustrophobic and agoraphobic, and his father was passive and frequently away from home on business.

David was not concerned about the three referral reasons, but he was concerned about his elaborate, time-consuming rituals. He had to perform many behaviors before going to bed because they prevented him from "getting sick." He once attempted to stop the rituals, but became ill the following day and never again considered stopping them. He experienced nightmares in which he was physically attacked and dismembered.

Hersen treated David once a week, using traditional psychoanalytic methods. After six months, genital pains were gone but nightmares, compulsions, and school absence continued. Hersen then used a behavior therapy approach with David and counseled his mother regarding her behavior, which was reinforcing David's avoidance of school.

A variation of implosive therapy was used, based on the idea that visualization of not performing rituals and not getting sick should lead to diminished anxiety. Contrary to usual implosive procedures, a hierarchy of scenes was used in order to lead David to gradual mastery. The following hierarchy was developed with David, who reported which ritual omissions would lead to the least (Item 1) anxiety and which to the most.

1. Put on both shoes before tying laces.
2. Open and close door to sister's room.
3. Displace and adjust rug in parents' room.
4. Turn shower on and off four times.
5. Thermometer placed in, out, in mouth, blow four times, count to four, four times.
6. Open and close car door two times, open and lock safety button six times.
7. Displace and adjust rug in hallway.
8. Open and close closet door.
9. Walk up and down stairs avoiding any stair being a multiple of four.
10. Open and close television knob three times.
11. Open and close water faucet two times.
12. Wash orthodontal plate three times, dry it three times before going to bed.
13. Wash body in rigid sequence.
14. Before going to sleep, displace and adjust window shade several times; put on and shut lamp two times; and open and shut closet three times.

David was instructed how to visualize scenes and asked to visualize Item 1. Acute anxiety quickly diminished and he was then asked to actually perform shoe lacing one at a time. At each session, one item on the hierarchy was visualized (at first with considerable anxiety, which then diminished), and David was told to omit that ritual during the week. By the tenth session, Item 7 was omitted and David spontaneously gave up all of the remaining rituals. During the sessions, David reported a decrease in nightmares of dismemberment. Three months more were spent in helping him in improving his relationship with his father. Follow-up revealed no recurrence of ritual behaviors.

Counseling with the mother began at the time when behavior therapy was initiated with David. She liked having David around during school days and she implied that his presence made her husband's absence more tolerable. Ten weekly one-hour counseling sessions were held. She was resistant to approaches that would lead to her independently finding ways to stop reinforcing David's avoidance of school. She expressed concern that she might send David to school with a real physical ailment and then feel guilty. She was instructed to never permit him to stay home unless a fever was over 100°. After some lapses and with reassurance from Hersen, she was able to follow the agreement. Six months later, David's school attendance was normal, minor symptoms were infrequent, and he was reportedly more independent and socially oriented.

COMMENTARY: Hersen believes that this case adds support to the assertion that symptom removal (with no symptom substitution) can be accomplished without going into underlying causes. The case offers a good example of one therapist doing therapy with a child and counseling with a parent. Hersen's approach appears useful with childhood fears and traumatic relationships. Visual imagery can be used to help children imagine various difficult situations that they can handle successfully.

SOURCE: Hersen, M. "Treatment of a Compulsive and Phobic Disorder Through a Total Behavior Therapy Program: A Case Study." *Psychotherapy: Theory, Research and Practice,* 1968, 5, 220–225.

Behavior Therapy with an Obsessive-Compulsive Boy

AUTHOR: Irving B. Weiner

PRECIS: Discovering positive reasons for rituals and substituting efficient, less extensive rituals, which are later spontaneously given up

INTRODUCTION: Weiner describes two approaches to treatment. One focuses solely on eliminating the compulsive habit itself (see following case study). The other seeks to decondition the anxiety or stimuli that elicits the maladaptive behavior.

CASE STUDY: One month before referral, a fifteen-year-old boy suddenly began pervasive compulsive rituals. Rituals involved washing, dressing, reading, writing, and compulsive placement of all objects. If the rituals were not performed, he believed, something horrible would happen to his parents or else he would be drafted into the army and eventually killed. When younger, the boy had been considered dependent and shy, with a compulsive personality, but without serious psychopathology.

In order to understand what stimuli elicited his compulsions, Weiner asked the boy to note the exact circumstances when he performed the rituals. This request led to an intensification of the rituals and greater anxiety. Weiner then decided to attack the motor symptoms directly and to make the pervasive rituals more limited and less interfering. The first step was to establish a *positive* reason for the ritual and to construct a more efficient substitute ritual.

One example was the boy's compulsive checking and rechecking of locking his school locker, because he might wind up in Viet Nam. When asked for a positive reason, he said he did it to protect his belongings. Checking only once would ensure this latter goal. He was told to step back and say to himself some sentences, to the effect that his possessions were safe, there was no reason to check again, and he was going to class. If he found he had to check, he was told not to worry about such lapses.

Other rituals were handled in the same manner. Each time, the boy agreed that far less extensive rituals would accomplish his stated positive reason for the behavior. Another example was the substitution of a timed three-minute morning face wash instead of his usual fifteen-minute wash. He had specified that three minutes was sufficient to ensure cleanliness. As the rituals lessened, he felt less dominated by unrealistic, uncontrollable urges and his anxiety diminished greatly. Follow-up revealed continued improvement and he spontaneously gave up the substitute rituals.

COMMENTARY: The procedures mentioned appear quite applicable to latency-age children. Weiner comments that instructing obsessive children to *do* rather than *think* decreases ruminations. The approach is an excellent example of helping a child feel good about himself by seeing results (lessened rituals) that he accomplishes. (Other theorists [see Bonnard, Gondor] suggest that focusing on his basic attitudes and feelings would result in his spontaneously giving up maladaptive behavior.) The rationale can be applied to other disorders, in that direct intervention is used to help the child change his behavior in a direction to which he agrees.

SOURCE: Weiner, I. B. "Behavior Therapy in Obsessive-Compulsive Neurosis: Treatment of an Adolescent Boy." *Psychotherapy: Theory, Research and Practice*, 1967, *4*, 27–29.

Additional Readings

Hallam, R. S. "Extinction of Ruminations: A Case Study." *Behavior Therapy*, 1974, *5*, 565–568.

An immature fifteen-year-old girl was successfully treated for compulsive questioning. Her deliberate manner and her habit of following people in order to ask them questions often resulted in teasing and social isolation. Treatment was aimed at improving her social skills (assertiveness, conversation, and so on) by role playing. Secondly, her questioning was extinguished by withdrawal of reassurance from others. Contingency rewards were used to further reduce her questioning.

Sherman, S. N. "Family Treatment: An Approach to Children's Problems." *Social Casework,* 1966, *47,* 368–372.

This article stresses the need to involve the family when treating children's problems. A case of a nine-year-old with obsessive thoughts about killing is described. The entire family was discovered to have a fear of violence. Various defensive maneuvers were used to avoid or deny violence. The author advocates flexible sessions with the whole family or in different combinations of members.

Hysterical Behavior

Hysteria is marked by emotional excitability and disturbances of psychic, visceral, sensory, or vasomotor functions. A large variety of physical symptoms are possible, with no organic basis. The symptoms often serve the function of reducing anxiety. Emotional conflicts are converted into symptoms. In children, hysterical symptoms may be seen as disturbed sensation or motility, isolated emotional outbursts, altered consciousness, or temporary loss of a sense of reality.

Conversion Hysteria in Latency

AUTHOR: Irving Kaufman

PRECIS: Psychoanalytic treatment of hysterical blindness by interpreting penis envy, resolving the oedipal conflict, and promoting feminine identification

INTRODUCTION: The following case illustrates the psychoanalytic treatment of hysterical blindness. The expression of sibling rivalry, castration anxiety, and hostility helped the client identify more fully with her femininity. Her wish for a penis was transformed to a more feminine wish for a baby. In conversion hysteria, major defense mechanisms are repression, displacement, and conversion. Erotic wishes associated with the genital area are often converted into a symptom such as blindness or paralysis. Kaufman also outlines further dynamic explanations and diagnostic difficulties.

CASE STUDY: At the age of eight and one half years, Catherine was referred for psychoanalysis because of hysterical blindness. She had two older sisters and two younger brothers. The analyst viewed Catherine's mother as feeling like a failure for not having a boy (instead of Catherine) and as seeing her daughter as a rival sibling. In treatment, Catherine's major problems were viewed as sibling rivalry and difficulty accepting a feminine role, a difficulty that was associated with castration anxiety.

Preceding the onset of hysterical blindness, two old women caught Catherine investigating a six-year-old boy's genitals and she was made to feel guilty about this forbidden activity. In the first few sessions, Catherine and the therapist conversed and drew pictures. A quick "transference cure" developed; she simultaneously gave the analyst lollipops and gave up her symptoms. Her drawings were of houses, with much concern over the safety of the structures and the openings. In games with the analyst, she always wanted to be first and discussed her feelings that her brothers and sisters were always first. The analyst interpreted her playing Chinese checkers as symbolical expression of her castration anxiety and penis envy.

Her wish for a phallus was transformed during therapy into a wish for Santa Claus to bring her a baby. Playing checkers and Monopoly was seen by the analyst as revealing her wish to be first, her not wanting to give unless getting something, and her guilt about her aggressive feelings. Catherine expressed castration anxiety in various ways—she saw the feet of a duck as too small; a doll lacked a nose; and she told the analyst she would pinch his finger off. Concern was expressed about the difference between boys and girls, about things being damaged, and about where babies came from.

In psychoanalytic terms, her unresolved wish for a penis from her father was expressed symbolically as a gift from Santa Claus. She felt damaged and castrated and wanted the analyst's finger as a substitute phallus. She expressed both hostility toward her mother and the accompanying fear of retaliation by being starved by her mother. The conflict aroused by repressed oedipal material was displaced to her eyes, resulting in the symptom of hysterical blindness. Neurotic conflict and the problems of sexual identity were resolved by analyzing the transference. Resolving the unconscious oedipal conflict (guilt and castration anxiety) furthered her process of developing a feminine identity.

COMMENTARY: The brief case description outlines the psychoanalytic approach to hysterical symptoms. Play and conversation are focused by the analyst in the areas believed to underlie the expression of the problem symptoms. Kaufman believes that some resolution of basic conflicts (unconscious wishes) is necessary for the disappearance of the symptom and for healthy personality development. This approach differs from theories that symptom removal can be accomplished without resolving underlying conflicts and that other positive consequences naturally follow symptom removal. The psychoanalytic approach usually takes a long time and follows a course of dealing with transference reactions and difficulties in psychosexual development.

SOURCE: Kaufman, I. "Conversion Hysteria in Latency." *Journal of Child Psychiatry,* 1962, *1,* 385–396.

Symptom Discouragement in Treating Hysterical Reactions

AUTHORS: Paul C. Laybourne and Stephen W. Churchill

PRECIS: Behavioral methods to eliminate hysterical symptoms followed by individual and family psychodynamic therapy

INTRODUCTION: In this article, hysterical conversion reactions are not seen as a disappearing disorder. In a pediatric setting, Laybourne and Churchill have seen children who have simulated blindness, deafness, paralysis, convulsions, and so on. They are dissatisfied with the traditional explanation of conversion reactions as unconscious conversion of a conflict to a somatic dysfunction. This explanation stresses the symbolic expression of the conflict in an illness, with unconscious secondary gains from heightened dependency. Laybourne and Churchill believe that the symptom defends the child against exposure to anxiety-provoking situations. Rather than being a secondary gain, the conversion is a security maneuver by the child to avoid a threatening situation. The child knows the reason for the conversion, but does not want to reveal the reason why he has chosen to become disabled.

Laybourne and Churchill feel that the first step is to get the child to give up the symptoms so that the conflict leading to the symptom can be revealed. Therapy is directed toward making the symptoms unrewarding and toward having the parents encourage the child to give up the sick role. Removing the symptom by behavioral techniques is necessary in ,order to learn what the child wishes to gain or avoid. Traditional therapy can then take place. The emphasis is on translating the symptoms into communication about problems, rather than making distinctions between conscious or unconscious processes.

CASE STUDY 1: Ten-year-old Bill was referred because he was unable to walk, feed himself, or care for himself in any way. He would only speak in a panting whisper. Prior to referral, he had been hospitalized for fecal retention and had witnessed his grandmother's painful progression of cancer. Bill was becoming weaker, was hospitalized, and diagnosed as having a conversion reaction. After a psychiatrist administered desoxyphedrine, he improved but quickly relapsed. His extremities were weak and he was enuretic, retained feces, panted, and whispered.

His parents' relationship was described as not good. Treatment began with Bill and his parents being told that his body was completely healthy and that he could walk and talk normally. The therapists told Bill that they expected him to behave normally, but he continued to drool and appear helpless. Bill used devices to make his urine appear red and then green. Bill and his parents were confronted with the therapists' knowledge of this, but the parents continued to help Bill dress and eat. The therapists decreased parental visiting hours, which angered the parents. After a week, Bill improved greatly. He talked more about anger toward his mother for being away and expressed fear that an exhibitionist man he had seen would murder him to keep him quiet. His fecal retention had led to a safe first hospitalization, but after discharge his weakness had developed, which the therapists saw as a simulation of his grandmother's cancer. Thus, Bill could not get well because he would be sent home and be killed. Marital therapy then helped the mother become less overprotective and seductive with Bill. A five-year follow-up revealed no symptoms and good school performance.

CASE STUDY 2: Betty, twelve years old, had had four hospitalizations and an exploratory laparotomy for three years of pain in the right side of her body. A psychiatrist told her that her body was healthy, and she agreed. She expressed some bizarre ideas regarding menstruation, which were not reinforced by the psychiatrist. Her mother was convinced, however, that Betty's problems were organic, as her own husband's previously misdiagnosed terminal cancer had in fact been. Betty was transferred to the psychiatric ward, where she spoke about her intolerable home. On the ward, she showed symptoms that impressed the psychiatrists—auditory hallucinations and suicidal ideation. She said that she wanted to be sick, because the alternative was going home. At that time, she was transferred to another hospital for continued treatment.

CASE STUDY 3: At times, a child can keep hidden his reason for his illness, in which case intravenous desoxyphedrine, with or without sodium amytal, may be used. The patient experiences euphoria and decreased anxiety under the drug and may then reveal his motivation. An eleven-year-old boy was referred for vomiting, headache, and abdominal pain. All medical tests were normal and he was therefore admitted to the psychiatric ward with a diagnosis of psychogenic vomiting. Parental visits were stopped and rectal thorazine was administered, but no improvement was seen. Desoxyphedrine and amytal were then administered. The boy was very suspicious during the interview. The therapist told him all people can remember what thoughts they had when they began vomiting and that he could only go home if he did remember. It developed that he was afraid of wetting his pants in school and being ridiculed. The therapist informed him that he presently had no kidney infection, that he would not wet his pants, and that the teacher would let him leave the room without asking permission. A four-month follow-up revealed no symptoms and an excellent adjustment.

COMMENTARY: Laybourne and Churchill state that therapy with the entire family should follow symptom removal. Their major point is that children know and can reveal the reason for their illness once their symptoms are eliminated. This article directly challenges (and includes a review of the literature) the belief that the child is unaware of the reasons for choosing to be ill. Laybourne and Churchill offer evidence that directly confronting the child and family can expedite the rapid disappearance of the illness. The cause of the child's need to avoid a healthy life can then be discussed and changed.

SOURCE: Laybourne, P. C., and Churchill, S. W. "Symptom Discouragement in Treating Hysterical Reactions of Childhood." *International Journal of Child Psychotherapy*, 1972, *1*, 111–123.

Hypnosis as a Therapeutic Adjunct in Treating Hysteria

AUTHORS: Daniel T. Williams and Manmohan Singh

PRECIS: Hypnotic relaxation exercises for increased self-control in hysterical conversion reactions

INTRODUCTION: Williams and Singh feel that hypnosis is under-utilized as a therapeutic adjunct in children, especially as children are relatively more hypnotizable than adults. They define hypnosis as "a response to a signal from another person or to an inner signal, which activates a capacity for a shift of awareness in the subject and permits a more intensive concentration upon a designated goal direction" (p. 327). Focal attention increases to a peak capacity. Hypnosis is seen as aiding in symptom resolution as a part of general psychotherapeutic procedures.

The authors assess hypnotizability by an eye-roll levitation method. Instructions for hypnosis depend on the age and individual characteristics of each child. The degree of responsiveness and compliance leads to a rating on a scale of hypnotizability. Under hypnosis, the patient can adopt a healthier adaptation provided by the supportive protective authority of the therapist. Organic pathology must first be ruled out and coercive symptom removal is to be avoided. Alternative adaptations are necessary to replace symptoms that serve a defensive function.

CASE STUDY 1: *Hysterical Amblyopia.* Eight-year-old Maria was referred for a progression of visual difficulties over a three-week period. Her diminished acuity in distance and peripheral vision made her unable to function in school. Complete medical examinations led to a diagnosis of a conversion reaction. Several traumatic events had happened to Maria; notably, a cousin had one eye removed after an injury; a new baby had been born into the family, and Maria had observed a television program about hysterical blindness. A hypnotic exercise and explanation were developed. Maria was helped to recognize the relationship between anxiety and loss of vision and to relinquish this symptom. The exercise was used first with Maria alone and then in a session with both her and her mother. While in a trance state, the therapist had her repeat the following statements aloud.

    1. "When people are very scared and upset, they may stop being able to see."

    2. "By relaxing, I can overcome my scared and upset feelings."

    3. "As soon as I am able to see better, I can go home and do all the things I like to do" (p. 332).

    Full vision was restored in two sessions over a three-day period. A ten-day follow-up showed no visual symptoms. Psychotherapy was continued, using the reinforcement provided by Maria's overcoming of her visual problems to convince her of her ability to handle other difficulties. Although therapy was discontinued prematurely, a follow-up one and a half years later revealed no visual difficulties.

CASE STUDY 2: *Possession by a Spirit.* Myra, thirteen years old, was referred for shaking and peculiar behavior. She was acting and talking like her deceased mother, whose death of cancer she had witnessed. Her mother had cried out and shook because of severe pain. After Myra had drunk some wine and heard a friend's comment on the resemblance between her and her deceased mother, she shook and fainted. The diagnosis was "hysterical reaction" and valium was administered.

    Myra was told that she would learn a "relaxation exercise" that would help her control her scary feelings. During the hypnotic trance, she would say

    1. "When I get upset I start feeling like my mother."

    2. "By using the relaxation exercise I can control this feeling and be myself" (p. 336).

    The sentences were written out for her and she was asked to practice them regularly, using self-hypnosis. After the session, immediate relief was noted. She felt like herself and stopped being overly dependent on her aunt. One last occurrence of shaking took place, which she controlled by using the relaxation exercise. Psychotherapy was continued for one year, focusing on resolving her feelings about the loss of her mother. No symptom recurrence took place.

COMMENTARY: Williams and Singh here used hypnosis with conversion reactions. They also describe uses with psychogenic urinary retention and abdominal pain. A brief appendix to the article presents the use of hypnosis in eight other cases, including psychophysiological reactions and behavior disorders. Williams and Singh believe that hypnosis can be combined with other techniques, such as family therapy, behavior therapy, and insight therapy, and that it can considerably accelerate treatment. The use of spoken, repeated phrases is quite compatible with the cognitively oriented behavior therapies presented in this book. Other therapists have had success using cognitive restructuring without using hypnosis (see Goodwin and Mahoney; Meichenbaum and Goodman).

SOURCE: Williams, D. T., and Singh, M. "Hypnosis as a Facilitating Therapeutic Adjunct in Child Psychiatry." *Journal of Child Psychiatry*, 1976, *15*, 327–342.

Additional Readings

Bradley, S., and Sloman, L. "Elective Mutism in Immigrant Families." *Journal of Child Psychiatry,* 1975, *14,* 510–514.

This article discusses the likelihood of elective mutism developing in immigrant families. Four Canadian immigrant families were treated. The hostile, dependent relationship between mother and child is exaggerated by the mother's remaining isolated and not learning the new language. Normal independence of the child is slowed by the fear of the unknown. Significantly, the parents often threatened to send the children back to their own country, where speaking would be no problem. Bradley and Sloman consider it essential to integrate the immigrant family into the general society.

Griffith, E. E., Schnelle, J. F., McNees, M. P., Bissinger, C., and Huff, T. M. "Elective Mutism in a First-Grader: The Remediation of a Complex Behavioral Problem." *Journal of Abnormal Child Psychology,* 1975, *3,* 127–134.

A technique is described for teachers to use in helping a child to overcome elective mutism. In the study reported, spontaneous and prompted speech were developed through the use of a reinforcement system. Points accumulated for speaking to a peer purchased free time. A three-month follow-up after the point system was terminated showed that the child was using average levels of prompted and spontaneous speech.

LaBarre, M. B., and LaBarre, W. "'The Worm in the Honeysuckle': A Case Study of a Child's Hysterical Blindness." *Social Casework*, 1965, *46*, 399–413.

The case of a ten-year-old Southern black girl highlights the interaction of external and internal stresses in the development of hysteria and the child's choice of a conversion symptom (blindness). The authors examine the meaning of blindness to the child, her family, and their social group. The social worker became involved in their community. The family's religious beliefs played a significant role in the course of treatment. The complex family and social dynamics are examined in detail, and treatment was based on this analysis.

Lebovici, S. "Child Hysteria." *Psychiatrie de l'Enfant*, 1974, *17*, 5–52.

Lebovici presents a detailed discussion of clinical and theoretical information regarding hysteria. Conversion hysteria is considered rare in children. Childhood hysteria may often form the basis for later adult neuroses. Hysteria in childhood must be differentiated from psychosomatic disorders.

Proctor, J. T. "Hysteria in Childhood." *American Journal of Orthopsychiatry*, 1958, *28*, 394–407.

Proctor reviews the literature on childhood hysteria and outlines psychoanalytic explanations and treatment approaches. Overdependence and ego weakness are characteristic. Constitutional factors and repressions occurring at the oedipal level are significant factors in hysteria. Affect-laden somatic expression is seen in cases of functional paralysis in childhood.

Rosenbaum, E., and Kellman, M. "Treatment of a Selectively Mute Third-Grade Child." *Journal of School Psychology*, 1973, *11*, 26–29.

Behavior modification principles were used to increase the speech of a third-grade girl who did not speak at all in school. Speech was reinforced in a one-to-one situation with a speech therapist, who gave her M & M's (candies) and social praise for verbal sounds and words. Later, M & M's were discontinued and only social praise was used. A step-by-step procedure (with elements similar to the classroom situation) was introduced. In the next phase, she invited children to come to the speech room with her. Two and one half months after treatment terminated, her speech in class was entirely normal.

Rosner, H. "Clinical and Prognostic Considerations in the Analysis of a Five-Year-Old Hysteric." *Journal of the American Psychoanalytic Association,* 1975, *23,* 507–534.

Rosner gives a detailed description of the psychoanalytic treatment of a five-year-old girl. She was perceived as needing to seduce her brother in order to gain possession of his penis. The analyst carried out this theme by giving her presents in the course of treatment. Her lack of satisfaction from receiving presents illustrated to her the futility of searching for something that could only be resolved intrapsychically. When dynamic and economic changes had occurred, treatment was terminated.

Depression

Depression is a state often marked by sadness, inactivity, and feelings of dejection. Suicidal behavior is most common in the presence of depression. Feelings of depression are extremely frequent reactions to deaths or loss of significant people. The depressed child commonly experiences difficulties in thinking and concentrating and has a reduction of vitality. Some theorists believe that depression underlies other childhood behavior disorders.

Attempted Suicide of a
Seven-and-a-Half-Year-Old Girl

AUTHOR: Malca K. Aleksandrowicz

PRECIS: Psychoanalytic treatment of a suicidal child who was considered temperamentally very different from her mother

INTRODUCTION: Aleksandrowicz notes that one theoretical system organizes suicidal behavior hierarchically: (1) nonserious, just talk; (2) a gesture that is a warning signal; (3) a threat; and (4) an actual attempt. Younger children usually attempt a more active means of suicide (jumping from a window) and the more aggressive child uses more aggressive means. Agitated depression is expressed by boredom, temper tantrums, restlessness, rebelliousness, defiance, somatic complaints, accident proneness, running away, and antisocial acts. Theorists quoted by Aleksandrowicz stress that a combination of factors underlie a suicidal threat or attempt. Some causes are an unconscious parental suggestion, rigid control by a parent, intense quarrels, brain damage, and reuniting with a loved one.

CASE STUDY: *Attempted Suicide.* Daphna was always tired, cried frequently, was moody, demanding, had headaches, and blinked her eyes frequently. After joining a group of children who stole candy from a store, she was caught and brought home. Her mother was angry and told her she could not leave the house for two weeks. While awake that night she opened the third-floor window and jumped. A sheet on a line broke her fall and she landed on bushes. After crawling back upstairs, she asked her parents not to be mad at her. She soon recovered from a fractured pelvis. At a psychiatric clinic, Daphna was described as irritable, moody, and explosively aggressive. She was diagnosed as having a hysterical personality and was administered thioridazine, with no effect. Two and a half years after the suicide attempt, Daphna was seen for psychotherapy. She had crying spells, fought with her parents and siblings, and walked in her sleep.

Daphna's parents attributed her accident to an evil eye spell cast by an enemy. They had come to Jerusalem from an Arabic country. Her mother was nondemonstrative, compulsively clean, and rigidly controlled her children. She did not get along well with her less-educated, temperamental, and impulsive husband, who was very attached to their three children.

Treatment. Daphna told the therapist about her fears and expressed much self-hatred. She was ambivalent toward her mother and blamed others for all her troubles. She related a daydream in which she was a caveman who become involved in stealing and violence. This was analyzed according to her wish to be an only child and return to the womb, the anal component of possessiveness and control, and the reality of growing up and mistrust. When Daphna understood her anger with her family and her wanting to hurt them, her symptoms decreased. Her relations with other children and mood swings improved. She told of a dream in which two hunters killed a she-elephant, and a boy with long hair would not allow a she-wolf to eat the elephant. This dream was interpreted as penis envy and the wish to be a boy, which underlay her concern about menstruation and sexual intercourse. After much discussion of her masturbation, voyeurism, and sex games with siblings, her sleepwalking and nighttime sweating disappeared. During the days, she was less tired and more relaxed.

The therapist was ill for a month and Daphna could not come for therapy. When therapy resumed, Daphna told a dream about being dead and talked about her attempted suicide for the first time. She was concerned that her angry wishes had made the therapist sick and could have killed her. Daphna expressed feelings of omnipotence; she believed that her curses could kill the therapist and her mother. The therapist found it difficult to get Daphna to accept the idea that grandiose omnipotent thoughts are not part of reality. Reluctantly and stormily, Daphna's feelings of omnipotence diminished. During the next few months, there was a gradual and consistent decrease in symptoms. The parents were satisfied and chose to terminate therapy after a total of fourteen months. The therapist reluctantly agreed to terminate, but thought that Daphna's infantile narcissistic fantasies and her oral aggressive impulses had not been dealt with adequately.

Daphna's case showed many features related to serious suicide attempts. She was the focus of long-standing family problems, was narcissistic, and was overwhelmed by guilt because of ambivalent relationships with her parents. She envied her brother and was furious over what she saw as loss of parental love. The precipitating suicidal factor was a sense of shame and rage and feeling trapped (not allowed to leave the house). She was unable to escape or vent her anger and had always been impulsive. Theoretically, the attempt was seen as a fusion of a destructive impulse with a desperate cry for help, in which annihilation was denied and death was seen as an act of rebirth.

Another factor was the mismatch between the child's characteristics and the mother's personality, which made them "biological strangers." Daphna was a vigorous, irritable baby and her mother was a quiet, reserved woman who resented her daughter's (and her husband's) exuberance. Having seen her mother lying naked and death-like following sexual intercourse, for Daphna, death became fused with love. She thus did not see death as an empty ending but as an ecstatic abandonment and magic union with the infantile love object. The therapist saw her suicidal attempt as the ultimate attempt to reunite with her love object and find the love that she could not evoke or give. Treatment helped her quiet down, change her behavior, and evoke less anxiety in her mother. Her mother withdrew less, expressed her discomfort more openly, and understood Daphna better.

COMMENTARY: This article provides a good example of a psychoanalytic approach used to diminish symptoms by focusing on "unconscious conflicts." Interpretations of dreams and daydreams were used to help the girl understand and accept herself. This approach might be used in many disorders where the practitioner perceives the operation of basic conflict as leading to ineffective or self-destructive behavior. Aleksandrowicz stresses the importance of the mother and daughter being very different in temperament (biological strangers). One might speculate about the possible efficacy of a counseling approach, where this problem was discussed and methods offered to the family. The mother could be counseled to accept her daughter's differences or even to positively reinforce quieter behavior. This direct approach would be in contrast to Alexsandrowicz's focus upon unconscious conflicts.

SOURCE: Aleksandrowicz, M. K. "The Biological Strangers: An Attempted Suicide of a Seven-and-a-Half-Year-Old Girl." *Bulletin of the Menninger Clinic,* 1975, *39,* 163–176.

Handling the Death of a Parent

AUTHORS: Diane Becker and Faith Margolin

PRECIS: Improving communication between children and their surviving parent

INTRODUCTION: The techniques described in this article are intended for children who do not appear to be in need of psychotherapy. The primary goal of the therapeutic intervention is to help parents work through their own grief and guide them in dealing effectively with their children's reaction to the loss of a parent. Individuals have different styles of mourning; intervention should take place only when a parent is having unusual difficulty dealing with the mourning process, when this difficulty interferes with the child's adaptation to the loss, and when a parent is concealing facts from his or her children. All the children discussed reacted with sadness, dejection, or confusion. A child's defense by denial is thought to be a valuable aid in the early stages of mourning.

PROBLEMS IN COMMUNICATION: The initial problem of informing a child of the death of a parent is uniformly experienced by the surviving parent. Moreover, it is very difficult for the surviving parent to deal effectively with denial by the children. Children may think that the deceased parent is alive in heaven and this belief may be intentionally or unintentionally encouraged by surviving parents. The inability of a parent to use the word *death* or to discuss the negative aspects of death reflects the difficulty that surviving parents have in accepting the death of their spouses. Some parents delay as long as possible telling their children that the deceased parent's body is buried. This delay discourages communication between the surviving parent and the child, because the parent's silence conveys a feeling that the subject is taboo. Once the parent is able to discuss the facts of burial with the child, communication improves. Parents want to spare their children the pain of loss and therefore do not initially share their sad feelings with their children.

Parental guilt feelings also impede open communication (by promoting or not correcting children's fantasies) with children about the death of a spouse. For example, one surviving father had had an ambivalent relationship with his wife. Only after she had been dead for three years could he admit to having negative feelings toward her.

BENEFITS OF RITUAL: In one family, formal religious and cultural observations of the anniversary of the death of the father facilitated the sharing of feelings about death. An unveiling of the tombstone ceremony (approximately one year after death) initiated family discussion. The experience proved to be so valuable that the widow committed herself to observe the anniversary of the death of her husband with her children. When a child is given adequate preparation, memorial observations and visits to the cemetery provide a valuable method that parents can use to help their children adjust to the loss.

COMMENTARY: Becker and Margolin studied nine families intensively to assess what *actually* occurred in response to a parent's death and which interventions were helpful in those situations. In the article, the authors therefore provide specific information. They also take a stand as to specific methods that will aid young children's adaptation to loss of a parent. Since a no-treatment control group was not involved, a study of the natural course of events in mourning the loss of a parent is therefore not available for comparison. Also, Becker and Margolin do not discuss the basis for deciding that the children did not require individual psychotherapy. If the study had begun immediately after the death (rather than within six months), more complete information would have resulted.

SOURCE: Becker, D., and Margolin, F. "How Surviving Parents Handled Their Young Children's Adaptation to the Crisis of Loss." *American Journal of Orthopsychiatry,* 1967, *37,* 753–757.

Art Therapy After Accidental Death
of a Sibling

AUTHOR: Felice W. Cohen

PRECIS: Use of spontaneous drawings to express grief and guilt

INTRODUCTION: Cohen feels that in drawing the person sketches a glimpse of his inner world, his attitudes, his behavioral characteristics, and his personality strengths and weaknesses. The degree to which inner resources are used to handle conflicts is revealed. Drawings employ the language of symbolism and tap primitive layers of the personality. Unlike projective drawings on psychological tests, drawings in art therapy are entirely spontaneous. Through drawings of recollections of dreams and fantasies, the patient can observe changes that occur in art therapy. The patient is encouraged to discover for himself the meaning of his productions, often through free association. In an atmosphere of acceptance, the patient draws what he does not dare put in words. Moreover, he cannot deny his drawn images. People often express their views unwittingly in their drawings. The therapist makes interpretive deductions only in the context of other information.

CASE STUDY: Mark's brother Scotty died one week after a fire that both inadvertently started. Feeling guilty, Mark disobeyed his parents, provoked fights with his friends, and apparently sought punishment. He ate compulsively, started fires, and hit and bit himself. Two years later, he was brought to a child guidance clinic and diagnosed as having neurotic anxiety and depressive reactions. Mark looked lonely and frightened, not like a boy who had lied, bullied, and asked to be punished. Presumably for two years he had had unsolved conflicts of self-accusation, self-forgiveness, anger, and confusion over his naturally ambivalent feelings toward his brother. His parents did not express grief openly. Mark was ignored and not given any consolation or opportunity to express his feelings.

Initially, in art therapy Mark was silent, responded in mono-syllables, and did not use the art materials. In a programed fashion, he mechanically told the story of Scotty's death, adding that he him-self should have also been burned. After four months of painting age-appropriate pictures, he began to accompany his drawings with talk about his dreams—red, hot fires that consumed him. While painting, he asked Cohen why he had not been allowed to go to the hospital or funeral, why his parents would not talk to him about Scotty, and why he also did not die. After two months of this type of material, Cohen suggested that he paint scenes about accidents. Evidently, no one had used the word *accident* with reference to the tragedy. Mark drew a series of stick figures on one large sheet. There were seven separate drawings. Cohen shows each drawing with captions describing the action. Each scene shows part of the accidental fire; the final one shows scarred Scotty being held by his mother. Mark complained that they took Scotty away and his parents never said anything about it again.

During each drawing, Mark cried as he relived the past trag-edy. Cohen encouraged him to continue talking about each scene. After saying that he could now see that he had not killed his brother, he accepted the accidental nature of the event. Presumably, he had felt guilty and defensively employed repression and denial. Mark re-mained in art therapy for an additional three months, by which time all referral problems had been eliminated.

Mark's parents were concomitantly seen for counseling by a social worker. At home, Mark and his parents began to express their feelings with each other. Mark was told that they had never actually held him responsible for Scotty's death. At one point, they openly expressed and shared their grief together.

COMMENTARY: This article illustrates in a concrete way how art therapy is used with a depressed boy who showed problem behavior. It is a good illustration of how therapists of any persua-sion can incorporate the use of spontaneous drawings in their work, especially with shy, nonverbal children, as a means of "breaking the ice." It is also a useful technique for aiding the child to express feel-ings when his talk appears overintellectualized or stilted. Rather than the use of art therapy, one could speculate on the possible efficacy of a few focused family sessions, where the accident was discussed directly.

SOURCE: Cohen, F. W. *Mark and the Paint Brush: How Art Therapy Helped One Little Boy.* Austin, Texas: Hogg Foundation for Mental Health, 1971.

Managing Suicidal Children

AUTHOR: Kurt Glaser

PRECIS: Counseling parents and promoting meaningful communication between suicidal children and significant adults

INTRODUCTION: Glaser notes that suicide in children prior to puberty is very rare. Consequently, the therapist can focus on the underlying psychopathology rather than on protection of these children from imminent danger to life. Suicidal statements, warnings, and threats are frequently made by young children and do not necessarily always indicate emotional disturbance. Therefore, the initial emphasis should be on separating the emotionally disturbed from the healthy child so that treatment may commence.

The children described in this report were seen in Glaser's private practice and represent a middle-class population. Therefore, caution should be used in regard to the generalizability of the findings.

ETIOLOGICAL FACTORS: As compared to adults, depression is relatively infrequent in children. Children may act out their need to punish parents and parental pressures concerning school performance by making suicidal statements and threats. An intellectually limited child with highly intelligent parents and siblings tends to become frustrated at not being able to fulfill the expectations of their parents and/or teachers. Additionally, premature as well as delayed social and psychosexual development may interfere with a child's adjustment and may lead to suicidal types of behavior. Another factor may be a single parent placing a child in a quasi-spouse relationship.

A child does not have the same concept of death as does an adult. Often a child does not see death as final and irreversible. Children who are seriously disturbed must be carefully guarded, because they may act out their suicidal thoughts, assuming that death is a reversible process.

A child's speech should be carefully evaluated. For example, a statement such as "I'll kill myself" may be a "casual statement," an indication of emotional instability, or a real warning of a possible suicide. Glaser considers a spontaneous threat to a parent or sibling less serious than a statement made to a professional person. It is also important to evaluate the extent of extrafamilial resources available to the child. For example, if a child has one close relationship with an adult he will be likely to have less reason for suicidal behavior than does the child who feels emotionally isolated.

MANAGEMENT CONCERNS: In treating the potentially suicidal child, it is essential to open up lines of communication within the family. The professional must not only establish a good working relationship with the child but must also make himself available without delay at all hours. The child should have the therapist's phone number so that he can reach the therapist without parental assistance. The therapist must develop a good working relationship with all significant members of the child's family. Direct advice giving is encouraged even at the first session. Glaser advocates a flexible therapeutic approach (individual, family, or group). The child's circle of significant others should be enriched through any available type of group membership. Additional sources of communication with others should be established. However, Glaser warns that, in some pathological family situations, contact with family members may exacerbate rather than diminish conflict. The therapist must therefore be willing to interrupt the process of increasing communication if it does not support the child's ego or reduce conflict.

Once a meaningful communication system has been developed between the child and a significant person, the danger of suicide is reduced. After this has been accomplished, the reasons for the suicidal behavior can be fully explored. Some environmental manipulation, such as a change in class, a transfer to a different school, or a change in scheduling of activities may be necessary. Treatment may also require parent counseling geared toward altering the parents' attitudes, helping them become more accepting of their child, and helping them provide emotional nurturance. Parents must be encouraged to listen to their children rather than to inhibit or actively forbid their children's expression of their thoughts and feelings.

If serious personality problems are present, a more traditional psychotherapeutic approach may be called for. Particular attention must be paid to such factors as missed appointments, mood swings, or marked changes in school behavior, which may all be signs that suicidal thoughts are returning.

COMMENTARY: Glaser stresses that the therapist should be available at all times and also stresses the need to consider interpersonal, as well as intrapersonal, factors. The suggestion that family, friends, and community clubs be involved can help balance the approach of a professional whose pattern might be one of treating children's fears from an intrapsychic viewpoint alone. We agree with Glaser that flexibility of approach (direct advice, environmental manipulation, and parent counseling) makes for a more individualized, creative effort. However, Glaser's speculation on causal factors in child suicide seems tenuous—parental pressure regarding school performance, premature or delayed development, and other stated causes can lead to a myriad of childhood problems other than suicidal thoughts. Glaser offers no clues for specific predictors that would alert parents. We would suggest that preventative (as well as during treatment) educational measures be taken to help children understand the irreversibility of death.

SOURCE: Glaser, K. "Suicidal Children: Management." *American Journal of Psychotherapy,* 1971, *25,* 27–36.

Handling Reactions to Death

AUTHOR: Bernard Rosenblatt

PRECIS: Case study helping a young boy cope with the death of his sister; changing parental approach and open discussion of religious beliefs

INTRODUCTION: Martin (age six and one half) had been referred for psychotherapy after the death of a younger sister (Suzy). She had died unexpectedly from an "asthma attack" and Martin subsequently appeared preoccupied with a "fear of dying." Martin's parents described him as not having many friends, preferring to play at home. It was the therapist's opinion that he had developed a strict and demanding superego.

INITIAL INTERVIEW: Martin appeared initially very comfortable and mentioned that he had become fearful of dying after seeing Suzy at her wake. The therapist pursued a line of inquiry to help Martin verbalize feelings—especially anger—and concerns about death. Martin was a religious child who identified with the punitive aspects of his religious belief. The therapist pointed out to Martin that he appeared frightened by some aspects of his belief; for example, that Jesus had taken Suzy "because he wanted to have an extra Angel." The therapist also pointed out many positive aspects of Martin's religious beliefs, such as the idea that God loves children, and this clarification was very comforting for Martin.

SUBSEQUENT VISITS AND TERMINATION: Martin mentioned that he was very concerned about the cost of psychotherapy and volunteered some money to pay for the cost. His feelings regarding God were further explored and clarified. The therapist reassured him and the emphasis on the comforting and positive "stories" in his religious instruction may have helped to reduce his anxiety. The therapist characterized God as being good, in an attempt to modulate Martin's aggressive superego development, he also offered the interpretation that God would understand a boy's death wishes. Religious teaching is viewed by Rosenblatt as being similar to societal or familial teachings to children regarding sex. Distortions in religious or sexual matters were corrected, and unconscious influences were pointed out by the therapist. The parents responded well to the therapist's statement that Martin's religious beliefs were defensive and misunderstood.

By the fourth appointment, Martin had become somewhat resistant to continuing. He mentioned that his visits to the therapist interfered with his play or watching television. The therapist interpreted the behavior as a mixture of rationalization to minimize the sense of loss regarding the ending of therapy and as resistance to further exploration of his conflicts. However, the sessions were terminated after this fourth visit. Martin appeared improved and the child and his parents felt that they could turn to the therapist in time of need. The therapist complimented the parents on their conduct and communicated to them that Martin's improvement was in part due to their behavior.

Rosenblatt believes that early, brief intervention favorably affected Martin's general development and prevented more rigid symptomatology. He feels that, without intervention, death of a close relative very frequently leads to the development of psychopathology in children.

COMMENTARY: Rosenblatt's article describes how brief intervention (four sessions) can be useful in helping a child cope with a death. Prior to therapy, the therapist openly discussed the negative effects of the boy's religious beliefs with his parents. Rather than avoiding religion as too sensitive an area, the therapist directly discussed and influenced the boy's fearful beliefs. Positive aspects of his religion were stressed (as in methods derived from learning theory, rational-emotive approaches, and so forth). Verbal positive reinforcement by the therapist was given to the parents for their improved approach with their child. However, the therapist's interpretation of resistance can be a two-edged sword. During the last session, the boy's lack of interest in therapy was interpreted as minimizing the importance of ending therapy and as resistance to further exploring his conflicts. This interpretation could lead to self-doubts on the part of the child and to fear of terminating; moreover, the interpretation may have been incorrect and based on the therapist's theoretical system. Even if it were correct, one could maintain that verbally reinforcing the gains in facing and adequately handling fears might be more effective than commenting on negative reasons for wanting to terminate.

SOURCE: Rosenblatt, B. "A Young Boy's Reaction to the Death of a Sister." *Journal of Child Psychiatry,* 1969, *8,* 321–325.

Additional Readings

Draughon, M. "Stepmother's Model of Identification in Relation to Mourning in the Child." *Psychological Reports,* 1975, *36,* 183–189.

Suggestions are made for the most effective role for stepmothers to assume. Being a "friend" is advantageous when the mother is still psychologically alive (incomplete mourning) to the child. Being a "primary" mother is best when mourning for the biological mother is complete. Adopting the role of "other" or "second" mother is seen as the most frequent model used and the least beneficial in either situation.

Graham, P. "Depression in Prepubertal Children." *Developmental Medical Child Neurology,* 1974, *16,* 340–349.

Depression in the preschool period is viewed as a reaction to a difficult situation. A four-year-old boy had ulcerative colitis and was withdrawn and depressed. Family tensions led to a recurrence of colitis; as the situation improved, he felt more understood and accepted and symptoms remitted. A twelve-year-old's mother became bedridden. His stealing money from his home was seen as comforting himself for the loss of an active mother. Therapy focusing on the acceptance (or resolution of) a stressful event leads to the disappearance of sadness.

Heard, D. H. "Crisis Intervention Guided by Attachment Concepts: A Case Study." *Journal of Child Psychology and Psychiatry,* 1974, *15,* 111–122.

The "assumptive world" was used in crisis intervention with a twelve-and-a-half-year-old boy. His fears, hopes, and expectations concerning different aspects of his life were explored. He discussed what he thought significant others (and his therapist) expected of him. Therapy focused on his contradictions and conflicting assumptions.

Hollon, T. H. "Poor School Performance as a Symptom of Masked Depression in Children and Adolescents." *American Journal of Psychotherapy*, 1970, *24*, 258–263.

Many children referred for poor school performance were found through psychological testing to have underlying depression, which was the actual cause of school failure. Hollon notes that efforts to motivate such children by pressure and criticism result in increased depression, and he presents illustrative cases. He feels modification of parental and teacher attitudes and appropriate treatment for the child are essential.

Kosky, R. "Severe Depression in Young Adolescents: A Report of Five Cases." *The Medical Journal of Australia*, 1975, *2*, 387–391.

This article presents five cases to demonstrate that depression can occur in fourteen- and fifteen-year-olds. Early signs are often not recognized because mood disturbance and impaired physical and mental functioning are concealed. Deterioration may occur, resulting in a serious suicide attempt. All five mothers of the children were dissatisfied with their marriages and the fathers were withdrawn and unaffectionate. Individual and family therapy were used in all five cases.

Ossofsky, H. J. "Endogenous Depression in Infancy and Childhood." *Comprehensive Psychiatry*, 1974, *15*, 19–25.

Ossofsky documents the need to recognize early childhood depression. Often, hyperactivity or behavior problems are the presenting complaint. Symptoms frequently associated with childhood depression are irritability, easy frustration, short attention span, sleep difficulties, and temper tantrums. Imipramine was prescribed for 220 depressed children from one through twelve years old. Ossofsky reports that results of imipramine treatment were seen as good, and presents analyses demonstrating improvement in intelligence test scores and in behavior.

Toolan, J. M. "Suicide in Children and Adolescents." *The American Journal of Psychotherapy*, 1975, *29*, 339–344.

According to Toolan, suicidal children are immature and impulsive and react excessively even to minor stress. He recommends a thorough evaluation for every child who attempts or seriously threatens suicide. An individualized treatment plan is necessary, using an approach suitable to patients who "act out." Intensive therapy, not crisis-oriented therapy, is considered essential. The youngsters are helped to realize that they are depressed and that denial and projection are defenses to avoid facing their depressive feelings. Toolan considers trust in the therapist necessary for the patient to face his painful feelings of loss and lowered self-esteem.

Shy, Withdrawn Behavior

Shy children are usually timid, retiring, reserved, and easily frightened. To withdraw is to remove oneself from participation and become socially or emotionally detached. Withdrawal serves the function of avoiding anxiety, which is aroused by anticipation of social failure or criticism. Lack of self-confidence, fear of new situations, and fear of being hurt are typical in shy, withdrawn children. (Also see section on Social Isolation.*)*

Broad-Spectrum Behavior Therapy with a Withdrawn Child

AUTHOR: Donald B. Keat

PRECIS: Case study of a withdrawn boy illustrating use of a therapeutic relationship, assertive training, behavioral rehearsal, relaxation, motor coordination training, cognitive restructuring, and training parents as behavior managers

INTRODUCTION: Keat reports that there has been little use of classical conditioning techniques with children. He presents a case to illustrate the "broad-spectrum" approach—using a wide range of techniques. In this case, Keat used classical and operant conditioning in outpatient treatment of an eleven-year-old child.

Charlie had had several operations for a cleft palate and had achieved only fair speech. He experienced some bedtime difficulties and occasional enuresis. His father had a distant relationship with him. His little sister, in contrast to Charlie, was lively, talkative, and aggressive. Charlie's main problems at the time of referral were social withdrawal and a lack of self-confidence. He was afraid to try new things, cautious, and fearful of being hurt. Charlie avoided group situations especially because he lacked athletic abilities. He kept his feelings inside and often daydreamed at school.

THERAPY: The following methods were used to help Charlie.

Relationship. The therapist's purpose in building a therapeutic relationship with Charlie was to gain his trust, communicate understanding, and gain his confidence. Principles followed by the therapist included (1) providing social approval and other rewarding contingencies, (2) indicating acceptance, (3) allowing expression of feelings, (4) encouraging recognition and reflection of feelings, (5) encouraging responsibility for choices, (6) allowing the child to lead, (7) conveying the idea that the process is gradual, and (8) setting limits. While he feels that the relationship is important, Keat also describes the utility of the following behavioral approaches that he used.

Assertiveness Training. Since Charlie was usually passive, the therapist continually encouraged him to take action on his own behalf. Theoretically, inhibition of anxiety is associated with action. Charlie was encouraged to express his suppressed angry feelings. With encouragement, he was more able to lead and determine the activities of the therapy hour. To increase generalization of his new learning to other situations, Charlie was given tasks to carry out in real life (insisting on his rights, speaking out, and so on). His parents were asked to support any change in this direction.

Behavioral Rehearsal. The therapist went over problems, discussed appropriate responses, and then rehearsed the responses. Some situations brought up by Charlie were problems with peers and approaching his father for help. The therapist would model a role and then Charlie would imitate him. This procedure was difficult and not productive. Keat notes that this technique is more effective with individuals over twelve years old.

Relaxation. Learning to relax deeply often helps children to overcome anxiety. The following techniques were used to help Charlie relax: (1) breathing, which is essential for relaxation and which was seen by Charlie as having practical use in competitive games; (2) isometric exercises, which help express aggression and relieve tension by directed muscular activity, and (3) relaxation, to relieve tension associated with bedtime.

Motor Coordination Training. As Charlie exhibited problems with motor coordination, model building was used to improve fine coordination and self-confidence. His gross coordination was also especially poor and numerous exercises were used to improve it, including catching and throwing.

Cognitive Restructuring. Several techniques were used to (1) help Charlie understand others' reactions to him and to change his internal sentences ("It's their problem if they have to scapegoat others"); (2) label and express feelings, often providing various choices for him, such as *glad* or *angry*; (3) employ "emotive imagery," especially of his hero image, an astronaut, to do what he wanted without anxiety; and (4) require books (bibliotherapy) for sex education, because his parents found it difficult to handle this area.

Parents as Behavior Managers. Monthly sessions were used to communicate the treatment procedures to Charlie's parents and to educate them in using behavioral methods. A programed text for parents was used to enable them to offer appropriate reinforcers to sustain behaviors such as increased assertiveness.

COMMENTARY: This article illustrates a clinician's use of several procedures, with the aim of achieving agreed-on goals, namely decreasing withdrawal and increasing self-confidence. Several times, Keat comments on the difficulty in assessing how effective each procedure was or was not. For the clinician, the question of which procedure was most effective is not as germane as the accomplishment of the goal by any combination of methods. The broad-spectrum approach described by Keat would seem to be utilizable with the other behavioral disorders covered in this book.

SOURCE: Keat, D. B. "Broad-Spectrum Behavior Therapy with Children: A Case Presentation." *Behavior Therapy*, 1972, *3*, 454–459.

Pet Psychotherapy for Increasing
Self-Confidence

AUTHOR: Boris M. Levinson

PRECIS: Promoting relaxation, trust, and feelings of adequacy in children through interaction with a pet animal

INTRODUCTION: Levinson suggests that a pet may be the only uniting interest of parents and children. While walking a dog, the child may feel a sense of belonging to a group of pet owners. Pets can be used as therapeutic agents; veterinarians may play a key role in such therapy. In discussing various stages of child development, Levinson notes that a pet can provide a soft, cuddly, yielding companion for the child. Pets provide continuity, especially for children who are taken care of by constantly changing, noncaring people. When a child does not meet parental expectations, the pet may play the role of a nonjudgmental, accepting friend, thus lessening the child's anxiety. Accompanied by a trusted pet, a child more freely explores his environment. Pets do not make excessive demands and do not reject the child. Taking care of a pet may aid the development of a sense of mastery over one's self and the world.

PET PSYCHOTHERAPY: Since many children are afraid of a clinician, a pet can serve to help the child feel relaxed. He can play spontaneously with an animal that is not associated in his mind with anxiety. Pets can be used in the therapist's office or in the child's home. Therapists should take walks with their patients and pets, thus moving therapy from the office to the child's natural environment.

When a child plays with a dog, desensitization occurs as the child learns trust. Accompanied by the dog, the child can risk relating to the therapist. The pet is an ally in the child's facing of his difficulties. A sense of adequacy, self-sufficiency, and self-confidence then develops through the usual therapeutic process. The child can participate in natural outdoor activities, accompanied by his pet. Because of his increased self-confidence and his alliance with the dog, he is more liked and accepted.

Introducing a pet into a family requires preparation. The pet should not be used by others as an opportunity to criticize the child who is not ready to care for the pet. When ready, the child will naturally accept responsibility. A pet may also be used to weaken an overprotective parental reaction: The child's mother may transfer some of her overattention from the child to the pet.

In residential settings, pets are recommended to induce a child to become active, thereby overcoming apathy and loss of interest. When a child is physically ill, a pet may enable a child to share his discomfort. The pet may also be an antidote to the fear of death. Levinson calls for broad state and federal programs encouraging the use of pets. He suggests using pets in hospitals, geriatric homes, nursing homes, residential schools, schools for delinquents, and prisons. Mental health centers should have veterinarians. Dogs should be used as therapeutic aids.

COMMENTARY: Levinson calls for the use of pets with many types of disturbed children. The article, which is quite broad, is included in this section because of its emphasis on increasing self-confidence and a more open type of personality. Shy, withdrawn children would be likely candidates for the types of approaches described. The desensitization aspect of play with pets would make the approaches applicable with anxious, fearful, and traumatized children.

SOURCE: Levinson, B. M. "Pets, Child Development, and Mental Illness." *The Journal of the American Veterinary Medical Association*, 1970, *157*, 1759–1766.

Additional Readings

Clement, P. W., and Milne, D. C. "Group Play Therapy and Tangible Reinforcers Used to Modify the Behavior of Eight-Year-Old Boys." *Behaviour Research and Therapy*, 1967, *5*, 301–312.

Three groups of shy, withdrawn boys were formed. One group received tangible reinforcements for social approach behavior from a therapist. A second group were treated similarly but no tangible reinforcers were used, only verbal reinforcers. The control group met without a therapist. After fourteen sessions, social approach behavior was greatest for the token group than for the verbal group. No change occurred for the control group. There was a decrease in discrete problem behavior in the token group. Brass tokens were used to purchase candy, trinkets, and small toys at the end of each fifty-minute session.

Gardner, R. A. "Psychotherapy of the Psychogenic Problems Secondary to Minimal Brain Dysfunction." *International Journal of Child Psychotherapy*, 1973, *2*, 224–256.

Conscious insight is not the primary goal in treating children with minimal brain dysfunction. Gardner uses confrontation, volitional control, allegorical communication, desensitization, emotionally corrective experiences, active parental participation in therapy, and audio- and videotapes. He discusses various psychogenic problems. Very frequently, children with brain dysfunction cope inefficiently with the world and therefore withdraw. The child is helped to be aware of his abilities and how to avoid failure. Withdrawal is reduced by the therapist making the child's environment less threatening and more inviting.

Hart, B. M., Allen, K. E., Buell, J. S., Harris, F. R., and Wolf, M. M. "Effects of Social Reinforcement on Operant Crying." *Journal of Experimental Child Psychology*, 1964, *1*, 145–153.

The authors feel that frequent crying is often largely a function of adult attention. Two preschool boys were helped to reduce crying and to develop more effective responses to frustration. Crying was ignored and appropriate responses to stress were verbally approved by the teachers.

Ludwig, L. D., and Lazarus, A. A. "A Cognitive and Behavioral Approach to the Treatment of Social Inhibition." *Psychotherapy: Theory, Research and Practice*, 1972, *9*, 204–206.

Socially inhibited individuals frequently have irrational cognitive beliefs—self-criticism, perfectionism, unrealistic approval needs, unrealistic labeling of aggressive and assertive behavior, and criticism of others. Various approaches are used to depropagandize the client against these irrational ideas. The client is urged to talk more, express disagreement, be more initiating, be more self-disclosing, tell more stories, and be more sensitive to others.

Mitchell, W. E. "The Use of College Student Volunteers in the Out-
    patient Treatment of Troubled Children." In H. R. Huessy
    (Ed.), *Mental Health with Limited Resources: Yankee Ingenuity.*
    New York: Grune & Stratton, 1966.

College students served as friends to children who were in
outpatient treatment at a family consultation center. Low self-
esteem adversely affected the children's social functioning and
school achievement. Companionship therapy enabled latency-age
youth to feel valued, respected, and unconditionally accepted by
a young adult. The relationship provided a noncompetitive setting
in which the child could gain competency and mastery experiences.
The college students were carefully supervised and taught to engage in enjoyable activities with the children assigned to them.

School Phobia

School phobia is an exaggerated, often illogical, fear of attending school. It may represent general fear of separation from mother. School phobia should be differentiated from nonattendance caused, for example, by truancy, boredom, or fear of academic failure. The child with school phobia protects himself from intense anxiety by not attending school. Reluctance to attend school is often a result of dreading some situation occurring in school. Somatic complaints are frequent and usually disappear once school has been successfully avoided.

Behavioral Management of School Phobia

AUTHORS: Teodoro Ayllon, Douglas Smith, and M. Rogers

PRECIS: Behavioral assessment and management of a school phobia in an eight-year-old girl: use of prompting-shaping of school attendance, withdrawing social consequences of not attending school, and aversive consequences for the mother

INTRODUCTION: There have been many speculations regarding causes of school phobia; for example, unrealistic self-image, the mother displacing her hostility onto the school, and hostile impulses of sadomasochistic school personnel. These hypotheses have not led to standardized treatment approaches. In contrast, an operant conditioning approach is now possible. School phobia can be described behaviorally as an observable event of low probability of occurrence. Behavioral procedures are applied to reinstate school attendance. Treatment in a therapist's office is avoided, since the phobia should be treated in the environment (the school) where it occurs.

CASE STUDY: Valerie, eight years old, came from a low-income area. In second grade, she gradually stopped attending school. In third grade, she refused to go to school and had violent temper tantrums. When Valerie was taken to school by her mother, she became stiff and began shaking and screaming. She said she was thinking about the time she was molested (when she was four years of age, a boy had played with her genitals). Advice from various professionals was ineffective in achieving her return to school. Valerie was described as having no friends, not interacting with peers, and being withdrawn in school. Psychological testing revealed variable functioning because of her extreme inability to concentrate and also revealed many fears, particularly of men. Her scores were 90 on the verbal IQ of the Weschler Intelligence Scale for Children (WISC) and 78 on performance component.

TREATMENT: Treatment involved the following preliminaries: (1) response definition—school phobia was defined as a low or zero level of school attendance; (2) reinforcement for not attending school—the consequences of her behavior were examined, and (3) redesigning the consequences—to minimize the probability of nonattendance and to maximize attendance. A systematic observation schedule was recorded from 7 A.M. to 9 A.M. for ten days by two assistant observers.

Behavior at home. Valerie slept an average of one hour later than her three siblings. After arising, she communicated with everyone except her father. Physical interaction of any type did not occur between Valerie and her siblings or father. Eighty percent of her time was spent closely following her mother around the house. Valerie was taken to a neighbor's apartment by her mother. On every occasion she followed her mother, until the mother literally had to run out of sight. All punishment efforts to stop this following were to no avail.

Behavior at neighbor's apartment. For three days, Valerie's behavior was recorded. She did whatever she pleased during the day, remaining outdoors unless it rained (when she would read a mail-order toy catalog). The neighbor very rarely interacted with her and no demands were made on her. She occasionally played with the neighbor's toddlers.

Behavior in school. After average kindergarten and first-grade attendance, she progressively attended less and less. Her academic achievement was average until absences became numerous.

Behavioral assessment. Valerie's school phobia was maintained by the pleasant and undemanding characteristics of the neighbor's apartment. A prompting-shaping procedure was planned. An assistant assessed Valerie's response to academic materials and found her interested and responsive. When taken for a ride by the assistant, she showed no resistance. The implications were that she could be taken directly to school (not in increasing steps) and that she should do academic work in class. Another possibility was removing the reinforcement of Valerie spending one hour alone with her mother after the other siblings had left for school.

SPECIFIC PROCEDURES: The following techniques were used to help Valerie.

Prompting-shaping of school attendance. First, Valerie visited school for one hour at the end of the day and left with the others. The assistant took her to school progressively earlier each day (extinguishing presumed fears). Because she was so far behind academically, a mutual agreement was reached to place her in a second-grade class. The teacher was given small prizes to give to her at the end of each day. When this procedure was terminated, Valerie remained at home. Sufficient motivation was necessary to ensure her leaving for school on her own. The article presents diagrams illustrating her school attendance under different conditions.

Withdrawing social consequences of nonattendance at school. The reinforcing consequences of one hour spent with her mother in the morning were eliminated. The mother informed her children that she was going to leave for work at the same time they left for school. For ten days thereafter, Valerie was taken to the neighbor's apartment, because she refused to go to school.

Prompting school attendance and home-based motivation. A source of reinforcement at home, to be contingent on school attendance, was sought. A chart was instituted, on which five stars would signify perfect voluntary school attendance and would lead to a special treat or trip on the weekend. Each child who voluntarily went to school would receive three favorite candies after school. Involuntary school attendance was rewarded with only one piece of candy. If Valerie did not leave for school with her sibs, her mother took her there fifteen minutes later. The mother was instructed to take her unless the thermometer reading was above 100°. Valerie went willingly when escorted, but not on her own (the escorting was perhaps reinforcing).

Aversive consequences for the mother. Since no irritation or inconvenience was experienced by Valerie or her mother, the following procedure was initiated. The mother went to school ten minutes before the children left. She met them there and gave them a reward. If Valerie did not arrive, the mother had to return home for her (a one-mile walk). The chart at home was continued. For two days the mother returned (once she hit Valerie on the way to school), but then Valerie went voluntarily and received a star each day. The mother stopped meeting them at school; the home motivational system was discontinued after one month. The follow-ups six and nine months later revealed no school attendance difficulties. No maladaptive behavior (symptom substitution) was reported. Instead, vastly improved attitude and behavior were noted.

COMMENTARY: The authors see this case study as supporting other reports that punishment without positive reinforcement is not effective. When punishment for an undesirable response occurs, an alternative competing response should be reinforced. A striking feature of the approach used is the negative consequences for the mother in having to return home and take her daughter to school. This is a concrete means of motivating the mother to convince her child that voluntary school attendance is very important. In this study, many specific behavioral techniques were used, following from the behavioral analysis, which is seen as an essential step. Behavioral analyses and strategies could be followed in altering other behavioral problems covered in this book.

SOURCE: Ayllon, T., Smith, D., and Rogers, M. "Behavioral Management of School Phobia." *Journal of Behavior Therapy and Experimental Psychiatry,* 1970, *1,* 125–138.

Rapid Treatment of School Phobia

AUTHOR: Wallace A. Kennedy

PRECIS: Differentiates two types of school phobia and specifies a successful rapid treatment program for the acute type

INTRODUCTION: Psychoanalytic theory stresses the mother's role in the development of school phobias. The mother presumably had an unsatisfactory relationship with her own mother. The father deprecates his wife and tries to outdo her and make himself look better. Possessive, domineering parents are seen as impeding the child's growing independence. The child feels guilty about his impulses and becomes depressed or anxious. If the phobia is viewed as a learned reaction, the symptom is attacked directly by desensitization. The rate of occurrence of school phobia is said to be seventeen cases per thousand school children.

TYPES OF SCHOOL PHOBIAS: Common symptoms are morbid fear of attending school, vague dread of disaster; frequent somatic complaints, such as headaches, nausea, and drowsiness; symbiotic relationship with mother; fear of separation; anxiety about darkness, crowds, noises, and so on; and parental conflict with the school administration. Of the following ten differential symptoms, a distinction between Type 1 and Type 2 can be made on the basis of any seven (p. 286).

Type 1	Type 2
1. First episode	1. Second, third, or fourth episode
2. Monday onset, following a Thursday or Friday illness	2. Monday onset (minor illness not prevalent)
3. Acute onset	3. Incipient onset
4. Mostly lower grades	4. Mostly upper grades
5. Expressed concern about death	5. No concern about death
6. Mother actually physically ill or child thinks she is	6. Mother's health not an issue

Type 1	*Type 2*
7. Parental communication good	7. Parental communication poor
8. Parents mostly well adjusted	8. Neurotic mother, character disordered father
9. Father competes with mother in household tasks	9. Father has little interest in household or children
10. Parents easily achieve understanding of dynamics	10. Parents very difficult to work with

RAPID TREATMENT FOR TYPE 1: Kennedy recommends the following treatment methods for Type 1 cases.

1. *Good Professional Public Relations.* Case should be referred no later than the second or third day of school avoidance. Good communication is necessary with school, physicians, and parent groups. All cases are followed up.

2. *Avoid Emphasis on Somatic Complaints.* The child's somatic complaints are handled matter-of-factly. An appointment is made for the child to see a physician after school hours.

3. *Forced School Attendance.* The child must be required to go to school. Parents have to believe in this requirement and be willing to use whatever force is necessary. Fathers who can kindly display authority take the child to school. The principal or attendance officer takes part in keeping the child in the classroom. Mother should not stay with the child but may be permitted to stand in the hall or visit in school in the morning.

4. *Structured Interview with the Parents.* The goal of the interview is to give the parents confidence in following the strategy regardless of how strongly the child resists.

a. *Lead the interview.* The interviewer anticipates seven out of ten symptoms, thereby gaining the parents' confidence.

b. *Be optimistic.* The transient nature of the problem is stressed. Monday is difficult, Tuesday better, and a problem-free Wednesday is predicted. Parental depression is thereby lessened.

c. *Emphasize success.* Type 1 cases always recover, with ninety percent attending school most of the first day.

d. *Present the formula.* The plan is stated simply, with repetition. If the referral is at the end of the school week, the interview takes place Thursday or Friday. The formula is as follows: School attendance or phobic symptoms are not discussed during the weekend. On Sunday evening the child is simply told that he goes back to school on Monday. The child is awakened, gets dressed, and is given a light breakfast (to reduce any nausea). Father matter-of-factly takes the child to school, presents him to school personnel, and leaves. No discussions or questions take place. (The child's therapist may see him after school on the first day). Regardless of what occurred (vomiting, crying, or so on), the child is complimented on Monday evening. He is told that Tuesday will be better and no further discussion takes place. On Tuesday evening, the child is encouraged and complimented. Wednesday should present no problems, and a party that evening should celebrate his overcoming the problem.

5. *Brief Interview with the Child.* Sessions should be brief and should be held after school hours. Various situations should be described, emphasizing doing things in spite of fear (immediate return after any type of accident). The therapist can describe overcoming temporary fear in his own childhood. Phobias are described as always being transitory.

6. *Follow-Up.* Phone interviews should be encouraging and not overly solicitous. Long-range follow-ups should include questions about progress in general and about any other problem areas.

COMMENTARY: Kennedy reports that fifty successive Type 1 cases were treated successfully, with complete remission of school phobia symptoms and no symptom substitution or recurrence. Type 2 requires a different approach, not addressed in this article. Many therapists have successfully used this approach, often with some modifications. Differentiating types of phobias and using different techniques fit the growing trend of specifying methods for specific problems. In cases fitting the Type 1 description, any lengthy procedure (where the child has not returned to school) would be inappropriate.

SOURCE: Kennedy, W. A. "School Phobia: Rapid Treatment of Fifty Cases." *Journal of Abnormal Psychology,* 1965, *70,* 285–289.

Returning School-Phobic Children to School

AUTHORS: Elisabeth Lassers, Robert Nordan, and Sheila Bladholm

PRECIS: Practical steps in quickly returning a school-phobic child to school, including use of a supportive, firm therapeutic ally

INTRODUCTION: For little or no reason, a child may refuse to go to school. He complains of aches and pains, and may cry, perspire, become pale and show other signs of panic. He may want to go to school but cannot, because of acute anxiety. The basic difficulty is usually a mutual hostile-dependent relationship between mother and child (or at times between father and child). Nonverbal cues given by the parents may reinforce the child's remaining at home. The child's fear that harm will come to a family member is interpreted as a fear that the hostile wish might be fulfilled.

STEPS FOR SCHOOL RETURN: Although different approaches are used, most authors believe that early return to school is essential. The following suggested steps are performed as quickly as possible.

Physical Examination. This step is required to rule out organically based problems. Chronic minor symptoms, such as headaches and stomach upsets, that keep a child out of school may mask a school phobia.

Psychiatric Evaluation. First, psychosis or other serious psychopathology must be ruled out. The authors discuss a case in which school avoidance by a thirteen-year-old boy was seen as a symptom of psychotic decompensation and hospitalization was recommended. The boy's chest pains were not organically based. His refusal to return to school was accompanied by nightmares, fears, and high anxiety. His delusions of grandeur and persecution and tenuous reality testing became evident.

Second, the family dynamics are assessed and the precipitating event is determined. The authors discuss the case of a six-and-a-half-year-old boy, who refused to attend school after a three-week hospitalization for a broken leg. The family was very disorganized, with eleven children and a divorced mother. While hospitalized, the boy was lonely and angry at his mother for not visiting him.

Feelings about past desertions added to his current anger and fear. Unexpressed anger and destructive fantasies about his mother were present. Unresolved castration anxiety was seen as related to his leg injury. The mother's background led to her dependence on him in spite of strong feelings of rejection toward him.

Finding a Therapeutic Ally. It is important to find one or more people who can exert external control and be supportive to the family. With eight-year-old Sally, the family physician provided the support necessary for her to return to school. The mother insisted that Sally's complaints were organically based (a reaction to penicillin). The physician told her that Sally's hyperventilation was producing the negative reaction and that her problems were emotional. He informed the mother that firm insistence on school attendance was the best course of action. Although the mother did not want to force a "sick" child to go to school, she followed her physician's advice. Once returned to school, Sally did well.

The Interpretive Interview. The focus of the interview is to discuss the problems with the family and to foster the expectation of immediate return to school. The therapist is sympathetic with any parental concern or guilt regarding forcing the child to return to school but remains firm in this objective. Less desirable alternatives are mentioned—a truancy petition or hospitalization. A mild tranquilizer may be temporarily used to reduce anxiety regarding school return.

Planning. When possible, a meeting with all concerned should take place. The plan could be gradual return or, in some cases, a return to all-day attendance. Jenny, age nine, was helped by school personnel, who took an active part in planning. Vomiting had interfered with school attendance. A successful solution was found by sending a change of clothes to school.

Support. The therapist must continue to be involved after return to school is accomplished. The therapist often makes telephone calls, has office visits, and makes home or school visits. Drug therapy may be necessary.

Follow-Up. The therapist should check regularly to assess progress after return to school is accomplished. This indicates interest and availability to the family. Involvement and consultation with the school is also maintained.

Psychotherapy. Although further therapy was recommended in the cases mentioned earlier, none of the families accepted. Once the child was back in school, the family was evidently satisfied.

COMMENTARY: The article outlines practical steps in a therapist's aiding in the child's quick return to school. An important aspect is the use of a "therapeutic ally" who provides support and firmness. The therapist is depicted as an active, involved, directive agent, who provides reassurance to the family that the child is not physically sick and must be returned to school immediately. The activity of the therapist is congruent with the community mental health approach, in which a therapist may involve a variety of community resources. This model of intervention is natural for children's problems that directly affect the community.

SOURCE: Lassers, E., Nordan, R., and Bladholm, S. "Steps in the Return to School of Children with School Phobia." *American Journal of Psychiatry,* 1973, *130,* 265–268.

Treating School Phobias
with Sodium Pentothal

AUTHOR: Richard W. Nice

PRECIS: One-session use of sodium pentothal to aid expression of problems in treatment of school phobia when progress is limited

INTRODUCTION: The phobic child has an irrational fear of some aspect of school, which leads to an inability to attend school. Truancy does not have the aspect of irrational panic and truant children (in contrast to phobic children) often come from broken homes or very deprived environments. The first signs of school phobia are usually seen in children between five and ten years of age who generally have adequate intelligence and academic ability. Pervasive anxiety and psychosomatic complaints and fears are typical. Tantrums, unhappiness at school, and habit disorders are frequently seen. The father of the children tends to be passive, dominated by his wife, and unable to clearly define his role in the family. Neurotic dependency struggles between mother and child are typical in the development of a school phobia. The child usually experiences intense dependency feelings, guilt-producing striving for independence, and frightening feelings of hostility toward the mother. A simple situation can arouse intense anxiety and school phobia in the child.

CASE STUDY: A ten-and-a-half-year-old girl had been out of school for one month. She had cried, threatened to kill herself, and once jumped from a moving car on the way to school. She also had temper tantrums and hysteria when school time came. She had run away from home, hidden in the woods, and run out of school.

She was hostile and resistant to coming for therapy and did not want to discuss school with the therapist. A home tutor successfully worked with her to maintain academic progress. Since therapeutic progress was not forthcoming, the parents agreed that a sodium pentothal interview would be conducted. The goal was to uncover the cause of the phobic reaction and to desensitize her to discussing her fears and anxieties. Although very resistant, she became calm before the injected drug took effect (500 mg of pentothal was mixed with 500 cc's of 5 percent dextrose and water).

Once she had reached a relatively deep state, the quality of the interaction changed. In response to questions, she expressed little concern about either of her parents deserting her. She did express concern and resentment about her younger sister being accorded the same privileges and status as she had. She also reported some dreams about dolls and fights. After the interview, the mother was seen and instructed to stress the patient's independence and to give her special privileges that her sister did not have. Making dinner alone was one of the privileges she enjoyed. Tutoring now took place at the clinic instead of at home and a gradual return to school was planned. She refused an offered opportunity to listen to the recorded drug interview.

Conflicts between the parents heightened but Nice advised the mother to not consider separation while the girl was in treatment. She returned to school on a half-day basis. She asked that she need not take the bus home, so the guidance counselor drove her. On one occasion, she ran away and refused to go to school but did return. Academic progress proceeded well and no school-phobic reaction appeared again.

COMMENTARY: Nice believes that a one-session use of sodium pentothal desensitized the patient's fearfulness in expressing concerns and provided material to the therapist that shortened treatment and return to school. In situations where therapy is not progressing, this approach may well alter the situation. Many therapists might prefer the use of hypnosis, relaxation techniques, or rational-emotive approaches that might lead to desensitization and the ability to express concerns.

SOURCE: Nice, R. W. "The Use of Sodium Pentothal in the Treatment of a School Phobic." *Journal of Learning Disabilities,* 1968, *1,* 35–41.

Treating School Phobia with Implosive Therapy

AUTHORS: Ronald E. Smith and Theodore M. Sharpe

PRECIS: Six sessions of vividly imagined anxiety-provoking scenes successfully returned a thirteen-year-old school-phobic boy to school

INTRODUCTION: Implosive therapy is based on the classical extinction model and consists of the patient imagining scenes evoking high anxiety. Evoking the conditioned stimulus in the absence of the primary aversive (unconditioned) stimulus results in extinction of anxiety.

CASE STUDY: Billy, thirteen years old, was referred because he had been absent from school for seven weeks. After being absent for three weeks because of illness, he had developed a phobia toward school. He became anxious, unable to eat, and complained of chest pains. Force, punishment, nor bribes led to a return to school. He said he was unaware of reasons for his fear of school.

Billy was the youngest of two children, and was described as submissive, tense, compulsive, perfectionistic, and very attached to his family. He had many physical illnesses and his mother was quite overprotective. Increased school competition and many absences apparently led to poorer grades and the development of chest pains. He appeared quite anxious in class. He was teased by peers because of academic difficulties and his weak and sickly appearance.

Standard interviewing could not determine the sources of his anxiety, so a behaviorally oriented assessment procedure was employed. Billy was asked to visualize and describe a typical school day and his behavioral indications of anxiety were noted and recorded, including flushing of the skin, body movements, muscular tension, vocal tremors, and tears. Mathematics and literature both were sources of intense anxiety. Being called on, unable to answer questions, and being teased evoked high anxiety. Leaving home and leaving his mother did not evoke anxiety.

Through interviews, it was apparent that Billy's mother was reinforcing school avoidance by allowing daytime television viewing and staying up late. The parents were instructed to structure a normal day, with awakening, doing schoolwork, and usual bed time. The basics of implosive therapy were explained to the parents. This was seen as a very important step in gaining their support. Billy's teachers were asked to welcome him back, but to call no other attention to him.

TREATMENT: Six consecutive daily sessions took place, in which Billy vividly imagined scenes involving anxiety-arousing cues. His description of the scene and description of his feelings aided focusing. Each scene that was imagined was presented until anxiety was visibly reduced.

Some of the scenes used follow:

1. During breakfast, his parents totally ignore him.

2. A cold and rejecting mother orders him into the car. His fears increase as the school approaches. Evil, laughing faces appear in the window.

3. He walks through silent halls to the auditorium, where a sadistic principal and audience taunt him. Teachers ask him quick and impossible-to-answer questions.

Throughout the many scenes presented, the parents are depicted by the therapist as cold and rejecting.

After the first implosive therapy session, Billy was told to attend the anxiety-provoking mathematics class the next day, followed by a gradual increase in number of classes attended each day. Billy described situations in school that made him anxious, which supplied the therapist with ideas for scenes to be imagined. The first session produced great anxiety, weeping, and chest pains. The next day, he was able to eat and attend the mathematics class. After the fourth session, he returned to school full-time with very little anxiety. Treatment was terminated after the sixth session. The therapist praised Billy's progress and stressed that Billy himself was primarily responsible for the improvement. A thirteen-week follow-up showed no reported anxiety, regular school attendance, and many other positive occurrences.

COMMENTARY: Smith and Sharpe see an advantage in having the child's anxiety take place in the therapist's office rather than during forced school attendance. Peer criticism is thus avoided. Implosive therapy is seen as a possible method for treating school phobias and other anxiety-based disorders. Implosive therapy is quick and therefore has the advantages of low cost and rapid return to school (which most therapists and parents believe is most desirable). Behavioral observation while the child describes a day at school is potentially very useful for therapists, as it is a quick and natural way for a nonverbal child to reveal areas of concern. As in other approaches, parental reduction of secondary gain is employed. The parents must avoid inadvertently reinforcing behavior which is satisfying to the child, while positively encouraging and reinforcing appropriate behavior (attending school).

SOURCE: Smith, R. E., and Sharpe, T. M. "Treatment of a School Phobia with Implosive Therapy." *Journal of Consulting and Clinical Psychology,* 1970, *35,* 239–243.

Additional Readings

Abe, K. "Sulpride in School Phobia." *Psychiatria Clinica,* 1975, *8,* 95–98.

Author notes that techniques not utilizing drugs fail to relieve anxiety and somatic symptoms in many cases of school phobia. Parental counseling and desensitization reportedly failed with twenty-one school-phobic children. Rather than imipramine, sulpride was administered. For children ten to fourteen years old, daily dosages were 100 mg given before breakfast. Children of other ages received varied dosages depending on weight and initial response. Abe feels sulpride is more rapid and effective and has fewer side effects than tricyclic antidepressants.

Blackham, G. J., and Eden, B. F. "Effective Reentry in a Long-Standing Case of School Phobia." *Devereux Forum,* 1973, *8,* 42–48.

Article specifies steps for successful reentry to school of a thirteen-year-old boy. Complete environmental control of reinforcing events that maintain the undesirable behavior is seen as essential. Interpersonal behaviors that are more adaptive are encouraged by using an extensive range of reinforcers. The parents must be helped to deal with their apprehension and guilt and helped to cope with practical problems. Absolute consistency of reinforcement is necessary and successive approximation into the phobic setting is suggested.

Coolidge, J. C., and Brodie, R. D. "Observations of Mothers of Forty-nine School-Phobic Children." *Journal of Child Psychiatry*, 1974, *13*, 275–285.

Mothers of school-phobic children are considered to have severe early unresolved conflicts and separation anxiety. Displacement, projection, and omnipotent attempts to control were uniformly present in the mothers studied. If a mother is able to look at herself and lower her projection and displacement, insight-oriented therapy is suggested. Mothers who are more disturbed require an ego-lending, supportive approach. Guarded, suspicious families might require an action-oriented approach with no personal inquiry.

Coolidge, J. C., and Grunebaum, M. G. "Individual and Group Therapy of a Latency-Age Child." *International Journal of Group Psychotherapy*, 1964, *14*, 84–96.

The authors advocate group and combined group and individual psychotherapy and discuss the case of a five-and-a-half-year-old girl with school-phobia symptoms. The family dynamics of this case and the functioning of activity group therapy are described in great detail. In the group, the girl was able to make considerable social progress and express herself (which she did not do in individual therapy). Various activities and materials are listed.

Eisenberg, L. "School Phobia: A Study in the Communication of Anxiety." *American Journal of Psychiatry*, 1958, *114*, 712–718.

Eisenberg discusses a program for rapid school return. The mother fosters the child's overdependence on her, yet resents the child's parasitic clinging. When firm handling is needed (illness, change of school), the parents often are distraught and not reassuring. The nonverbal message is that the situation is extraordinarily frightening. Parental behavior is seen as contradictory and as causing the school-phobic symptoms. The author suggests active participation by the therapist and community personnel and describes continuing therapy with the family.

Gittelman-Klein, R., and Klein, D. F. "School Phobia: Diagnostic
    Considerations in the Light of Imipramine Effects." *The
    Journal of Nervous and Mental Disease*, 1973, *156*, 199–215.

The authors conducted a double blind study (imipramine and
placebo) with thirty-five school-phobic children, ages six to fourteen. The usual therapeutic procedures were also followed with the
family. In six weeks, imipramine was significantly superior to
placebo in inducing school return and in measured general therapeutic efficacy. Drug dosages varied from 100 to 200 mg per day.
The article reports the results of psychiatrist and mother rating
scales and discusses the dynamics of school phobia. Imipramine
reduces primary anxiety and parental pressure then exposes the
child to the fearful situation, where the child's anxiety dissipates
through extinction.

Hersen, M. "Behavior Modification Approach to a School Phobia
    Case." *Journal of Clinical Psychology*, 1970, *26*, 128–132.

Hersen describes the treatment of a twelve-and-a-half-year-
old boy with a school phobia by training his parents to use behavioral
techniques. Guidelines for therapists are presented. Resistance to
behavioral techniques are dealt with in a positive manner, which
includes the imparting of information regarding operant principles.
Seeing the boy in therapy sessions permits the therapist to observe
progress and reinforce changes and it also enables the patient to
express anger about the altered responses from the environment.
Hersen feels that school phobias and other deviant behaviors are
inadvertently learned by children and are then reinforced by adults.

Machler, T. J. "Pinocchio in the Treatment of School Phobia."
    Bulletin of the Menninger Clinic, 1965, *29*, 212–219.

Machler briefly treated a ten-year-old girl for school phobia.
He used hand puppets and the Pinocchio theme for diagnosis
and treatment, together with play therapy and casework with the
parents. Machler sees the Pinocchio character as a kindred spirit
to children: Pinocchio acts on impulse, behaves irresponsibly, is
punished, and emerges whole and better. The girl's infantile omnipotence and search for a magic wand were revealed in puppet
play with Pinocchio, through which she was able to give up her
illusory goals.

Marine, E. "School Refusal—Who Should Intervene? (Diagnostic and treatment categories)." *Journal of School Psychology,* 1968–69, *7,* 63–70.

Marine presents four cases to illustrate four proposed categories of school refusal. Simple separation anxiety is handled by the teacher and principal. Mild school refusal responds to crisis intervention that uses a structured approach by teacher, principal, school nurse, pediatrician and guidance counselor. Chronic severe school refusal requires family therapy and collaboration with the school social worker, school psychologist, and mental health team. Childhood psychosis with school refusal symptoms is treated in residential treatment and special class by a psychiatric team.

Miller, D. L. "School Phobia: Diagnosis, Emotional Genesis, and Management." *New York State Journal of Medicine,* 1972, *72,* 1160–1165.

The author discusses the cases of five elementary school children, to illustrate dynamic understanding and treatment of school phobia. The roles of the physician, school principal, school nurse, and teacher are described. A rapid somatic work-up is stressed so that the physician is certain that no disease is present. Plans must be based on an understanding both of the family dynamics and of the school's organizational structure.

Newman, M. R., and Stern, E. M. "The Age Game." *The Psychoanalytic Review,* 1964, *51,* 300–313.

Newman and Stern feel that therapeutically controlled regression is helpful in treating emotionally disturbed children. The authors describe "The Age Game" and present a successful illustrative case of a ten-year-old girl with a severe school phobia. In the game, the child pretends to be much younger—he or she chooses an age and is told to act as if she were that age. Typically, the child pretends to be a baby who gets cuddled. Yearning to return to helplessness is seen by the authors as a desire for earlier gratification. Facing aloneness and separation from an all-caring mother leads to self-realization. Regression helps the child realize that earlier conflicts can be dealt with and psychological growth can occur.

Olsen, I. A., and Coleman, H. S. "Treatment of School Phobia as a Case of Separation Anxiety." *Psychology in the Schools,* 1967, *4,* 151–154.

In a clinic, the authors treated a six-year-old boy for a school phobia. Separation was achieved first as a gesture and then for increasing time intervals. The therapists first used a stopwatch to help the boy control the amount of separation from his father, the parent on whom he was the least dependent. Because of the parents' and principal's anxiety, all agreed that the psychologist would return him to school. After twenty minutes, the psychologist left, and the boy seemed to do well. The child learned to associate separation with mastery and independence rather than anxiety.

Pritchard, C., and Ward, R. I. "The Family Dynamics of School Phobics." *British Journal of Social Work,* 1974, *4,* 61–94.

This article gives a detailed description of a casework method of assessing family dynamics. Significant differences in family interaction are described between male (forty-one cases) and female (twenty-six cases) school phobics. Oedipal problems are seen as significant factors that must be dealt with in treatment.

Rines, W. B. "Behavior Therapy Before Institutionalization." *Psychotherapy: Theory, Research and Practice,* 1973, *10,* 284–286.

Rines describes a twelve-year-old girl who had a Kennedy Type II (way of life) school phobia. In spite of Kennedy's suggestions that behavioral therapy is only appropriate for Type I, a successful behavioral approach was carried out. Type II phobias are said to require lengthy psychodynamically oriented treatment. A crucial element was the active involvement of school personnel. Rines speculates that the mother's interference resulted from a need to have a socially inept child (as seen in other cases). Behavioral approaches to accomplish school return are recommended for both Type I and II school phobias and avoiding institutionalization is seen as beneficial whenever possible.

Skynner, A. C. R. "School Phobia: A Reappraisal." *British Journal of Medical Psychology,* 1974, *47,* 1–16.

This article emphasizes the neglected role of the father in conjoint family therapy. Skynner describes four types of situations in school phobia: (1) parents present the developmental challenge to the child; (2) therapist shares the presentation of the challenge with the parents; (3) parents are fully colluding with the child; and (4) truants referred as school phobics. The father must help loosen the exclusive mutual attachment between mother and child. Authority and control are crucial issues. Therapy focuses on confronting and weakening fantasies of omnipotence in the child and parents. Medication (librium) is routinely employed.

Smith, S. L. "School Refusal with Anxiety: A Review of Sixty-three Cases." *Canadian Psychiatric Association Journal,* 1970, *15,* 257–264.

Smith reviewed cases of English children with school phobias. Peak incidence was between eleven and twelve years of age, with a high proportion of youngest sibling. Three syndromes were found: separation anxiety of young children; school phobia in older children with no previous episode; and depression or withdrawal in adolescents. Various treatment modalities were used—twenty-four were treated as outpatients, twelve were treated on a hospital ward, and fifteen were transferred to a different school.

Spain, J. L., Attkisson, C. C., and Fine, H. J. " 'Never Scold a Little Tin Soldier': Case Conceptualization in School Phobia." *Psychotherapy: Theory, Research and Practice,* 1970, *7,* 95–98.

The authors use the case of a ten-year-old boy with a school phobia to illustrate therapeutic approaches and characterological phenomena. Prompt school return and treatment of the defects in development are both necessary. A poem about a tin soldier written by the boy reflected his heightened sensitivity to criticism and his feelings of vulnerability. The authors note that in treatment it is important to understand the parental dynamics, the child's image of his parents, and the factors that precipitated the school phobia.

Sperling, M. "School Phobias: Classification, Dynamics, and Treatment." *The Psychoanalytic Study of the Child,* 1967, *22,* 375–401.

Sperling examines causal, dynamic, and therapeutic factors in school phobia. She considers school phobia as a fixation at the anal-sadistic phase of development, with ambivalence, narcissism, and magical thinking (omnipotence). A pathological parent-child relationship can lead to an insidious trauma of an induced school phobia. The common school phobia follows trauma. Differential treatment is based on differential diagnosis. Sperling advocates treating the total neurosis, not simply treating symptoms and quickly returning the child to school.

Veltkamp, L. J. "School Phobia." *Journal of Family Counseling*, 1975,
    3, 47–51.

This article defines school phobia (acute and chronic) and
presents three cases. Children afraid of separation find a weak link
among significant adults, and exploit the weakness to avoid school.
Veltkamp describes cases in which separation anxiety was inadvertently reinforced. Immediate physical evaluation, family interviews,
and intervention with school personnel were 85 percent effective
in returning the acute school phobic to school. Chronic school
phobics were returned only 20 percent of the time.

Waldron, S., Shrier, D. K., Stone, B., and Tobin, F. "School Phobia
    and Other Childhood Neuroses: A Systematic Study of the
    Children and Their Families." *American Journal of Psychiatry*,
    1975, *132*, 802–808.

The authors call for the use of rating scales to better understand clinical concepts such as school phobias. Their rating scales
revealed mutually hostile-dependent relationships between mother
and child, as well as the mother's overconcern for the child. The
child shows a high degree of separation anxiety and faulty development of autonomy and self-esteem. School attendance requires considerable capacity for independent functioning. One significant
research finding is that neurotic parents have more neurotic children than do normal parents. The school-phobic children were
involved in neurotic patterns with their parents.

Westman, J. C., Kansky, E. W., Erikson, M. E., Arthur, B., and
    Vroom, A. L. "Parallel Group Psychotherapy with the Parents
    of Emotionally Disturbed Children." *International Journal of
    Group Psychotherapy*, 1963, *13*, 52–60.

Parallel group insight psychotherapy opens conscious verbal
communication between parents. Separate mothers' and fathers'
groups meet, with periodic joint meetings. Families in parallel
group psychotherapy go through five phases: family neurosis,
displacement to the group, mirroring in the groups, intrapersonal
change, and interpersonal change. The authors describe an illustrative case of a family in which a six-year-old girl developed a school
phobia. The girl's return to school and the changes in the family
are detailed.

Childhood Fears

Fear is an unpleasant emotion caused by anticipation of danger. Fears of the dark, heights, transportation, animals, and monsters are typical in childhood. Dreams often reflect children's fears. A neurotic phobic reaction is more severe and exaggerated than normal. A phobia may be defined as an irrational and persistent fear.

Modeling and the Fear of Dentistry

AUTHORS: Richard Adelson and Marvin R. Goldfried

PRECIS: Having a fearful child observe a nonfearful child, to eliminate fear

INTRODUCTION: The first visit to the dentist often provokes fear in a child. Awesome dental equipment, a new experience, peers and sibling stories, and parental fears often make for a difficult visit. Prior writings suggest: (1) allowing the child to visit many times and get acquainted with procedures; (2) a "tell, show, then do" procedure; and (3) premedication to make the child more compliant. The authors explain why Methods 1 and 2 are not the most effective and often do not work with the very fearful child. Method 3 may have negative or dangerous consequences.

Adelson and Goldfried describe the use of pleasurable activities and gradual habituation to eliminate children's fears. Systematic desensitization and emotive imagery have also been employed. In managing the apprehensive child dental patient, the authors use modeling—the observation of a nonfearful child in the same situation. Learning through modeling is particularly effective when the observer is aroused, when the model has high status, and when there are positive consequences for the model's behavior.

Amy (four years) and Penny (three-and-a-half years) were scheduled for office visits. Amy was outgoing and had had a prior pleasant dental experience. Penny was shy, withdrawn, and worried about her first dental examination. She was invited to sit in the back of the room and watch Amy's examination (mouth mirror and explorer, visual examination, radiographs, and soft tissue examination). As expected, Amy was cheerful and cooperative throughout. Since she had been so cooperative, she was allowed to select a special prize from a small treasure chest. Amy stood on the chair and jumped loudly to the floor with both feet.

After Amy left, Penny was examined. Although reticent, she willingly cooperated. Before receiving her reward, she jumped to the floor exactly as her "model" had. Six months later, Penny very cooperatively received polishing and fluoride treatments, and got down from the chair in the same manner. The authors interpret that Penny was aroused (worried and apprehensive), the model had high status (somewhat older, gregarious, and sociable), and the model's behavior resulted in positive consequences (a reward).

The authors consider modeling particularly effective in introducing children in a large clinic setting. A film may be shown where the child vicariously views a favorable model. The dentist himself is also seen as a powerful model and should be calm, relaxed, confident, and positive. Modeling (live or film) is seen as very effective in producing a more favorable response to the administration of actual analgesia.

COMMENTARY: This article is obviously applicable in allaying fears of children in dental situations. Because the therapist sees many fearful children, the therapist might contact the parent and/or dentist, and expedite this approach. Possibly, the therapist could use modeling or a film in his own office to help children cope more effectively with upcoming stressful situations. Like other techniques in this book, it provides another example for the therapist to use when speaking to audiences about generally helpful approaches in child development.

SOURCE: Adelson, R., and Goldfried, M. R. "Modeling and the Fearful Child Patient." *Journal of Dentistry for Children,* 1970, *37,* 34–47.

Treating Fearful Children

AUTHOR: Jacob H. Conn

PRECIS: Play interviews to help children express themselves and overcome their fears

INTRODUCTION: Most timid, fearful children conceal their feelings after having been embarrassed or ridiculed. The psychiatrist respectfully listens to the parents and helps relieve the burden placed on them by unjust accusation or excessive self-criticism. A method of play interview has been developed to give an opportunity for the child to express himself. In an experimental play situation, the fearful child can present his point of view, interests, and complaints.

PROCEDURES: Before the child is seen, a parent is interviewed, in order to get a description of the child's behavior. This interview also helps decrease some tension and overconcern. After the parent interview, the child is invited to inspect the various toys in the playroom. The mother's complaints are not discussed with the child. After the child's spontaneous play is observed, he is asked to sit next to a toy house that contains a concealed microphone. A stenographer records all dialog. Others can observe through a one-way screen. The child is not told what he may or may not say or do. Whatever he says about parents or siblings is accepted in a sympathetic, encouraging manner. He is repeatedly put at ease and therefore he more and more feels that he has found someone with whom he can converse freely—directly or through the medium of dolls. The play interview is not a fixed technique, but rather an opportunity for the child to express himself and reveal problems to himself by pretending it is not he himself who is fearful, envious, or angry, but the doll character. By explaining the doll's motives and imagination, he can reveal his own. The child's life situation gives the therapist clues as to possible arrangements of dolls and furniture.

CASE STUDY: Nine-year-old Harriet was brought by her over-solicitous mother. She cried at night and wanted her father to sleep with her. After hearing about three little girls who had been kid-napped and killed, she became quite frightened. She had always been afraid of the dark and used to scream until one of her parents came in to quiet her. Two years previously, she had heard of a kid-napping and was afraid that there was a man in the room who would kidnap her younger sister. She was timid with strangers, cried easily, and was in a remedial reading disabilities class (having an "average" IQ score).

The article presents a verbatim interview related to Harriet's playing with two girl dolls "who had been kidnapped." Harriet spoke for each doll and the psychiatrist asked leading questions. One doll expressed a wish to not have a sister who was bothersome and who prevented the doll from having everything. The other doll expressed the positive aspects of having a sister. A detailed question-and-answer period followed, in which the two girl dolls were in beds and a black male doll was standing nearby. Harriet answered ques-tions that had the theme of the kidnapper removing his mask and really being her father. The story was discussed with Harriet through leading questions, and her wish to have her sister kidnapped was revealed. During the third play interview, Harriet revealed her fear of kidnapping, her understanding of her wish to get rid of her sister, and her not wanting to think of removing her sister anymore. Harriet said that she had not been afraid recently, because there was nothing in the dark to scare her.

The mother reported dramatic improvement. Harriet was not fearful, did not talk of kidnappers, and did not call for her father. In the fourth interview, Harriet discussed not being afraid and real-ized that her fears were only her imagination.

The article presents the questions and answers. In all, nine sessions were conducted over a ten-month period. A one-and-a-half-year follow-up revealed improvement in all areas.

The procedure uses the capacity for self-scrutiny, provides for a personal reorientation and a synthesis of seemingly unrelated experiences. The child can view the whole story and see himself as others see him. No attempt is made to arouse antagonistic or hostile feelings. Guns, knives, soldiers, and so on are not included in the play materials. Therefore, aggression and anxiety situations occur very infrequently and in no case has a therapist been attacked by a patient. Termination is decided with the consent of the patient, who also decides when to return after each session (in one, two, or three weeks).

COMMENTARY: Conn presents a type of play interview in which the child is helped to express motivation and feelings. It is apparent that the theoretical framework of the therapist determines the direction of the interview. The article describes a good example of a situation in which the child is able to make the connection between fears and unexpressed or unaccepted wishes or "bad" thoughts. The focus is on fearful children, but the method is typical of a type of interpretive play interview used by many therapists with children having various behavioral problems. Conn's comment that improvement almost always occurs after the first few interviews is significant, since nonimprovement would be a cue that this type of approach is not appropriate in that situation.

SOURCE: Conn, J. H. "The Treatment of Fearful Children." *American Journal of Orthopsychiatry,* 1941, *11,* 744–752.

Eliminating a High Building Phobia by Desensitization and Game Playing

AUTHORS: Leo Croghan and Gerard J. Musante

PRECIS: Six sessions of behavior therapy with a seven-year-old boy: playing games in the presence of the feared object

INTRODUCTION: Imagined situations reportedly do not arouse emotional responses equivalent to responses evoked by live situations. The following case involved an in vivo desensitization of a boy with a high building phobia, using game playing as the method of reciprocal inhibition.

CASE STUDY: B. R., seven years old, had an isolated phobia that began while viewing skyscrapers. In a small city, he showed fear of the two tallest structures. While viewing tall buildings, he closed his eyes and refused to move. If led inside, his fear subsided.

Six sessions, averaging forty minutes each, took place over a two-and-a-half-month period. The therapist walked with the boy toward a tall building. At forty yards, when the building became visible, the boy closed his eyes and pulled the therapist away from the building. Several games were then introduced as counterconditioners. First they played "jumping the cracks in the sidewalk." Then B. R. looked at the building twenty-five times. They then approached the building, which the therapist kicked. B. R. was asked to kick it five times. The therapist said that the building could not kick back and could not hurt B. R. After each session, B. R. was given a soft drink and candy and was asked to report progress to his mother.

During the second session, B. R. was fortunately able to observe the behavior of young children touring the building. The therapist and B. R. threw snowballs at the building during the third session. Spontaneous talking, number of glances, and kicks increased with each session. Although there was improvement, B. R. was still somewhat phobic while going to the hotel where he was staying with his mother. The therapist drove B. R. to the hotel for the final two sessions. As the hotel came into view, B. R. counted a hundred glances at the hotel, but he refused to get out and kick the hotel, so the therapist did it. B. R. stated he would do so during the next visit, which he did. Both of them then kicked the building together. From that point on, he displayed no fear of tall buildings.

Croghan and Musante speculate that traditional game therapy might be successful because the child plays games with, or in the presence of, a feared object, thus becoming desensitized.

COMMENTARY: This article describes a therapist's use of playing games with a child, outside the office, in the presence of a feared object. Many psychotherapists only have children play in an office. One implication is that the described method might be used when an office approach does not work in a few sessions. Another implication is that game playing or discussions might take place in the surroundings that elicit anxiety. Therapists might be more effective with some fearful children in the children's own homes.

SOURCE: Croghan, L., and Musante, G. J. "The Elimination of a Boy's High Building Phobia by In Vivo Desensitization and Game Playing." *Journal of Behavior Therapy and Experimental Psychiatry,* 1975, *6,* 87–88.

Systematic Desensitization of a Dog Phobia

AUTHOR: Stanley Kissel

PRECIS: Use of pictures, reading, and storytelling about dogs with an eleven-year-old girl with a dog phobia

INTRODUCTION: Although Kissel successfully used classical systematic desensitization with adolescents, latency-age children (five to twelve years old) did not respond well. With this latter age group, modifications are suggested to deal with (1) difficulties with imagery, (2) concerns of fear of failure and loss of control, and (3) the anxiety-reducing nature of interpersonal relationships. It is pointed out that the busy practitioner in an outpatient clinic may not be able to use the actual objects of fear often used in desensitization.

CASE STUDY: Eleven-year-old Yvonne was not doing well in school. She was shy and lacked confidence, but was not intellectually retarded. Her terror of dogs was the reason for referral. Yvonne was initially afraid that the therapist would show her a large dog. She attributed her fear to an incident at two years of age when a visitor threw a large stuffed bulldog into her playpen.

At the initial session, she was told that she could learn to not fear dogs just as she had learned to fear them. A portable radio would be her prize for being able to pet a dog. Muscle relaxation was demonstrated, and she was taught about imagery. During the six additional sessions, she continually glanced and fidgeted. Since she was unable to relax, the desensitization technique was modified. The interpersonal relationship was substituted for muscle relaxation as the anxiety inhibitor. Instead of imagery, more concrete pictures of dogs were used.

Three books were used, ranked in order of fewest to most pictures of dogs. With the therapist keeping score, Yvonne pointed to every picture of a dog. She was given homework in which she would write a story about a dog. School-age children expect homework and it gave her more opportunity to work on her fear. However, this time Yvonne forgot her homework, which led to a final modification of procedure.

Yvonne was asked to make up a story about a dog and tape-record it. While playing it, she imagined what was happening and afterward described the images for the therapist. At the end of another replay, the therapist added more fearful events, which she imagined (for example, a dog on a leash ran off, played with her, licked her, and so on). After each session, she was asked to draw a picture of the dog she imagined. Homework was also hierarchical, in that numbers of dog pictures had to be cut out and put in a scrapbook. Other assignments were sketching or photographing a live dog. Kissel also suggests visiting a pet shop and finally petting a dog.

COMMENTARY: Kissel presents a rationale for modification of desensitization with young children. Clinicians may have to make specific modifications, depending on the child's response. Within the framework of desensitizing fears, the techniques of telling stories, taking pictures, doing homework, and so forth have been useful to different theorists. The many different storytelling techniques may serve the purpose of desensitization along with other purposes seen by the therapist. Hyperkinetic behavior may well be influenced by the procedures described. For example, modifications of stories could be made in which the child is less restless, less impulsive, and so forth. Homework could then be given in keeping with modified actual behavior.

SOURCE: Kissel, S. "Systematic Desensitization Therapy with Children: A Case Study and Some Suggested Modifications." *Professional Psychology*, 1972, *3*, 164–168.

Deconditioning Children's Phobias

AUTHOR: Arnold A. Lazarus

PRECIS: Reducing fears by systematic use of food, relaxation, drugs, and conditioned avoidance

INTRODUCTION: This article describes an application of Wolpe's methods to the field of child therapy. Feeding responses have been employed in overcoming neurotic anxieties in children. Wolpe has shown that many other responses are capable of inhibiting anxiety. Lazarus used feeding, relaxation, drugs and conditioned avoidance, in deconditioning children's phobias. These techniques were applied to the following case studies.

DECONDITIONING BASED ON FEEDING RESPONSES: John, eight years old, developed a fear of moving vehicles two years after he and his parents had been in an automobile accident. He refused to enter any vehicle and became hysterical when his father once tried to force him into his car. The therapist spoke to John about trains, airplanes, buses, and so on, which made him anxious. When John made any type of positive comment, he was given his favorite chocolate. During the third interview, there was no overt anxiety. Deliberate "accidents" with toy cars were played, resulting in fairly high anxiety. John was given chocolate after each "accident" and his anxiety soon diminished. Then the accident was discussed (and chocolates given) while sitting together in a stationary car. John then took short trips in a car with the therapist and then with his parents.

SYSTEMATIC DESENSITIZATION BASED ON RELAXATION: Carol, nine and a half years old, became enuretic, developed fear of the dark, and had night terrors and "psychosomatic ailments." Just prior to these developments a school friend had drowned, Carol's next-door playmate had died of meningitis, and she had witnessed a fatal car accident. During an interview, her mother stated that she read that the maturation of nine-year-old children would be hindered by any overt affection. The therapist suggested the necessity of deliberate, overt love and warmth. While on a three-week vacation, Carol's behavior was normal, but on return her behavior worsened. It became apparent that Carol feared losing her mother through death. An anxiety hierarchy of seven steps was constructed (separation from mother for a first step of five minutes to one week for the seventh). While relaxed, Carol was told to imagine that she would not see her mother for five minutes, and so forth. Repeated reciprocal inhibition led to the development of conditioned inhibition. Five sessions over ten consecutive days desensitized Carol to the threat of maternal deprivation.

DRUGS IN DECONDITIONING: Douglas, three and a half years old, had had severe phobic reactions to dogs since being bitten by a dog five months before therapy. His parents' purchase of a puppy worsened his fears—fear of cats, birds, and outdoors then developed. His overactivity precluded the use of relaxation techniques. A satisfactory level of sedation was reached by administration of small doses of amobarbital and phenaglycodol over a three-day period. Gradual introduction to animals did not lead to anxiety. Drugs were gradually reduced over a five-week period, and a one-year follow-up revealed no relapses.

DECONDITIONING BY CONDITIONED AVOIDANCE RESPONSES: Since learning to walk, ten-year-old Brian had always woken early in the morning and gone to his mother's bed. Punishments, threats, and rewards had not changed this behavior. When questioned, Brian said that he wanted to sleep in his own bed but when he awoke, he would become very anxious unless he went to his mother's bed (the bed being the source of anxiety relief). Avoidance conditioning with a mild electric shock was used. Brian was asked to imagine himself in his mother's bed and to say "mother's bed" when he saw a clear image. A mild electric shock was applied to his forearm until he could not tolerate it. At that point he said "my bed" and current was turned off. This occurred fourteen times for approximately ten minutes. A week later, Brian reported with great pride that he had slept in his own bed every night. Although he awoke for the first five nights, he merely went back to sleep. A six-month follow-up showed no relapse. Brian's ability to sleep in his own bed led to many other positive changes reported by the parents.

COMMENTARY: This article appeared early in the development of behavior therapy approaches with children. One might prefer to avoid the use of food to inhibit anxiety, since eating for comfort is often philosophically opposed by parents. One might also avoid aversive procedures for philosophical reasons or because of a preference for using positive reinforcers. However, this article exemplifies the attempt to tailor treatment to the individual client and situation. The target is clearly the reduction of undesirable behavior. Evidence is given here and in the later literature for the absence of symptom substitution and the frequent appearance of other positive changes. Variations of these basic procedures have been used for most childhood behavior problems.

SOURCE: Lazarus, A. A. "The Elimination of Children's Phobias by Deconditioning." *Medical Proceedings* [South Africa], 1959, 5, 261–265.

Emotive Imagery in Treating Phobias

AUTHORS: Arnold A. Lazarus and Arnold Abramovitz

PRECIS: Two cases using imagined hero figures or wish-fulfilling situations to reduce fears and inhibit anxiety

INTRODUCTION: Removing fears (learned, unadaptive responses) can be eliminated by repeatedly evoking incompatible responses. Systematic desensitization gradually habituates the imagined stimuli through the anxiety-inhibiting response of relaxation. This article describes the use of inducing anxiety-inhibiting *emotive* images, without training the child to relax. Emotive images are images that arouse feelings of self-assertion, pride, affection, mirth, and similar anxiety-inhibiting responses. As in usual systematic desensitization, the range, intensity, and circumstances of the child's fears are assessed and a most- to least-feared hierarchy is established. In conversation, the therapist asks about and establishes the child's hero images and the accompanying wish fulfillments. Nine phobic children, ages seven through fourteen, were treated using emotive imagery. Seven recovered, in a mean of 3.3 sessions. Follow-ups up to twelve months later showed no relapses or symptom substitution.

CASE STUDY 1: Stanley, age fourteen, had had an intense fear of dogs for three years. Training in relaxation was ineffective. Because of his inarticulateness, the nature of Stanley's aspirations was difficult to ascertain. After much discussion, the topic of greatest interest to him turned out to be racing cars. The therapist presented to Stanley a detailed story in which Stanley owns his long-desired Alfa Romeo sports car. Concrete driving events were described by the therapist. In the midst of these thrilling experiences, a little dog is seen from the car. Later while Stanley and his car are being admired at a cafe, a large dog comes up to him. While this story was told, Stanley signaled anxiety as traditionally indicated, by raising his finger.

After three sessions with this method, a marked improvement in reaction to dogs was reported. During the next two sessions, a few field assignments were given and then therapy was terminated. A twelve-month follow-up revealed no trace of the dog phobia.

CASE STUDY 2: A ten-year-old boy was excessively afraid of the dark. He felt acute anxiety when his parents left and even when they were home he had to be accompanied when entering any darkened room. This fear presumably originated after he viewed a frightening film and had been warned about burglars and kidnappers. A previous therapist had ameliorated some interpersonal difficulties, but the fear of darkness remained.

After a thirty-minute conversation, this boy's great interest was revealed in two radio heroes—Superman and Captain Silver. He was asked to imagine that Superman and Captain Silver appointed him as their agent. A detailed story was told by the therapist: While at home, the boy receives a signal on his wrist radio. He waits for the heroes, alone, in a dimly lit lounge. If anxiety was indicated in any scene, the story was terminated. An anxiety-arousing image was represented to be less threatening or more positively challenging. By the third session, he could imagine himself alone in his darkened bathroom, awaiting Superman's communication.

At the end of treatment, his phobia was gone, school work reportedly had improved, and he had lost his previous insecurity. Gains were being maintained at an eleven-month follow-up.

COMMENTARY: This early work using "emotive imagery" is an excellent example of attempts to tailor specific methods to specific problems. Since they did not consider relaxation and the use of food as efficacious, Lazarus and Abramovitz used the anxiety-inhibiting method of having children imagine stories related to their own hero images. Since then, other therapists have used imaginative stories in a variety of ways to aid children in coping with various neuroses and with other problems covered in this book.

SOURCE: Lazarus, A. A., and Abramovitz, A. "The Use of 'Emotive Imagery' in the Treatment of Children's Phobias." *Journal of Mental Science*, 1962, *108*, 191–195.

Treating a Noise Phobia by Flooding

AUTHORS: William Yule, Ben Sacks, and Lionel Hersov

PRECIS: Two sessions of performing the feared activity in eliminating a noise phobia in a nine-year-old boy

INTRODUCTION: Uncomplicated phobias in childhood are often treated with systematic desensitization. The following example illustrates the use of flooding when systematic desensitization is not successful.

CASE STUDY: Bill, nine years old, was referred because he feared sudden, loud noises—bursting balloons, cap guns, motorcycles, and pneumatic drills. These fears prevented normal play with peers and siblings. He sulked, felt people were against him, and was self-conscious.

Desensitization was used for twenty-two sessions, each lasting from thirty minutes to one hour. The hierarchy consisted of firing caps to bursting balloons and hearing cars backfiring. Actually firing a cap gun, while relaxing, conversing, and eating candy, was successful in eliminating that fear. Treatment was discontinued, although other fears persisted.

Nine months later, Bill was still worried about his balloon phobia. The therapist explained that treatment would be unpleasant for a short time, but Bill wanted to try it. Fifty inflated balloons were brought into a small room, frightening Bill very much. He refused to burst any, so the therapist burst six, making loud noises. Bill cried, but the therapist continued bursting ballons until Bill did not flinch at all. With much persuasion, Bill pushed balloons against a nail held by the therapist. Steps followed of bursting balloons by hand with one hand over his ear, then bursting balloons with both ears uncovered. In this first session, 220 balloons were burst and, although shaken, he agreed to return the next day. During the second session, 320 balloons were burst, after initial encouraging and prompting. By the end, he burst them enthusiastically.

A two-year follow-up showed no noise phobias and better peer relationships. The authors prefer to try desensitization first and to use flooding if desensitization is unsuccessful. They caution that sufficiently prolonged exposure to fearful stimuli is necessary. Treatment should not be terminated until the person is quite confident of his ability to tolerate the fearful situation.

COMMENTARY: Recently, flooding techniques have been increasingly used to overcome fears. This case is a good example of a patient successfully overcoming a specific fear in two sessions. Flooding techniques appear compatible with other methods, in that specific fears may be handled while other problems are approached using other theoretical models.

SOURCE: Yule, W., Sacks, B., and Hersov, L. "Successful Flooding Treatment of a Noise Phobia in an Eleven-Year-Old." *Journal of Behavior Therapy and Experimental Psychiatry*, 1974, *5*, 209–211.

Additional Readings

Freeman, B. J., Roy, R. R., and Hemmick, S. "Extinction of a Phobia of Physical Examination in a Seven-Year-Old Mentally Retarded Boy: A Case Study." *Behaviour Research and Therapy*, 1976, *14*, 63–64.

The authors describe a treatment in which a social relationship was used as an antianxiety agent for a seven-and-a-half-year-old retarded boy with a phobic response to physical examinations. The traditional counterconditioning procedures (relaxation or positive imagery) were not used. The examination by a male physician was paired with a very comfortable relationship that the boy had with a ward nurse. The article outlines eleven steps for the treatment, in which the nurse performed parts of the examination or was present during the examination. Generalization did occur to other physicians.

Hampe, E., Noble, H., Miller, L. C., and Barrett, C. L. "Phobic Children One and Two Years Posttreatment." *Journal of Abnormal Psychology*, 1973, *82*, 446–453.

Follow-up studies revealed that 80 percent of sixty-two phobic children treated were free of symptoms or significantly improved. Only 7 percent had severe phobias. Other deviant behavior (symptom substitution) was not developed by the successfully treated group. The two-year follow-up showed no difference in outcome effect between psychotherapy and reciprocal inhibition therapy. Time-limited therapy of two months' duration was effective for approximately 60 percent of the phobic children.

Jones, M. C. "The Elimination of Children's Fears." *Journal of Experimental Psychology*, 1924, *7*, 382–390.

Jones reports that two preschoolers' fearful responses were successfully removed by conditioning procedures. The fear object was associated with a craved object. The boys participated in play groups of selected children under supervision (social imitation). Other methods employed were verbal appeal, elimination through disuse, negative adaptation, repression, and distraction.

Kanfer, F. H., Koroly, P., and Newman, A. "Reduction of Children's Fear of the Dark by Competence-Related and Situation Threat-Related Verbal Cues." *Journal of Consulting and Clinical Psychology*, 1975, *43*, 251–258.

Forty-five five- and six-year-old children were treated for fear of the dark. Three types of verbal controlling responses were employed in developing tolerance for darkness. The children, grouped by response, repeated sentences that (1) emphasized competence (active control), (2) reduced the negative qualities of darkness, and (3) were neutral. The amount of illumination was controlled by the child. Ability to tolerate darkness was best accomplished by the group using competency responses (Type 1).

Kelley, C. K. "Play Desensitization of Fear of Darkness in Preschool Children." *Behaviour Research and Therapy*, 1976, *14*, 79–81.

Kelley's study concluded that modifying darkness avoidance is produced most quickly and effectively by direct instruction. High demand is seen as being similar to in vivo implosive therapy. None of the following treatment conditions significantly reduced fear of darkness: (1) no-treatment control, (2) play placebo, (3) play desensitization, (4) play desensitization with noncontingent M & M candies, and (5) play desensitization with contingent M & M's.

Kelly, D., and others. "Treatment of Phobic States with Antidepressants: A Retrospective Study of 246 Patients." *British Journal of Psychiatry*, 1970, *116*, 387–398.

Regardless of personality or type of phobia, wide improvement and results superior to those of behavior therapy or psychotherapy were found as a result of administration of monoamine oxidase inhibitor alone or combined with chlordiazepoxide or a tricyclic antidepressant. Children improved as much as adults, but long-term maintenance therapy was usually not necessary.

Kornhaber, R. C., and Schroeder, H. E. "Importance of Model Similarity on Extinction of Avoidance Behavior in Children." *Journal of Consulting and Clinical Psychology*, 1975, *43*, 601–607.

Forty second- and third-grade girls who were afraid of snakes viewed one of four types of models—fearless child, fearful child, fearless adult, fearful adult. Kornhaber and Schroeder report that model similarity regarding fear was not significantly related to overt snake avoidance, although similarity of age was. Regarding the girls' attitudes, the most similar model (fearful child) produced the greatest change.

Leitenberg, H., and Callahan, E. J. "Reinforced Practice and Reduction of Different Kinds of Fears in Adults and Children." *Behaviour Research and Therapy*, 1973, *11*, 19–30.

Reinforced practice is a combination of a number of therapeutic procedures previously found to be successful in reducing fears. Leitenberg and Callahan report treatment in which they graduated the procedures and provided repeated practice in approaching actual phobic stimuli, reinforcement for gains in performance, feedback of measurable progress, and instructions intended to arouse expectations of gradual success. Significant gains were found for individuals with fear of heights, snakes, and electric shock in adults, and fear of darkness in young children. The authors note that regardless of whether fears are rational or irrational, transitory or long-lasting reinforced practice can be effective in reducing escape and avoidance behavior.

MacDonald, M. L. "Multiple-Impact Behavior Therapy in a Child's Dog Phobia." *Journal of Behavior Therapy and Experimental Psychiatry*, 1975, *6*, 317–322.

After three separate incidents, a boy developed an intense fear of dogs. At eleven years of age, he was successfully treated by various learning-based procedures. Techniques included imaginal desensitization, desensitization adjuncts (photographs, writing stories, and tape recordings), dog interaction skill training, programed outdoor activity, and social environmental restructuring. The multiple treatment strategy was indicated because the phobia was maintained by conditioned anxiety, parental expectation of fearfulness, and his own expectations and use of his fear.

Miller, L. C., Barrett, C. L., Hampe, E., and Noble, H. "Comparison of Reciprocal Inhibition, Psychotherapy, and Waiting-List Control for Phobic Children." *Journal of Abnormal Psychology,* 1972, *79,* 269–279.

Sixty-seven phobic children, ages six to fifteen, were randomly assigned to twenty-four sessions of reciprocal inhibition, psychotherapy, and waiting-list control (three months). Systematic desensitization or traditional therapy (affective expression and cognitive awareness) were employed. Parents reported effects on both target fear and general fearfulness. The two approaches were found to be equally effective.

Mintz, I. L. "Fleeting Phobias." *Journal of the American Academy of Child Psychiatry,* 1970, *9,* 394–395.

An eight-and-a-half-year-old boy became very frightened after reading about an eleven-year-old boy who was dying of "old age." The father, on advice from his own psychoanalyst, interpreted his son's fears: Anger was leading the boy to see his father as a monster. He was told that, rather than seeing monsters, he could get angry at his father. Anxiety diminished rapidly, and there was no return of fear of monsters, baths, or the dark.

O'Reilly, P. P. "Desensitization of Fire Bell Phobia." *Journal of School Psychology,* 1971, *9,* 55–57.

A six-year-old girl developed psychosomatic pains and anxiety when anticipating or hearing a bell for a fire drill. Her classmates were distressed and showed undue concern about fire drills. Systematic desensitization techniques were successfully used with the girl and her classmates. The bell was paired with a pleasure-producing auditory stimulus—tape recordings of children's songs and stories. It is hypothesized that the group's positive responses to the stories aided in the elimination of the girl's phobia.

Reactions to Trauma

Trauma may be defined as a disordered mental or behavioral state resulting from physical injury or emotional stress. In infectious trauma, physically noxious stimuli cause abnormal behavior by damaging the central nervous system. Here we are dealing with noninfectious trauma—maladaptive reactions caused by psychologically noxious stimuli. Traumatic events are characterized by the child's experience of helplessness and a lack of preparedness for coping with stress.

129

Preparing a Child for Surgery

AUTHORS: Foster W. Cline and Michael B. Rothenberg

PRECIS: Play therapy and parent counseling to help a child cope with physical trauma

INTRODUCTION: Physical traumas often involve mistaken ideas. Children often view surgery as punishment or as a consequence of being naughty. Younger children fear separation, whereas older children often fear attack. Preadolescents begin to view death as adults do and fear loss of control. Many mothers feel responsible for having produced a defective child.

Open-heart surgery had been performed on seven-year-old Bobby. His parents had many conflicts with each other—especially religious differences. After the first operation, the father had said that Bobby's defect was God's punishment for the mother's premarital promiscuity. The parents often disagreed about child-rearing methods and the mother was considering a divorce after the necessary second operation. When Mr. J., a seaman, was away, Mrs. J. was quite happy. Angry emotional arguments took place frequently. The surgeon was concerned about the possibility of depression slowing Bobby's recovery, and recommended therapy.

THERAPY: Mr. J. had been away and had come back sooner than expected. He and Mrs. J. quarrelled severely, especially about Mr. J.'s concerns over his wife's sexual activities. The parents agreed to come with Bobby for presurgical therapy. The therapeutic goals were: (1) to have Bobby form a warm therapeutic relationship with Mr. J.; (2) to stress parental support for Bobby during stress (to help them be therapeutic, not destructive); and (3) to help the parents tell Bobby about the operation in a supportive manner.

When the parents were seen together, they discussed divorce, but agreed to provide a united and supportive stand. Even though Bobby had made comments about operations, they had not yet told him about the impending operation. They agreed to tell him about the operation and to bring him for play therapy one week later.

Bobby was seen after this session and poignantly expressed feelings of being caught in a chronic marital conflict. Cline and Rothenberg present some verbatim material in which Bobby talked of being caught in the middle of their fights. He expressed his helplessness at not being able to stop their fights and saw his father as starting most arguments. At next week's session, the parents reported that they had not fought less and said that there had been no time to tell Bobby about the operation. While Bobby waited outside, the therapist discussed with the parents how they would all meet with Bobby. Mr. J. was given the job of telling his son.

Family Session. The authors present a verbatim report of how Mr. J. told Bobby about the "bad news." Throughout the session, Bobby sat on his father's lap, cried, and said nothing. Mr. J. tried to explain about fixing the hole in his heart so he could play normally. The therapist asked Bobby how he felt and what he felt worst about, with no response. The parents left with instructions to "hold Bobby and be with him."

Play Therapy. A week later, seven weekly directive play therapy sessions were begun prior to the operation. The goals were: (1) to help Bobby work through his anxieties about surgery; (2) to help him feel more confident by familiarizing him with the surgical procedure; and (3) to help him share his feelings and anxieties with a supportive person—the therapist.

A toy doctor's kit, clay, and pieces of cloth were placed on the play table. The therapist discussed how unhappy Bobby was, how operations are not fun, and asked how things were at home. He said his parents continued to fight and he appeared resigned to the operation. During the next five sessions, he played with the doctor's kit and appeared to work on his anxiety in play surgery.

Verbatim material is presented from the sixth session. He "blocked" when speaking about recatheterization and talked of his fears of reoperation and death. A doll's septal defect was described as too big to repair, so the doll had to die. The therapist verbalized the action and made comments such as: "You mean, if you can't plug up the hole he's going to die?" "He's going to die! Oh dear, how did you decide that, doctor?" "We might be able to patch that. I think the hole is being plugged." (Bobby said, "It is.") "Oh, how does he feel about that?"

AFTER THE OPERATION: The parents continued their battle. Mr. J. visited the hospital smelling of alcohol and openly fought with Mrs. J. She said she had to separate and Mr. J. told his son that "Mommy's leaving Daddy because she doesn't love either of us anymore." The therapist attempted to be a source of stability for Bobby during this time. Bobby felt guilty about not living with his father. The guilt was increased by Mr. J.'s telling him that he knew Bobby wants to live with Mommy more than Daddy, but Daddy will get over it somehow.

Twenty-five days after the operation, Bobby was discharged without problems. One week later, he was brought to the emergency room by his mother because he complained of abdominal and chest pains. Examination showed no problems; a diagnosis of gastro-enteritis was suggested. That night Bobby told his mother that he was tired of fighting it all and said, "I'm just worn out." Next morning, he was found dead in his bed.

Parental conflict should be resolved prior to elective surgery. In this case, the date of surgery was accepted as a given. The authors suggest possible alternatives: The operation could have been sched-uled during the father's absence or Bobby might have adjusted to parental separation (with therapy) prior to surgery. During the week between discharge and his death, he was subjected to parental conflict without any support from the therapist or hospital person-nel. The shattering of his fantasies of parental reconciliation could have led to his depression and his loss of the "will to live."

The authors discuss the therapist's own difficulty in facing Bobby's possible death. When the doll "had to die," the therapist only supported the option of successful surgery and did not ex-plore with Bobby reactions to dying.

COMMENTARY: Cline and Rothenberg dramatically stress the importance of parental conflict influencing a child's reaction to surgery. In similar situations, therapeutic contact should be intensi-fied after discharge. Preparing for an operation is one issue; coping with difficulties afterward is another. From a psychological point of view, a case could be made that all families should receive help when a child is undergoing a serious physical trauma. Some families might require one session, while others might benefit from daily sessions following an operation. Family therapy might be the treatment of choice in many situations.

SOURCE: Cline, F. W., and Rothenberg, M. B. "Preparation of a Child for Major Surgery: A Case Report." *Journal of the American Academy of Child Psychiatry,* 1974, *13,* 78–94.

Trance Therapy with Severely Burned Children

AUTHOR: Wallace L. LaBaw

PRECIS: Hypnotic relaxing games to reduce negative behavioral relations to physical trauma

INTRODUCTION: The management of badly burned children (six months to sixteen years of age) involves many professional disciplines. Latent trance capabilities of the children can be used therapeutically. Because of the acute problem and desperate need, it was not necessary to establish a relationship before using the suggestion. Reluctance to be hypnotized does not make the child a poor hypnotic subject for an "omnipotent" hypnotist, because the therapist is simply a catalyst for the patient's employing his own trance capability.

METHODS: LaBaw reports that, for babies, rhythmical touch or sounds have been used successfully to induce comfort and a trance-like stare. Therapists have used such methods as patting, rocking, rubbing, crooning, and so on. For children, a highly successful technique is to insinuate a rhythmical suggestive routine into the child's activity or game. A formal game used is "Doctor Says," which is a variation of Simon Says. The child only does what is requested if the request is preceded by "Doctor Says." Some requests are eyes open or closed, arms relaxed or tense, and necks bent or straight. Suggestions for relaxation are given more and more frequently. A good index of successful trance induction is the child's responding less and less to requests and often showing a characteristic fluttering of the eyelids. At this point, attention has presumably shifted from the context of the words to the rhythmical sound of the therapist's voice. A mannikin is often used to relax a child; the mannikin makes stupid mistakes and does not know how to play the game.

Adolescents were found to respond favorably to relaxing games, because they responded to their burns by regressing to an earlier state of mind. Using two or more children in a trance induction is suggested. Parents are often included as observers.

USES: Trance techniques help the child develop greater tolerance for performing prescribed exercises. When nurses employed suggestions, painful dressing changes were tolerated better. Suggestions play an important role in diminishing anticipatory fear. Other uses are to facilitate transition to sleep and to get basic instructions through to a delirious child. Also, oral intake of food and water can be increased through suggestive techniques. Finally, LaBaw sees trance therapy as the most effective means of stopping traumatic enuresis and encopresis.

CASE STUDY 1: A six-year-old boy and a seven-year-old girl had survived a fire they had set that had killed the girl's younger sister. Both children showed guilt depression, enuresis, encopresis, and anorexia with lowered fluid intake. Hypnosis was employed with them together once each day for thirty minutes, focusing on soiling. One stopped in three days, the other in four. Then trance therapy was used twice a week for the other symptoms and to help them tolerate discomfort. The phrases used in the trance state are positive, being urged to keep dry or clean. The family's terminology for excretion is used.

CASE STUDY 2: A fourteen-year-old boy had been inadvertently set afire with gasoline by his younger brother. At the hospital, he did not improve and developed ulcers. He was emaciated, enuretic, encopretic, dehydrated, infected, and depressed. After the first suggestive session, his appetite improved and weight loss stopped. The therapist spent each session giving a suggestive, monotonous monolog. He was urged to keep dry, to "feel it when he had to go," to feel hungry and thirsty, and to feel confident and good and not "down." He recovered completely.

CASE STUDY 3: While fixing a furnace, a sixteen-year-old boy had been severely burned. He was delirious and communication with him was impossible, as he was in critical condition. Only verbal suggestion appeared to lull him into a more relaxed state, in which he could respond to simple directions. His restlessness and oppositional behavior diminished greatly. Until his death, his only contact with reality was through his altered state of consciousness.

CASE STUDY 4: Trapped in her burning home, a five-year-old had suffered severe burns. In the hospital, her withdrawal was so great that she seemed autistic. She was encopretic, anorexic, and dehydrated and did not respond to rhythmical movement, music, or verbalization. Her father was found to have been sexually using her; he had tried to kill her by burning the house down before she could report it. When the father was removed from frequently being in her room, she responded successfully to trance induction.

COMMENTARY: LaBaw stresses that it is not necessary for the hypnotist to specify the details of what patients should do. The goals desired by the patient and therapist are clearly agreed upon before the use of a trance. Progress naturally occurs in the trance toward accomplishment of the goal, as the patient is able to use good judgment just as he would in the wakeful state. This emphasis accounts for the lack of many specifics in the illustrative cases. Although the article only advocates trance therapy in burned children, one might easily speculate that this approach would be useful in other physical traumas.

SOURCE: LaBaw, W. L. "Adjunctive Trance Therapy with Severely Burned Children." *International Journal of Child Psychotherapy*, 1973, *2*, 80–92.

Additional Readings

Drotar, D. "The Treatment of a Severe Anxiety Reaction in an Adolescent Boy Following Renal Transplantation." *Journal of Child Psychiatry*, 1975, *14*, 451–464.

A sixteen-year-old boy developed a severe anxiety reaction eighteen months after a renal transplant. Treatment consisted of individual psychotherapy three times a week, group and occupational therapy, and weekly family interviews. After a seven-week hospital stay, the boy's anxiety diminished and adaptive abilities improved. The author discusses impulse control and body image, and notes that regression occurs in life-threatening illnesses and strong guilt feelings are stimulated.

LaBaw, W. L. "Regular Use of Suggestibility by Pediatric Bleeders." *Haematologia*, 1970, *4*, 419–425.

A group of children with hemophilia were treated by encouraging routine use of suggestibility (rather than the use of suggestibility only in emergencies). Suggestive therapy was used to promote relaxation and diminish tension. The children were taught control of trance ability and practiced at home. Trance induction by telephone was quite successful. Stress, depression, and other psychological reactions to hemophilia were successfully treated. LaBaw reports that lower morbidity rates result from suggestibility treatment.

LaBaw, W., Holton, C., Tewell, K., and Eccles, D. "The Use of Self-Hypnosis by Children with Cancer." *The American Journal of Clinical Hypnosis*, 1975, *17*, 233–238.

Twenty-seven children with cancer were trained in groups to use self-induced trances. The induction techniques included the progressive body relaxation method followed by restful imagery of idyllic scenes, such as a tranquil mountain view. The common experience of anxiety is usually poorly handled by denial. Trance states often led to more rest, better sleep, and better food and fluid intake and retention. Greater tolerance was shown for diagnostic and therapeutic procedures. Anticipatory vomiting, fear, anxiety, and depression were diminished.

Melamed, B. G., and Siegel, L. J. "Reduction of Anxiety in Children Facing Hospitalization and Surgery by Use of Filmed Modeling." *Journal of Consulting and Clinical Psychology*, 1975, *43*, 511–521.

Surgery for hernias, tonsillectomies, or urinary-genital difficulties were scheduled for sixty children, ages four through twelve. A relevant peer modeling film of a child being hospitalized and receiving surgery was very effective in reducing anxiety. Preoperative (night before) and postoperative (three to four weeks) fearfulness were significantly reduced, compared to a control group, who observed an unrelated film. The children who observed the modeling film had fewer behavior problems postoperatively (as reported by parents).

Robertson, M., and Barford, F. "Story-Making in Psychotherapy with a Chronically Ill Child." *Psychotherapy: Theory, Research and Practice*, 1970, *7*, 104–107.

Story-making psychotherapy offers children a means of expressing feelings, especially when they are chronically ill and/or immobilized. Stories written for hospitalized children serve the purposes of releasing feelings and reinforcing the goal of getting well. The authors present stories that were written to reflect the agony of a six-year-old boy, for whom separation from a respirator was a significant event. The stories reflected ways of overcoming adversity. Animal characters were used to express resolution of different problems. For example, Secret Squirrel became more open in expressing feelings. The hero copes with stress and emerges successfully. The boy requested stories concerning tubes and bad dreams about choking. Storytelling may diminish the negative short- or long-term effects of trauma.

Sampson, T. F. "The Child in Renal Failure: Emotional Impact of Treatment on the Child and His Family." *Journal of Child Psychiatry,* 1975, *14,* 462–476.

Twenty-two children, aged nine to eighteen, with end-stage renal failure were studied. The majority of these children had relatively serious social and emotional difficulties. Depression and anxiety aroused by fear of pain were common, as was altered body image among the group receiving dialysis. Part of this latter group became withdrawn, while the other part strongly desired social interaction. Sampson stresses the need for the children to attend regular classrooms with their friends. In children receiving transplants, better adjustment was noted, but anxiety and fearfulness were aroused by minimal or nonexistent signs of rejection. Stress led to increased sibling rivalry, husband-wife conflicts, and detrimental, intense donor-patient relationships. Sampson considers that better preparation and therapeutic intervention are necessary.

2

Habit Disorders

A habit can be defined as: (1) "a constant, often unconscious inclination to perform some act, acquired through its frequent repetition [and] (2) an established trend of the mind or character" (*American Heritage Dictionary*, 1969). This chapter concerns habits that are maladaptive, dysfunctional, or viewed in a negative manner by the child and/or adults in the child's life.

Long-established habits tend to be overlearned and become rather isolated or "walled off" within the psyche. They develop an automatic or semiconscious life of their own below the conscious awareness or control of the individual. Clients usually report that they begin the act without awareness and "catch themselves doing it." Some investigators have noted that when parents or professionals have tried actively to break the habit, it has become worse and more deeply entrenched. (See D. A. Thom, *Everyday Problems of the Everyday Child.* New York, Appleton-Century-Crofts, 1970.)

For these reasons, nervous habits have proven remarkably resistant to therapeutic treatment—particularly traditional psychotherapeutic methods (psychoanalytic and nondirective therapy). They represent a challenge of the highest order for the practicing therapist. At the very least, it takes a great deal of patience, persistence, and flexibility to treat habit disorders of long standing. The greatest success to date has occurred with behavioral methods, especially conditioning techniques. Accordingly, a number of the more promising behavioral techniques are presented in this chapter.

Learning theorists view maladaptive habits as learned responses that can occur in normal as well as disturbed children; they state that these separate clinical entities can best be unlearned by behavioral principles. Psychodynamic therapists, on the other hand, consider these habits to be manifestations of underlying personality conflicts. And family therapists view such disorders as indices of dysfunctional family interaction patterns. The latter two approaches expect symptom substitution to occur unless the underlying conflict is resolved. The symptom substitution hypothesis states that underlying anxiety or conflict continues to be experienced after symptom relief and shortly emerges again in the form of a new symptom, that is, as behavior judged to be socially or personally maladjustive. After reviewing the literature on symptom substitution, Montgomery and Crowder note that a general conclusion is not possible; that is, the occurrence of substitute symptoms depends on the kind of treatment and/or kind of initial symptom (G. T. Montgomery and J. E. Crowder, "The Symptom Substitution Hypothesis and the Evidence," *Psychotherapy: Theory, Research and Practice,* 1972, *9,* 98–102). For certain maladaptive habits, such as enuresis and encopresis, the weight of evidence to date strongly supports the behavioral position—that no symptom substitution occurs.

With such habits as enuresis and encopresis, then, the learning theorists point to three major justifications for treating symptoms rather than the "cause" of the disorder:

1. Symptom substitution does not usually occur with these symptoms.

2. The symptom may create more psychological difficulties than the problem that caused the symptom.

3. A symptom can persist after the psychogenic forces that produced it have abated.

Other theorists, on the contrary, point out that enuretic or encopretic children typically exhibit other emotional problems, such as immaturity, and that the intensity of parental reactions to these symptoms, such as disgust and revulsion, tends to create long-lasting "distancing" effects on the parent-child relationship that need to be resolved by family counseling. It would seem, then, that clinical judgment is still needed to decide whether to treat the overt symptom or to treat a postulated underlying cause. All theorists agree on the need for long-term follow-up data to investigate the possibility of symptom substitution.

The reader will note that in treating certain "psychosomatic" disorders such as enuresis and encopresis, some of the authors utilize techniques based both on psychological and on physiological knowledge. In treating cases of encopresis, for example, Wright (1973) combined reinforcement contingencies with the use of cathartics (suppositories and enemas) to relieve the congested colon. This is an example of a multidimensional approach involving expert clinical knowledge of both physiological and behavioral principles. The most effective treatment for psychosomatic disorders may often involve an integration of organic, psychological, and social principles and techniques. Indeed, most psychological disorders seem to have multiple determinants and a disorder that originated from psychological causes can, under persistent stress, develop an organic basis.

Tics

A tic can be briefly described as follows: "(1) An intermittent but recurring muscle spasm limited to a single muscle group; (2) tends to occur whenever the patient feels anxious or tense; (3) patient may be unaware when the tic occurs; (4) etiology—most tics are of psychological origin, although local muscle and neurological pathology must be ruled out; [and] (5) more common in children than adults" (H. A. Storrow, Outline of Clinical Psychiatry, *New York: Appleton-Century-Crofts, 1969, p. 174). The following four methods are representative of the current treatment approaches to tics that traditionally have proved refractory to most forms of clinical intervention.*

Eliminating Nervous Habits
and Tics by Habit Reversal

AUTHORS: Nathan H. Azrin and Robert G. Nunn

PRECIS: Rapid treatment of tics by combining several behavioral methods, especially by providing competing physical exercises

INTRODUCTION: Azrin and Nunn note that nervous habits and tics (head jerking, tongue pushing, nail biting, and so on) have proved notoriously resistant to almost every form of treatment. Three main theoretical explanations have been offered in the past for the etiology of tics. Viewing tics as erotic and aggressive instinctual impulses which are continually escaping through pathological discharge, psychoanalysts try to persuade (give insight to) the client that these impulses are causing his problem and then attempt to channel these impulses elsewhere. Others view nervous habits as being caused by tension and either prescribe drugs to relieve it or suggest negative practice. The latter procedure requires the client to perform the tic rapidly, thereby preventing the tension discharge that would otherwise result (A. J. Yates, "The Application of Learning Theory to the Treatment of Tics, *Journal of Abnormal and Social Psychology*, 1958, *56*, 175–182). A third position is held by behavior modification theorists who assert that nervous habits are learned responses that are maintained by operant reinforcement.

RATIONALE: The rationale offered by Azrin and Nunn is that a nervous habit begins as a normal reaction, often to physical or psychological trauma of a transitory nature. The movement then becomes part of the typical behavior pattern of the person—without either the individual's or society's conscious awareness. Once established as a strong habit, the movement further resists personal awareness because of its automatic nature. With frequent use, specific muscles are strengthened and opposing muscles are weakened. Social reinforcement in the form of sympathy or attention sometimes contributes to the problem.

TREATMENT: Azrin and Nunn describe the treatment of twelve clients with a variety of nervous habits. The ages of the clients ranged from five to sixty-four years. The three children in the group had been referred by their parents at the suggestion of their teacher. The habits were all long-standing problems of at least three years' duration and seriously interfered with the client's functioning.

The first step in treatment was to require all the clients (or their parents) to record the incidence of the nervous habit, that is, to keep a record of how often the habit occurred, in terms of number of times per minute/day or the percentage of time each day that the habit was experienced. After two weeks of daily recording, this record-keeping requirement was reduced to twice a week and, a few weeks later, to only about twice a month.

Step Two consisted of awareness training. Several procedures were used to make the habit more conscious. The response description procedure required the client to describe the details of the nervous movement to the counselor, using a mirror if needed, while reenacting several instances of the typical movement. A second procedure, response detection, involved teaching the client to detect each occurrence of a movement by alerting him to when it happened. A third procedure—early warning—gave the client practice in noting the earliest sign of the habit movement, such as when the hand of a nail biter first approached the face. The competing response practice is described in the following section. The fifth procedure, situation awareness training, was designed to heighten awareness of situations, persons, and places wherein the habit was likely to emerge, by having the client describe how he performed the habit in each situation.

Competing Response Practice. Each client was taught a specific movement pattern that was opposite to or incompatible with the nervous habit. These competing responses were selected for being socially inconspicuous, comfortably compatible with normal ongoing activities, and for strengthening the muscles antagonistic to the tic movement for the muscle tics. The clients were told to perform the competing responses for about three minutes following either the temptation to perform a tic or the actual occurrence of a tic.

For a backward head-jerking tic, the client practiced isometrically contracting the neck flexors by pulling the chin in and down. Once he had the necessary strength to control the backward jerk, he isometrically tensed the neck flexors, rather than conspicuously moving his chin onto his sternum. For an upward jerking of the shoulder, the client isometrically contracted the shoulder depressors so as to strengthen the muscles that work in opposition to the upward jerking movement. The client who constantly sucked the roof of her mouth was instructed to press her tongue against the roof of her mouth (in a different position from the habit) and against the bottom of her mouth for each incidence of the habit. For clients with thumbsucking, nail-biting and eyelash-picking habits, the competing response consisted of placing their hands down by their sides and to clench their fists until they could feel tension in their hands and arms. If this movement interfered with their ongoing activities, they were to grasp an object appropriate to that situation and squeeze until some tension was felt. In the case of small children with thumbsucking problems, their parents were advised to manually guide their child's hands through an open-and-close exercise twenty times.

Habit Control Motivation. Previous experience had convinced Azrin and Nunn that little success would result if the client was only casually interested in eliminating the habit. Thus, several procedures were used to strengthen a client's motivation. In the first procedure, habit inconvenience review, the counselor reviewed with the client, in detail, the inconveniences, embarrassment, and suffering that resulted from the habit. Once a client was able to control his nervous habit during a counseling session, the social support procedure was instituted. The family and close friends of the clients were advised to bolster the clients' resolve by (1) remarking favorably on their efforts and improved appearance when refraining from the habit and (2) reminding them of a need to practice their exercises when they observed a habit going uncorrected. The counselor also telephoned the clients regularly after treatment to praise the clients for their efforts in inhibiting the habit, as well as to obtain data regarding the frequency of the habit.

A special motivational problem existed with children, because the parents rather than the children desired to eliminate the habit. It was felt that adversive consequences were needed to motivate these children. For very young children, the parents would manually guide the child through the required exercises when necessary. Uncooperative older children were required to perform their exercises in a bedroom when they failed to initiate the exercise themselves.

Another special motivational problem was present with certain tics that seemed neurologically caused and thus not subject to voluntary control, such as neck and shoulder jerks. A public display procedure was used for this problem; the family was required to observe demonstrations of self-control during the counseling sessions. Immediately after the counseling session, the counselor also notified friends and teachers of the client's ability to control the tic.

Generalization Training. During the counseling sessions, how to control the nervous habit in everyday situations was discussed. After the clients were observed to be correctly practicing their exercises, they were taught, by a symbolic rehearsal procedure, to be more aware of the habit movement in many other situations. The clients were asked to imagine common habit-inducing situations and to imagine that they detected a habit move and were performing the required exercise. The situation awareness procedure previously described was used to obtain a list of problem situations. Also, the counselor engaged the client in casual conversation for about half an hour to give the habit a chance to appear and the client an opportunity to notice it and perform his exercise for three minutes. If the client failed to notice his nervous movement, the counselor would remind him or her, using as little suggestion as possible, such as staring, saying "hmm," or raising both eyebrows. When prompted, the client was to initiate the competing response while continuing the conversation.

RESULTS: The pretreatment occurrence of the habits ranged from 20 per day or 50 percent of the day to 8,000 per day and 100 percent of the day. After treatment, the habit was reduced by at least 90 percent for every client; for ten of the twelve clients, the habit was completely absent during the third week after treatment. The seven clients for whom five-month follow-up data were available maintained an average reduction in habit frequency of about 99 percent. The habit reversal training worked rapidly, requiring only one counseling session for all clients. Two clients were given a second session a few months following the first one. One client, a twenty-one-year-old female nail biter, decided to stop her successful efforts after three weeks of work. The eleven continuing clients stated that the exercises seemed meaningful and were easy to perform. They all stated that no new habits appeared when the treated habit was eliminated.

COMMENTARY: Azrin and Nunn's multidimensional approach highlights the respect they have for the tenacity of nervous habits. The need to reinforce the client's motivation and to involve significant family members in treatment seems most significant. The method seems suitable as a general treatment approach for many types of nervous habits, with both children and adults, males and females. Azrin and Nunn assert that the present method appears clinically more useful than other treatment methods, because it proved effective for virtually all clients and required only one or two sessions. Further research is clearly needed to evaluate this claim, which appears to be based on only a handful of cases.

SOURCE: Azrin, N. H., and Nunn, R. G. "Habit Reversal: A Method of Eliminating Nervous Habits and Tics." *Behaviour Research and Therapy*, 1973, *11*, 619–628.

Involving Parents in the
Treatment of Childhood Tics

AUTHOR: David M. Zausmer

PRECIS: Treating tics by a dynamically oriented approach consisting of brief parental counseling

INTRODUCTION: Zausmer's study evaluates the treatment of ninety-six children with tics referred to the Psychiatric Department of the Royal Liverpool Children's Hospital over a five-year period. Inspection of background data revealed that boys outnumbered girls by a ratio of two to one. Age at onset of the tic ranged from three and one-half to twelve and one-half years, with a well-defined peak at seven years. The mean duration of tics for this group was four and one-half years; range, one and one-half to eleven years. It was further discovered that the children had a number of common personality traits; in descending order of frequency, they were found to be restless, sensitive, stubborn, excitable, phobic, apprehensive, and quick tempered. In regard to body build, most of the children were asthenic, wiry children. A high proportion of the parents exhibited symptoms of pathological anxiety, psychoneurosis, and tics. Moreover, they tended to be rigid and restrictive in child rearing. In particular, a disturbed mother-child relationship was found to be a major cause of anxiety in the child.

TREATMENT: Brief parental guidance (two to three sessions) was the treatment of choice for most of the families. After a physical and mental examination of the child, the informant (usually the mother) was encouraged to ventilate her anxieties. Rapport with the child was gained by showing an interest in both his or her health, worries, ambitions, and problems of home and school adjustment. The parents were typically reassured by the therapist about the child's physical and mental health. Also, they were offered a simple explanation of the cause of the tic; the tic was interpreted as a safety valve for tension resulting most commonly from parental criticism and restriction. The parents were advised to ignore the tic and not to punish its occurrence or call the child's attention to it in any way. Practical advice on child rearing was given the parents in some cases. For a small number of the most severe cases, prolonged psychotherapy was offered, consisting of play therapy for the child and of parental guidance. The latter focused on promoting more harmonious, enjoyable interactions between mother and child. Drugs were not prescribed for any cases unless indicated for a complicating physical ailment.

FOLLOW-UP AND CONCLUSION: The results of treatment for a group of fifty children were evaluated by means of a follow-up inquiry two to three years after termination. The data reveal that 76 percent showed marked improvement, with 24 percent of the cases completely free of tics for at least a year. A total of 24 percent of the cases were found to be unimproved at follow-up. Most of these latter cases improved with additional treatment. Although more girls showed improvement than boys, there was no significant relationship between improvement and intelligence, age of onset, or duration of tic before treatment.

Zausmer concludes from this research that the role of the mother is of paramount importance in the etiology and treatment of tics. The clients were found to be nervous, overdependent children who readily absorbed maternal anxiety. For most of the cases, improvement of the tics and anxiety symptoms was achieved by modifying parental attitudes, increasing the mother's insight, and attending to the mother's and the child's health. Brief therapy was effective for the majority of cases, with the more severe emotional disturbances requiring prolonged psychotherapy on a weekly basis.

COMMENTARY: The research and evaluation emphasis of Zausmer's article supports the validity of the treatment approach. According to the findings of this study, a childhood tic that persists for an extended period should be a warning sign to parents and professionals that anxiety is present in the child, probably caused by a dysfunctional mother-child relationship. Brief therapy involving both parents and child would seem to be an effective treatment approach for most children with this disorder.

SOURCE: Zausmer, D. M. "The Treatment of Tics in Childhood: A Review and Follow-Up Study." *Archives of Diseases of Childhood*, 1954, *29*, 537–542.

Treating Tourette's Syndrome
with Haloperidol

AUTHORS: James L. Chapel, Noel Brown, and Richard L. Jenkins

PRECIS: Drug treatment of four children with tics resulting from Tourette's syndrome

INTRODUCTION: In 1885, Gilles de la Tourette described a "nervous affliction characterized by motor incoordination, accompanied by echolalia (repeating what others just said) and coprolalia (compulsive speaking or shouting obscene words)" (de la Tourette, G. *Archives of Neurology,* Paris, 1885, *9,* 19). Typically this disorder begins in childhood with tics that progress to involve the upper limbs (for example, arm jerking), trunk (for example, squatting), or the entire body. Subsequently, vocal tics become consistent symptoms, such as frequent coughing, clearing the throat, grunting, and then coprolalia. Although temporary remission of the symptoms is not uncommon, the condition has generally been resistant to nearly all forms of treatment—including psychotherapy and drug treatment. It is still unclear whether the etiology is primarily psychological, organic, or both.

DRUG TREATMENT: Chapel, Brown, and Jenkins describe the treatment of four children with the drug haloperidol—trade name, Haldol. This drug is a butyrophenone compound classified as a neuroleptic agent. It has pharmacological actions similar to the phenothiazines and has proved especially effective with symptoms of hallucinations, compulsions, and aggressive tendencies. The four cases presented were all hospitalized with a diagnosis of Tourette's syndrome. The age of onset ranged from seven to eleven years and the symptoms at the time of treatment had been present from two to nine years. The frequency of the tics ranged from 100 a day to 200 an hour. Initially, the children were given dosage levels of haloperidol of 0.2 to 0.3 mg, which were gradually increased by daily increments of 0.3 to 0.4 mg, until levels of from 4.8 to 6.0 mg were reached. The latter dosage levels resulted in the children either losing their symptoms or exhibiting only infrequent tics (one to five a day). Only one child showed adverse side effects, namely mild parkinsonian effects. The authors report that a follow-up showed that two of the children had been discharged for over a year and, under maintenance dosages of 1.5 and 3.2 mg of haloperidol daily, were either free of symptoms or showed only an occasional verbal tic (explosive bark). Both were functioning well in the community and were attending regular public schools.

COMMENTARY: The goal of this drug treatment was simply to remove or control the tics so that the child could function in the community and/or benefit from psychotherapy. There can be little argument with the authors' observation that the control of this disrupting symptom is of the "greatest importance in creating a situation more favorable for the effective readjustment of the patient" (p. 610). Haloperidol appears to be the only drug to date that has been used successfully in the treatment of Tourette's syndrome. In a recent review of cases with Tourette's syndrome (see *Psychiatric Drugs* by G. Honigfeld and A. Howard [New York: Academic Press, 1973, p. 100]), it was found that over 80 percent of the haloperidol-treated cases were helped, compared with less than 40 percent for all other forms of treatment.

SOURCE: Chapel, J. L., Brown, N., and Jenkins, R. L. "Tourette's Disease: Symptomatic Relief with Haloperidol." *American Journal of Psychiatry*, 1964, *121*, 608–610.

Behavior Modification Techniques
for Tourette's Syndrome

AUTHOR: Arnold L. Miller

PRECIS: Training parents and teacher to use positive and negative reinforcement to eliminate body tics and barking noises in a young boy

INTRODUCTION: This case involved a five-year-old boy who often made barking noises, accompanied by frequent eye blinking, facial grimaces, jerking, neck twisting, and writhing. Compulsive cursing was not evident. The rapid, staccato bark had begun two years earlier, as a chronic throat clearing. The noises had grown in both frequency and intensity to the point of being most disrupting to the home and school environments. As usual, no evidence of neurological or organic impairment was discovered. Previous treatment by a physical therapist had not helped. The child's parents reported that ignoring the child's symptoms had no effect, nor did paying more attention to the boy.

TREATMENT: The boy was seen on an outpatient basis. Initially, the goal of therapy was to ascertain the extent of voluntary control of the barking noises. To this end, a game was devised from prior research using massed trials in treating tics. The boy was instructed to make as many noises as he wanted, in succession, until he became tired, when he could stop. He was further advised that the therapist would use a stopwatch to time the period when he made no noises. For each one-minute interval in which he made no barking noises he would receive two M & M's (candies). This part of the game could be ended at the discretion of the boy.

The boy appeared to enjoy both the game and his rewards for being quiet. During the next four sessions he would go ten or fifteen minutes at a time with no barking noises and for the remainder of the session he would emit no more than half a dozen "barks." The parents were seen separately during the boy's sessions. They reported that the boy would begin with mild coughing, either at the supper table or watching television, and would gradually show body writhing and louder voice volume until the parents could no longer stand it. His mother would typically react by criticism, showing worry and concern or leaving the room crying. The parents were advised that the boy seemed to be receiving intermittent reinforcement by their attention, which meant that extinction would prove difficult and recurrence of symptoms should be expected.

PARENTS AS COTHERAPISTS: The parents were advised to handle the boy in the following manner. First, they were to instruct the child that his loud noises were disturbing them while eating supper and while watching television. Accordingly, they were going to help him learn to be calmer and quiet down so as not to disturb others. The parents were also instructed to give the boy a quiet verbal warning early in the behavior sequence—before he had become unbearably disruptive. If the warning proved unsuccessful, the child was to go to his room and close the door. In the room, he was encouraged to make all the noises or gestures he wished. When he felt tired, he was free to return immediately to the supper table or television set.

Moreover, the parents were instructed to give the boy attention and other forms of positive reinforcement for times when he was not abnormally disruptive. For example, they were advised to praise the boy and give him a small treat (gum) whenever he had gotten through a day without having to be sent to his room. They were also to make comments like "You're nice to have around when you're not being real loud."

The parents and the boy were seen in therapy for twenty-two sessions over the course of the next year. During the first month of treatment, a marked improvement was noted in the boy's behavior. The mother needed considerable support to deal with recurrences of symptoms and to continue to give the boy consistent warnings and penalties when he became noisy. Positive comments from neighbors also helped the parents endure the difficult first two months of therapy. They noticed how much happier and friendlier the boy had become. Both the barking noises and the tics continued to diminish over the next six months, at which time the noises returned in the classroom only. The teacher was then advised to explain to the boy that this behavior was disrupting the class and making it difficult for everyone to work. She was also counseled to remove the boy from the room if the disruption continued. Each day he was not removed from the class he was to earn a token (poker chip) and the parents agreed that if he earned three chips over the course of a week he would receive his choice of three rewards (buying a hot dog at a local store; getting ice cream; or shopping at the Army-Navy store). Subsequently, the requirement of three tokens a week was raised to four. Within a period of two weeks he was no longer causing a classroom disturbance and his grades remained as high as ever.

A follow-up telephone call eighteen months after clinic contacts had terminated revealed that he remained practically free of symptoms; that is, he needed reminding about bizarre noises about once a month. His school adjustment continued to be free of problems.

COMMENTARY: This report demonstrates that behavior modification procedures (positive and negative reinforcement) offer a promising alternative to the use of drugs with Tourette's syndrome. Miller also suggests that involvement of parents and teachers in the treatment may be a crucial aspect of effective intervention. Without the involvement of significant adults in a child's life, there appears to be little generalization from the therapy session.

SOURCE: Miller, A. L. "Treatment of a Child with Gilles de la Tourette's Syndrome Using Behavior Modification Techniques." *Journal of Behavior Therapy and Experimental Psychiatry*, 1970, *1*, 319–321.

Additional Readings

Feldman, R. B., and Werry, J. S. "An Unsuccessful Attempt to Treat a Tiqueur by Massed Practice." *Behaviour Research and Therapy*, 1966, *4*, 111–117.

A thirteen-year-old boy with multiple tics of the head was treated by massed practice of one tic three times daily for ten weeks after a preliminary observation period of five weeks' duration.

Another tic was left untreated as a control. Over the course of treatment, both tics increased in their involuntary frequency, but fell quickly to pretreatment levels with cessation of massed practice. There was a similar increment in the number of voluntary performances of the tic during the 200 practice sessions. A tic that has been absent for several months reappeared during treatment. It appeared that treatment temporarily increased the patient's drive level, thus neutralizing reactive inhibition. Feldman and Werry conclude that massed practice can be unsuitable for patients prone to develop anxiety unless systematic attempts are made to reduce anxiety as it arises in treatment.

Hersen, M., and Eisler, R. M. "Behavioral Approaches to Study and Treatment of Psychogenic Tics." *Genetic Psychology Monographs,* ·1973, *87,* 289–312.

Hersen and Eisler review the behavioral approach to treating psychogenic tics with respect to the use of massed practice, operant, feedback, desensitization, and aversion techniques. Methods for recording tic frequency are outlined, with particular attention to precise self-monitoring and the use of videotape equipment.

Lahey, B. B., McNees, M. P., and McNees, M. C. "Control of an Obscene 'Verbal Tic' Through Time Out in an Elementary School Classroom." *Journal of Applied Behavior Analysis,* 1973, *6,* 101–104.

A classroom teacher successfully modified the behavior of a ten-year-old student who had a high rate of obscene vocalizations accompanied by facial twitches. In the first phase, the subject was instructed to repeat rapidly the most frequent obscene word in four daily fifteen-minute sessions. This procedure reduced the frequency of obscene vocalizations, but not to an acceptable level. Later the teacher was able to control the target behavior using a time-out procedure. The subject was immediately placed in a time-out room for a minimum of five minutes and until he was quiet for one minute after every target behavior. The room was stripped of all objects and locked to prevent further disruption while he was in time out.

Yates, A. J. "The Application of Learning Theory to the Treatment of Tics." *Journal of Abnormal and Social Psychology,* 1958, *56,* 175–182.

Yates conceptualizes some tics as drive-reducing conditioned avoidance responses originally evoked in a traumatic situation and derived a method of treatment from this theoretical model. He predicted that if the tics were evoked voluntarily under conditions of massed practice, a negative habit of "not doing the tic" would be built up, which would ultimately result in the extinction of the tics. The results of a number of experiments supported this theory. According to Yates, the optimum condition for the growth of the negative habit is the combination of very prolonged massed practice followed by prolonged rest.

Eating Difficulty

Eating difficulty in children has been found to be a very common disorder. Estimates vary, but there seems to be some consensus that about one child in three experiences some form of eating difficulty, such as over- or undereating, finicky eating, or tantrums while eating. Most of the articles in this section focus on the treatment of a life-threatening disorder—failure of the child to retain sufficient food, which results in severe weight loss.

Outpatient Management of Anorexia Nervosa

AUTHORS: John Reinhart, Marita Kenna, and Ruth Succop

PRECIS: Treating girls with severe weight loss by outpatient counseling of parents and child

INTRODUCTION: Reinhart, Kenna, and Succop report that the typical anorexia nervosa patient is a preadolescent or adolescent girl who is in poor health because of a great deal of weight loss. Such girls have a history of food avoidance for various reasons and commonly show symptoms of amenorrhea and hyperactivity. The patients are often so physically emaciated that they look like concentration camp victims. Typically, the patient is unconcerned about her weight loss and is actually trying to avoid weight gain, although her parents are greatly upset and anxious about this condition. The usual treatment reported in the literature is hospitalization; the goal is the preservation of life and the restoration of physiologic homeostasis. Most of these patients are diagnosed hysterical-manipulative, although a few are seen as compulsive or schizophrenic.

OUTPATIENT TREATMENT: Basing their conclusions on fifteen years' experience, the authors report that outpatient treatment of anorexia nervosa cases is as effective as inpatient care. Only rarely have they found it necessary to hospitalize a child for a brief period, to separate the child from extremely anxious and frightened parents. As the authors view anorexia nervosa as a psychological problem, they treat it primarily with psychotherapy. The child and the parents are usually seen by different therapists. Finding the natural ambivalence of the pediatrician too disruptive, the authors insist on assuming complete responsibility for both the psychological and physiological management of the case. Showing no alarm at the physical condition of the patient, they begin by confronting her (occasionally him) with their belief that her unhappiness is their concern but her eating is her own province. In terms of the dynamics of the situation, they view giving the child responsibility for eating as confronting the child with autonomy and independence. The patient is encouraged to separate herself from her worried and anxious parents. Moreover, the child is told that unhappy feelings such as anger, resentment, or hopelessness can cause her to have no appetite for food or life. She is warned that death can occur if she starves herself long enough and that, although concerned, the therapists cannot stop her.

At the same time, the parents are advised to let their daughter assume responsibility for deciding what and when she wants to eat and, indeed, for whether she wants to live or not. Parents typically report relief at being reassured that eating is the child's responsibility and often relate critical incidents wherein they are able to communicate this to a patient. For example, one mother shouted at her child, "If you're going to die, it's upon your head, not mine" (p. 124). Recently, the authors have asked mothers of treated cases to talk to families of girls currently anorexic.

CASE STUDY: Susie was an eight-year-old girl who was referred by her pediatrician for refusing to eat shortly after the birth of a baby brother. She became irritable, withdrawn, and cried easily. Becoming preoccupied with food, she reduced her eating drastically. Her weight loss continued for a month after outpatient treatment commenced. The parents were seen by a social worker and the child by a psychiatrist in weekly sessions. Although she generally refused to talk about feelings, Susie was able to express some negative feelings about her siblings and her mother. The parents' anxieties and conflicts were also revealed through their therapy sessions. Because of Susie's continuing weight loss during the first month, her pediatrician often called to ask if the therapists were "sure she didn't need to be in the hospital—she looks terrible!" (p. 121). During the second month of treatment, her weight loss leveled off and during the third month there was definite weight gain. Susie became more verbal and animated in the therapy sessions. Her eating increased and weight gain continued from then on. An isolated, bizarre incident occurred during the fourth month of treatment. She presented her mother with a ball of feces wrapped as a present. She also defecated on the kitchen floor. Early in the fifth month of treatment, Susie and her parents became quiet during the sessions. Because Susie then stated that she and her parents had decided that they did not want to come any more, that things were going well, treatment was discontinued in the sixth month. A follow-up two years later revealed that there had been no recurrence of the anorexia. Susie had regained her normal weight (she had been at the third percentile on the weight chart) and her behavior was said to be normal.

COMMENTARY: Contrary to traditional practice, Reinhart, Kenna, and Succop use hospitalization only as a last resort in treating the anorectic child. In lieu of prolonged hospitalization, medication, special diets, or forced feedings, they advocate outpatient psychotherapy to resolve the underlying conflict between child and family. However, if the parents prove unable to tolerate the symptoms of anorexia, they will use brief hospitalization (less than two weeks), followed by outpatient therapy. They report that only two children of the thirty-two treated to date required prolonged hospitalization. These two cases were extremely disturbed youth who were experiencing psychotic breaks with reality.

SOURCE: Reinhart, J., Kenna, M., and Succop, R. "Anorexia Nervosa in Children: Outpatient Management." *Journal of Child Psychiatry,* 1972, *11,* 114–131.

Extinction of Vomiting Behavior

AUTHOR: Marilyn G. Komechak

PRECIS: Teaching parents to eliminate vomiting in a young boy by systematically withdrawing attention

INTRODUCTION: Komechak reports the treatment of Jack, a four-year-old boy who had been diagnosed mentally retarded, hyperactive, and brain damaged. During the diagnostic observations he exhibited the rather unique ability to vomit as often as fifteen times in an hour and a half. The vomiting behavior became a prime goal of treatment, because it was interfering with the plan to place Jack in a day-care center several times a week. This plan would offer Jack educational and socialization experiences and provide the mother with some much-needed relief.

PARENT COUNSELING: The results of several parent conferences supported the hypothesis that the vomiting was a conditioned response reinforced by the parents' attention. The parents would usually respond to Jack's vomiting with affection and attention, that is, they would approach him, say his name, and express sympathy while removing the vomitus from his face and clothing. When the parents then proceeded to clean the floor, Jack would often kick them in the shins because they were interrupting his play. Although somewhat skeptical that the way to stop Jack's vomiting was to let him vomit as much as he wanted, his parents agreed to give it a try. They were instructed to ignore the vomiting by not looking at him, speaking to, or touching him. They were only to clean the floor to ensure he did not reconsume his mess. They were further advised to give Jack considerable affection and attention at other times.

Each day the parents counted the number of vomits and sent the data to the counselor. These data revealed that the extinction procedure was effective. Over a four-week period, the daily vomiting incidents declined from thirty to once a day. Then Jack had a relapse and vomited about ten times a day, so a conference with the parents was arranged. They confided at this time that they did not really believe that their ignoring the behavior had decreased its rate. In thinking about his relapse, the parents related that most of Jack's vomiting now occurred in the evening while they were watching their new color television set. To get attention, Jack would run across the room and vomit in their laps or on the television set. This always provoked a response from the parents. After analyzing the situation for themselves, the parents felt somewhat more confident that their behavior had been effective in extinguishing the vomiting, and they agreed to try again. Their renewed efforts quickly reduced the incidence of vomiting to about once a day over the next three weeks.

COMMENTARY: The parents' recordings of vomiting incidence clearly demonstrated in this study that it was being reinforced and thus maintained by their attention (looking at the boy, touching him, and speaking his name). For some children, then, the key to resolving this particularly disruptive and annoying behavior is to discover what exactly the parents (or relatives or teachers) are doing to reinforce the behavior.

SOURCE: Komechak, M. G. "Extinction of Vomiting Behavior in a Retarded Child." *JSAS* [Journal Supplement Abstract Service] *Catalog of Selected Documents in Psychology,* 1972, 2, 69. Published by the American Psychological Association.

Treating a Child's Refusal to Eat by the Use of Learning Theory

AUTHOR: John G. White

PRECIS: Reviving a five-year-old girl's appetite for solid food by conditioning (stimulus substitution) and play therapy techniques

INTRODUCTION: This paper represents an early attempt to apply learning theory principles to the treatment of childhood disorders. White made no attempt to explain or treat the child by the psychodynamic procedures that were currently popular.

CASE STUDY: A five-and-a-half-year-old girl was admitted to the hospital because of her refusal to eat and her suffering from what seemed to be rheumatic pain.

A clinical history revealed that the child was the youngest of two girls and had clearly become "Daddy's baby." Her father not only lavished attention on her but also fed her from the time she was born. Between ages three and four, the child's appetite became capricious. She would insist on waiting until her father came home at night so she could sit on his lap and be fed by him. Similarly, the bedtime ritual in the home involved her father reading to her until she fell asleep. A month before her fifth birthday, her father became seriously ill and four months later died at home. Since her mother told her that Daddy had gone to "God's hospital," the child expected him to return one day.

Shortly thereafter the mother went to work and the child was left with relatives during the day. These relatives were soon hard pressed to feed her lunch. For example, one of the relatives would perform a dance while her grandmother tried to feed her with a spoon. Her appetite quickly deteriorated and she became ill with what was diagnosed as acute rheumatism. Confined to bed for six weeks, she continued to refuse more and more food, until eventually she would only take milk and fruit drinks. At this time the child commented to her mother, "Dr. B. says if I don't eat I'll never be a big girl. If I grow into a big girl, my daddy won't recognize me, will he?" The child was then hospitalized, but forced feeding by the nurses also proved unsuccessful.

TREATMENT: Reviving appetite became the urgent task of treatment. From the child's history, it was clear that the father had become the conditioned stimulus for eating, with reinforcement coming from both hunger satisfaction and anxiety reduction through the father's attention. Thus, stimulus substitution was attempted by having a male psychologist initially replace the father; later, uncles, the father's sister, and finally her mother played this role. For the first week, the psychologist saw the child an hour a day for play therapy sessions. The first session involved attending to the needs of dolls and feeding them with a toy tea set. The next afternoon, the child ate some miniature biscuits and drank a doll's cup full of milk laced with stout, a drink her father had liked. Daily play sessions with dolls and tea parties continued that week and one evening the child accepted a sausage from an uncle. At the end of the week, it was decided that the child would be returned home and would continue as an outpatient.

During the next three weeks, play sessions continued four times a week with larger cups substituted for the doll's cups and full-sized biscuits introduced. The child often prepared the meals she and the therapist ate together and determined their other activities. During this period, the child was eating regularly at neighbors' houses. At the end of the month, she had eaten lunch at home with her mother and sister.

About this time, the psychologist decided to be a little less submissive to the child's every whim. Thus, a play session was abruptly terminated when she refused to play alone and allow the therapist to talk to her mother. Thereafter, every cooperative response by the child in the play session, such as fixing broken toys, was reinforced by the therapist. The child continued to eat better; she took a regular breakfast and informed her mother when she was hungry.

Three months after treatment started, a relapse occurred when her mother had to return to work. Fortunately, the relapse only lasted three or four days, during which time she would only take fluids. For the next six weeks, no therapeutic contact occurred because she contracted first measles and then chicken pox. Five months after the referral, the child was showing an interest in food and developing special tastes. A month later, her eating was no longer a problem to her relatives. By this time, the therapist had succeeded in transferring a large part of the "father role" to two of the child's uncles, one of whom (husband of father's sister) the child said she loved "nearly as much as Daddy."

After seven months, the treatment was terminated. A three-year follow-up revealed that the child had remained free of symptoms and was fairly well-adjusted at home, school, and with her peers.

COMMENTARY: White successfully used learning theory principles in the treatment of a childhood eating problem. Stimulus substitution and generalization were the main techniques employed. Clearly, the child in this study benefited from temporary father surrogates in adapting to loss of her father. The medium of play was also used effectively as a natural way of communicating with and relating to this young child. Therapist availability was also a crucial factor: The therapist not only saw the child quite often but also was available at any time by phone to consult with the mother.

SOURCE: White, J. G. "The Use of Learning Theory in the Psychological Treatment of Children." *Journal of Clinical Psychology*, 1959, *15*, 227–229.

Treating Anorexia Nervosa
by the Family Lunch Session

AUTHORS: Bernice L. Rosman, Salvador Minuchin, and Ronald Liebman

PRECIS: Use of a family therapy technique (lunch sessions) to initiate weight gain in eight cases

INTRODUCTION: Following a family systems orientation, Rosman, Minuchin, and Liebman present the application of a particular type of session with anorexia nervosa cases. The family therapy lunch session is used to involve the anorectic's family in treatment. By eating with the family, the therapist has a golden opportunity to make direct observations and interventions.

STRATEGIES: Three types of therapeutic lunch sessions are described, each applicable to a different type of case. In the first approach, "Increasing Parental Executive Effectiveness," each parent in turn is requested to get the child to eat. They are told that it is their responsibility as parents to ensure that the child eats. The problem is defined as one of management of a balky rather than sick child. Because one parent will often undermine the efforts of the other, these unilateral efforts usually fail. However, the parents by this time have been so encouraged by the therapist and enraged at the intransigence of the child that they unite and take a firm stand together. This often results in their successfully feeding the child or the child spontaneously beginning to eat.

Strategy Two, "Increasing Distance Between Parents and Child," begins in a similar manner, with the therapist instructing one parent, and then the other, to get the child to eat. The child refuses. Usually a stormy scene then develops, with the parents imploring, coaxing, or threatening the child. These unsuccessful efforts are stopped by the therapist when the power of this supposedly sick child to defeat her parents is apparent. The therapist then disengages the parents from further direct involvement in the conflict by making this into a private issue between child and therapist.

In Strategy Three, "Neutralizing Family Interaction with Respect to Eating," no effort is made to confront the parents and child around the eating issue. Instead, all parental attention to the child's eating behavior is discouraged. The therapist models a casual or indifferent attitude toward the child's eating. He involves the family in discussions about family background, interpersonal relationships, or family problems. Characteristic modes of family interaction patterns are noted, as well as the typical kinds of roles each family member plays. Sometimes the therapist will comment on other members of the family who show symptoms, especially siblings, in order to broaden the therapeutic focus to other family members. The anorectic child will usually begin to eat at some point during this session.

Strategies One and Two tend to provoke a crisis and are recommended for rigid families where the child is overtly resisting the parents. In this conflict situation, the interpersonal negotiation patterns of the parents and children become evident. Strategy One is used more often with younger and preadolescent youth, in order to highlight the issue of control and to strengthen the competence of the parents. Strategy Two is advocated for use with older adolescents, for whom autonomy and independence are important behaviors to reinforce. Where there is a flexible family, or where the child is already eating a little, Strategy Three is recommended, to provide the family with the experience of eating without a power struggle.

BASIC GOALS OF TREATMENT: According to Rosman, Minuchin, and Liebman, the following three goals must be met if a lunch session is to result in remission of symptoms and the beginning of therapeutic change within the family.

Changing the concept of the identified patient within the family. Typically, the family will present the anorectic child as the only one who has a problem and will portray the rest of the family as basically normal and untroubled. An important objective of the lunch session, then, is to help each family member begin thinking in terms of "*We* have a problem here." Explorations of problems and symptoms of other family members often help the family see the problem as a dysfunction of the family system rather than an isolated problem of one member.

Transforming an eating problem into an interpersonal problem. A second major task of the family therapist is to transform this specific "eating" problem into a more general interpersonal problem. Family systems theory postulates that the eating difficulty is a sign of an underlying conflict or dysfunction among family members. The therapist therefore redefines the problem in interpersonal terms—as parent-child problems in communication, as adolescent rebellion against parental overcontrol, and so forth.

Disengagement of the parents from using the child's eating behavior as a conflict-detouring device. A major assumption made by Rosman, Minuchin, and Liebman is that the eating difficulty provides a mechanism through which the family can avoid interpersonal conflict—particularly conflict between spouses. The symptom is viewed as a maladaptive attempt by one family member to deal with conflict. A primary goal of the lunch session is to bring to light this underlying conflict and to help the parents deal with it more directly and effectively. The usual pattern of parent-child interactions around the symptom are therefore changed, in order to bring about a separation or distancing between parents and child. Freed from their obsessive concern with the child's eating, the parents are helped to face unresolved conflict between themselves or with their children.

EFFECTIVENESS OF THE LUNCH SESSION: The article presents data that support the subjective impressions of family therapists that, following a lunch session, their patients begin to eat more and gain weight. The authors caution, however, that symptom remission in the index patient is only the first step in the therapeutic process. They feel that family members must proceed to develop new interaction patterns that promote self-enhancement in each member if a more permanent and meaningful recovery is to result.

COMMENTARY: As opposed to the behaviorist, who deals directly with the eating disorder, or to the psychodynamic therapist, who tries to give the child "insight" into the early roots of his eating difficulty (for example, a maladaptive mother-child relationship), the family systems worker approaches the eating problem by attempting to uncover and change current dysfunctional interaction patterns among family members. Although family therapists employ this general approach with a wide variety of childhood behavior problems, they reserve the use of the family lunch session technique for eating difficulties. Because they consider the eating difficulty to be a defense the family uses to avoid conflict, they see symptom remission as necessarily creating a crisis situation to be resolved by ongoing family therapy.

SOURCE: Rosman, B. L., Minuchin, S., and Liebman, R. "Family Lunch Session: An Introduction to Family Therapy in Anorexia Nervosa." *American Journal of Orthopsychiatry*, 1975, *45*, 846–853.

Behavioral Treatment of a Child's Eating Problem

AUTHOR: Martha E. Bernal

PRECIS: Use of a shaping procedure (rewarding gradual steps toward goal) to motivate a four-year-old girl to eat solid foods

INTRODUCTION: Bernal employs a direct behavioral approach to treating a child's eating problem, applying the successive approximation technique. This technique involves reinforcing in a sequential order the small steps that lead to the desired outcome.

CASE STUDY: Sandy, the four-year-old girl studied, would eat only strained foods, consisting exclusively of oatmeal, cottage cheese, and occasionally some types of fruit. She refused to eat strained vegetables or meats, as well as any regular adult table foods. At nine months, she had begun to eat finger foods, but had choked on a string bean, and thereafter she reverted to eating only strained foods. Many subsequent battles over food between Sandy and her mother were won by Sandy. At twenty months, for example, her mother withdrew the strained foods and offered her only table foods, on advice of the pediatrician. After thirty-six hours of not eating, Sandy began dry heaving and crying for her strained foods. Her frightened parents gave in to her request. At a typical meal, Sandy would feed herself a few mouthfuls of strained foods and then coerce her parents into feeding her the food they did not wish her to eat. The parents stated that their concern for her health— she had had a congenital heart defect—was an important factor in her gaining her own way. Fortunately, the defect had been corrected two months before treatment was started. At the time of referral, her pediatrician offered reassurance that her angry outbursts would not damage her health in any way and agreed to cooperate fully with the behavioral program. Because Sandy's weight at the time was only thirty pounds, he prescribed multivitamins to maintain her health.

TREATMENT: The treatment goal was for Sandy to eat by herself a variety of basic table food groups, including meats, vegetables, fruits, cereals, and dairy products. Bernal decided to work toward a gradual introduction of table foods, rather than risk another failure with a drastic withdrawal of strained foods. Accordingly, breakfast remained as usual except that intake was curtailed—as were between-meal snacks—to increase her appetite during the rest of the day. Rather than trying to coax, threaten, or nag her into eating, her parents allowed Sandy to earn social reinforcers and food rewards for eating. Also, as a precaution against dehydration and anemia, eight weeks before treatment a routine was instituted in which she was required to drink four tall glasses of water with her two daily vitamin pills.

Videotapes of previous lunch sessions in the home revealed that Sandy received much social attention—but not for self-feeding. Rather, her parents' attention consisted of coaxing and lecturing her for refusing to eat and for playing with her food. As a result, the mother was trained to alter her interaction patterns at the table and the father was advised to leave all care relating to food management to his wife. During the early phase of treatment, the mother was instructed to offer Sandy only positive attention at the table, such as smiling, looking, and pleasant talk, and to give this briefly when Sandy had taken a swallow of food. The mother agreed to practice this behavior and to study her performance on videotape. She was cautioned not to force Sandy to eat and to clean her only after the meal was finished. Sandy fed herself both cottage cheese and several types of preferred fruit during the first and subsequent training sessions. She also reminded her mother when smiles and conversation were due her.

During Sessions Two, Three, and Four, Sandy was allowed to eat cottage cheese only if she first ate the half jar of nonpreferred strained vegetables or fruits that were on her plate. Eating a "full meal" at lunch and dinner was defined as eating a half jar each of strained vegetables and either cottage cheese or fruit. By the eleventh week, the mother's records indicated that Sandy was eating two whole jars of strained fruits and vegetables as selected by the mother at both lunch and dinner. From the thirteenth to the twenty-first week, all types of strained foods were made contingent on eating new table foods. Because putting table foods on her plate without any urging to eat during the seventh to tenth weeks had produced no effect, at the twelfth week it was also decided to make viewing of a television program contingent on her eating even a tiny bite of some new table food. This resulted in Sandy's trying her first new table foods—a cupcake, french fries, and a cookie—between mealtimes. However, Sandy generally made no attempt to get the television set turned on and spent much time sulking during the week. At this point, Sandy was allowed a "free" half jar of previously nonpreferred baby food at lunch and dinner, but was required to earn the rest of her baby food by eating a small portion of new table food. The mother was advised to ignore the temper tantrums she threw to get the rest of her baby food. During the fourteenth week she tried three new foods, all sweets, and earned two television programs and one complete baby food meal. The sweet foods were then used as rewards for nonsweet foods. During the sixteenth week, television was dropped as a reinforcer because it did not prove to be very powerful. For the next three weeks, Sandy ate only her breakfast and the half jar of baby food at the other meals. Because it was discovered that her mother was yielding to her pleas during this period and giving her chocolate milk, Kool-Aid, and chewing gum, a consultation with the pediatrician was held. It was decided that the mother would discontinue the chewing gum and Kool-Aid and give her only four glasses of plain milk a day.

During the nineteenth week, Sandy finally requested and ate a portion of her father's oatmeal and this was gradually substituted for her strained oatmeal at breakfast. No reinforcers were given because it was felt that any attention given to her eating habits only strengthened her resistance to eating. At about the twentieth week, Sandy began to eat a new food—for example, peanut butter on a cracker—and then would insist on having only this food. Her mother was advised to ignore her whining and to continue to vary the table food. During the twenty-second week she was allowed peanut butter and jelly sandwiches (her favorite food at the time) whenever she ate any portion of the regular table food served the family. The first nonsweet table food (canned spaghetti) was taken during lunchtime of the twenty-fourth week. Having taken this step, she then continued trying new foods. Because it was apparent by the twenty-fifth week that Sandy could be expected to eat a regular family meal, it was recommended that a very small portion of the regular meal be put on her plate and that eating be rewarded with small amounts of preferred adult food and dessert. Sandy continued to eat most new foods after trying them and her diet by the thirty-second week (end of program) included all food groups. Her weight at the end of the program was thirty-three pounds and her mother reported she was eating very well. She had added about fifty different foods to her diet from the twelfth to the thirty-second week of the program.

COMMENTARY: Bernal's paper demonstrates the effectiveness of a behavioral treatment method for children who develop eating habits that are detrimental to their physical health. The literature attests to the fact that behavior modification techniques have proven successful in relieving a wide variety of eating difficulties in youth. Training parents in the use of behavioral procedures reflects the current trend toward using parents as therapists for their own children. Another important collaborator in this team approach is the medical doctor, who offers safeguards against possible ill health if food is refused.

A major difficulty in the use of this approach is that mothers find it very difficult to ignore the pleas and manipulations of a hungry child. Bernal reports that even with extensive videotape training on how to ignore her child's whining and tantrums, the mother in this study found it very hard to carry out. Consequently, her behavior had to be even more carefully monitored than the child's. She also needed ongoing therapist support, as reflected in the fact that she often telephoned her whenever she felt she could not handle Sandy's coercive behaviors. Once the mother was able to consistently ignore these coercive behaviors, they gradually ceased.

SOURCE: Bernal, M. E. "Behavioral Treatment of a Child's Eating Problem." *Journal of Behavior Therapy and Experimental Psychiatry,* 1972, *3,* 43–50.

Additional Readings

Aragona, J., Cassady, J., and Drabman, R. S. "Treating Overweight
     Children Through Parental Training and Contingency Con-
     tracting." *Journal of Applied Behavior Analysis,* 1975, *8,* 269–278.

Fifteen overweight girls, ages five to eleven years, were randomly assigned to one of two weight reduction treatments: response
cost plus reinforcement; response cost only; or a no-treatment
control group. In the group treated by response cost plus reinforcement, parents contracted to facilitate their child's weight loss by
carrying out reinforcement and stimulus control techniques, completing weekly charts and graphs, and encouraging their child to
exercise. The child received a reward for losing the predetermined
weight each week, while the parents paid a monetary fine if the
child did not lose the weight. The response cost group did not contract to reinforce their child's performance. The response cost
program was conducted in weekly meetings in which parents lost
previously deposited sums of money: 25 percent for missing the
weekly meeting, 25 percent for failing to fill out charts and graphs,
and 50 percent if their child failed to meet her specified weekly
weight loss goal. At the end of the twelve-week treatment period,
both experimental groups had lost significantly more weight than
the control group. A thirty-one-week, no-contract follow-up failed
to show a treatment effect, but did show a trend toward slower
weight gain by the response cost plus reinforcement group.

Bhanji, S., and Thompson, J. "Operant Conditioning in the Treat-
     ment of Anorexia Nervosa: A Review and Retrospective Study
     of Eleven Cases." *British Journal of Psychiatry,* 1974, *124,* 166–
     172.

The operant conditioning regime was discussed with the
patients and their parents before or at the time of admission to the
hospital. On admission the patients were not allowed to get out of
bed except to be weighed and were denied visiting and correspon-
dence privileges. When asked to specify a hierarchy of seven rewards, all the patients chose permission to have visitors as the most
desirable reward. The initial criterion of successful eating behavior
was eight consecutive meals, each consumed within sixty minutes
of presentation. When this had been achieved the patient received

her least desired reward from the hierarchy. When the patient had eaten eight consecutive meals, each within thirty minutes, and so obtained her seventh reward, a new hierarchy of rewards was drawn up. The total daily calorie intake was 2,000 to 3,000 calories, with vitamin supplements. Almost all the patients regained their weight loss in a period ranging from thirty-one to eighty-six days. A limited follow-up suggested that the operant procedures were often inadequate for long-term maintenance of normal eating habits and weight and should probably be combined with long-term psychotherapy.

Bruch, H. "Conceptual Confusion in Eating Disorders." *Journal of Nervous and Mental Disease*, 1961, *133*, 46–54.

Bruch states that the inability to correctly identify hunger and other bodily sensations should be recognized in patients with eating disorders. Some such patients live chiefly by responding to stimuli from others. They tend to respond with passive compliance or rigid negativism, without experiencing sensations, thoughts, or feelings as originating from within. This same lack of self-effectiveness and sense of external control also occurs in schizophrenic development. Traditional insight-giving therapy only reinforces the patient's experience of being influenced by others. To be effective, therapy must evoke an awareness of self-initiated thinking and doing.

Palmer, S., Thompson, R. J., and Linscheid, T. R. "Applied Behavior Analysis in the Treatment of Childhood Feeding Problems." *Developmental Medicine and Child Neurology*, 1975, *17*, 333–339.

This study reports the use of applied behavior analysis to treat a six-year-old boy who was subsisting almost entirely on pureed foods at the time of his referral. Whenever the boy took a bite of minced and bite-sized food, he was praised and given his preferred pureed food. If the boy refused food or avoided eating by making irrelevant comments, the therapist immediately turned his back until the boy stopped the inappropriate behavior. During the fifth session, it was necessary to ignore the boy's crying and pleading for more than three hours! After this session, the boy began to eat more and more solid foods. The authors report that they have successfully used the applied behavior analysis approach with a variety of childhood feeding problems.

Wright, L., and Thalassinos, P. A. "Success with Electroshock in Habitual Vomiting." *Clinical Pediatrics,* 1973, *12,* 594–597.

A four-year-old retarded girl who was becoming dehydrated because of severe vomiting was administered an electroshock via electrodes attached to her thigh after every incidence of retching, ruminating, or regurgitating during the first fifteen minutes following feeding. After twelve conditioning sessions, her vomiting behavior was dramatically reduced. A six-month follow-up revealed that some retching still occurred but that the incidence had been reduced from fifteen attempts per meal to only one or two a week.

Enuresis

Nocturnal enuresis is usually defined as urinary incontinence during sleep in children three years of age or older who show no signs of congenital or acquired physical defects or disease of the nervous or urogenital systems. As opposed to primary enuresis, *the term* secondary enuresis *refers to the fact that the child established and maintained control of his bladder for at least one year before relapsing. About 19 percent of the normal five- and six-year-old population wet the bed at night.*

As enuresis or bedwetting has a high spontaneous cure rate, claims of successful treatment must be viewed with caution. Studies have revealed that the annual spontaneous cure rate in children between the ages of five and nine is 14 percent; between ten and twenty years, the rate is 16 percent. Accordingly, treatment procedures must considerably improve on these rates to be regarded as effective. About 3 percent of children with this problem will still be wetting at age twenty.

Only nocturnal enuresis will be discussed in this section. It is noteworthy, however, that when children who exhibit both day and night wetting are successfully treated for the nighttime wetting, about 50 percent of them simultaneously cease their daytime enuresis.

Treating Enuresis by
Retention Control Training

AUTHORS: Herbert D. Kimmel and Ellen Kimmel

PRECIS: Parents trained three enuretic girls to hold their urine for increasingly long periods during the day

INTRODUCTION: Because the goal of the bell-and-pad conditioning method is nighttime awakening on awareness of the sensation of a full bladder, the Kimmels consider it a less than optimal method for nocturnal enuresis. They therefore devised a method of training a child to hold his or her urine and thereby sleep through the night.

RETENTION CONTROL TRAINING: On the first day of training, the parent instructs the child to "hold it in" for about five minutes when the child reports the urge to urinate. A young child may be told to hold it in until the "big hand on the clock gets to here." The child is promised a reward if this can be done. The reinforcer (for example, candy, soda, cookies) is decided on by the parent ahead of time, according to the parent's knowledge of the child. As soon as it becomes clear that the time demand has become easy for the child, it is gradually increased, always in small steps (for example, for three- to five-minute intervals) to preclude failure or refusal to cooperate. Usually, the time can be increased to as much as thirty minutes in only a few days. This may necessitate an increase in the amount of the reward as well. Contrary to conventional practice, the child is encouraged to drink liquids freely at any hour. Typically, the first sign that the procedure is working is a decrease in the frequency of daytime urination. Later, a reduction in nighttime bedwetting typically occurs.

The Kimmels report that this procedure successfully eliminated bedwetting in two four-year-old girls with a week of training. Similarly, a ten-year-old girl stopped her bedwetting after two weeks of this procedure and maintained her control thereafter.

COMMENTARY: The obvious advantages of this procedure are that it is simple, inexpensive, easy to administer, and quickly effective. Several later studies have documented the effectiveness of retention training alone and as part of an overall training program. The procedure is described as an instrumental conditioning technique designed to increase the amount of bladder distension that serves as a stimulus for voiding.

SOURCE: Kimmel, H. D., and Kimmel, E. "An Instrumental Conditioning Method for the Treatment of Enuresis." *Journal of Behavior Therapy and Experimental Psychiatry,* 1970, *1,* 121–123.

Treating Nocturnal Enuresis by
Classical Bell-and-Pad Conditioning

AUTHORS: Peter D. Taylor and R. Keith Turner

PRECIS: Research study of relapse rate supports an "overlearning" modification of the standard bell-and-pad treatment schedule for enuretic youth

INTRODUCTION: More than thirty years have now elapsed since Mowrer and Mowrer first reported the use of bell-and-pad conditioning procedures in treating enuresis. Although research efforts have consistently indicated a high success rate (65 to 100 percent) for the bell-and-pad method, high relapse rates continue to be reported. Lovibond, for example, found as many as 50 percent of patients successfully treated with the classical Mowrer conditioning procedure relapse within the first three months following treatment. The present study investigates the effectiveness of different schedules of reinforcement with the bell and pad.

TREATMENT: A total of eighty-two children (sixty-eight males, fourteen females) who had an enuresis problem, as reported by their parents, participated in this research study. A physician examined each child, to rule out any possibility of organic etiology. The age range of the subjects was four to fifteen years. The mothers of the children conducted the treatment and kept records of the incidence of wet and dry nights, time when child retired, time(s) when alarm was triggered, size of wet patch on bed, and any occurrence of spontaneous waking. The children were randomly assigned to one of three treatment conditions. In the continuous reinforcement treatment, the alarm was set to go off 100 percent of the times the child wet. In the intermittent reinforcement condition, the mother set the alarm to go off on a 50 percent random reinforcement schedule. For the overlearning treatment, the child's fluid intake one hour before bedtime was increased one to two pints as soon as seven consecutive dry nights had been achieved. All three treatment procedures continued until the criterion of no more than one wetting incidence occurred in twenty-eight consecutive nights.

Prior to treatment, the bell-and-pad apparatus was demonstrated to both mother and child. The apparatus, consisting of a rubber pad with electrodes embedded in it, was placed under the child's sheet at night. The child wore only the top part of his or her pajamas. When the child urinated, a loud bell was immediately activated, because an electrical grid was shorted by the moisture on the pad. An extension buzzer was available for those children who did not wake to the bell. The mother changed the wet bedding after each wetting and reset the instrument. On the activation of the apparatus, the child was fully awakened by the mother and taken to the toilet to finish voiding.

The results indicated an overall success rate of 57 percent, with no significant difference between treatments. On the other hand, only 23 percent of the overlearning group relapsed, while 69 percent of the continuous group, and 44 percent of the intermittent group relapsed. A case was considered relapsed if the child wet more than once per week at any stage during the eight- to fifteen-month follow-up.

COMMENTARY: The results of this study, together with similar findings by other investigators, suggest that the overlearning modification of the standard bell-and-pad procedure offers a promising way of minimizing the relapse problem. Taylor and Turner speculate that the overlearning is effective because the child gains confidence from the fact that he passed the "test" of an extra drink. In the present study, the stringent criterion of success (four weeks with one accident allowed) did not result in an overall reduction in the relapse rate as compared with the usual criterion of fourteen consecutive dry nights. On the basis of this and other studies conducted in special clinics, it appears that the bell-and-pad method is the single most effective form of treatment for enuresis.

SOURCE: Taylor, P. D., and Turner, R. K. "A Clinical Trial of Continuous, Intermittent and Overlearning 'Bell-and-Pad' Treatments for Nocturnal Enuresis." *Behaviour Research and Therapy*, 1975, *13*, 281–293.

Controlling Nocturnal Enuresis
by Operant Conditioning

AUTHOR: Makram Samaan

PRECIS: After unsuccessful treatment by classical bell-and-pad conditioning, the enuresis of a young girl was successfully treated by positive reinforcement for appropriate urination

INTRODUCTION: Samaan reports a case of a seven-year-old girl who had always been enuretic at night and had sometimes been so during the day when playing with her peers. She exhibited other deviant behaviors as well, such as being inattentive in class, complaining about peers, and always putting herself down. Previous efforts at treatment had proved futile, including two years with a psychoanalytic psychiatrist, the classical bell-and-pad procedure, dexedrine to produce light sleep, and restriction of fluids after supper. Another treatment strategy was therefore decided on.

OPERANT CONDITIONING: Parental interviews disclosed that the child liked both chocolate candy and body touch. She would also wet within one or two hours after retiring, and she usually wet two or three times every night, within two to three hours of going to bed. The treatment plan comprised three steps: (1) the child was to urinate every night just before retiring; (2) after the first hour in bed, the parents were to gently awaken her and lead her to the toilet—as soon as the child started urinating, she was to receive a piece of chocolate; and (3) Step 2 was to be repeated three times every night at two- to three-hour intervals. The parents were advised to prompt urination by making a "shh" sound or by opening a water faucet as soon as the child sat on the toilet. On the fourth day, the chocolate was to be put on the water tank for the child to take herself. To obtain additional verbal reinforcement, the child was requested to make a daily telephone call to the therapist.

After ten days of successful control, the child started to go by herself to urinate before retiring. If she did not spontaneously awaken to urinate after the first hour in bed, her parents followed the usual treatment. During the second week, only intermittent awakening by the parents was needed. During the fourth week, the child started getting up on her own while her parents intermittently praised her. Every morning they hugged and praised her profusely. From the fifth to the seventh week, the candy reinforcement was made intermittent on a variable ratio schedule. When the child asked about the absence of candy, her parents explained that they had forgotten or overslept and gave her candy coupled with praise. The candy at night was gradually phased out until by the eighth week the child did not receive candy until the morning. This positive reinforcement procedure resulted in the child being dry every night except on three occasions when the parents neglected to fulfill the requirements. The parents were advised to continue the established procedure for about a year, until the child developed self-confidence in her bladder control. A two-year follow-up revealed that no relapse had occurred and the child showed greater self-esteem and better emotional adjustment.

COMMENTARY: The success of this operant procedure seems related to the fact that the child received clear prompts and directions as to the desired behavior and immediate reinforcement when the behavior occurred. A total of seven behavior therapy sessions produced the outcome that had proven so resistant for other modes of treatment.

SOURCE: Samaan, M. "The Control of Nocturnal Enuresis by Operant Conditioning." *Journal of Behavior Therapy and Experimental Psychiatry*, 1972, *3*, 103–105.

Drugs for Bedwetting

AUTHOR: Roy Meadow

PRECIS: Discussion of the "pros" and "cons" of treating enuresis with antidepressant drugs

INTRODUCTION: Basing his conclusions on a review of the literature, Meadow states that the most effective treatment for enuresis and bladder control is the bell-and-pad method. However, he concludes that drugs do have a place in treating enuresis despite the fact that they tend to be expensive, addictive, and dangerous. The tricyclic antidepressants, he asserts, are the only drugs that have consistently been found to be superior to placebo. The two most frequently used are imipramine (Tofranil) and amitriptyline (Tryptizol). Their mode of action remains uncertain but is most likely related to their anticholinergic activity. Up to 40 percent of children may become dry after taking these drugs, but the relapse rate is much higher than it is with other forms of treatment. A reduction in the number of wet nights, rather than complete cessation of wetting, is the most likely result. Meadow favors the use of drugs when a child needs to be dry for a particular occasion (a night spent away from home) or for children who cannot use the buzzer alarm because of their age (typically, below the age of seven) or situation.

DRUG TREATMENT PLAN: A common drug treatment procedure is to use a starting dose of 25 mg of imipramine. At fortnightly intervals, the dosage is increased by 25 mg, until a maximum level of 75 mg is reached. The effective dosage level will vary widely among children. The drug is often stopped if a mood or sleep disturbance results. If a child regularly wets before midnight, it seems best to give the drug at 4 P.M.

COMMENTARY: Because of adverse side effects and high relapse rates, drugs have fallen into disrepute for the treatment of enuresis.

Meadow points out, however, that there remain some occasions when drugs seem the treatment of choice for the suppression of this troublesome behavior.

SOURCE: Meadow, R. "Drugs for Bed-Wetting." *Archives of Disease in Childhood,* 1974, *49,* 257–258.

Using a Staggered-Wakening Procedure to Control Enuresis in an Institutional Setting

AUTHORS: Thomas L. Creer and Margaret H. Davis

PRECIS: Successful application of staggered wakening technique using a variable-interval schedule

INTRODUCTION: Despite its impressive record of success, the bell-and-pad procedure has certain disadvantages in an institutional setting; for example, the alarm usually awakens others sleeping near the subject. At the institution with which Creer and Davis are affiliated, a residential treatment center for children with chronic bronchial asthma, previous efforts to eliminate enuresis by the use of drugs or awakening the children once each night at a fixed time had proven unsuccessful. It was therefore decided to try a new approach.

STAGGERED WAKENING PROCEDURE: A total of nine enuretic children (three from three different residential cottages) were awakened to void by the night attendants. Initially, they were awakened three times each night, according to a variable-interval (VI) schedule. The exact times were selected by drawing numbers from a hat. After two weeks, a fading procedure was initiated, whereby the children were only awakened twice a night. The third stage, begun two weeks later, involved awakening the children only once each night for a period of two weeks. The final one-month period consisted of allowing the children to sleep undisturbed at night.

The results disclosed that the staggered wakening approach produced a significant decrease in bedwetting both during the treatment period and over the one-month follow-up. This change was achieved with a minimal amount of disturbance to the other residents. Although systematic follow-up data were not available, Creer and Davis report that most of the children maintained their gains when they returned home.

COMMENTARY: Most residential treatment institutions for children treat enuresis by the practice of waking the children up at a fixed time to void. Unfortunately, the prolonged use of this procedure can lead to the maintenance of the habit. This is demonstrated by the rapid increase in bedwetting that usually occurs when this procedure is halted. The use of the staggered wakening procedure, then, appears to be a more promising approach for institutional populations. Creer and Davis hypothesize that the method is effective because the children find it quite aversive to be awakened on a frequent and unpredictable basis.

SOURCE: Creer, T. L., and Davis, M. H. "Using a Staggered-Wakening Procedure with Enuretic Children in an Institutional Setting." *Journal of Behavior Therapy and Experimental Psychiatry*, 1975, *6*, 23–25.

The Responsibility-Reinforcement
Technique for Enuresis

AUTHORS: Sumner Marshall, Hermine H. Marshall, and Richards P. Lyons

PRECIS: Research-supported strategy of making children responsible for their own treatment rather than making them passive participants in the process

INTRODUCTION: The authors point out that the child is a *passive* participant in most forms of enuresis therapy, including surgery, medication, and conditioning devices. They recommend a procedure whereby the child takes *active* responsibility for achieving change and is supported in his efforts by reinforcement from his family and therapist. The details of their responsibility-reinforcement approach follow.

RESPONSIBILITY-REINFORCEMENT TREATMENT: A study is reported in which 300 enuretic children, ages three to fourteen years, were treated by one of four different techniques: bell-and-pad conditioning, medication, instrumentation—which involved urethral dilation or meatotomy, and responsibility-reinforcement training. The last approach used principles derived from Glasser's "reality therapy" approach and from the behavior modification approach of Skinner. The basic assumption of this method is that the child himself must want to change his bedwetting behavior and to take responsibility for achieving this goal. The following techniques are used to help the child reach his goal. First, he is given a progress record, on which he notes the days he wets and possible causes for this wetting (for example, emotional stress during the day). On dry days, he places a star on the chart. The therapist offers praise for the successes achieved and discusses with the child how he can cope with the environmental and psychological factors that can contribute to wetting.

A "response-shaping" technique is also employed; the child is helped to gain rewards for each step-by-step improvement toward a goal. For example, to promote gradual control over the ability to hold urine, the child is advised to set an alarm clock so that he can awaken and empty his bladder at longer and longer intervals. Recording these intervals and knowing that this achievement is his own is in itself reinforcing to the child. Family and therapist provide additional reinforcement by praise and approval.

The "sensation awareness" technique is another aspect of this approach. It is felt that the child must become more aware of the sensation of a full bladder so that he can gain greater control over voiding and thereby gain mastery of his own body. To this end, the child is encouraged to hold his urine as long as possible and then void into a measuring cup so as to measure the volume. Furthermore, by stopping and starting his micturition at will, he gains awareness of his power to control the act of voiding.

RESULTS OF DIFFERENT APPROACHES: The results of this study reveal that when a child played an active role in his therapy through the responsibility-reinforcement method, the overall reduction in his bedwetting was greater than for the other three approaches. The relapse rate was also lower (5 percent). The improvement took longer with the responsibility technique but it proved to be more consistent. In addition, the families of the children were able to continue the technique at home.

COMMENTARY: In view of its growth-producing potential, the responsibility-reinforcement technique offers great promise as the initial form of treatment for enuresis. According to the Marshalls and Lyons, the approach results in the least disruption to the child's physiological, psychological, and social functioning. However, further research is clearly needed to evaluate the effectiveness of this approach.

SOURCE: Marshall, S., Marshall, H. H., and Lyons, R. P. "Enuresis: An Analysis of Various Therapeutic Approaches." *Pediatrics,* 1973, *52,* 813–817.

The Implicit Use of Operant
Conditioning to Night Train Children

AUTHORS: Lorna Benjamin, William Serdahely, and Thomas Geppert

PRECIS: Questionnaire study indicating that positive reinforcement from parents is most effective in training children to be dry at night

INTRODUCTION: The authors conducted a study to answer the question, How do most children learn not to wet during the night? They sent a questionnaire to 90 parents of normal children who, during a routine pediatric visit, indicated that they had night trained a child under the age of nine. The questionnaire contained a number of specific parent-child interactions that seemed related to night training. It was hypothesized that—following the operant conditioning model—the desired response of remaining dry through the night was emitted and then, if rewarded, was more likely to be repeated.

FINDINGS: The results gave no support to the popular idea that night training is helped by restricting fluids after supper, by waking the child before the parents retire, or by stopping the night bottle. Although the parents reported that there was no real "training," the results indicated that operant conditioning was implicitly present. The data demonstrated that efficient night training was related to the following procedures: (1) the presence of a discriminative stimulus, such as switching from diapers at night to training pants or pajamas; (2) having a motivated, responsible child—for example, the parent said, "It was really the child's idea that it was time to begin night training" (p. 964); (3) maximizing conditions to elicit the desired response—"I had him urinate immediately after he woke up in the morning" (p. 965); and (4) rewarding success with positive reinforcers—"I said in a pleased manner, 'You can keep dry pants all by yourself'" (p. 965). On the other hand, it was found that negative parental reinforcers, such as shaming, spanking, rejecting, and name calling, retarded night training.

COMMENTARY: The results support the common knowledge that children generally are influenced by positive evaluations of themselves by their parents. It is also apparent from the data that children resist being "put down" by such power-oriented strategies as shame and punishment. When children have a sense of internal control and mastery of their own affairs, they will not only show more efficient learning but also better emotional adjustment.

SOURCE: Benjamin, L., Serdahely, W., and Geppert, T. "Night Training Through Parents' Implicit Use of Operant Conditioning." *Child Development,* 1971, *42,* 963–966.

Dry-Bed Training

AUTHORS: N. H. Azrin, T. J. Sneed, and R. M. Foxx

PRECIS: Rapid elimination of enuresis in thirteen children by supplementing the bell-and-pad apparatus with inhibition training, positive reinforcement, rapid awakening training, increased fluid intake, increased motivation, self-correction of accidents, and toileting practice

INTRODUCTION: Because the standard bell-and-pad apparatus did not prove particularly successful with profoundly retarded adult enuretics, Azrin and his associates developed a method of dry-bed training. On the average, this procedure required only one night of intensive training for results and proved equally successful with children. The one night of intensive training is, however, quite elaborate and exhausting for both parent and child. The dry-bed procedure, which is used in conjunction with the bell-and-pad, is described by the authors (pp. 150–151) as follows:

I. *Intensive training (one night)*

  A. *One hour before bedtime*
   1. Child informed of all phases of training procedure
   2. Alarm placed on bed
   3. Positive practice in toileting (twenty practice trials)
    a. Child lies down in bed
    b. Child counts to fifty
    c. Child arises and attempts to urinate in toilet
    d. Child returns to bed
    e. Steps a, b, c and d repeated twenty times
  B. *At bedtime*
   1. Child drinks fluids
   2. Child repeats training instructions to trainer
   3. Child retires for the night
  C. *Hourly awakenings*
   1. Minimal prompt used to awaken child
   2. Child walks to bathroom

      3. At bathroom door (*before* urination), child is asked to inhibit urination for one hour (omit for children under six)
        a. If child could not inhibit urination
          (1) Child urinates in toilet
          (2) Trainer praises child for correct toileting
          (3) Child returns to bed
        b. If child indicates that he could inhibit urination for one hour
          (1) Trainer praises child for his urinary control
          (2) Child returns to bed
      4. At bedside, the child feels the bed sheets and comments on their dryness
      5. Trainer praises child for having a dry bed
      6. Child is given fluids to drink
      7. Child returns to sleep
   D. *When an accident occurs*
      1. Trainer disconnects alarm
      2. Trainer awakens child and reprimands him for wetting
      3. Trainer directs child to bathroom to finish urinating
      4. Child is given cleanliness training
        a. Child is required to change night clothes
        b. Child is required to remove wet bed sheet and place it with dirty laundry
        c. Trainer reactivates alarm
        d. Child obtains clean sheets and remakes bed
      5. Positive practice in correct toileting (twenty practice trials) performed immediately after the cleanliness training
      6. Positive practice in correct toileting (twenty practice trials) performed the following evening *before* bedtime

II. *Posttraining supervision (begins the night after training)*

   A. *Before bedtime*
      1. Alarm is placed on bed
      2. Positive practice given (*if* an accident occurred the previous night)
      3. Child is reminded of need to remain dry and of the need

for cleanliness training and positive practice if wetting
occurred
4. Child is asked to repeat the parent's instructions
B. *Nighttime toileting*
1. At parents' bedtime, they awaken child and send him to
toilet
2. After each dry night, parent awakens child thirty minutes
earlier than on previous night
3. Awakening discontinued when they are scheduled to
occur within one hour of child's bedtime
C. *When accidents occur, child receives cleanliness training and
positive practice immediately on wetting and at bedtime the next day*
D. *After a dry night*
1. Both parents praise child for not wetting his bed
2. Parents praise child at least five times during the day
3. Child's favorite relatives are encouraged to praise him

III. *Normal routine—initiated after seven consecutive dry nights*

A. *Urine-alarm is no longer placed on bed*
B. *Parents inspect child's bed each morning*
1. If bed is wet, child receives cleanliness training
immediately and positive practice the following evening
2. If bed is dry, child receives praise for keeping his bed dry
C. *If two accidents occur within a week, the posttraining supervision is
reinstated*

Azrin, Sneed, and Foxx state that each of the thirteen children
receiving dry-bed training was given lengthy verbal instructions
and explanations. The children were also trained to deliberately
delay their urination, as in the Kimmel and Kimmel (1970) procedure. To ensure that the parents would awaken, a buzzer was placed
in the parents' bedroom as well as in the child's room. Moreover,
the parents were given a complete description of the dry-bed training, the rationale for each step, and a discussion of the advantages
of eliminating the bed-wetting problem.

In order to increase the frequency of urination, the child was
given a glass of his favorite drink just before bedtime. He then performed the positive practice routine by himself in his darkened

room. Then the child was asked to again drink as much as he could of his favorite drink. If, after each hourly awakening, the child did not immediately walk to the bathroom, the parent pointed toward the bathroom and asked the child, "What did you promise to do when I woke you?" If the child continued to delay, the parent quickly led him into the bathroom saying, "You have to hurry to the bathroom if you don't want to wet your bed!" At the bathroom door, the child was asked if he could hold his urine for another hour. If the child said no, he was asked to inhibit it for a few minutes and then was praised immediately after urination for correct toileting. After a nighttime accident, the child was required to wash his face to ensure complete awakening. A trainer stayed in the home during the first night of intensive training.

RESULTS: For the thirteen children in the dry-bed training, the results indicated that the median number of bedtime accidents fell from seven a week to one during the first week, one during the second week, and none after the third week for the duration of the six-month follow-up. The number of accidents with the dry-bed trained children was found to be significantly less than for a control group trained with the standard bell-and-pad procedure. Although none of the dry-bed children relapsed to their former level of bedwetting during the six months of observation, about half of these children did require the use of the bed-and-pad a second time.

COMMENTARY: Dry-bed training seems to achieve results much quicker than the usual bell-and-pad procedure, but it requires much more work, especially during the first night of training. If quick results are not essential, it would seem more humane to employ the traditional Mowrer and Mowrer bell-and-pad procedure. In the event the usual bell-and-pad approach fails, then one should probably employ the more intense dry-bed training. However, there is a clear need for independent replications of Azrin's findings concerning dry-bed training.

SOURCE: Azrin, N. H., Sneed, T. J., and Foxx, R. M. "Dry-Bed Training: Rapid Elimination of Childhood Enuresis." *Behaviour Research and Therapy*, 1974, *12*, 147–156.

Treating 1,000 Consecutive Cases of Enuresis

AUTHOR: Margaret White

PRECIS: Describes a "placebo plus reassurance" procedure as the initial method of choice for younger enuretic children

INTRODUCTION: Basing her conclusions on an extensive review of the literature, White notes that there is a greater incidence of enuresis in boys than girls (the ratio is about two to one) and that there is a higher incidence of enuresis, past and present, among the immediate family of enuretics than among the immediate family of controls. Notwithstanding the popular "organic" and "emotional disturbance" theories concerning the origin of enuresis, White concludes that the cause in most cases is originally a slow developmental control of the bladder, which is largely hereditary. If the problem was completely ignored, it would show spontaneous remission by age seven or eight. Unfortunately, parents never ignore it. Indeed, 30 percent of the mothers reported scolding or beating the child. Other parents found different ways to express their disapproval or disgust. The result of this reaction is that the child anxiously tries to meet parental expectations, an attempt that only leads to depression, more anxiety, and lowered self-esteem. The habit some mothers have of "lifting" their child on to the toilet to urinate without awakening them only serves to train the child to wet his bed.

TREATMENT: The following was the treatment of choice for the 1,000 enuretic children who attended the White's clinic in London during the period studied. First, the therapist would get to know the child and explain why he wets the bed—great care was placed on the fact that it was *not the child's fault.* The child was asked to mark on a card when he had dry nights and bring this card to his monthly meetings with the therapist. By doing so, the child was subconsciously bringing a gift of so many dry beds per month to a friend. The child was also given a placebo tablet of lactose. The tablets were given for the benefit of mothers as much as for the child, because many mothers would not return to the clinic if they did not receive medication. No limit on fluid intake was imposed. The child was told that he would not get better immediately—that the treatment would take about six months. He was reassured that he would get a bit better each month, so that by the end of one month he would have four or five dry beds, at the end of two months eight or nine, and so on. If the child did not respond to this procedure, he was placed on the bell-and-pad apparatus. The bell and pad was also the treatment of choice for older subjects (teen-agers), because it produces quicker results (2.5 months average length of treatment) than the placebo plus reassurance (5.8 months). The bell and pad does, however, have a higher relapse rate (33 percent) than the placebo method (10 percent). The results of treatment have been quite impressive at this clinic: 728 of the 1,000 children were discharged as dry (73 percent); 168 (17 percent) were discharged for nonattendance; and only five (.05 percent) were discharged as still enuretic. About 5 percent of the cases discharged as dry subsequently relapsed and returned to the clinic for further treatment. The bell-and-pad procedure was used in about a third of the cases.

COMMENTARY: White's flexibility in selecting a treatment technique depending on the age of the child seems sensible. Because teen-age children are more resistant to treatment, they should be given a "fast-action" mode of treatment to prevent nonattendance after a few sessions. Too often therapists adopt a favorite therapeutic approach and apply it rigidly to all cases showing a similar problem. Giving the child and his parents encouragement and confidence seemed to be the key aspect of therapy in the majority of the cases reported in this study.

SOURCE: White, M. "A Thousand Consecutive Cases of Enuresis: Results of Treatment." *Child and Family,* 1971, *10,* 198–209.

Additional Readings

Catalina, D. "Enuresis: Parent-Mediated Modification." Paper presented at the annual Eastern Psychological Association Convention, New York, April 1976.

The purpose of Catalina's study was to investigate the effect of a parent mediated training procedure on children's bedwetting.

Parents checked the child's bed three times nightly; if wet, the child was awakened, sent to the bathroom, and helped to remake his bed. Since only 35 percent of the twenty children stopped wetting as a result of this procedure, Catalina concludes that the traditional bell-and-pad apparatus is not only quicker but more effective; that is, it yields 65 percent to 100 percent success in most studies.

Doleys, D. M., and Wells, K. C. "Changes in Functional Bladder Capacity and Bedwetting During and After Retention Control Training: A Case Study." *Behavior Therapy,* 1975, *6,* 685–688.

Changes in functional bladder capacity and frequency of bedwetting were recorded during retention control training with a forty-two-month-old girl. Bladder capacity increased and remained above baseline levels. Bedwetting decreased and did not occur during the final eight weeks of the fourteen-week follow-up period. The girl was reinforced with food and a variety of trinkets for drinking fluids and withholding urination until the preset retention interval time ended. The initial retention interval was set at five minutes and was systematically increased in increments of three minutes. After the seventh day of training, fluids were no longer forced, because the child showed excessive emotional behavior during the retention interval. Retention trials continued to be imposed. At this point, Azrin's "positive practice" procedure was started, which required the child to lie on the bed for twenty seconds, walk to the bathroom, sit on the toilet without urinating, and return to the bed. About five to ten positive practice trials occurred after each retention period. The child was allowed to urinate at the last trial. Also, the girl's parents began to awaken her every hour on the hour after 10 P.M. and had her perform five to ten positive practice trials until she voided on the toilet.

Edgar, C. L., Kohler, H. F., and Harman, S. "A New Method for Toilet Training Developmentally Disabled Children." *Perceptual and Motor Skills,* 1975, *41,* 63–69.

A number of profoundly retarded children (four to twelve years old) were successfully toilet trained by using a variety of relaxation and tension activities designed to help them differentiate and gain control of their lower abdominal muscles. Operant techniques were used to reinforce appropriate urination.

Finley, W. W., Besserman, R. L., Bennet, L. F., Clapp, R. K., and Finley, P. M. "The Effect of Continuous, Intermittent, and "Placebo" Reinforcement on the Effectiveness of the Conditioning Treatment for Enuresis Nocturna." *Behaviour Research and Therapy,* 1973, *11,* 289–297.

The authors conducted an experiment with thirty enuretic boys to investigate the acquisition and extinction parameters of continuous (100 percent), intermittent (70 percent variable ratio), and "placebo" (0 percent) reinforcement schedules. Reinforced trials were administered, as in the typical Mowrer conditioning procedure. Nonreinforced trials were achieved by means of a time delay with the subsequent alarm being activated in the parents' room rather than in the child's room. The results of this study revealed that the continuous reinforcement (CR) and intermittent reinforcement (IR) groups attained acquisition in approximately the same number of trials and with essentially the same success rate. Relapse rate was significantly greater in the CR group than in the IR group. The placebo group showed no improvement during the six weeks of treatment. The findings suggest that IR may be of value in reducing the rate of relapse in bedwetting conditioning therapy.

Gladston, R., and Perlmutter, A. D. "The Urinary Manifestations of Anxiety in Children." *Pediatrics,* 1973, *52,* 818–822.

Experience with children hospitalized for urinary disorders indicates that anxiety can alter the frequency and disturb the adequacy of voiding to a degree sufficient to dispose the child to urinary tract infection.

Johnson, J. H., and Thompson, D. J. "Modeling in the Treatment of Enuresis: A Case Study." *Journal of Behavior Therapy and Experimental Psychiatry,* 1974, *5,* 93–94.

This paper reports on the successful treatment of a child with enuresis, in which modeling procedures were thought to have played a major role. Tommy, age five, was wetting both day and night at least eight times a day. By accident, Tommy then observed his mother begin to toilet train his two-year-old brother. The mother hugged and praised the younger sibling for successfully urinating on the toilet. Tommy then asked if he could urinate on the toilet to make his mother proud and was promptly praised when he did so. The mother then carefully arranged similar scenes wherein

Tommy would observe his brother successfully urinating in the bathroom and received praise and candy. This produced a rapid decrease in the enuresis to about once a day (occurring primarily at night), and finally a complete cessation of both day and night wetting. This case suggests that modeling procedures may be of value in the treatment of enuresis.

McConaghy, N. "A Controlled Trial of Imipramine, Amphetamine, Pad-and-Bell Conditioning, and Random Awakening in the Treatment of Nocturnal Enuresis." *Medical Journal of Australia,* 1969, *2,* 237–239.

In a controlled study of methods of treating nocturnal enuresis in otherwise healthy children, bell-and-pad conditioning produced the best results, both initially and at a one-year follow-up. Imipramine initially produced a significantly superior response than did placebo, but there was a considerable relapse rate with gradual withdrawal. Amphetamine proved of little value.

Morgan, R. T. T., and Young, G. C. "Case Histories and Shorter Communications." *Behaviour Research and Therapy,* 1975, *13,* 197–199.

Measures of tolerance of enuresis and the "nuisance value" attached to the disorder were obtained from the mothers of children entering treatment for enuresis. Mothers regarding enuresis as a greater nuisance tended to have enuretic children who were more anxious and mothers from lower socioeconomic levels were found to be less tolerant of the problem and to rate it as a greater nuisance. The attitudinal variables measured were not found to be relevant to rate of therapeutic response, but tolerant mothers were more likely to withdraw their children prematurely from treatment.

Nergardh, A., Hendenberg, C., Hellstrom, B., and Ericsson, N. "Continence Training of Children with Neurogenic Bladder Dysfunction." *Developmental Medicine and Child Neurology,* 1974, *16,* 47–51.

Thirty children with neurogenic bladder dysfunction were included in a continence training experiment. The dysfunction was primarily caused by myelomeningocele. Training consisted of bladder elimination every three to four hours during the day, supported by drug therapy to help contract and relax different muscles in the urinary tract. After two training sessions about one half of the children had become socially continent, that is, had regular dry periods between micturition every three to four hours. With one exception, all the other children also showed improvement. The importance of supporting and encouraging the patients during this training was stressed.

Olness, K. "The Use of Self-Hypnosis in the Treatment of Childhood Nocturnal Enuresis." *Clinical Pediatrics,* 1975, *14,* 273–279.

Forty enuretic children were taught the technique of self-hypnosis or self-conditioning. After teaching the children how to stare at an object and become relaxed, they were told to relax themselves every night and tell themselves: "When I need to urinate I will wake up all by myself, go to the bathroom all by myself, urinate in the toilet, and return to my dry bed. When I wake up, my bed will be dry and I will be very happy" (p. 275). This procedure resulted in thirty-one of the forty children being cured; six improved markedly and three did not improve. The technique requires no medications, gadgets, or charts, and does not appear to have side effects. Olness reports that children develop new self-confidence from having achieved the cure on their own.

Paschalis, A. P., Kimmel, H. D., and Kimmel. E. "Further Study of Diurnal Instrumental Conditioning in the Treatment of Enuresis Nocturna." *Journal of Behavior Therapy and Experimental Psychiatry,* 1972, *3,* 253–256.

Prolongation of urine retention was rewarded during waking hours in thirty-one enuretic children who had never experienced a dry night. Training continued until a forty-five-minute prolongation was attained. Training took twenty days. At a three-month follow-up, fifteen of the thirty-one children were completely free of enuresis and eight more showed significant improvement. This result was deemed especially impressive in that the treatment was administered by parents with only two hours of training by the experimenter. Possible applications of the method to other behavioral problems involving autonomic mediation are suggested in this article.

Young, G. C., and Morgan, R. T. "Overlearning in the Conditioning Treatment of Enuresis: A Long-Term Follow-Up Study." *Behaviour Research and Therapy,* 1972, *10,* 419–420.

Various studies have reported high rates of relapse following the otherwise highly successful conditioning treatment of childhood nocturnal enuresis. Relapse seems to be a hazard inherent in this form of treatment, independent of patient variables. Use of the technique of intermittent reinforcement schedules and of central nervous system stimulant drugs to counteract the relapse problem have failed to achieve satisfactory results. Young and Morgan have demonstrated the success of overlearning therapy in reducing the relapse rate. This regime requires the child to maintain or regain his learned nocturnal bladder control, to a success criterion of fourteen consecutive dry nights, while drinking up to two pints of liquid in the hour before retiring. This paper reports that overlearning reduces the relapse rate from about 50 to 25 percent.

Encopresis

Encopresis has been defined as any voluntary or involuntary defecation that results in soiled clothes. The incidence of encopresis is higher in boys than in girls, by a ratio of more than three to one. Children with primary encopresis have never developed bowel control, whereas children who established bowel control for a period of time but later regressed to fecal soiling are considered to have secondary encopresis. Secondary encopresis has a better prognosis and is usually the result of a child's response to psychic stress. In America, the child is considered capable of exercising voluntary control at age two, although therapeutic treatment is usually deferred until age five. The overall incidence of encopresis in the general population in western civilization is reported to be 1.5 percent.

203

Handling Encopresis With a Combination of Behavior Modification Procedures and Laxatives

AUTHOR: Logan Wright

PRECIS: Treating psychogenic encopresis with an economical, effective, and widely applicable procedure that can be administered by parents at home

INTRODUCTION: From his experience with encopretic children, Wright devised a standardized treatment program with wide applicability. Prior to treatment, Wright recommends a comprehensive diagnostic assessment that gathers both medical and psychological information.

TREATMENT: The first step in treatment involves "selling" the parents on the efficacy of conditioning methods, to establish in them the expectation that treatment will be successful. The parents are warned that lack of consistency in strictly following the conditioning program is a common cause of failure. Consistency is defined as something that happens 100 percent of the time; 90 percent consistency is seen as no better than 10 percent. To promote consistency, daily written records and at least weekly check-ins with the therapist are required.

Next, three reinforcers (two positive and one negative) are identified for the conditioning program. The most common positive reinforcer, in Wright's experience, has been the opportunity to earn time alone with parents, during which period the child determines the nature of the activity, such as playing a game, going for a ride. Other rewards include tokens for purchase of toys, money, toys themselves, trips, and tickets to movies. Negative reinforcers include such consequences as thirty minutes in the bathtub, extra chores, and loss of free play time. Any incidence of defecation on the toilet is then positively reinforced, as is going for one day without soiling. A punishment is administered after each soiling episode.

The child is told he must try to defecate on arising in the morning. If he cannot, he is given glycerin suppositories (no prescription needed) and allowed to eat breakfast. By the end of breakfast, the child will usually need to defecate. If not, he is given a Fleet enema before going to school. This absolute predictability of defecation at a fixed time is considered essential to treatment. The daily defecation also allows the child's colon to regain its normal shape and muscle tone and prevents soiling.

The final and most difficult step of the program involves weaning the child from the suppositories after daily bowel movements are established for two weeks and soiling discontinued. Initially, one day of the week is chosen and all external aids to defecation are eliminated for that day. With each additional week without soiling, another day's cathartics (external aids) are discontinued. If soiling occurs during the weaning process, one day's cathartics are added for each soiling episode until the child is receiving cathartics every day or until he again goes a week without soiling. At this point, the weaning process begins anew. If a child goes two weeks without soiling after all cathartics are discontinued, the program is terminated.

Wright reports that the program has generally been effective in alleviating encopresis in an average of fifteen to twenty weeks.

COMMENTARY: This program, which can be administered by parents at home, seems to offer a practical, economical, and efficient means of treating the encopretic child. As in any home management program, the parents' ability to follow the routine rigorously is a crucial aspect of successful treatment. Parental ability to calmly and effectively administer enemas to children is an important aspect to consider, as is the possibility of either child or parent showing hostile or erotic feelings from the use of suppositories or enemas.

SOURCE: Wright, L. "Handling the Encopretic Child." *Professional Psychology,* 1973, *4,* 137–144.

A Triadic Behavioral Approach to Encopresis

AUTHOR: Marc Sheinbein

PRECIS: Combining behavior modification with conjoint family therapy to treat psychogenic encopresis

INTRODUCTION: Sheinbein is strongly convinced that both the encopretic child and his family should be included in the treatment plan. Thus, he advocates a novel triadic approach that combines behavior modification principles with conjoint family therapy. Before treatment, of course, neurological causes, such as Hirschsprung's disease, must be ruled out. (Hirschsprung's disease is a primarily neurological disorder where the colon is unable to respond to pressure with the appropriate defecation reflex.)

TRIADIC BEHAVIORAL APPROACH: In the triadic behavioral approach, the therapist first provides the family with a positive reinforcement procedure that gives the child material and/or social rewards for appropriate defecation. The child is made an ally in the process and encouraged to be responsible for its success. The parents are involved in this procedure as monitors and reinforcers. The child no longer fears the parents, as he knows exactly what to expect and feels that it is up to him now.

Once the encopresis problem is under control and the family members are able to relax, the therapist seeks to resolve the underlying causes of the symptom by conjoint family sessions. Typically, the parents are compulsive, overly intellectualizing people who isolate feelings and have trouble becoming close to one another. The therapist therefore encourages the family members to be more honest and open with each other by disclosing feelings and making clear, direct statements of needs and wishes. Through this process, they reveal their individuality and become more lovable to one another. It is important that the therapist serve as a model for giving support, for negotiating, and for providing firm, consistent limits. He must also demonstrate confidence that the treatment will work. The family will attempt to undermine his efforts by diverse strategies, including a proclivity to complain rather than to solve problems, but the therapist should not be put off. The parent-child-therapist triad must continue to struggle to overcome interpersonal distance and misunderstanding.

COMMENTARY: In the triadic behavioral approach, the therapist seeks to change the family interaction patterns as well as the child. The basic premise is that if the goals of open and honest communication among family members are achieved, then deviant behaviors become unnecessary and disappear. The theory is based on the triad-based family therapy approach of G. H. Zuk.

SOURCE: Sheinbein, M. "A Triadic-Behavioral Approach to Encopresis." *Journal of Family Counseling*, 1975, *3*, 58–61.

Eliminating Soiling Behavior Through Aversive Techniques

AUTHORS: William Ferinden and Donald Van Handel

PRECIS: Case study illustrating the use of aversive techniques by school personnel

INTRODUCTION: Ferinden and Van Handel present the case of George, a seven-year-old boy diagnosed as emotionally immature and having psychogenic megacolon (dilation of the colon) with a five-year history of soiling and chronic constipation. George was referred to the school psychologist because he soiled almost daily and sometimes as often as three times in a school day. After each mishap, George had been sent home to be cleaned up and obtain fresh clothing.

TREATMENT: The following punishment procedure was implemented. George was not only required to bring a change of clothing to school, but also to clean himself and wash his soiled clothes in cold water with a mildly abrasive soap. In addition, he had to make up time lost from the classroom after school hours.

Simultaneously, George met with the psychologist to discuss the social implications of his behavior. In one of these sessions, he admitted that he was acting like a baby because he would like to stay home all the time with his mother and watch television.

The aversive procedure produced a marked reduction in the incidence of classroom soiling and George soiled himself only nine more times after the procedure was initiated. In addition to the elimination of soiling in school and at home (no relapse after six months), the boy also showed more positive peer relationships.

COMMENTARY: Although the punishment and counseling procedure proved very effective in this case, one wonders if comparable results could not have been obtained through the use of positive reinforcers. Because of possible adverse side effects, punishment should only be used when alternative forms of treatment are clearly inappropriate or have failed to produce change.

SOURCE: Ferinden, W., and Van Handel, D. "Elimination of Soiling Behavior in an Elementary School Child Through the Application of Aversive Techniques." *Journal of School Psychology,* 1970, *8,* 267–269.

Dynamic Treatment of Encopresis

AUTHORS: Samuel R. Warson, Marilyn R. Caldwell, Alice Warinner, A'Lelia J. Kirk, and Reynold A. Jensen

PRECIS: Use of play therapy and parent counseling to treat psychogenic encopresis in a young girl

INTRODUCTION: The authors present a case study involving a six-year-old girl who exhibited an encopresis problem since infancy. She was the second of three children. Her upper-middle-class parents were highly intellectual, compulsive persons who revealed little warmth. They were disgusted with her soiling and emphasized the need for their child to conform and show normal cleanliness. The mother was preoccupied with feelings of inadequacy and failure as a parent.

When the child was two, her older brother required hospitalization and extended home care because of an illness; at the same time, her father was transferred to another city, so that the family had to move. During this hectic period, the child received little parental attention and changed from a happy child to a whiny, fearful, demanding one. At age three, the child strained to avoid bowel movements and began almost continuous fecal soiling. She seemed indifferent to the problem and refused to cooperate with her mother, who spent a great deal of time keeping her clean. No physical basis for the problem was discovered. The child and her mother were seen in parallel treatment sessions over the course of a year.

TREATMENT: The child was seen in a permissive form of play therapy for forty-two sessions over the period of fourteen months. During the initial sessions, her compulsive, critical traits were evident in her calling toys "dirty," "black," "nasty brown," or "broken." After touching any of these condemned items, she would run to the playroom sink to wash her hands. Her critical comments soon switched to her siblings and she began to attack them verbally while smearing with finger paints. Although she seemed excited and delighted with finger painting, she would quickly become anxious and rush to scrub her hands. Gradually she was able to spend a whole hour pushing a "brother doll" through a mound of brown finger paint. Next, mother dolls, who were viewed as being angry and punishing, were rubbed with sand and water in a hostile manner. In a later session, the child expressed verbal anger toward her mother for the first time and then became very frightened about this. In subsequent sessions, she became more spontaneous about verbalizing such feelings as fears about being sent away from home; her panic on one occasion in early childhood when she had flushed the toilet and it had overflowed; and hostile-competitive feelings toward her sibling and mother. She also began enjoying making messes with clay and finger paints. She remarked, for example, how wonderful the "soft, squishy mud" felt. The patient then began having the dolls make bowel movements with clay and finger paints. She talked about some mothers who did not want their children ever to have bowel movements. After asking the therapist to clean up the mess made by the dolls, she seemed to relax when it was done in a matter-of-fact manner. During the final sessions, she began playing in a constructive fashion with the paints and expressed the desire to terminate therapy because she was not soiling anymore.

In separate sessions, the child's mother was able to express pent-up feelings of inadequacy, resentment, and hostility toward both her husband and mother. She was helped to see that her own mother raised her in a strict, perfectionistic, overly controlled way, just as she was raising her own daughter. With a great deal of acceptance, understanding, and support, the mother seemed to gain more confidence in herself as a parent.

Follow-ups two and twelve months after the termination of therapy revealed that the child remained free of symptoms and she was described as a "changed" child. Both she and her mother seemed happy, friendly, and more self-confident.

COMMENTARY: The authors attribute much of the success of treatment to the changes in the mother made possible by the acceptance and support of the therapist and the removal of the stigma of maternal inadequacy suggested by having a nonconforming child. It is doubtful whether the child could have been helped in therapy without the mother undertaking parallel treatment. The roots of the problem seemed to be in the anger and resentment the child and mother felt toward each other but were unable to express. Play therapy offered the child the opportunity to release her hostility, while at the same time it reduced the inhibitions she felt against such instinctual pleasures as mud play.

SOURCE: Warson, S. R., Caldwell, M. R., Warinner, A., Kirk, A. J., and Jensen, R. A. "The Dynamics of Encopresis." *American Journal of Orthopsychiatry,* 1954, *24,* 402–415.

Additional Readings

Anthony, E. J. "An Experimental Approach to the Psychopathology of Childhood Encopresis." *British Journal of Medical Psychology,* 1957, *30,* 146–175.

Anthony distinguishes between two types of encopretic children. The "continuous" (never had control) child is a dirty child coming from a dirty family, burdened with every conceivable sort of social problem. Much external pressure is needed before the mother will agree to treatment. This child does not need psychotherapy, but rather consistent habit training administered by a warm, interested person. By identifying with a normal adult, he can develop some degree of disgust for the symptom. He can be reasonably stabilized in a period of three to five months. The "discontinuous" (had control but lost it) child, on the other hand, is the compulsive child of a compulsive family. He is overcontrolled and inhibited in his emotional life and scrupulous in his habits. He is very defensive about his symptom and difficult to treat. He tends to be a deeply disturbed child who needs prolonged psychotherapy and some measure of protection from his mother and their sadomasochistic relationship. A disappearance of an exaggerated disgust reaction is the first hopeful therapeutic sign.

Ashkenazi, Z. "The Treatment of Encopresis Using a Discriminative Stimulus and Positive Reinforcement." *Journal of Behavior Therapy and Experimental Psychiatry,* 1975, *6,* 155–157.

Sixteen of eighteen cases of encopresis in children were successfully treated by using glycerine suppositories to increase the discrimination control of rectal pressure for elimination. Social and material reinforcers were added for appropriate toileting behavior. Follow-up after six months showed that the behavior was maintained in all cases.

Ayllon, T., Simon, S. J., and Wildman, R. W. "Instructions and Reinforcement in the Elimination of Encopresis: A Case Study." *Journal of Behavior Therapy and Experimental Psychiatry,* 1975, *6,* 235–238.

A seven-year-old encopretic boy was rewarded by a trip with his therapist for every week of symptom-free behavior. His mother recorded and charted his behavior. Within ten days, fecal soiling was eliminated and his mother assumed the responsibility for reinforcing his appropriate behavior. An eleven-month follow-up revealed no evidence of a relapse or symptom substitution.

Bach, R., and Moylan, J. J. "Parents Administer Behavior Therapy for Inappropriate Urination and Encopresis: A Case Study." *Journal of Behavior Therapy and Experimental Psychiatry,* 1975, *6,* 239–241.

A six-year-old boy with a long history of inappropriate urination and secondary reactive encopresis was treated by his disturbed parents with an operant approach. The parents administered money rewards on a continuous schedule for appropriate defecation and ignored soiling. The rate of urine incontinence dropped immediately, but the encopresis continued, perhaps because the child had no sensation of a full colon. Accordingly, the parents began to prompt the boy to attempt defecation and rewarded him for trying. This latter procedure reduced the soiling rate to nearly zero. The money rewards were reduced and then faded into a weekly allowance. A two-year follow-up revealed no remission.

Baird, M. "Characteristic Interaction Patterns in Families of Encopretic Children." *Bulletin of the Menninger Clinic,* 1974, *38,* 144–153.

Families of encopretic children were found to exhibit the following behaviors: the withholding of vital information, an aspect of the relationship, or of tangible things from the child; the propensity to infantilize the child; the presence of anger and its denial; and a general distortion of communication. Therefore the correction of the dysfunctional family patterns should be the first step in a child's treatment.

Barrett, B. H. "Behavior Modification in the Home: Parents Adapt Laboratory-Developed Tactics to Bowel-Train a Five-and-a-Half-Year-Old." *Psychotherapy: Theory, Research and Practice,* 1969, *3,* 172–176.

Parents of a five-and-a-half-year-old retarded, hyperactive, "autistic" child rapidly eliminated his encopresis by punishing soiling with isolation and restraint in a special chair. They rewarded appropriate bowel movements by praise and food. When the child held his feces for four days, they terminated this behavior with suppositories. Their successful treatment enabled the child to participate in training programs previously denied him because of his encopresis.

Doleys, D. M., and Arnold, S. "Treatment of Childhood Encopresis: Full Cleanliness Training." *Mental Retardation,* 1975, *13,* 14–16.

The use of "full cleanliness training" in combination with positive reinforcement effectively stopped the encopresis of a retarded male after sixteen weeks of treatment. Full cleanliness training, contingent on inappropriate soiling, requires the child to clean himself and his clothing. This procedure involved three steps: (1) parents expressed displeasure about the soiling; (2) the child was required to scrub his soiled underwear for at least fifteen minutes; and (3) he was then required to bathe and clean himself. The child was not released from the cleaning task if he was crying or being disruptive when the required time elapsed.

Edelman, R. I. "Operant Conditioning Treatment of Encopresis." *Journal of Behavior Therapy and Experimental Psychiatry,* 1971, *2,* 71–73.

A twelve-year-old girl with a history of chronic encopresis was treated by being given periods of isolation as a punishment for fecal soiling, and later, in addition, by relieving her of dishwashing chores when she did not soil. The undesirable behavior virtually ceased after forty-one weeks of this management in the home situation.

Keehn, J. D. "Brief Case Report: Reinforcement Therapy of Incontinence." *Behaviour Research and Therapy,* 1965, *2,* 239.

A normal five-year-old boy frequently soiled himself over a period of several months. On psychological advice, the mother repeatedly told the child that whenever he emptied his bowel on the toilet she would give him a piece of chocolate. This procedure worked immediately and there was no sign of relapse two months later, when the frequency of chocolate reinforcement had been reduced to almost zero.

Neale, D. H. "Behavior Therapy and Encopresis in Children." *Behaviour Research and Therapy*, 1963, *1*, 139–149.

Neale reports four cases of psychogenic encopresis in children ages seven to ten. Because the soiling was of long standing and resistant to other forms of treatment, the children were all inpatients in a psychiatric hospital. After each main meal and at bedtime, the children were taken to the toilet by a warm, friendly nurse. The procedure was explained to the children and they were given comic books to read on the toilet if they wished. After successful passing of feces, the child was rewarded by adult approval and the knowledge of progress toward greater self-control. In addition, the children were given a reward of sweets, peanuts, pennies, or stars in a book. Two of the children were orally given a dried mucilage of tropical seeds that gave additional bulk for the colon to work on and made the stools soft and easy to pass. Once a child was free from soiling, he was instructed to go whenever he felt the sensation of rectal fullness (which had returned at this stage). No punishment was given for dirty pants nor any reward for clean ones. This operant procedure resulted in rapid elimination of encopresis in three of the four children.

Perdini, B. C., and Perdini, D. T. "Reinforcement Procedures in the Control of Encopresis: A Case Study." *Psychological Reports,* 1971, *28*, 937–938.

An eleven-year-old boy frequently defecated in class. His mother reported that he had never been toilet trained. Because the boy enjoyed reading, it was decided to reinforce symptom-free behavior in the classroom with coupons toward book purchases. The boy could earn eight coupons a day; he needed forty coupons to buy the first book, fifty-five for the second book, and so on. The soiling was immediately eliminated by this procedure, and follow-up seven months after the elimination of book coupons revealed only one accident.

Perzan, R. S., Boulander, F., and Fischer, D. G. "Complex Factors in Inhibition of Defecation: A Review and Case Study." *Journal of Behavior Therapy and Experimental Psychiatry*, 1972, *3*, 129–133.

This article briefly reviews the control of elimination problems in children through planned reinforcement. Constipation can be less amenable than frequent soiling to modification by strictly operant methodology, which raises the possibility of congenital anomalies. Since birth, a four-year-old boy had been subjected to several hospitalizations, numerous inconclusive medical examinations, daily laxatives, and suppositories for chronic constipation. With the introduction of repetitive suggestions and a material reinforcer, bowel movements were accelerated from zero unless suppositories were used, to a terminal rate of one per day without suppositories or laxatives of any kind. Suggestions consisted of holding the child after an involuntary elimination using a suppository, and saying in a hypnotic monotone, "You will soon be able to go potty by yourself every day; it will feel good, no more suppositories will be used, you will not have to go to the hospital anymore" (p. 131).

Tomlinson, J. R. "The Treatment of Bowel Retention by Operant Procedures: A Case Study." *Journal of Behavior Therapy and Experimental Psychiatry*, 1970, *1*, 83–85.

A long-standing problem of bowel retention in a three-year-old child was treated by an operant approach. A contingency was established in which the response of voluntary elimination was the only available instrumental response that would be followed by a bubble gum reinforcer. The sole task of the parents was to check the adequacy of the child's response and to dispense the gum. The rate of voluntary defecation increased from a base rate of once per week to six times per week by the end of the third week. The rate was maintained at this level at the end of a two-year period, although a new reinforcer was introduced at the end of the first year. During the fourteenth week, when the contingency was removed, the rate fell to its original level.

Young, G. C. "The Treatment of Childhood Encopresis by Conditioned Gastroileal Reflex Training." *Behaviour Research and Therapy*, 1973, *11*, 499–503.

Mass movements of the colon occur usually after a meal or fluid intake because of increased colonic motor activity (gastrocolic reflex) and hyperactive terminal ileum (gastroileal reflex). Mass movements of the colon empty the contents of the proximal colon into the more distal sections and frequently these movements result in an increased urge to defecate. It takes about twenty to thirty minutes after ingesting food or drink for the colonic sensation to occur and the most common time for the reflex to appear is during the first hour after arising in the morning. Accumulated feces in the rectum are removed before treating an encopretic child, to increase perception of the reflexes. After a child awakens in the morning, his parents give him or her a warm drink or food. After twenty to thirty minutes, the child is taken to the toilet and the parents suggest bowel action. The child is allowed to sit on the toilet for no more than ten minutes. If successful, he is given approval; if not, a nonchalant attitude is shown. This procedure is repeated after other meals, if possible. To relieve colonic inertia and assist the gastroileal reflex, most of the twenty-four children in this study were given Senokot (one-half to two tablets) before going to bed at night. The results indicated that nineteen children were successfully treated within twelve months, three were successful in over twelve months, and two children did not respond. During follow-up, four children suffered relapses that were successfully treated by repeating the procedure.

Young, I. L., and Goldsmith, A. O. "Treatment of Encopresis in a Day Treatment Program." *Psychotherapy: Theory, Research and Practice*, 1972, *9*, 231–235.

An eight-year-old boy who had regressed to frequent encopresis at age seven was successfully treated by the use of concrete rewards for appropriate elimination during the school day. Other treatment efforts during the previous two years had failed, including psychotherapy for the child and casework with the parents within a comprehensive therapeutic milieu.

Glue Sniffing

Glue sniffing can be defined as the deliberate inhaling of glue vapors for the purpose of getting "high." In recent years, its incidence has increased among children and adolescents. The following two papers present two opposing positions as to its seriousness and treatment.

Psychotherapy with Glue Sniffers

AUTHOR: Gabriel V. Laury

PRECIS: Recommends psychotherapy for the juvenile glue sniffer and his parents

INTRODUCTION: According to Laury, who worked extensively with the problem, glue sniffing appeals to youth because it is cheap, readily available, inconspicuous, and legal to buy. The usual procedure is to empty a tube of cement into a small paper bag that has been wrinkled and massaged beforehand so that breathing in and out of the bag will result in no distracting noise to the user. Placing the bag over the mouth and nose, the user breathes in and out rapidly for about fifteen minutes while massaging the glue to keep it from drying too fast. Glue sniffing tends to produce effects quite similar to alcohol intoxication—ranging from pleasant relaxation to a feeling of inebriation, exhilaration, and euphoria and, in the extreme, to drowsiness and unconsciousness. In addition to this "high," visual hallucinations such as bright colors are common. Typically, glue sniffing is done with a group of peers, is associated with emotional problems, and leads to later heroin use among young people.

TREATMENT: Efforts to remove the opportunity to inhale vapors are usually unsuccessful. Laury, who treated thirty glue sniffers, recommends psychotherapy for both child and parent. Identification with the therapist should be used to channel the child's energy into constructive pursuits. By engaging in some community activity, such as band, cadets, scouts, choir, athletic team, or big brothers, the child not only overcomes his boredom but also forms new friendships. His resistance to joining these "square" activities and deserting his old friends must be overcome.

The parents of the child often choose to ignore his behavior and find it convenient to have him out of the house after school. They tend to ignore the child's late arrivals, inebriated behavior, and glue stains on the nose and hair. Through counseling, the parents must be made to realize that they have to spend more time with the child and communicate with him. The child's efforts and accomplishments should also be noticed and appreciated. Finally, the parents should give clear and consistent messages as to behaviors they consider right and wrong.

Laury presents a case study of a twelve-year-old boy who had been sniffing glue for six months because of parental neglect. His mother spent her time watching television rather than her five children, while his father was a heavy drinker who was rarely home because of his job. Glue sniffing brought on hallucinations in the boy and made it difficult for him to study, so he eventually gave up his schoolwork altogether. He felt very guilty about his actions and agreed with his father's judgment that he had brought "shame" on the family. He also expressed fears about the effect of his sniffing on his physical health.

In therapy, the boy ventilated considerable anger and resentment toward his parents for not supervising him more closely. The therapist helped him appreciate the problems of his parents; he then felt closer to them and his hostility decreased. Although expressing guilt feelings about deserting his friends, he eventually joined the band and was able to make new friends there. As a result of individual sessions with each parent, they were able to appreciate their involvement in the problem and began to become somewhat more involved with their children. One year after the start of treatment, the boy was free of symptoms and doing well at home, in school, and with his peers.

COMMENTARY: Laury reports good success in treating glue sniffing with dynamically oriented psychotherapy. He cautions, however, that a major pitfall in working with these clients is that depression often sets in when the sniffing is discontinued. Two of his patients even attempted suicide between the time they were required to give up sniffing and the start of psychotherapy. As with any other drug addiction, a person going "cold turkey" needs considerable support and encouragement to overcome the habit.

SOURCE: Laury, G. V. "Psychotherapy with Glue Sniffers." *International Journal of Child Psychotherapy,* 1972, *1,* 98–110.

Glue Sniffing in Children: A Position Paper

AUTHORS: Norman E. Silberberg and Margaret C. Silberberg

PRECIS: Recommends that remedial efforts be directed at relieving school failure—the major stress underlying glue sniffing

INTRODUCTION: The Silberbergs review the literature in an attempt to separate fact from myth in regard to glue sniffing. Studies of its physiological effects have revealed no clear evidence of chronic brain damage, kidney or liver impairment, or injury to bone marrow. Physiological addiction apparently does not occur, but psychological dependency is common. Most studies revealed no marked transition to alcohol, marijuana, barbiturates, or opiates. Typically, the sniffer is a thirteen-year-old, nonblack male with an IQ in the lower half of the normal range. Most sniffers come from low-income families, tend to be truants, and have difficulty with reading, writing, and arithmetic. It is felt that drug use does not indicate that there is something terribly wrong with the youth, either morally or psychologically. The use of glue in childhood to escape certain stressful situations is similar to the use of drugs and alcohol by millions of adults when confronted with frustration, anxiety, or failure. In our culture, children are taught that drugs are an effective way to make one feel better. As a remedy, children need to find "something better," that is, a satisfying experience outside of the chemical realm.

SOME RECOMMENDATIONS: Rather than spending a great deal of money on psychotherapy, incarceration, or drug education programs (which may turn some nonusers on to glue by describing "how to do it"), the Silberbergs suggest that much of the money could be better spent by applying it to the underlying cause of sniffing—feelings of worthlessness. School failure is seen as one major cause of these feelings of inadequacy. The Silberbergs state that it is essential to develop new school curricula that maximize school success by taking into account the learning style of the many youngsters who are failing in the present system. Furthermore, they suggest that parents and professionals be more understanding of the stresses placed on children and that they begin doing something to change those institutions in our society that help destroy children.

COMMENTARY: The Silberbergs' point that—like marijuana— the fears surrounding glue sniffing and the methods used to prevent it may do more harm than good is well taken. Forbidding the possession of certain glue products by youth and thereby criminalizing the practice would probably be as ineffective as prohibiting the possession of marijuana. The Silberbergs also make a contribution by pointing out that school failure is often one of the prime causes of glue addiction. Efforts directed at changing school curricula so as to provide more success experience would undoubtedly help reduce the glue-sniffing problem.

SOURCE: Silberberg, N. E., and Silberberg, M. C. "Glue Sniffing in Children: A Position Paper." *Journal of Drug Education,* 1974, *4,* 301–307.

Additional Readings

Chapel, J. L., and Taylor, D. W. "Drugs for Kicks." *Crime and Delinquency,* 1970, *16,* 1–35.

Chapel and Taylor describe the effects on, personality characteristics of, and treatment of children who inhale the noxious vapors of glue, gasoline, thinners, and lighter fluid. To treat acute intoxication, the authors recommend fresh air or oxygen with or without 5 percent carbon dioxide. Tests to determine any damage to the blood, bone marrow, liver, and kidneys should also be made. Cases involving repeated glue sniffing should be referred for therapy. The importance of uncovering the underlying cause is stressed, lest the youth turn to other drugs for kicks, such as alcohol and heroin. The immediate effect of inhaling glue is an acute brain syndrome that resembles alcohol intoxication but with the addition of more serious side effects such as hallucinations, delusions of omnipotence (a common feeling is that of being able to fly), and insensitivity to physical pain.

Sleep Disturbance

As with eating disorders, children show a very high incidence of sleep problems. About half of all sleep disturbances can be classified as being minor in nature—for example, restlessness, mumbling, talking, teeth grinding, early or frequent waking, and difficulty in falling asleep. According to the literature, the more serious sleep disorders include nocturnal enuresis, whose incidence accounts for about a quarter of all sleep problems; nightmares (7 percent incidence); night terrors (2 percent); and sleepwalking (1 percent). The reader is referred to other sections of this book for discussions of enuresis, nightmares, and night terrors. This section presents various treatment techniques for treating some of the other disorders of sleep, especially insomnia and sleepwalking.

Drug Treatment of Somnambulism

AUTHORS: Richard B. Pesikoff and Parma C. Davis

PRECIS: Five sleepwalking children were successfully treated with imipramine

INTRODUCTION: Somnambulism or sleepwalking usually occurs in children one to three hours after they have fallen asleep. Pesikoff and Davis state that the child arises quietly and walks about in a confused way. Soon, however, his actions may become more coordinated and it is difficult to waken the somnambulist. The child may simply walk around his room, other parts of the house, or outdoors. Sometimes the child engages in complex tasks, such as taking toys apart and reassembling them. The next morning the child remembers nothing of these actions, which may last from a few minutes to a half hour. As with *pavor nocturnus,* somnambulism usually occurs during slow-wave sleep, that is, in Stages Three and Four.

TREATMENT: The drug imipramine was selected as the treatment of choice because of its reported success with enuresis, a disorder that is also associated with Sleep Stages Three and Four. All five somnambulist patients were eleven years old or less. Written parental consent was obtained prior to treatment, because at the time imipramine was not cleared for use with children below the age of twelve. All the children were given a complete physical and psychiatric evaluation before treatment. The medication was given orally at bedtime in doses ranging from 10 mg to 50 mg, depending on the weight of the child. All of the children took the drug for a minimum of eight weeks and received bimonthly reevaluations during the course of the study.

Pesikoff and Davis present several case studies. For example, one three-year-old girl had been sleepwalking for the past year and a half. Every night she would get out of bed after sleeping for a few hours and wander aimlessly about the home. About fifteen to twenty minutes later, the girl would return to bed and remain in the bed for the rest of the night. In the morning, she remembered nothing of the previous evening's events. Mental status and physical and laboratory evaluations were all normal for this child. She was started on 25 mg of imipramine at bedtime. Since the frequency of sleepwalking remained unchanged for the first week, her dosage was increased to 50 mg. This immediately terminated the somnambulism. She remained on this dosage for eight weeks with no recurrence of symptoms.

The authors report similar results for the other four sleepwalkers they treated, as well as for two cases of night terrors. Without exception, all the children showed complete cessation of their sleep disorders when treated with imipramine. The reason why the drug is successful with sleep abnormalities is still not clear. Studies show that it does not decrease the amount of time spent in Sleep Stages Three and Four.

COMMENTARY: Pesikoff and Davis found no evidence to support the hypothesis that symptom removal often leads to symptom substitution. Rather than exhibiting any new emotional problems, the treated children tended to be less anxious and more agreeable at home. However, it cannot be definitely concluded that imipramine was responsible for the treatment's effectiveness, because this study was neither double blind nor controlled. The authors report that they are conducting further studies to investigate this question.

SOURCE: Pesikoff, R. B., and Davis, P. C. "Treatment of Pavor Nocturnus and Somnambulism in Children." *American Journal of Psychiatry*, 1971, *128*, 778–781.

Parent Guidance in Child Treatment

AUTHORS: Marvin Ack, Estela Beale, and Lucille Ware

PRECIS: Analytically oriented therapy directed at helping parents become aware of unconscious factors underlying sleep and other behavior disorders in children

INTRODUCTION: The authors point out that the special technique of treating children by having their parents act as therapists is not new—Freud, for example, used it in his famous study "The Analysis of a Phobia in a Five-Year-Old Boy." Most therapists who have employed this psychoanalytically oriented method of parent guidance have reported considerable success. The authors reserve the term *parent guidance* for cases where the parents do supervised therapy with their child under age five. Except for the diagnostic interview, the therapist does not see the child. Rather, one or both parents are seen weekly to discuss significant events in the child's life.

The major therapeutic technique is to make the parents aware of the unconscious forces at work in the child and to help the parents use this new awareness in the interpretation of the difficulties. Through specific situations recounted by parents, they are given explanations of the operation of defense mechanisms; for example, they are told how aggressiveness in a child may be a protection against intense anxiety, sadness, or fear of failure. Parents are also helped to recognize that all behavior in a child is motivated and has meaning, rather than being the result of a coincidence unrelated to past events or being a temporary phase that will pass.

Contraindications for the use of parent guidance include cases of full-blown neurosis or psychosis in child or parent; unmotivated parents who come only because of external pressure; and families currently experiencing severe environmental stresses, such as impending divorce or constant parental discord. In the latter cases, the authors feel that crisis intervention is more appropriate than parent guidance.

TREATMENT: Since the therapeutic focus is to resolve the child's problem, discussion of a parent's feelings or attitudes are explored only insofar as they pertain to the child's current difficulty. In forming a working alliance, the parents (usually only the mother is able to attend regularly) must be made to feel respected as an integral part of the therapy team. The therapist tries to be empathically understanding of the parents' dilemma, rather than critical or judgmental. Therapeutic advice is given in slow increments, to avoid making the parents feel stupid or attacked. On the other hand, if the therapist remains a passive, sympathetic listener, the parents will feel they are not being helped.

Transference. The authors feel that a mild, positive transference is the best climate for guidance. Often, however, the parents will either act helpless, as if in the presence of an all-knowing parent figure, or will seem fearful, lest they be criticized by a harsh authority figure. Because of this fear, they will avoid revealing facts that will place them in an unfavorable light. By interpreting transference resistances, the therapist helps the parents to understand maladaptive interactions with their own parents that currently interfere with child-rearing practices.

For example, one mother entered parent guidance because she was experiencing a number of problems with her four-year-old son, including separation difficulties. After seven months of guidance, the child had improved in all areas except separation. When the therapist then stated that he would be absent for the next two weeks, the mother asked to be reassigned to another therapist for those weeks. This led to a discussion of whether she was denying the importance of the relationship with the therapist. In this connection, the mother realized that her own mother had left her to go to work when there was no economic reason to do so. She had reacted to this original separation by becoming self-sufficient and independent. She then realized how many times she had left her son without any empathy for his feelings.

Other cases involve parental mismanagement or situations where the conflict is the same as a parent experienced as a child. In such cases, the authors state, only when the parents, especially the mother, can meaningfully appreciate the way their own past conflicts and experiences are dictating their current parenting practices can they alter these maladaptive methods.

CASE STUDY: According to the authors, parent guidance is most appropriate for cases of developmental difficulties caused by environmental trauma or for children whose problems seem more related to parental neglect or harsh treatment. As an example of the former, the authors present the case of a four-year-old boy with a sleep disorder. Since age two, the child had not spent a dozen undisturbed nights in his own bed. Even after falling asleep, the boy would often arise and go into his parents' bedroom to check on their presence. The case history revealed that the boy's father had suddenly been hospitalized on three occasions because of a heart condition. Because of the father's condition, the mother had been forced to leave the boy with a sitter and go to work. Discussion of these events led the mother and therapist to connect the boy's reluctance to going to sleep with a fear of awakening in a fatherless house. The mother was encouraged to discuss with her son how upset and fearful he must still feel about waking up and finding his father in the hospital and his mother so upset. Gradually the boy was able to express his feelings and to connect the past with the present. Within four months, the boy was sleeping through the night and did not experience a regression.

COMMENTARY: Parental guidance is a method that can be used with children displaying not only sleeping difficulty but a wide variety of other behavior disorders. Rather than restricting the use of this method to children under five, however, a number of therapists are now experimenting with its use for children of all ages. Apart from analytically oriented therapists, parental guidance is employed quite commonly by therapists with training in learning theory, nondirective counseling, and Adlerian principles. The content of the guidance, of course, varies markedly depending on the therapeutic approach.

SOURCE: Ack, M., Beale, E., and Ware, L. "Parent Guidance: Psychotherapy of the Young Child Via the Parent." *Bulletin of the Menninger Clinic,* 1975, *39,* 436–447.

Psychic Trauma and Somnambulism in Children

AUTHORS: Helen Kurtz and Samai Davidson

PRECIS: Dynamically oriented, short-term therapy for a somnambulistic boy who was traumatized by an injury to his father

INTRODUCTION: Kurtz and Davidson point out that nervous habits, such as sleeplessness, are often triggered by some trauma to the psyche. A psychic trauma is defined as an "experience of helplessness on the part of the ego when faced with an overwhelming intensive onslaught of excitation emanating either from external sources or from the unconscious drives" (p. 438). It typically occurs in a sudden, unexpected manner that prevents a defensive action (with the exception of swift and severe repression). Psychoanalysts agree, however, that no event is traumatic in and of itself. In certain vulnerable persons, it can touch off deep-seated anxiety or symbolize the fulfillment of an unconscious wish. An example of the latter is a situation in which a traumatic event symbolizes the fulfillment of a repressed death wish toward a parent or sibling, which often results in the child experiencing severe fear of an aggressive attack on himself. Also, a child who suffered partial object loss in the past—for example, separation from a parent because of illness or job demands—is often vulnerable to a trauma that symbolizes total loss of a parent.

CASE REPORT: An eleven-year-old boy was referred for treatment because of severe episodes of somnambulism, which had continued for the past two and a half years. His frequent sleepwalking episodes were characterized by frantic racing and searching about the home, which on at least one occasion had resulted in his climbing on the barrier of a third-floor balcony. The boy's parents were not aware of any outstanding event that could have triggered the symptom. However, during the initial interview they remarked that, two months prior to the onset of the boy's symptoms, the father, an officer in the Israeli army, had participated in a security action, which had left him badly wounded. The boy had first learned of this incident from peers who shouted to him from the street, "Your father has been killed." His somnambulism began as soon as the father returned home from the hospital. After this incident, the boy became restless and easily distracted, which resulted in a deterioration of his school grades. The case history revealed that the boy and his father had never been close, partly because of the fact that the father's army position kept him away from home for long periods of time. Lacking a strong male identification figure, the boy showed signs of difficulty in developing a masculine identity. Contributing to the problem was the fact that the boy's mother had become overly involved with the boy and intrusive in his activiites. Diagnostic testing of the boy revealed signs of a severe neurosis with hysterical features.

TREATMENT: Using focused, dynamic, short-term therapy, a female therapist saw the boy and his parents separately in weekly sessions at a mental health clinic. The therapist's goal with the boy was to make him aware of his strengths and repressed emotions. In the first session, she helped the boy see that a sleepwalker was neither "strange" nor "not sane," as the boy had thought, but a person expressing the emotions he does not allow himself to express when he is fully conscious. The boy appeared to absorb and relate to the therapist's interpretations, but in a rather passive, hesitant way. After the first month of treatment, the sleepwalking incidents only occurred on Friday nights, when the father was regularly absent from the home. When the therapist asked the boy what could happen to the family with the father away at night, the boy recited a long litany of fears, such as the house collapsing. The therapist accepted these fears as understandable emotions. After this session, the somnambulism episodes disappeared. Regular sessions were continued for three months, to allow the boy opportunities to further express his fears and angry feelings. During one of these sessions, abreaction occurred when the boy relived the moment of panic he experienced when he first learned that his father had been hurt.

Therapy sessions with the parents were focused on helping them understand the boy's denial and repression of his emotions, his need for a closer relationship with his father, and a need for freedom from his mother's overprotection and overinterference. As a result of these sessions, the boy and his father were partially able to work through their problematic relationship. An eighteen-month follow-up revealed that the boy was continuing to develop increased competence in the social and academic areas. Sleepwalking did not recur.

COMMENTARY: This case illustrates that when parents ignore sleep disturbances in a child for an extended period, there is a likelihood that the child's underlying anxiety will become internalized in the form of a full-blown neurosis. When adults bottle up their emotions during times of external stress, such as in wars and natural disasters, while demanding that their children repress their frightened feelings, then the children will be prone to psychological disturbance. It is better to honestly and openly discuss the situation with the children, face it together as a family, and encourage the children to ventilate their feelings in an accepting atmosphere.

SOURCE: Kurtz, H., and Davidson, S. "Psychic Trauma in an Israeli Child: Relationship to Environmental Security." *American Journal of Psychotherapy,* 1974, *28,* 438–444.

Treating Insomnia by Self-Relaxation

AUTHORS: Gabriel Weil and Marvin R. Goldfried

PRECIS: Demonstrates the use of in vivo relaxation training to treat insomnia in an eleven-year-old girl

INTRODUCTION: Weil and Goldfried present a case wherein a school nurse referred Susan, an eleven-year-old girl, for outpatient treatment because of her fatigued condition. The parents reported that the girl was well-adjusted at home and in school except for two problems: She had trouble falling asleep at night and she resisted remaining home alone, even with a babysitter. Usually it would take the girl about two hours to fall asleep in the evening, because she would ruminate about the events of the day, and she was sensitive to external noises. The insomnia problem was the initial focus of treatment because of its serious effect on her health and schoolwork.

TREATMENT: The following relaxation procedure was set up after two assessment interviews and a home visit. The therapist went to the girl's home in the evening and, while she was lying in bed, instructed her to relax by alternately tensing and relaxing the various muscle groups. Susan responded favorably to the relaxation and fell asleep an hour later. Using a thirty-minute tape recording of the therapist's relaxation instructions, during the next two weeks she fell asleep either halfway through or immediately after the tape was completed. Her mother and teachers also reported that Susan seemed more relaxed and rested during the day. After this two-week period, a new tape was made, eliminating the tension phase and requesting only relaxation of muscles. Since this proved equally effective, Susan was provided with a fifteen-minute version of the tape a week later. Use of this recording for the next two weeks produced similarly good results. During this time, her parents had left her alone on a few occasions (both during the day and in the evening), which the girl accepted without any difficulty. Susan was then given a five-minute tape that consisted of instructions for self-relaxation. She used this for another week and reported no difficulty going to sleep after the tape was completed. At this point the tapes were eliminated completely, and Susan was simply instructed to shut out all ruminations and external noises by concentrating on self-relaxation when she went to bed. She tried this for the next few weeks and reported that this procedure helped her to get to sleep almost immediately. Her parents confirmed that the two presenting problems were no longer present at that point. Follow-ups six and twelve months later revealed that these gains were maintained. Susan was generally relaxed during the day and continued to put relaxation skills to good use in falling asleep at night. Her mother remarked, "It's another Susan! It's as if she matured three years in one year" (p. 283).

COMMENTARY: This case demonstrates the effectiveness of an in vivo relaxation procedure for insomnia. The efficiency of the method is seen in the fact that it not only produced results in a brief period, but with a minimum of therapist time. The tape recordings afforded the client over forty relaxation "sessions" during the two-month treatment, thus necessitating only seven meetings between therapist and family. The tapes also offered the client self-control over her own therapy—an important feature. In other words, the therapist did not use "magic" or manipulation on the client, just logical, learnable methods of self-control. Apart from efficiency, this relaxation procedure has the advantage of wide applicability. Relaxation skills have been employed to systematically desensitize a wide variety of anxiety symptoms in both children and adults.

SOURCE: Weil, G., and Goldfried, M. R. "Treatment of Insomnia in an Eleven-Year-Old Child Through Self-Relaxation." *Behavior Therapy*, 1973, *4*, 282–284.

Additional Readings

Anthony, J. "An Experimental Approach to the Psychopathology of Childhood: Sleep Disturbances." *British Journal of Medical Psychology*, 1959, *32*, 19–37.

Anthony presents a detailed discussion of the etiology, types, and correlates of sleep disturbances in children. He found that underlying sleep disturbances was a background of anxiety, insecurity, instability, overstimulation, and traumatization. A highly anxious, phobic mother was predominant in the family background, as was a history of parental sexual stimulation via sharing the parental bed with the child. Anthony also found that the types of sleep disturbances are related to the child's capacity for imagery: Sleepwalkers were found to be more prone to motor activities such as athletics, while children with nightmares or night terrors were prone to visual imagery.

Porter, J. "Guided Fantasy as a Treatment for Childhood Insomnia." *Australian and New Zealand Journal of Psychiatry*, 1965, *9*, 169–172.

Porter describes a technique to relieve insomnia in children without chemotherapy or hypnotherapy. In children who are still prone to fantasize and who enjoy make-believe play, relaxed sleep is induced through listening to a tape-recorded story created from the child's favorite fantasy figures and everyday likes and dislikes. The recording is presented by the parents as a bedtime story rather than by the therapist as therapy. The child is allowed to feel that he or she has a controlling influence in putting a favorite figure to sleep within the story and is gently led to accept sleep by choice. Porter gives excerpts from a story used with an eight-year-old girl.

Sperling, M. "Etiology and Treatment of Sleep Disturbances in Children." *Psychoanalytic Quarterly*, 1955, *24*, 358–368.

During the preschool years, the occurrence of mild and temporary sleep disturbances, such as difficulty falling asleep and occasional nightmares, is a rather common experience. Sperling cautions, however, that severe and persistent sleeplessness is the earliest warning sign of emotional turmoil in children. She recommends immediate treatment of these persistent sleep disturbances, lest this nervous habit become internalized and lead to subsequent neuroses or psychoses. Sperling considers the treatment of choice to be guidance of the mother, to relieve the child's underlying insecurity or anxiety. She strongly advises parents not to reinforce nighttime crying or bad dreams by taking the child into their bed. Several case illustrations are presented.

Yen, S., McIntire, R. W., and Berkowitz, S. "Extinction of Inappropriate Sleeping Behavior: Multiple Assessment." *Psychological Reports*, 1972, *30*, 375–378.

A seventeen-year-old boy who found it difficult to fall asleep unless he talked to his mother about his worries just before going to bed was effectively treated with behavior modification procedures. The opportunity to talk with his mother in the living room about his worries early in the evening was made contingent on his not entering her bedroom just before retiring in the evening.

Obscene Language

This section discusses the compulsive use of "dirty words," strong words, or swearwords by children. The use of dirty words by children seems to serve a variety of purposes: the discharge of aggressive tension, infantile sexual pleasure, the expression of nonconformity by opposing a taboo of society, and a sense of power. In regard to the last item, children tend to use words in a very concrete, magical, and primitive way. In some primitive societies, for example, it is felt that making sounds of an object results in one becoming the object and thereby obtaining power over it. Since coprolalia or compulsive cursing is a common symptom of Tourette's syndrome, the reader is referred to the section in this book dealing with tics for a further discussion of this disturbance.

The Use of Dirty Words by Children

AUTHOR: Lawrence Hartmann

PRECIS: Dynamically oriented case study of the therapeutic use of obscene language in an eight-year-old boy

INTRODUCTION: Hartmann describes the constructive use of dirty words in therapeutic work with children. With a young encopretic boy, for example, it was clearly evident that as he was able to increase his verbal expression of dirty words in the therapy session his fecal soiling decreased. Hartmann also reports the following case, in which the expression of dirty words served a therapeutic purpose for a child.

CASE STUDY: An eight-year-old boy was hospitalized because of bizarre behavior and poor reality testing. In school Roger would crawl on the floor and bark like a dog. His parents were intolerant of any messy, boyish behavior in their only son and were quite upset by his strange, primitive behavior at home and in school.

Since Roger was informed that he was free to swear or not to in the therapist's office, just as he pleased, the therapy room became his "swearing place." At first he expressed the primitive sexual and aggressive drives that his parents found so offensive through crude body noises, such as farts and belches. He then began very tentatively to use strong language, such as "I'll break your bones" and "Drop dead." His play and drawings were also full of aggression, including sadism, murder, and chaos. Gradually the boy began using swearwords and street words for *penis*. During the few years he was in therapy (first as an inpatient and then as an outpatient), Roger swore remarkably little at home and at school, while swearing profusely in the therapist's office.

Roger continued to enlarge his use of swearwords and dirty words until he began saying combinations, such as "damn fucking thing" and "shit-head asshole." In time he started to direct these dirty words at the therapist himself and at his parents. He experimented with writing out swearwords, as if trying to gain a new kind of magical control. For the first year or two of therapy, he often asked to hear himself on the dictaphone using dirty words. While listening, he showed feelings of self-admiration and power that seemed to alternate with a tendency to reject his old noisy, dirty self.

Roger gradually went to the local public school from the ward. He did well in school and was therefore discharged from the hospital to outpatient status. He continued to see his therapist, who helped him with his concern that he would give in to his continuing urge to swear in public. At home he accepted the fact that his mother would not let him put up on the kitchen wall a list of swearwords. He continued to do well at home, in school, and with his friends. With his therapist, his swearing first tapered off and then almost completely disappeared. He told the therapist that he was not having to act crazy anymore or even swear—except a little with his friends, because they swore too.

COMMENTARY: This study indicates that the conscious use of swearing can be an important part of the therapeutic process with certain children. Swearing seems not only to afford a safety valve for the release of emotional tension, but also to assist the ego gain control of primitive sexual and aggressive impulses. Hartmann cautions parents not to establish very strong taboos against the use of dirty words at home, because this only seems to add to their power and significance. According to Hartmann, a child who swears is, in effect, saying to adults, "I am dirty, angry, regressed; I have dirty and forbidden things inside me such as fantasies and wishes about sex and aggression. I want to be able to express them and am afraid and in conflict. I want reassurance that you can stand me with them so that I can stand me with them and master them" (p. 118).

SOURCE: Hartmann, L. "Some Uses of Dirty Words by Children." *Journal of Child Psychiatry*, 1973, *12*, 108–121.

Treating a Case of Compulsive Cursing

AUTHOR: Max Hammer

PRECIS: Dynamically oriented treatment of coprolalia in an adolescent boy

INTRODUCTION: Hammer reports a case study involving Mike, a sixteen-year-old boy who exhibited coprolalia (compulsive cursing without any ability to control the torrent of foul and obscene words that continuously flowed from his mouth). Although he used almost every curse word you could imagine, he most frequently spat out three words: "fuck-fuck-fuck." The unacceptability of this behavior to the boy was apparent from his desperate but futile efforts to control his foul language by covering his mouth with his hands, clenching his teeth, and attempting to pretend he was coughing or clearing his throat. He even cursed when he was alone. The cursing was often accompanied by other ticlike behaviors, including grimaces, wild flailing of his arms, and compulsive spitting.

A detailed case history revealed that Mike was the oldest of five boys in a home characterized by a passive father and an aggressive mother. The developmental history was normal, except that at age six the boy had exhibited compulsive fire-setting behavior, which spontaneously disappeared in the latency period. Constant beating by his parents had done little to stop the fire setting. The father brought the boy in for treatment and recounted that the boy and his mother were constantly engaged in angry fighting with each other. Through a letter, the mother informed the therapist that she thought cursing was a deliberate attempt to embarrass her and that she thought the boy was a "hopeless case."

The boy stated that the cursing started at age thirteen, shortly after he had lost control of his bicycle going down a hill and smashed into a car. Although the boy was not seriously hurt, the anxiety resulting from this accident seemed to trigger off his unconscious desire to attack his mother both sexually and aggressively. The obscene language not only achieved this end but also seemed to provide some oral-libidinal gratification. Furthermore, the embarrassment caused him by the symptom seemed to placate a sadistic superego in the boy.

TREATMENT: Because the boy and his mother seemed to be involved in an intense sadomasochistic relationship, the therapist attempted to involve the mother in treatment. These efforts were steadfastly resisted by the mother, so an effort was made to remove Mike from the home. Initially, she did allow the boy to live with a relative for a few weeks but then insisted he return home. Toward the end of the year of treatment, the therapist persuaded the father to let Mike stay at the local state hospital while he attended treatment at the clinic. However, the mother visited him after a short period and, seeing that his symptoms had almost completely disappeared, she not only removed him from the hospital but refused to let him continue any form of treatment.

The goal of treatment had been to assist Mike to bring his rejected impulses under the conscious control of his ego. He was urged to make a deliberate effort to curse and get angry. As this was difficult for him, the therapist would help by role playing various family members who were needling him into a rage. Mike soon learned that when he was able to express his anger, his compulsive cursing stopped. This strategy, together with interpretations of his unconscious anger, helped him establish control over his aggressive feelings. Consequently, his symptoms were significantly reduced and whenever Mike was able to get in touch with his anger his compulsive cursing stopped.

COMMENTARY: This case illustrates a psychodynamic approach to treating coprolalia, together with the use of paradoxical intention. The multiple-tic symptom pattern suggests a diagnosis of Tourette's syndrome. Unfortunately, the mother's resistance to treatment proved to be insurmountable in this case, despite the fact that the treatment seemed effective with a long-standing and deeply entrenched cursing habit.

SOURCE: Hammer, M. "A Case of Coprolalia in an Adolescent Boy." *Psychotherapy: Theory, Research and Practice,* 1965, 2(4), 169–170.

Self-Injurious Behavior

Incidents of severe self-injurious behaviors, such as head banging, hair pulling, and scratching, tend to produce a spell-binding effect on professionals and nonprofessionals alike. The extremely primitive nature of the acts usually results in strong emotional reactions in adults—typically disgust and/or pity. The following studies describe diverse techniques that have been employed to systematically eliminate self-destructive behaviors in children.

241

Treating Compulsive Hair Pulling

AUTHORS: Julia G. McLaughlin and W. Robert Nay

PRECIS: Behavioral treatment (rewards and penalties) of tricho-tillomania by an adolescent girl

INTRODUCTION: The incidence of compulsive hair pulling, according to McLaughlin and Nay, occurs most frequently among children and adolescents and has proved most resistant to traditional forms of treatment. In institutions, the usual treatment for this disorder is to clip the hair short. This study reports the outpatient treatment of a seventeen-year-old girl with a six-year history of hair pulling.

CASE STUDY: Despite several years of traditional therapy and threats of punishment by her parents, the subject had failed to stop hair pulling. The girl was currently pulling out two or three hairs every day, usually when she was alone in her room studying or reading. She was not aware of beginning the pulling and stated that she typically "found herself doing it." She wore a wig to hide the baldness covering the front third of her scalp.

The subject and the therapist signed the following treatment contract:

1. Whenever she felt tense, the subject was to systematically relax herself, using a Jacobson-type procedure for large muscle relaxation.

2. Every time she successfully resisted an urge to pull, she was to reward herself by imagining one of a predetermined number of pleasant scenes, such as picturing herself with a full head of normal hair, imagining a desirable man stroking her hair, and so on.

3. Each time she pulled she was to impose a response cost of recording detailed information (time, place, conditions, and so on) in a log book. In addition, all hairs pulled during each full day were to be placed in an envelope and mailed to the therapist. (Every month, during treatment, the therapist also measured the amount and length of hair on top of her head.)

During the weekly therapy sessions, the subject received supportive counseling designed to relieve anxieties about her rather perfectionistic parents and school conflicts. The therapist helped her express her feelings about these issues and develop more adaptive ways of resolving them. Because it was evident one month into treatment that her hair pulling remained at a high rate, it was decided to make the response cost or aversive consequences more severe. The new agreement stipulated that each time she pulled a hair she was to immediately go to the bathroom to look at the spot in the mirror and then record the time and the area pulled from. During the therapy sessions she was enthusiastically praised for her progress, which became evident in the monthly scalp checks.

The rate of hair pulling decreased steadily through the first three months of therapy. By the eighteenth week it was completely eliminated, and she no longer required a wig. A three-month follow-up indicated that the hair pulling did not return.

COMMENTARY: In this study both the specific behavioral treatment procedures and the warm interpersonal counseling relationship seemed to contribute to the successful result. The client remarked that she felt it was important that she had specific "things to do" and had the feeling of being "in control" during the course of treatment. She also stated that the relaxation and response cost and positive imagery procedures were helpful to her in breaking this long-standing habit.

SOURCE: McLaughlin, J. G., and Nay, W. R. "Treatment of Trichotillomania Using Positive Coverants and Response Cost: A Case Study." *Behavior Therapy*, 1975, *6*, 87–91.

Eliminating Severe Head-Slapping Behavior

AUTHORS: Donald T. Saposnek and Luke S. Watson, Jr.

PRECIS: Rage-reduction treatment of a severely disturbed boy's self-destructive behavior

INTRODUCTION: Because Saposnek and Watson regarded extinction procedures too slow to be effective with self-destructive behavior and considered the electric shock technique too controversial, they turned to Zaslow's "rage-reduction" method for treating self-injurious behavior in children (Zaslow, R. W., and Breger, L. "A Theory and Treatment of Autism," in L. Breger (Ed.), *Clinical-Cognitive Psychology: Models and Integrations.* New Jersey: Prentice-Hall, 1969, pp. 246–291.)

CASE STUDY: Saposnek and Watson sought to eliminate a very specific behavior—chronic, severe head slapping—in a ten-year-old boy. The boy was institutionalized, with a diagnosis of autism and mental retardation. Whenever he was released from his arm restraints, he would immediately begin to rapidly and vigorously slap himself in the temple regions of the head with both hands until restrained by someone. Not only did his slapping result in severe contusions to his temples, but this behavior seemed to be creating the imminent danger of his retinas being detached and his middle ear becoming damaged.

The treatment procedure involved the therapist first sitting in a chair and then holding the boy in his lap in a horizontal, cradling position in which the therapist's arms were loosely positioned under the child's neck and knees (the child's weight was on the therapist's lap). The boy would respond to this by screaming, flailing, kicking, and, initially, head slapping. The therapist prevented the head slapping by blocking the child's arms. Moreover, he encouraged the boy to hit the therapist's hand by instructing him to "Hit my hand" while physically moving the child's arm through the motions of hitting his hand. After the second session, the child began voluntarily to hit the therapist's hand when enraged. When the child's body became relaxed and he stopped squirming, hitting, and crying, the therapist ended the treatment by placing him back down on his feet. The duration of this treatment procedure ranged from forty-five minutes in the beginning to two minutes in the last sessions, averaging about ten to fifteen minutes for each administration. A total of thirty-four training sessions comprised the formal treatment, with about two rage-reduction procedures employed in each session. During the final fourteen sessions, which were held on the ward, the therapist administered the rage-reduction technique contingent on the child exhibiting head-slapping behavior.

A gradual decrease in the head-slapping behavior was noted during the course of treatment, from an initial level of almost constant, intense slapping when free from restraint (eighty-five slaps per thirty-second interval observed) to the final level of not a single head slap during the last eight sessions. At this time, two ward attendants were trained to administer the treatment procedure— primarily on a noncontingent basis—to the child as often as they could during their daily schedules (typically, two small sessions a day). Within a few days, the occurrences of head-slapping behavior were reduced to less than one per day; within six months, the frequency of head-slapping incidents was only one or two per week. Such incidents were relatively weak in intensity and were easily controlled by simply telling the child to stop. The child no longer required arm restraints on the ward. Also, he was now amenable to the regular treatment program consisting of positive reinforcement for socially appropriate behavior, such as dressing himself and playing constructively with toys.

COMMENTARY: This case illustrates the successful application of a technique for eliminating a strongly entrenched habit involving self-destructive behavior in a severely disturbed child. For example, prior to treatment the child's mother had observed the child engage in head slapping for forty-five consecutive minutes. In this case, it was necessary to train regular staff attendants to use the technique, to ensure that learning generalized to the ward. In the authors' judgment, the treatment was successful because "slapping anything" had become pleasurable to the child and the hand slapping offered an acceptable alternative to the head slapping.

SOURCE: Saposnek, D. T., and Watson, L. S., Jr. "The Elimination of the Self-Destructive Behavior of a Psychotic Child: A Case Study." *Behavior Therapy*, 1974, *5*, 79–89.

Treating Head Banging by
a Punishment Technique

AUTHOR: Delmont Morrison

PRECIS: Aversive control of self-injurious behavior in a retarded girl

INTRODUCTION: Morrison reports the case of Ann, an eight-year-old girl, who for over a year had frequently struck her head on hard surfaces. The force of these blows had resulted in the formation of large hematomas on both sides of her forehead, making serious neurological damage likely. The ward staff attending this mute, mentally retarded girl were at a loss as to how to stop the self-injurious behavior. With the aid of two students in a behavior modification course, Morrison attempted to decrease this behavior.

Careful observation of the frequency, antecedents, and consequences of the girl's head-banging behavior revealed that the head banging occurred most frequently just before mealtime and during toilet time. On such occasions, Ann was tied down for about a half hour, because of a shortage of ward attendants. The head banging during these two periods became the target of treatment.

TREATMENT: Initially, Ann was given a food reward for intervals in which she did not bang her head. Although this produced a slight decrease in the maladaptive behavior, it was decided that this procedure would take too long to become effective. Thus, a switch was made to saying the word *no* followed by a slight tap on Ann's head. The students tried this punishment technique with Ann for a two-week period. The results were dramatic: The head banging during both toilet time and before meals showed about a ninety percent reduction from baseline. Regular staff members were instructed in the use of this procedure, as well as on the advisability of combining the punishment with positive reinforcement for periods in which Ann did not bang her head.

COMMENTARY: As Morrison points out, nonprofessional adults typically show strong emotional reactions to self-injurious behavior in children. Parents in particular tend to feel not only anger and disgust for the child, but also guilt and embarrassment over their ineffectual efforts to stop it. The use of punishment raises additional emotional reactions in some adults who feel the child needs love and kindness, not more pain. In comparison to the real possibility of permanent central nervous system damage if head banging continues unabated, however, the use of punishment in a controlled, carefully planned way seems more humanitarian.

Although generally efficient and effective, punishment has many drawbacks as Morrison clearly indicates. Indiscriminate use of punishment, for example, can produce a general inhibitory and suppressive effect on the behavior of a child. Punishment should only be used as part of a total treatment approach that emphasizes positive reinforcement for prosocial behaviors.

SOURCE: Morrison, D. "Issues in the Application of Reinforcement Theory in the Treatment of a Child's Self-Injurious Behavior." *Psychotherapy: Theory, Research and Practice*, 1972, *9*, 40–45.

Treating Hair Pulling by Brief Psychotherapy

AUTHOR: Eva P. Lester

PRECIS: Brief, dynamically oriented psychotherapy involving parents and child

INTRODUCTION: Lester describes the rationale for and application of brief, dynamic psychotherapy with children. Brief psychotherapy has two main characteristics: Its goals are limited and well-defined and the therapist assumes an active role. The main technique of dynamic therapy is interpretation of transference and symbolic fantasy material to the child, to promote self-understanding. With the parents, the main techniques are clarification, explanation, direction, and reeducation. In the initial interview, Lester states, it is important for the therapist to be understanding and supportive of the child, who usually manifests considerable anxiety in the form of denial and indifference. Through the medium of play and drawing, the therapist can often establish affective contact with the resistant child. In brief psychotherapy, it is usually best for one therapist to see both the child and his parents. Conjoint sessions are preferable with preschoolers, whereas with latency-age children individual sessions seem to work well.

CASE STUDY: Lynn, a seven-year-old girl, was referred by her dermatologist for hair-pulling behavior. The pulling, which only occurred in the girl's sleep, had resulted in the child being completely bald, with only a fluff of young hair on her head. The problem had existed, off and on, since the girl was eighteen months old. Lynn, the oldest of four children, was described as industrious, orderly, and family minded. Her mother, a very tense and competitive woman, admitted to being particularly hard on Lynn in terms of child rearing. During the usually hectic bedtime ritual in the home, Lynn received no attention from her mother; rather, she was assigned several chores to do. The mother's efforts to stop the hair pulling by tying up her arms and putting a cap on her head had proved futile.

The parents and the child were seen separately during four weekly sessions. Lynn spent most of her time drawing during the sessions. The following themes emerged from these contacts. First, despite an outward show of independence, both Lynn and her mother exhibited strong dependency feelings for their mothers. Second, the mother's strict, restrictive parenting practices had given Lynn little opportunity for obtaining instinctual pleasure. Neatness, orderliness, and usefulness were the mother's main values, which meant that she gave Lynn few chances to make a mess, have fun, or be a child. The mother showed very little inclination to play with her child. Lynn's longing for more help and emotional closeness with her mother was pointed out to her parents, as was her need for individual attention and quiet comforting at bedtime. The parents seemed eager to try this different approach and her mother called a few months after the termination of the brief therapy session to report that Lynn was doing well and only pulled her hair on rare occasions.

COMMENTARY: As Lester points out, brief treatment has a long history in child therapy. In the early child guidance clinics, children were typically treated in three or four sessions. Also, the first recorded cases of child analysis lasted only a few months. The key to the successful use of brief, dynamically oriented therapy seems to be the openness of the parents to new information and their willingness to change their approach to the child. The main thrust of treatment is to uncover the underlying forces that are causing the problem and to provide the child with a brief corrective emotional experience through the use of play and fantasy.

SOURCE: Lester, E. P. "Brief Psychotherapies in Child Psychiatry," *Canadian Psychiatric Association Journal,* 1968, *13,* 301–309.

Additional Readings

Adams, K. M., Klinge, V., and Keiser, T. W. "Case Histories and Shorter Communications." *Behaviour Research and Therapy,* 1973, *11,* 351–365.

To gain attention, a fourteen-year-old hospitalized girl suddenly began to fall to either side of her chair when sitting alone or with others for more than twenty minutes. Several times these falls resulted in severe bruises. Treatment consisted of applying rewards (playing cards or with a tape recorder) and punishments (wearing a football helmet or brief isolation in a quiet room), to decrease the falling and increase incompatible behavior. The girl was told exactly why the rewards and punishments were being given. No falls occurred six weeks after the application of this program.

Allen, K. E., and Harris, F. R. "Elimination of a Child's Excessive Scratching by Training the Mother in Reinforcement Procedures." *Behaviour Research and Therapy*, 1966, *4*, 79–84.

A five-year-old girl whose face and neck as well as other parts of her body were covered with open sores from a year's scratching behavior was treated by her mother. The mother was trained to withhold all reinforcement, including attention, contingent on the child's scratching herself but to reinforce other desirable behavior. For every twenty- to thirty-minute period of no scratching behavior at home, the child was to be warmly praised and given a gold star to paste in a booklet. For every second or third gold star, she was to receive a primary reinforcer such as candy, cookie, or beverage. The stars were to be counted twice a day and her achievement reinforced by a presentation of an inexpensive trinket. As the scratching decreased, the mother was instructed in appropriate techniques for thinning out the reinforcement schedule. By six weeks, the scabs and scars had disappeared.

Freeman, B. J., Graham, V., and Ritvo, E. R. "Reduction of Self-Destructive Behavior by Overcorrection." *Psychological Reports*, 1975, *37*, 446.

The rationale of the overcorrection or restitution procedure is to teach a child to assume responsibility for disruptive behavior by requiring him or her to restore the disturbed situation to an improved state. For ritualistic behaviors, the child is required to make a response incompatible with the ritualistic movement. The six-year-old girl in this study continually picked her nails, which often caused bleeding. The procedure employed was to hold the child's hands down by her side for one minute each time she picked her nails. Lavish praise and positive reinforcement was given whenever she was engaging in appropriate behavior.

Rubin, G., Griswald, K., Smith, I., and DeLeonardo, C. D. "A Case Study in the Remediation of Severe Self-Destructive Behavior in a Six-Year-Old Mentally Retarded Girl." *Journal of Clinical Psychology*, 1972, *28*, 424–426.

For over a year, Susan beat herself so severely about the face that imminent death was possible. Treatment involved conditioning her to associate a positive reinforcer (favorite staff member) with a neutral one (kickball), to gradually expand her repertoire of positive interests. She was also required to talk before her two wishes were granted—food and having people leave the room. As her life space expanded, Susan decreased her self-destructive gestures.

Stabler, B., and Warren, A. B. "Behavioral Contracting in Treating Trichotillomania: Case Note." *Psychological Reports*, 1974, *34*, 401–402.

Trichotillomania—compulsive pulling of one's hair so that actual hair loss occurs—was treated in a fourteen-year-old girl with a two-year history of the disorder. Because behavioral contracting had proven so successful with other obsessive-compulsive disorders, the authors tried it with this outpatient, who referred herself for treatment. The girl agreed to collect all the hairs pulled and bring them to the therapist each week. If no hairs were pulled for a week (validated by visual inspection of the scalp by the therapist), she earned 10 points; the payoff for 140 points consisted of her choice of a new dress, dinner out, or a visit to a beauty parlor. Back-up reinforcers included soda and crackers with the therapist for a week of no hair pulling and the opportunity to discuss with the therapist for ten minutes any topic of her choice (unrelated to her symptom). The hair pulling decreased from twenty-five a day to zero a day after the first week of therapy where it remained for fourteen consecutive weekly visits. She then selected the payoff of a trip to the beauty parlor.

Weiher, R. G., and Harman, R. E. "The Use of Omission Training to Reduce Self-Injurious Behavior in a Retarded Child." *Behavior Therapy*, 1975, *6*, 261–268.

This case involved the complete elimination of head banging in a fourteen-year-old boy by the use of omission training, that is, the positive reinforcement of periods in which no head-banging behavior occurred. The reinforcer was a half teaspoon of applesauce. Initially these time intervals with no head banging were short (three seconds) and were gradually lengthened to three minutes. Social reinforcement, that is, saying the word *good* was added to the concrete rewards at the twenty-third session. The subject wore a padded helmet until the forty-sixth session.

Thumbsucking

About 46 percent of the child population from birth to sixteen years of age are reported to be thumbsuckers. The desirability of eliminating this habit is indicated by its apparent social inappropriateness and its association with dental malocclusion. In the home, diverse management procedures have been tried, including sucking pacifiers, prolonged sucking from the breast or bottle, wearing special mittens or restraints, applying bitter-tasting chemicals to the thumb, ignoring the sucking, verbal and physical punishment, and making parental attention contingent on not sucking. The following articles explore the systematic application of some of these techniques.

Parent Control of Thumbsucking in the Home

AUTHORS: James M. Kauffman and T. R. Scranton

PRECIS: Elimination of thumbsucking in a two-year-old by the application of positive reinforcement

INTRODUCTION: Kauffman and Scranton report a case in which the parents of a girl two years and nine months old attempted to decrease her frequent thumbsucking, which had appeared shortly after birth. The sucking had caused a large blister and callus on the girl's right thumb. In the first home study, the effect of punishment was investigated by each parent making the reading of stories to the child contingent on no thumbsucking. Every day the mother read to the child for ten minutes in the morning and ten minutes in the evening; the father read to her for ten minutes in the evening. Whenever sucking occurred during the reading, the parent immediately closed the book and said, "I'll read when you take your thumb out." With this procedure, the sucking was quickly reduced to near zero during the reading sessions. The results, however, failed to generalize to other situations and the sucking immediately resumed during the reading sessions when the contingency was removed.

POSITIVE REINFORCEMENT: It was decided to try a new procedure involving differential positive reinforcement. During the mother's evening reading session, then, the girl was given a colorful sticker to paste on a "big girl" chart whenever she kept her thumb out of her mouth during the reading. Five stickers were worth a "birthday party" with a cake and candles. Whenever she turned the page of the book, the mother also gave the girl praise ("That's a big girl") for not sucking. After a week, the praise was provided after every second page. During the beginning of the other two reading sessions, the child was reminded to be a "big girl" and not suck her thumb. At the end of these two sessions, she was praised contingent on having shown no thumbsucking behavior. After about two weeks, the stickers and chart were discontinued and frequent praise for not sucking was substituted by the mother. After a month of this procedure, the parents gave intermittent praise for not sucking at other times and in other settings during the day. The results of this second study indicate that the differential positive reinforcement procedure applied by the mother in the evening immediately reduced the thumbsucking to zero during these sessions; within a few days this dramatic result generalized to other reading sessions. The child earned two birthday parties as a result of the procedure. A thirty-day follow-up revealed that the callus on the girl's thumb had disappeared. Moreover, no evidence of emotional disturbance or substitute behavior was apparent to the parents.

COMMENTARY: This study demonstrates that parents can control thumbsucking in very young children by the simple technique of rewarding other behavior. By carefully observing the frequency of the habit during different times and situations during the day, the parents were able to evaluate the effects of differential treatment approaches. Generalization of the effect was achieved in this study when some aspect of the differential reinforcement procedure (prompt as well as delayed social reinforcement) was replicated in different settings. This finding is in keeping with other research that has shown that generalization is not likely to occur unless specific steps are taken to facilitate it.

SOURCE: Kauffman, J. M., and Scranton, T. R. "Parent Control of Thumbsucking in the Home." *Child Study Journal*, 1974, *4*, 1–10.

Reducing Chronic Thumbsucking
by Behavior Techniques

AUTHOR: Daun Martin

PRECIS: Six-year-old "behaviorist" solves the thumbsucking problem of her younger sister

INTRODUCTION: Martin reports the case of Mindee, a four-year-old girl from a middle-class family who wished to get rid of her chronic thumbsucking problem. Previous attempts to stop the sucking by use of bandaids, ace bandages, and wool gloves during bedtime had proven unsuccessful. Her parents had established stimulus control over the problem by sending her to bed and giving her a blanket to suck whenever she put a thumb in her mouth. The following procedure was established by Mindee's six-year-old sister, who acted as a consultant.

TREATMENT: Mindee was told that she would receive a nickel and a star for her Thumb Chart for each dry-thumb night. After twenty to thirty dry-thumb nights, she could select a movie of her choice. The Thumb Chart, which had the numbers 1 to 30 printed on it, was taped to the refrigerator door. A star was placed on the chart in the morning if, prior to retiring late in the evening, her mother found that Mindee's thumb was not in her mouth nor was it "wet or soggy." If Mindee's thumb was out of her mouth and dry, the mother would say, while the child was sleeping, "Very good for having your thumb out of your mouth." The placement of a star in the morning was accompanied by a great deal of verbal praise by all family members and the presentation of a nickel. At bedtime, Mindee's older sister would remind her not to suck her thumb. In addition, at the start of the experiment, Mindee's mother removed her security blanket on Mindee's request and comment that "the blanket makes me do it."

The results indicated that Mindee only exhibited bedtime thumbsucking five times during the one-month experiment (Days 3, 4, 6, 7, and 21). A one-year follow-up revealed that there had been no recurrence of the thumbsucking problem.

COMMENTARY: The most remarkable aspect of this study was the fact that the girl's six-year-old sister designed most of the components of the token program, including defining the problem, contracting, charting, and identifying short-term reinforcers and the long-term reward. This sister was quite familiar with this procedure, because she had personally participated in similar programs to control her own behaviors, such as toothbrushing, bed making, and candy eating. The program has the advantage of being simple, easy to supervise, and applicable to a wide variety of behavior problems in childhood.

SOURCE: Martin, D. "A Six-Year-Old "Behaviorist" Solves Her Sibling's Chronic Thumbsucking Problem." *Corrective and Social Psychiatry and Journal of Behavior Technology Methods and Therapy*, 1975, *21*, 19–21.

Treating Chronic Thumbsucking Through
the Use of Dental Appliances

AUTHORS: R. D. Haryett, F. C. Hansen, P. O. Davidson, and M. L. Sandilands

PRECIS: Research study of the effectiveness of dental devices in stopping thumbsucking

INTRODUCTION: This study of sixty-six children reports on the use of dental appliances to stop thumbsucking. One group of children received a dental crib, a metal device with prongs like "hayrakes," which deter the child from putting his fingers in his mouth. Another group received a palatal arch, a stainless steel bar on the upper molars that is similar to the crib except it does not have a vertical, fencelike portion. These devices extend across the roof of the mouth and prevent sucking action. Both groups wore the appliances for a ten-month period. Half of the children in each of these appliance groups received psychological support from a dentist. This support consisted of motivating the child to break the habit by showing him pictures of what happens to his own teeth and those of others because of the habit. In addition, the child's mother was instructed to reward with attention the periods when the child did not suck his thumb and ignore all incidents of thumbsucking behavior. A no-treatment control group was also included in the study.

The results of the study revealed that all the twenty-two children with dental cribs stopped their thumbsucking, while only six of the remaining children were able to stop. Those children in the crib group who received supplementary psychological support exhibited no sign of symptom substitution. On the other hand, a number of children in the crib, no-psychological-support group developed other nervous habits, such as nail biting and chewing bedclothes. Over 80 percent of the children with the dental crib stopped sucking within seven days. In contrast, most of the children in the other treatment groups who were successful required three months or more to break the thumbsucking habit. It was also found that none of the treatment methods produced any adverse side effects on the children's general emotional well-being. Although there were three disadvantages to the use of the crib (a period of irritability, lisping, and difficulty in eating) for some of the children, these drawbacks were not universal and, for the most part, the inconvenience proved to be only temporary in duration.

COMMENTARY: The control of thumbsucking remains an enigma to many parents because of conflicting reports they receive from professionals. In this well-controlled study, the use of dental devices to discourage thumbsucking produced dramatic results in a remarkably short period of time. Psychological support of both parent and dentist was needed to prevent symptom substitution. There is clearly a need for more studies of this nature, not only to compare the success of dental appliances with that of behavioral approaches but also to provide long-term follow-up data.

SOURCE: Haryett, R. D., Hansen, F. C., Davidson, P. O., and Sandilands, M. L. "Chronic Thumb-Sucking: The Psychological Effects and the Relative Effectiveness of Various Methods of Treatment." *American Journal of Orthodontics,* 1967, *53*(8), 569–585.

Suppressing Thumbsucking by the Use of Oral Overcorrection

AUTHORS: Larry A. Doke and Leonard H. Epstein

PRECIS: Use of punishment (contingent toothbrushing with an oral antiseptic) to control thumbsucking in a young retarded girl

INTRODUCTION: The persistent thumbsucking of May, a four-year-old retarded girl attending a daycare program, was the treatment target in one phase of this study. Her hand-mouthing behavior was deemed unacceptable because it interfered with the child's speech and responsiveness, decreased her use of manipulative materials, threatened dental malformation, and seemed to promote inattentiveness to scheduled activities. Previous attempts to terminate the hand-mouthing behavior had proved unsuccessful, including direct commands to stop, time-out procedures, and differential reinforcement (adult attention contingent on no mouthing behavior).

TREATMENT: Doke and Epstein selected a form of Foxx and Azrin's restitutional overcorrection procedure. Entitled "overcorrective oral hygiene," this punishment technique involved the following procedure: Each time May put her hand to her mouth, during "language time" in the classroom, a caretaker approached her, instructed her not to suck her thumb, and then brushed her teeth briskly for two minutes with an oral antiseptic (undiluted Listerine). Except for instructions to expectorate, the caretakers did not speak to the child during each treatment episode. They were careful not to injure the child's gums or tongue. Every ten to twenty seconds the soft-bristled toothbrush was dipped into a 2 oz. solution of Listerine. May's face was dried with a protective towel after each overcorrection incident. May received ten days of treatment, with the mean number of daily treatments being 2.1 (a 0 to 7 range). She was then unavoidably transferred to another center.

    The treatment produced an abrupt reduction in thumbsucking incidents during language time. A series of ten observations revealed that the median incidence of hand mouthing decreased from 80 percent to 10 percent. On the other hand, hand-to-mouth behavior quickly returned when the treatment was stopped. Doke and Epstein found, however, that the use of contingent verbal warnings or threats ("I'll have to use the toothbrush if you put your hand in your mouth") could be used to maintain reduced levels of hand mouthing in other children. They also found that the use of this procedure produced a favorable vicarious effect on other children who observed its operation (Foxx, R. M., and Azrin, N. H. "The Elimination of Self-Stimulatory Behavior by Overcorrection." *Journal of Applied Behavior Analysis,* 1973, *6,* 7–78).

COMMENTARY: This study illustrates that a simple punishment technique can quickly suppress thumbsucking behavior in children. Doke and Epstein caution, however, that oral correction should not be used as the first approach to thumbsucking problems. In view of the possible negative effects of this aversive procedure, they present it as a treatment alternative when positive contingencies or milder forms of punishment have proven ineffectual. Extreme care must be taken to ensure that the procedure is not misused.

SOURCE: Doke, L. A., and Epstein, L. H. "Oral Overcorrection: Side Effects and Extended Applications." *Journal of Experimental Child Psychology,* 1975, *20,* 496–511.

Additional Readings

Baer, D. M. "Laboratory Control of Thumbsucking by Withdrawal and Representation of Reinforcement." *Journal of the Experimental Analysis of Behavior,* 1962, *5,* 25–28.

A five-year-old boy was punished for thumbsucking during alternate presentation of cartoons by turning off all the cartoons for as long as his thumb remained in his mouth. The incidence of thumbsucking was less during such periods. During alternate periods of uninterrupted cartoons, the thumbsucking promptly returned, which suggested a quick discrimination process.

Knight, M. F., and McKenzie, H. S. "Elimination of Bedtime Thumbsucking in Home Settings Through Contingent Reading." *Journal of Applied Behavior Analysis,* 1974, *7,* 33–38.

Story reading at bedtime was made contingent on not sucking thumbs for girls three, six, and eight years old. All had been persistent thumbsuckers since infancy. During the experimental period, reading stopped whenever thumbsucking was observed and resumed immediately when it ceased. This procedure proved effective and bedtime thumbsucking was eliminated for all three girls.

Ross, J. A. "Use of Teacher and Peers to Control Classroom Thumbsucking." *Psychological Reports,* 1974, *34,* 327–330.

A child who continually sucked his thumb in class was rewarded if the teacher or any of his classmates did not catch him sucking for a specified period of time. Each time the child was caught by a peer, the peer was reinforced. The incidence of thumbsucking decreased markedly after the reinforcement contingencies were introduced.

Ross, J. A., and Levine, B. A. "Control of Thumbsucking in the Classroom: Case Study." *Perceptual and Motor Skills,* 1972, *34,* 584–586.

Reinforcement of peers in class was made contingent on a child's not sucking his thumb. A significant decrease in thumbsucking was observed after instituting the reinforcement contingency. Removal and reinstatement of the contingency substantiated this observation.

3

Antisocial Behaviors

This chapter focuses on children who show an active, antisocial pattern of aggressiveness that results in conflict with parents, peers, or social institutions. Many of these children lack the necessary ego strength to control the overt expression of aggressive impulses. In the words of Fritz Redl, these are the "children who hate" (F. Redl and D. Wineman, *Children Who Hate,* New York: Free Press, 1951). Since the basic causes of antisocial behaviors vary widely, one cannot speak of *the* delinquent or antisocial child. Some delinquent acts are transient situational reactions to stress, while others reflect deep seated personality or ego defects. Also, important differences have long been recognized between behaviors of delinquent gang members and the actions of the lone, hostile, resentful type of delinquent. Studies comparing the delinquent behavior of the gang with that of the hostile loner have indicated that the former represents adaptive behavior learned from delinquent peers. Typically, the background factors of the socialized delinquent include an overcrowded home or alcoholic father. Finding little parental guidance at home, the child seeks recognition and support from his delinquent peers. Exposure to group experiences with prosocial peers can be of substantial help to these children.

In contrast, the aggressiveness of the loner tends to be a frustration response that is associated with a long-standing rejection by the child's parents. Often the parents are inconsistent in their parenting practices; they are typically quite punitive with the child but they can also be very permissive at times. A critical, rejecting mother or stepmother is a common feature. Family therapy seems indicated with this type of child.

Some children also exhibit antisocial behaviors that seem to be primarily related to minimal brain dysfunction. Such children are the impulsive, hyperactive, and distractible children whose capacity to delay gratification is impaired. Behavior modification procedures and/or chemotherapy seem to work best with children who display this diffuse, primitive type of aggressiveness. Knowledge of the etiology of antisocial behavior can assist the clinician in selecting the most appropriate intervention strategy.

This chapter presents some methods for helping antisocial children find better ways of coping with their impulses than acting them out. The overall goal is to help the practitioner discover specific techniques for handling different manifestations of antisocial behaviors by different types of aggressive children, including a number of the more common patterns of acting-out behaviors, such as temper tantrums, destruction of property, fighting, stealing, fire setting, and running away. Hopefully, the approaches described in this chapter will help overcome some of the apathy, defeatism, and lack of imagination that have characterized clinical interventions in the past. Traditionally, clinicians have reported much greater success in treating neurotic behaviors (phobias and inhibitions) than in treating aggressively delinquent acts. Redl states this is because aggressive children lack the minimum ego strengths, such as frustration tolerance or readiness to relate, to profit from orthodox treatment (*Children Who Hate*, 1951).

Penal methods, such as state training schools, have an even worse track record with antisocial children. These usually succeed only in making a delinquent into a more hardened criminal. Consequently, criminologists keep looking to clinicians for new solutions to the problem of rehabilitating the aggressive child. In regard to criminal justice, liberal thinkers condemn the conservatives for advocating cruel and inhumane punishment, which overlooks the root causes of violence, while the conservatives criticize liberals for using overly permissive, ineffectual approaches. Meanwhile, the incidence of violent crimes by youth keeps rising. We need to recognize how tentative our knowledge in this area is, and to work diligently toward the development of innovative approaches. Recognizing the complexity of the problem, Redl maintains that the clinician must somehow give the child "ego support and ego repair," while simultaneously performing "value surgery and superego repair" (*Children Who Hate*, 1951).

One of the most promising and comprehensive approaches for treating children with multiple, persistent antisocial behaviors is an intervention that combines behavioral, relationship, and cognitive approaches. Achievement Place, for example, has become a model for community-based group homes that treat predelinquent boys who have committed such offenses as stealing, vandalism, running away, assault, and chronic school disruption. The group residence is run by two teaching parents who seek to build self-esteem and teach self-control skills in the boys. The program uses behavioral methods (token economy, contracts, behavioral rehearsal); relationship-building methods (lots of love, warmth, and caring in a home environment); and cognitive approaches (teaching such problem-solving skills as identifying problems, assuming responsibility for the behavior of self and others, discovering other alternative ways of behaviors, deciding on a course of action, and monitoring and evaluating progress). In brief, Achievement Place attempts to systematically apply good parenting practices in an effort to effect multimodal change in the child's thoughts, feelings, behaviors, and relationships.

Another recent trend is to consider direct intervention with families as important as individual work with the child. Gerald Patterson and his colleagues at the Oregon Research Institute have been among the pioneers in this regard. They have attempted to treat the aggressive child, for instance, by teaching the child's parents more effective child-rearing techniques based on behavioral principles.

A variety of individual, family, and group therapy approaches for helping the antisocial child are offered in this chapter. The goals of these approaches include helping the child "talk out" rather than "act out" his impulses and frustrations; helping children learn to trust adults; and helping the child's family clearly spell out expectations, rules, and the positive and negative consequences of a child's behaviors. A number of more innovative techniques are also described in this chapter, such as Hare-Mustin's use of "paradoxical intention" (1975).

Temper Tantrums

A temper tantrum is a violent outbreak of anger characterized by complete loss of control, screaming, and kicking. Temper tantrums by children are very distressing to parents because such behavior makes adults appear helpless and incompetent not only in their own eyes but also in the eyes of others. Thus, tantrums tend to arouse in parents intense feelings (hostility and fearfulness) that are difficult to keep under control. For some children, tantrums are the best way they know for coping with an emotional crisis. Tantrums only become a sign of abnormality when a child uses them frequently and over a prolonged period of time. (Also see sections on Destructiveness *and* Aggressiveness.*)*

The "Barb" Technique

AUTHORS: Leon M. Kaufmann and Bernard R. Wagner

PRECIS: Teaching children alternatives to temper tantrums

INTRODUCTION: After reviewing published case studies and research dealing with the elimination of temper tantrums in children, Kaufmann and Wagner felt that a systematic approach to teaching children *alternate* approaches for handling frustrating situations needed to be developed. This article attempts to present a temper control technique that has particular applicability to pre-adolescents and adolescents. Within a positive learning context, the "barb" technique is designed to teach alternate ways of coping with provoking situations. The technique was developed at a residential center for adolescents with conduct problems. A token economy based on positive reinforcement principles was the main treatment strategy at this center.

BARB TECHNOLOGY FOR TEMPER DISTURBANCES: Kaufmann and Wagner maintain that youths with poor temper control respond with extreme anger, verbal abuse, or physical violence to adults who constitute a threat to them. The form of the threat varies from a parent yelling at a child for coming in late to a teacher asking why the child is in the hall rather than in the classroom where he belongs. The "barb," named after a provoking verbal statement from an adult, is an individual programing technique that consists of three key elements: systematic presentation of provoking verbal stimuli; specification of appropriate responses to these stimuli; and positive reinforcement for socially appropriate responses. Among the subtechniques employed as part of the barb program are rapport building, modeling, role playing, cueing, cue fading, intermittent reinforcement, and negative reinforcement. Generalizing appropriate behaviors to different situations is also an integral part of the program.

CASE STUDY: The authors report the following case history, which illustrates the barb procedure. Unintimidated by the constant

threats of his father and stepmother, Ed, a fourteen-year-old delinquent, responded with angry outbursts when they attempted to
set limits at home. After striking teachers and fighting with a high
school principal, he was expelled from school and became involved
in gang fights and theft. He was referred from jail after being in-
carcerated for illegal trespass.

The first stage of Ed's program consisted of building rapport
through individual sessions in which the program coordinator
attempted to establish trust and gain Ed's cooperation. In these
initial sessions, Ed was helped to explore and identify (1) the situations that triggered his temper problems, (2) his actual behavior
responses, and (3) the consequences of these behaviors. The second
stage consisted of Ed's role playing his typical responses to authority
figures and then rehearsing more socially adaptive responses.
Reverse role playing was then used to provide him with a mirror
of himself. He found it uproariously funny when the therapist
role played his typical temper reactions. Stage Three consisted of
offering Ed a cue phrase before each barb, such as "Ed, I'm going
to give you a barb." Ed earned a token (exchangeable for privileges
and concrete rewards) for exhibiting any of three socially adaptive
responses to a barb: eye contact, moderate tone of voice, or a socially
cooperative verbal response (for example, if asked where his assigned homework was, a cooperative type of response would be,
"My mistake—I'll get it from my locker where I left it."). In Stage
Four, the cue was gradually phased out: "Ed, a barb's coming";
then, "Ed, watch out"; then simply "Ed"; then no cue. One token
for each behavior requirement was still given, this time by two additional staff members who administered barbs. In later stages,
stimulus generalization was further achieved by having all staff
members on the unit deliver barbs, then teachers, administrators,
and finally, Ed's parents. The barbs became less obvious and more
subtle or tricky. Soon Ed had to evidence all three socially appropriate responses to earn a token—all or none. Later the tokens were
gradually eliminated (intermittent reinforcement) and social praise
was substituted when Ed successfully coped with a barb. As he progressed through the stages, the frequency with which Ed was placed
in isolation or time out for temper tantrums (negative reinforcement) diminished from almost daily to less than once per month.

Once this success had stabilized, Ed was returned to the community. Kaufmann and Wagner report that he was doing well after five months at home.

COMMENTARY: The authors caution that one or more of the following pitfalls may weaken or destroy the effectiveness of barbs:

1. Using a barb program unsystematically.

2. Giving unplanned barbs, barbs used as punishers, and barbs given in anger.

3. Telling a student he failed to meet barb requirements after an outburst unrelated to a barb.

4. Moving too slowly or too quickly through the program stages.

The most distinctive feature of this article is its presentation of a very comprehensive approach to treating temper disturbances. Employing a very specific, systematic, and sequential procedure, Kaufmann and Wagner describe the application of a broad spectrum of behavioral principles. Particularly noteworthy is the fact that the parents of the boy were able to understand and apply the barb procedure at home. Although the authors have used the technique primarily with adolescents, it seems appropriate for use with preadolescent children as well. One of the prerequisites for use of this approach might be a clear understanding of learning theory principles, especially of reinforcement and generalization concepts.

SOURCE: Kaufmann, L. M., and Wagner, B. R. "Barb: A Systematic Treatment Technology for Temper Control Disorders." *Behavior Therapy,* 1972, *3,* 84–90.

Observations on Temper
Tantrums in Children

AUTHOR: Elizabeth R. Geleerd

PRECIS: Understanding the dynamics of special types of childhood tantrums

INTRODUCTION: Geleerd notes that the prevailing opinion on how to handle temper tantrums is to be firm and under no circumstances to comply with the child's demands. Although concurring in general with this view, Geleerd indicates that ignoring the outburst, coupled with noncompliance with the child's demands, is not the best approach for certain types of childhood tantrums. She then cites several case studies that describe how she arrives at a dynamic understanding of the individual child's behavior.

TYPES OF CHILDREN WHO EXHIBIT TANTRUMS: Geleerd feels that the most commonly observed tantrums are produced by children with good reality orientation who are trying to overcome a frustrating situation. These temper outbursts typically disappear when parents consistently enforce limits by using time out from positive reinforcement when the child misbehaves. This procedure should be coupled with reward and praise for appropriate behavior. In addition to this standard procedure, Geleerd frequently recommends parent and child counseling to relieve a disturbed interpersonal situation.

In Geleerd's experience as a child analyst, there is a second type of child who often displays tantrums: a severely disturbed child with poor reality testing. Typically this child has not developed beyond the stage of the early infant-mother relationship. His tenuous hold on reality can only be maintained as long as he feels secure in the love of a mother figure. When thwarted, such children project their hostile, destructive fantasies onto the uncontrollable adult. These fantasies of being persecuted and attacked are experienced as reality. Routine handling of these tantrums by strictness and isolation only tends to exacerbate the intensity of the outburst.

Geleerd notes that when these children are affectionately held and reassured by their mothers they quickly quiet down and return to reality, just as a very young child stops crying when his absent mother returns.

Residential treatment for these children, Geleerd states, should be aimed at helping them to develop beyond the stage of complete dependence on a mother figure by supplying them with this love and nurturance all the time. This means the undivided attention of one adult—preferably a woman. Loving words and physical holding, as with an infant, are given when they have a tantrum. In one of the eight cases cited by Geleerd, this procedure, used in conjunction with child analysis, helped the child mature enough to return home and enter a regular public school.

COMMENTARY: In reporting her careful observations about a qualitative difference in maturity among children who exhibit tantrums, Geleerd has made a major contribution to the literature. Some children clearly do not respond to firmness and isolation because they have never developed beyond the infant level. Deficient in basic trust, they experience—in a paranoid fashion—adult frustrations as hostile acts and they feel unloved. Such a child is typically diagnosed as "borderline" because the severity of disturbance falls between the neurotic and psychotic levels. To place these children in isolation is comparable to ignoring the cries of a hungry newborn. Although some children may remain fixated at this infantile level, they can be made more secure by being given consistent love and affection when they become upset. A crucial diagnostic indicator of this type of infantile, psychotic child is that his temper tantrums get worse (more intense and prolonged) when strictness and social isolation are used by parent figures.

SOURCE: Geleerd, E. R. "Observations on Temper Tantrums in Children." *American Journal of Orthopsychiatry,* 1945, *15,* 238–246.

A Behavioral Approach to Temper Tantrums

AUTHOR: William C. Coe

PRECIS: Parents' modification of a child's temper tantrums

INTRODUCTION: Coe presents a detailed case study involving parental use of a behavior modification program to reduce temper tantrums in their twelve-year-old son Dick. During the tantrums, this neurologically handicapped boy would curse, yell, and run away from home. Once he threatened to attack his mother with a knife. Previous attempts at therapeutic intervention by means of individual therapy, family counseling, and chemotherapy had proven unsuccessful with Dick. The boy's behavior had become so unmanageable at home and in school that the parents were on the verge of sending him to a residential treatment center.

FAMILY OPERANT PROGRAM: At the end of the first family session, in which both parents and the boy were present, Coe suggested that faulty family interaction patterns rather than the boy's neurological impairment seemed to be the major cause of the problem. To establish clearer lines of communication and improve problem-solving skills in the family, the therapist asked the family to reach consensus on three lists of concrete, observable behaviors:

1. *Don't*—Behaviors that both parents and the boy agreed that he did, but should not do.
2. *Do*—Behaviors that all agreed the child should do, but had trouble doing.
3. *Reinforcers*—behaviors or things that the child liked, whether or not his parents liked them.

Dick stated that he did not want to have temper tantrums—a behavior that all agreed should be on the "Don't" list. Everyone also concurred with his mother's suggestion that attendance at school was an appropriate "Do" behavior, as the school was restricting his attendance because of his misbehavior. Reinforcer behaviors were television watching, eating popcorn, and staying up after his regular bedtime. The first session was ended with the therapist outlining the "financial plan": A predetermined number of points was to be paid Dick for all the "Do" behaviors, whereas he would lose points for behaviors on the "Don't" list. Thus, if he wanted to have a temper tantrum he would lose a point a minute up to a half hour. Dick was required to pay for the things he liked; for example, a bowl of popcorn was worth a specified number of points. The family was instructed to come to agreement before the next session on the number of points each "Do" and "Don't" was worth. To balance the income and outflow, the family was advised first to assign points to the "Don't" and "Reinforcer" columns and then to balance the income for the "Do" behaviors so that the boy could afford a reasonable number of "Reinforcers." The second session was devoted to further clarifying the agreed-on behaviors and assigned points. Points were to be recorded on a conspicuously posted chart in the home.

The third session began with Dick triumphantly announcing he was "worth 400 points." His usual daily temper tantrums had been absent all week. At this session, his parents were assisted in devising a "trade-in" program wherein his excess points could be traded for other things, such as money or special activities.

Two weeks later, the mother called in great distress because Dick had thrown a "wing-dinger" of a temper tantrum. This had caused him to go into considerable debt in terms of points. As it turned out, his mother had prompted the tantrum by failing to follow the program. She had refused his request to stay up late one night and to pay the necessary points. It was then decided that Dick could earn double points for his positive behaviors; 80 percent of his total earnings would go toward paying off the debt or state of bankruptcy. In the future, it was agreed that Dick would pay for the first half hour of a tantrum and then he would be spanked by his father. His mother promised that Dick could have any of the reinforcers in the future if he had the capital.

A few additional problems arose during the course of treatment but most were easily handled over the phone and the sessions were set increasingly farther apart. All the family members became quite adept at creatively solving problem situations. With the cooperation of his classroom teacher, Dick began earning points for his behavior in school. These points were recorded on the home behavior chart and used to purchase reinforcers. Feedback from the parents over the course of the next year revealed that the family was now working together effectively, free from guilt, hostility, and hopelessness.

COMMENTARY: By clearly specifying approved and disapproved behaviors and their consequences, the parents in this study were able to employ a better way of parenting than their usual habit of "riding" the child. Moreover, the child was motivated because he was shown a way of receiving many of the things he wanted at home. Coe states that this approach seems indicated when the family interaction pattern is characterized by a number of parental complaints about a child's behavior, frequent but futile use of punishment by the parents to control the child, and the child's feeling that his parents are restrictive and oppressive and that he cannot "get through" to them. The parents must be strongly motivated and willing to rigorously follow a detailed program. Frequent therapist-parent communication by telephone and office visits was a key to the success of this behavior modification program.

SOURCE: Coe, W. C. "A Behavioral Approach to Disrupted Family Interactions." *Psychotherapy: Theory, Research and Practice,* 1972, *9,* 80–85.

Treatment of Temper Tantrums
by Paradoxical Intention

AUTHOR: Rachel T. Hare-Mustin

PRECIS: Reducing temper tantrums by encouraging their occurrence in special places and at special times (paradoxical intention)

INTRODUCTION: Hare-Mustin reports a use of Frankl's technique of paradoxical intention, involving replacing the usual restrictions on a child's undesirable behavior with intentional and
even exaggerated urgings by adults to perform the misdeed (Frankl,
V. E. "Paradoxical Intention: A Logotherapeutic Technique."
American Journal of Psychotherapy, 1960, *40*, 520–535). Typically, a
child prone to temper tantrums is locked in an intense power struggle with his parents. The child's resistance to the paradoxical directions given by the parents produces a change in the desired direction.
The case described by Hare-Mustin involved Tommy, age four, a
rather small, immature child. His parents tended to overprotect
him and typically used "reasoning" to influence his behavior. The
parents reported feeling helpless and frantic in the face of Tommy's
daily temper tantrums.

TREATMENT: During the eight consecutive weekly sessions with
the family, Tommy and his seven-year-old sister were present
for all or part of each session. Tommy's tantrums were treated in
the first three sessions. Initially, the therapist obtained a detailed
description of when and where the tantrums occurred and what
seemed to prompt them. The therapist then noted that the tantrums
were particularly disturbing because of their unpredictability—
they could occur anywhere and at any time. She then said that she
wanted Tommy to continue to have his tantrums but only in a selected "tantrum place" at home. Tommy and his family decided
that the upstairs hall was the best place. If Tommy started to have
a tantrum in any other place, he was to go or be taken to the "tantrum place." In the event he was away from home when he wanted
to have a tantrum, he would have to wait until he got home to have it.

At the second session, the family reported that Tommy threw only one tantrum during the week and this was held in the "tantrum place." On another occasion, he stopped this behavior when his mother started to take him to the place. No tantrums occurred outside the home. The therapist now informed the family that it was necessary to agree on a time of day for the tantrums to occur. While the family was considering this question, the therapist mentioned that the usual time of occurrence had been the two-hour period between 5:00 and 7:00 P.M. The family then selected this time. It was pointed out that should Tommy start to have a tantrum at another time he was to be reminded that he had to wait until 5:00 P.M., when tantrum time started.

By the third week, the family members reported that they could not remember Tommy having any tantrums that week. The therapist expressed some concern that the progress had been too rapid and remarked, in an off-hand way, that Tommy might want to have a tantrum the next week. Although the tantrum must be in the "tantrum place" and at the "tantrum time," he could choose the day of the week himself. No further temper tantrums were reported during the subsequent five weeks of treatment. Because of this change, the family felt that they could be more relaxed about giving greater responsibility and independence to both siblings. A nine-month follow-up revealed no recurrence of the temper tantrums.

COMMENTARY: According to Hare-Mustin, a dramatic reduction or disappearance of problem behavior is not unusual when paradoxical intention is employed. In her experience, most patients accept the rather incongruous procedure without much question. Of course, the therapist must present this procedure in a matter-of-fact and confident manner to dispel anxiety in the clients and to convey the message that this method is an accepted practice. By expressing concern that the progress is too rapid, Hare-Mustin deliberately gives her patients a further paradoxical intention directive, which often increases the rate of improvement.

SOURCE: Hare-Mustin, R. T. "Treatment of Temper Tantrums by a Paradoxical Intention." *Family Process,* 1975, *14,* 481–485.

Elimination of Middle-of-the-Night Tantrums

AUTHORS: Jerry A. Martin and Diane M. Iagulli

PRECIS: Extinction and delayed bedtime strategies in reducing tantrums

INTRODUCTION: In this study, behavioral techniques were used to eliminate prolonged tantrums that occurred from midnight until dawn. The subject was a four-year-old mentally retarded girl who would go to sleep soon after her parents put her to bed at 8:00 P.M. but who would then awaken shortly after midnight and start screaming and crying. Eventually, her parents would give in and go to her room to comfort her.

TREATMENT: The subject was admitted on a short-term basis to a residential facility. During the first fifteen days of treatment, she was put to bed at her usual time and the staff was instructed to ignore her middle-of-the-night tantrums while keeping her awake at all times during the day. Ignoring her tantrums, however, produced no effect; she continued to awaken before 1:00 A.M. and screamed or cried off and on for at least three hours and often for the rest of the night. Accordingly, from Day 16 to 27, the girl was kept awake each evening until midnight by a staff member. For the first four nights, she awoke between 3:00 and 5:00 A.M. and had a tantrum that lasted the remainder of the night. On the twentieth day, she slept the entire night (midnight to rising time at 7:00 A.M.). From this day until Day 27, she had a tantrum on only one night.

From Day 28 to Day 40, the girl was again put to bed between 7:30 and 8:00 P.M. She slept the entire night during this period without a tantrum. She was then discharged to her parents who continued to put her to bed at the usual time. They were instructed to ignore a nighttime tantrum but to keep her awake all the following day until midnight. Follow-up reports over the next six months revealed that the child had had a tantrum on only two nights; on both occasions, the parents had followed the recommended procedure.

COMMENTARY: The extinction strategy initially employed in this study showed no sign of producing an effect in the time allowed. This is not surprising, because ignoring misbehavior generally takes a long time to be successful when there is a history of intermittent reinforcement. Although some therapists have reported successful treatment of tantrums by extinction, some form of positive and/or negative reinforcement contingency seems to be a generally more efficient method.

SOURCE: Martin, J. A., and Iagulli, D. M. "Elimination of Middle-of-the-Night Tantrums in a Blind, Retarded Child." *Behavior Therapy*, 1974, 5, 420–422.

Therapeutic Use of a Child Management Task

AUTHORS: Laurie Chassin, Michael Perelman, and Gerald Weinberger

PRECIS: Helping parents see their role in maintaining a child's deviant behaviors

INTRODUCTION: A seven-year-old girl was brought to outpatient treatment by her parents because of a variety of problems, including severe temper tantrums and disobedience at home. During the initial session with the family, the child exhibited many of the deviant behaviors described by her parents. Rather than expressing disapproval of the child's unusual, bizarre actions (such as rocking in her chair and waving her arms), the parents seemed to reinforce them by smiling and showing approval. When the child was seen individually during the second session, she showed little deviant behavior and tended to relate to the therapists in a mature and organized manner. The therapeutic goal then became to convince the parents that the child was not the severely disturbed child they perceived her to be and that parent-child interactions were related to the child's difficulties. To this end, the parents were asked to attempt a task that would illustrate to them that the child's behavior was a function of their management skills.

CHILD MANAGEMENT TASK: Since the child's tantrums had become so extreme as to put the family in imminent danger of eviction from their apartment, the temper tantrums were selected for modification. A contingency management "game" (the "Going-to-Bed Game") was instituted, wherein appropriate bedtime behaviors were broken down into discrete steps, such as brushing teeth. Whenever the child successfully performed one of the steps, she was to be reinforced with pennies as well as with expressions of approval from parents and therapists. The child's behavior was recorded on a chart cross-listing the days of the week with specific, discrete responses required at bedtime. The required responses and reinforcers were clearly stated in a contract that was signed by the child and her parents. The mother had the responsibility of monitoring the agreement, while the father was given the task of giving the child ten cents each morning when she successfully completed all of the tasks the previous evening.

For the next two weeks, the game was highly successful. Unfortunately there was a rapid deterioration in the plan and return of tantrums following a family excursion after bedtime to buy the child a toy. This behavior by the parents was explicitly contrary to therapeutic directions. At this point, the parents directed bitter recriminations against each other because the management scheme had collapsed. This gave the therapists the opportunity to point out that the parents were jointly responsible for undermining the child's improvement. It was also suggested that having a "sick" child precluded the need for them to resolve their hostile feelings toward one another. The parents were now willing to renegotiate a contract wherein the main focus of therapy was a discussion of family interactions, particularly the marriage relationship.

COMMENTARY: This study underscores the careful strategy that must be employed by therapists when dealing with parents who maintain that their own relationship and parenting skills are unrelated to their child's problems. To explore this area in therapy without explicit parental agreement may lead the parents to abruptly terminate therapy. The task is to keep the parents in therapy while gradually unfolding to them their role in maintaining the deviant behavior of the child.

SOURCE: Chassin, L., Perelman, M., and Weinberger, G. "Reducing Parental Resistance to Examining Family Relationships: The Therapeutic Use of a Child Management Task." *Psychotherapy: Theory, Research and Practice,* 1974, *11,* 387–390.

Additional Readings

Freeman, B. J., Somerset, T., and Ritvo, E. R. "Effect of Duration of Time Out in Suppressing Disruptive Behavior of a Severely Autistic Child." *Psychological Reports,* 1976, *38,* 124–126.

Tantrums in a four-year-old boy were suppressed by placing him in a small time-out room. This severely disturbed child's disruptiveness was best reduced by a fifteen-minute time out, as opposed to three minutes or one hour.

Hardt, F. A. "Modification of a Temper Tantrum." Experimental Publication System, American Psychological Association, 1971, *10,* Ms. No. 383-335.

An eleven-year-old boy exhibited severe tantrums at the dinner table and in the classroom. Treatment consisted of a combination of negative consequences (immediate removal to a time-out room) and positive reinforcement for acceptable behavior. The boy was given points for periods of acceptable behavior. These points were exchangeable for concrete rewards.

Lewis, M., and Stark, M. H. "Family-Centered Diagnosis and Treatment in a Pediatric Clinic." *Social Casework,* January 1966, 13–18.

The sudden and severe temper tantrums of a six-year-old boy seemed to be related to a family crisis. The boy's mother was sick and depressed and the father was debt-ridden and prone to desert the family. The parents engaged in violent quarrels and a sibling had recently been born. Treatment consisted of family counseling and supportive services. The father was given legal help in declaring bankruptcy, welfare assistance was obtained until the father could locate work, visiting nurse and homemaker services were provided when the mother was hospitalized for a hysterectomy, and so on. By helping the family through this crisis period, the boy's fears of abandonment lessened and he exhibited little need to obtain attention by temper tantrums.

Novaco, R. W. *Anger Control: The Development and Evaluation of an Experimental Treatment.* Lexington, Mass.: Lexington Books, 1975.

Novaco designed a treatment program involving self-instruction (after Meichenbaum) and desensitization/relaxation (after Jacobsen and Wolpe). Empirical studies of this cognitive-behavioral approach support its effectiveness in anger control.

Smith, R. E. "The Use of Humor in the Counterconditioning of Anger Responses: A Case Study." *Behavior Therapy,* 1973, *4,* 576–580.

Counterconditioning procedures were successfully applied to the reduction of strong, maladaptive anger responses. Although muscle relaxation procedures proved ineffective in inhibiting anger responses, the introduction of humor into the hierarchy of items proved highly effective.

Sulzbacher, S. I. "The Learning-Disabled or Hyperactive Child." *Journal of the American Medical Association,* 1975, *234,* 838–841.

Sulzbacher found that impulsive children did not seem to be aware of when they were becoming irritated or frustrated and rarely communicated these feelings to others, except by a full-blown tantrum (which often appeared hours after the initial provocation). To avoid an "all-or-none" expression of anger, Sulzbacher encouraged these children to communicate minor irritations in a socially acceptable way. The children were taught specific sets of verbal responses (p. 840) to early warning signs: (1) "I am becoming irritated and I wish you would change this situation" and (2) "If you don't do something about my complaint right now I will ———— (leave, hit, throw a fit, and so on)." The child was also instructed always to follow through on his threats and only to make threats he intended to carry out. Sulzbacher does not view this technique as condoning the behavior, because the tantrums are occurring anyway. This approach seems to work best with five- to eight-year-old children.

Webster, D. R., and Azrin, N. H. "Required Relaxation: A Method of Inhibiting Agitative-Disruptive Behavior of Retardates." *Behaviour Research and Therapy,* 1973, *11,* 67–78.

Webster and Azrin developed a procedure in which overcorrective practice in relaxation was given to disruptive retardates. The agitated patient was required to spend two hours relaxing on his bed following each temper outburst. Any disruption in the final fifteen minutes of relaxation resulted in a fifteen-minute extension. No eating, listening to the radio, playing with objects, and so on was permitted during relaxation. The patient was told that he was upset and needed to lie down for a while to relax.

Williams, C. D. "The Elimination of Tantrum Behavior by Extinction Procedures." *Journal of Abnormal and Social Psychology,* 1959, *59,* 269.

Tyrannical tantrums in a twenty-one-month-old boy were eliminated by the removal of reinforcement. The parents were instructed to immediately leave the child's bedroom after placing him in bed, close the door, and to ignore the child's screaming. He screamed for forty-five minutes the first night but bedtime crying was extinguished after eight nights. No side effects or aftereffects of this treatment were observed.

Destructiveness

In this section, we are concerned with children who destroy their own or other people's property, either deliberately, out of ignorance, or in a fit of anger. The usual punishment for vandalism is to require the child to make restitution, that is, to restore or replace the damaged property or to make a monetary payment to compensate the victim. (Also see sections on Temper Tantrums *and* Aggressiveness.*)*

Modifying Destructive and
Disruptive Behavior

AUTHORS: John Burchard and Vernon Tyler, Jr.

PRECIS: Behavior modification with a boy who exhibited multiple antisocial behaviors

INTRODUCTION: Using operant conditioning principles, Burchard and Tyler developed a program to eliminate the general antisocial behavior of Donny, a thirteen-year-old boy. Donny had been in a residential treatment institution for a period of four-and-a-half years. Various therapeutic interventions had failed to modify his "destructive and disruptive" acts, which included destruction of property, stealing, fire setting, glue sniffing, and cruelty to animals and small children. In an effort to reverse the general deterioration in his behavior, Burchard and Tyler instituted the following procedure.

OPERANT PROGRAM: First, Donny was to be placed in an isolation room whenever he displayed any antisocial behaviors. He was to remain there for a period of three hours unless he was placed there in the late evening, in which case he was to remain in the room until 7:00 A.M. (overnight). The following instructions were given to all staff members in his cottage:

> Whenever Donny displays any unacceptable behavior, he is to be immediately placed in isolation. Unacceptable behavior is defined as any behavior which would normally require a sanction, verbal or otherwise. If you don't feel the behavior should warrant isolation, then the behavior should be ignored. However, if any action is taken to modify or eliminate the behavior, it should be isolation. The use of isolation should be on an all-or-none basis; that is, he should never be threatened with the possibility of being sent into isolation. He should be told in simple terms why he is being sent and any further verbal interaction with Donny should be held to a minimum. It

is important that you do not become too emotionally involved with Donny. Anyone who feels guilty or for some reason does not send Donny to isolation when his behavior warrants it is not participating in the treatment plan. As long as Donny is "fouling up," the more he is sent to isolation, the more effective the treatment program will be [p. 247]

Aside from a metal bed without a mattress and a toilet, there were no objects in the isolation room. During an overnight isolation, Donny was given a mattress and blankets at 10:00 P.M. To preclude the possibility of Donny talking to boys in adjacent rooms, a radio placed immediately above his room was played at a moderate volume during the daytime. Whenever Donny acted out while in isolation, his length of stay in isolation was extended by an hour.

To provide positive reinforcement, Donny was given a poker chip for each hour he remained out of isolation between the hours of 7:00 A.M. and 10:00 P.M. If he remained in the cottage for an entire overnight period, he was given three tokens in the morning. The tokens were redeemable for such items as soda pop, trips to town, recreational activities, cigarettes, movies, and so on. These privileges were only offered to Donny in exchange for a specified number of tokens.

After two months of this behavior modification procedure, the following changes were made. First, Donny was required to stay out of isolation for two hours rather than one in order to receive a token. Whenever he remained out of isolation for a twenty-four-hour period, he received a bonus of seven tokens. Also, his time in isolation was reduced from three hours to two hours.

The results of this procedure revealed a gradual but steady reduction in the frequency of unacceptable behavior. The boy was placed in isolation eighteen times during the first month and twelve times during the fifth month, a decline of 33 percent. Moreover, the seriousness of his destructive and disruptive behaviors decreased during the five-month period. Burchard and Tyler conclude that the attention Donny had been receiving from others prior to the program had been contributing to the frequency of the antisocial acts.

COMMENTARY: A period of social isolation appears to be a logical consequence for the antisocial behaviors of children. However, one wonders if a period of two or three hours in isolation is any more effective than a briefer interval. Also, several states have recently established regulations that prohibit the use of isolation with institutionalized children. It is noteworthy that isolation or punishment was employed in this study only after various treatment modalities, including medication and two years of "regressive therapy," had failed to control the child's delinquent acts. Also, provision was made in this program to ensure that the child was rewarded for appropriate behavior.

SOURCE: Burchard, J., and Tyler, V., Jr. "The Modification of Delinquent Behaviour Through Operant Conditioning." *Behaviour Research and Therapy*, 1965, 2, 245–250.

The Efficacy of Time-Out Procedures

AUTHOR: David A. Sachs

PRECIS: Use of a time-out room to reduce disruptive classroom behavior

INTRODUCTION: Sachs describes several variations of time out from positive reinforcement procedures for reducing inappropriate behaviors. In one case, Mark, a ten-year-old boy, was referred for a variety of disruptive behaviors in the classroom, including damaging classroom equipment.

TIME OUT: Treatment was initiated when the teacher informed the class that anyone who (1) disrupted the class, (2) destroyed school equipment, or (3) injured or attempted to injure anyone else would be placed in the time-out room and have to remain there for "five minutes straight without making a sound" (p. 238). The time-out apparatus was a four- by six-foot sound-insulated room that had no inside handle for the child to open. The room was barren except for a microphone in the ceiling that was connected to a voice-operated relay. Any sound in the room actuated the relay, which sent a reset pulse to the timer.

Whenever Mark was sent to the time-out room, he was told for what specific behavior he was being punished and was reminded that he had to be quiet for five consecutive minutes before he could leave. A buzzer sounded in the classroom whenever the timer in the time-out room had operated for five minutes. After ten days of this procedure, the average number of inappropriate behaviors Mark exhibited during a five-minute period declined from about twenty to only one.

COMMENTARY: This study shows that a time-out procedure can dramatically reduce the incidence of disruptive and destructive behaviors in the classroom. One wonders, however, if confining a child to the apparatus described in this experiment is really necessary for effective time out. The small, closetlike room described by Sachs reminds one of a sensory deprivation room. Needless to say, time-out procedures are not meant to be so severe as to border on child abuse. Even the old classroom cloakroom would seem to be a better choice for time out than the apparatus in this study.

SOURCE: Sachs, D. A. "The Efficacy of Time-Out Procedures in a Variety of Behavior Problems." *Journal of Behavior Therapy and Experimental Psychiatry,* 1973, *4,* 237–242.

Additional Readings

Felder, R. "The Therapist at Home." *Voices,* 1965, Fall, 116.

After discovering that his son had shot holes through a valuable family painting with a BB gun, Felder required his son to write an essay about "Vandalism in the House."

Foxx, R. M., and Azrin, N. H. "Restitution: A Method of Eliminating Aggressive-Disruptive Behavior of Retarded and Brain-Damaged Patients." *Behaviour Research and Therapy,* 1972, *10,* 15–27.

Foxx and Azrin developed a procedure that provided disruptive offenders with reeducation, removal of the reinforcement for the offense, time out from general positive reinforcement, and an effort requirement. The offender was required by instructions or physical guidance to overcorrect the general psychological and physical disturbance created by the offense. For example, if a child threw a chair or turned over a table or bed, he was required not only to restore that object to its correct position but also to straighten all other chairs, tables, or beds in the area, as well as related objects. If property was damaged, the child was required to spend considerable time repairing it (or working to obtain money to replace it). The results showed that the restitution training procedures were effective in eliminating several disruptive and aggressive behaviors. The effects of restitution training were immediate and endured over several months.

Aggressiveness

This section discusses children's general aggressiveness toward others, that is, trying to dominate others by unprovoked verbal and physical attacks. In other sections, a more focused type of aggression will be discussed. (Since there is considerable overlap between these behaviors, the reader should also see sections on Temper Tantrums, Impulsiveness and Low Frustration Tolerance, Overt Hostility Toward Peers, Sibling Rivalry, *and* Overt Hostility Toward Parents.*)*

Analysis of Aggression in a Five-Year-Old Girl

AUTHOR: Elizabeth Seeberg

PRECIS: Psychoanalytic interpretation in reducing overt aggression

INTRODUCTION: Seeberg describes a psychoanalytic case study involving Jane, a five-year-old girl who was displaying violent behaviors toward her mother—for example, hitting, pinching, and biting. Formerly quite affectionate, the girl now cursed her parents and her belligerence had spread to other female relatives. She also was "mean" to her peers. A fourteen-year-old stepsister had lived at home but was placed away two months after the initial therapy session. The sixty-nine treatment sessions consisted primarily of psychoanalytically oriented play therapy. The parents were asked to do three things at home: Fill out a behavior chart, remove Jane's bed from their bedroom into her own room, and cease the daily whippings Jane had been receiving.

OEDIPUS CONFLICT: Rapport was easily established with Jane, who was a model of good behavior with the therapist. The prime goal of therapy was to discover the motive underlying her aggressiveness toward her mother and help her gain control over it. After being told that it was acceptable to express her "bad" feelings with the therapist, Jane freely expressed her thoughts and feelings both verbally and through the medium of play. The following themes dominated her responses and clearly pointed to the presence of an oedipal conflict. First, she revealed the desire to possess the sexual attributes of adult women. Thus she would ask both her mother and the therapist if she could wear their rings and purses. In her play, she would often decorate herself with makeup and jewelry while talking about going out on dates with men. She also showed a strong preoccupation with "being married" and with the sex relationship between husband and wife, which she viewed as being exciting yet repulsive. Another theme was aggressive attack, which she seemed to connect with sexual intercourse. Related to this content was a preoccupation with the sadistic use of phallic symbols.

Treatment consisted of encouraging the release of hateful, jealous feelings and sexual interest, so that Jane could gain more control over them. In addition to correcting Jane's misinformation about sex and relieving her guilt about masturbation, the therapist tried to interpret for her some of her fantasies and feelings. Jane was helped to see that she was jealous of her mother and did not want her parents to be alone together. Finally, in the twenty-fifth session, the therapist pointed out to Jane that there was marked similarity between the aggression she displayed toward her mother and her play scenes in which a man aggressively attacks a woman during intercourse. The therapist explained to Jane that a man does not really injure a woman in the sex relationship and that to believe so may be a reflection of her jealousy toward her mother and desire to be like her father. She seemed to be identifying with her father, whom she believed was physically injuring her mother during intercourse. After this last interpretation, Jane's behavior took a decided turn for the better. She stopped pinching, kicking, and cursing her mother and did not do so again.

Noting this improvement, her parents terminated therapy, even though the therapist advised that the control of physical aggression was just the first goal of therapy. Contact with the parents three years later revealed that there had been no relapse in the aggressiveness nor had there been further improvement. Jane's disobedience at home continued to be a problem.

COMMENTARY: In this study, interpretation was the main therapeutic tool for inhibiting the overt expression of aggression. The insights gained by the child seemed to give her more conscious control of an underlying oedipal conflict. One wonders, however, if the limited behavioral gain noted could not have been achieved with less cost and effort by more brief interventions, such as behavioral management. This study is a classic example of the application of psychoanalytic methods for the resolution of childhood behavior problems.

SOURCE: Seeberg, E. "Analysis of Aggression in a Five-Year-Old Girl." *American Journal of Orthopsychiatry,* 1943, *13,* 53–62.

Use of Fantasy as a Therapeutic Technique

AUTHOR: Thomas Scheidler

PRECIS: Guided stimulation of fantasy in alleviating aggression—
a technique for children's groups

INTRODUCTION: Scheidler describes the use of Hammer's
"directed daydream" technique in a group context with latency-
age youth (Hammer, M. "The Directed Daydream Technique."
Psychotherapy: Theory, Research and Practice, 1967, *4,* 173–181). Two
groups of six children, with a mean age of twelve and ten, respec-
tively, were employed in this study. One or two girls were included
in each group. Aggressive acting out and poor peer relations were
the main reasons for referral.

GROUP ACTIVITY: Most of the group members elected to keep
their eyes open during the directed daydream exercise. The first
step was a relaxation exercise. The therapist described a bitterly cold
winter scene with "icy cold snow blowing into our noses and ears"
and a "chill going into our bodies." Then a suggestion of warmth
and relaxation was proposed: entering a cabin with a "thick, deep,
soft rug" in front of a roaring fireplace and a "cup of steaming hot
chocolate" on a nearby table (p. 299). Once the children were relaxed, they were asked to visualize and describe a predetermined
symbolic object in the cabin: a sword for the boys and a vase for the
girls. The therapist asked each group member in turn various questions about the imagined object; for example, "What does it look
like?" "How does it feel?" At the end of this twenty-minute warmup
and dream activity, the therapist stimulated group discussion by
touching on a common theme of the daydreams: "I wonder if sometimes we disappoint ourselves by the way we act?" (p. 300). A lively
interaction resulted from this stimulus question; the children talked
about how they were aware of their unacceptable behavior and
their frustrations and how they felt rejected by foster parents and
stepparents. The therapist helped them connect these two aspects
of their experiences. During subsequent sessions, the directed
daydream technique was used only periodically; for example, when

the discussion slowed or became redundant the therapist would suggest that they "try dreaming again." Over the course of the seven sessions, the children's fantasies improved and lengthened.

Follow-up contacts indicated that there was substantial improvement in the mischievous acting out of the older group members. One boy, who had been referred by his father because of an aggressively manifested adjustment reaction to his mother's death, was reported much more sensitive and concerned about other family members. A school principal of two of the other boys reported that their aggressive behavior in school had decreased substantially. The younger group's improvements were also positive but less dramatic.

COMMENTARY: The "directed daydream" technique, which was originally designed for individual use, was employed effectively in this study to "break the ice" in group therapy. By first asking group members to imagine symbolic nonthreatening objects, the therapist created an emotional climate that allowed easy transition to the exploration of conscious problem areas and attitudes. Also, the daydream exercise gave the group members the experience of sharing a deep part of themselves with others. As Scheidler observes, this sharing evoked a feeling of community that allowed meaningful group interaction. In Jungian terms, the group intuitively sensed their unification around an archetypal symbol. By encouraging exploration of a deeper layer of the human psyche, the daydream technique seemed to promote greater personality integration in the group members.

SOURCE: Scheidler, T. "Use of Fantasy as a Therapeutic Agent in Latency-Age Groups." *Psychotherapy: Theory, Research and Practice*, 1972, *9*, 299–302.

Behavior Contracting and Group Therapy

AUTHOR: Donald Bardill

PRECIS: Behavior modification with a group of acting out, pre-adolescent boys

INTRODUCTION: From his personal experiences with acting out preadolescent boys in group therapy, Bardill observed the need for more structure. Quite often the weekly group sessions were disrupted by fights between group members, destruction of office furniture, and failure to attend sessions. He therefore decided to use behavior contracting techniques during his therapy sessions with nine- to thirteen-year-old boys at a residential treatment center. Characteristically, the boys were impulsive, acted out their aggressive feelings, and lacked skills necessary for engaging in cooperative interpersonal transactions.

BEHAVIOR CONTRACTING: In brief, behavioral contracting is a procedure for scheduling the exchange of positive reinforcements between two or more persons. It clearly specifies the expectations of each person in a transaction. The contracting in this study involved a point system in which each boy was awarded points for certain specified behaviors during the therapy sessions. Each boy could earn a maximum of fifteen points for appropriate conduct and up to ten points for "therapeutic responses." The therapist and cotherapist met at the end of each session to agree on the total points for each child. Conduct points were earned for (1) arriving for therapy at the scheduled time, (2) not taking items from the office, (3) not physically hurting or abusing anyone, and (4) obeying the institutional rules regarding such behaviors as cursing and smoking. Therapy points were earned by (1) listening to others, (2) making verbal comments designed to be helpful to others, and (3) talking about one's own concerns. Specific explanations and examples of each of these guidelines were given to each boy. The goal of the therapy points was a traditional one—to get the boys to talk out rather than act out their negative feelings, as well as to learn more positive ways of relating to others.

Each boy could earn an extra two points by correctly guessing, within two points, the number of points awarded to him for each session. The therapists met with each boy individually after each treatment session to discuss his points. This guessing procedure was intended to encourage a more realistic appraisal of their behavior during therapy. Moreover, a sponsor system was established whereby each boy acted as a sponsor for two other boys in the group. Whenever a sponsoree earned top conduct and therapy points (twenty-five) for a session, his sponsor earned three extra points. It was hoped that the sponsor or buddy system would instill in the boys a sense of responsibility for the behavior of others and for the formation of common goals. A listing of the points earned by each boy was posted on the office bulletin board every week.

On earning fifty or more points during the calendar month a boy became eligible to convert the points into money at the rate of one cent per point. He also qualified for a monthly off-campus trip to spend his money. The off-campus trips were considered part of the group therapy and a boy's behavior off campus was subject to the same point rules as the other therapy sessions.

Throughout the eight months of this group program, the therapists made a conscious effort to present the program with a positive orientation, that is, to show the boys a way of earning points and rewards rather than to emphasize the misbehaviors that would result in the loss of points. The program was successful almost immediately in eliminating physical fights among the boys, destruction of furniture, and thefts of office items. The boys did "test" the program with minor breaches of conduct but this testing became less noticeable as the program continued. Often more prosocial leaders emerged in the therapy groups, in contrast to the delinquent-type leaders who often reigned in the larger institutional program by physical power and threats.

COMMENTARY: Bardill concludes that the behavior-contracting group therapy model was dramatically successful not only in reducing blatant disruptive behavior during the sessions but also in fostering the development of cooperative social behavior during the therapy sessions. Unfortunately, there was no provision in this study for assessing the generalization, if any, of the positive interpersonal behavior during group sessions to the general overall behavior patterns of the boys. Nevertheless, any procedure that offers predelinquent boys a means of controlling their own behavior in a group situation is clearly a welcome addition to the literature.

SOURCE: Bardill, D. "Behavior Contracting and Group Therapy with Preadolescent Males in a Residential Treatment Setting." *International Journal of Group Psychotherapy*, 1972, *22*, 333–342.

Additional Readings

Blackwood, R. O. "The Operant Conditioning of Verbally Mediated Self-Control in the Classroom." *Journal of School Psychology*, 1970, *8*, 251–258.

Blackwood hypothesized that words emitted by a child can mediate between temptation and the target response. To teach children to say the right words to themselves when tempted to act out in class, he required children to copy or paraphrase an essay while in detention. The one-paragraph mediation essay contained four questions and their answers. The questions were "What did I do wrong?" "Why was this inappropriate?" "What should I have done?' and "Why should I act differently; what good things will happen to me?" (p. 253). Children who cooperated in writing this essay were released early from detention. Occasionally the children were asked to role play, that is, to act out both misbehavior and alternate behaviors while verbalizing the consequences of each course of action. This mediation training was found to be effective in reducing aggressiveness to peers and teachers.

Gittleman, M. "Behavior Rehearsal as a Technique in Child Treatment." *Journal of Child Psychology and Psychiatry*, 1965, *6*, 251–255.

Gittleman presents a technique for treating aggressive, acting-out children in an outpatient setting. The method involves the use of role playing or behavior rehearsal, wherein various instigatory situations are played out by the child and other group members. While the technique is similar in many respects to psychodrama, an effort has been made to introduce certain learning theory concepts, particularly that of desensitization.

Patterson, G. R., and Brodsky, G. "A Behaviour Modification Pro-
gramme for a Child with Multiple Problem Behaviours."
Journal of Child Psychology and Psychiatry, 1966, 7, 277–295.

Patterson and Brodsky describe the treatment of an intensely
aggressive five-year-old boy. He threw temper tantrums to avoid
the anxiety of separation from his mother in school. This behavior
was being reinforced by the mother staying with him or the teacher
giving him extra attention. Treatment involved extinguishing the
positive reinforcements following a tantrum, while strengthening
more adaptive responses to separation. Thus the boy was sent to a
time-out room where he was physically restrained every time he
threw a temper fit. On the other hand, he was praised and given
candy every time he stated appropriate alternatives for handling
separation, such as playing. His mother was trained to reinforce
him for times when he separated from her in an appropriate manner. Group therapy, involving group reinforcement contingencies,
was also used to train the boy to play cooperatively with his peers.
Finally, the parents were trained to use behavioral contingencies
at home.

Stealing

This section focuses on stealing, that is, taking the money or possessions of others without permission. Typically, stealing is done in a secret or surreptitious manner. Studies have shown that the children most frequently involved in "aggressive" stealing are diagnosed as showing "group delinquent reaction." Aggressive stealing, such as burglary, involves some degree of courage, in contrast to the furtive stealing of the sneak thief.

Treating Compulsive Stealing with Behavioral Techniques

AUTHOR: Ralph Wetzel

PRECIS: Training adults to systematically withdraw positive reinforcement for stealing episodes

INTRODUCTION: Wetzel's study illustrates the use of behavioral methods in the treatment of deviant behavior. The compulsive stealing of Mike, a ten-year-old boy at a home for mildly disturbed children, was the focus of this intervention. Mike was described by staff as "charming" but with little conscience and a tendency to project his faults onto others. A psychiatric report indicated that he was on the verge of becoming a "full-blown psychopath." For the past five years, complaints of his stealing had increased. Various attempts to curb his stealing had been tried. Since Mike usually gave the stolen objects to others, one caseworker had suggested to him that his stealing represented an attempt to buy affection from others. Although Mike repeatedly had said he was sorry and that it would not happen again, his stealing continued and had now spread to the school. He frequently brought home school toys, books, and assorted objects from the teacher's desk and school bulletin board.

TREATMENT: First, the child-care staff working with Mike was trained in behavioral principles through a series of four conferences. After a discussion of the application of these principles to Mike, it was decided to withdraw some positive reinforcement contingent on stealing. Mike's relationship with a female cook was selected as the positive reinforcer. Initially, the casual relationship was strengthened by scheduling daily interactions, such as shopping trips and visits to the cook's home. Then the cook was instructed to tell Mike after he had stolen something: "I'm sorry that you took so-and-so's ——— because now I can't let you come home with me tonight" (p. 370). After saying this, she was to immediately turn and walk away without listening to any excuses or explanations.

The next day she was to resume her usual warm relationship with the boy and continue it until the next stealing episode. The child-care staff kept a record of Mike's stealing, that is, of other people's property found on his person, in his locker, or in his room. In addition, the staff praised Mike highly for periods or incidents of non-stealing behavior.

The incidence of Mike's stealing was reduced dramatically once the removal of positive reinforcement was instituted. During the fourth and final month of recordings, Mike reminded the staff that he had not stolen or lied. Since Mike's relationship with his peers had also improved, his visits with the cook had dropped to only two or three times a week. There had been some problems with the child-care staff not recording certain stealing episodes and being too lenient in interpreting stealing, but these difficulties were finally resolved by additional conferences with the staff.

COMMENTARY: Even though Wetzel had given the child-care staff prior instruction in the theory of behavioral intervention, he still discovered that the staff found it difficult to understand the need for immediate and consistent reinforcement. Reinforcement was quite inconsistent at the beginning of the program. This highlights the need for close supervision and monitoring of behavioral programs by the consultant. It also points out the need for a long-term training program for institutional staff.

SOURCE: Wetzel, R. "Use of Behavioral Techniques in a Case of Compulsive Stealing." *Journal of Consulting Psychology,* 1966, *30,* 367–374.

Behavioral Rehearsal with Children

AUTHOR: Martin Gittleman

PRECIS: Behavior rehearsal—a systematic method of eliciting maladaptive behavior and then helping a child learn more appropriate responses

INTRODUCTION: Gittleman has found behavior rehearsal to be very effective in working with predelinquent children from ghetto backgrounds. Basically, the technique involves presenting cues that prompt maladaptive responses in the child; the child is then assisted in practicing more appropriate responses. Role playing is used initially to elicit from the child a complete picture of the troublesome stimuli and the child's response to them. The therapist, for example, may play the role of the bully who instills fear in the child, while the child is encouraged to give his typical response to the bully. The stressful situations are then reenacted in a hierarchical sequence, the mildest situations being presented first. As the child learns to tolerate and cope with the milder situations, the more stressful ones are gradually introduced. Often the therapist will model or act out more adaptive responses to the situation.

GROUP BEHAVIOR REHEARSAL: Usually a child is seen first in individual sessions. After a number of private sessions the child is seen jointly with another child; finally, he is introduced to a group behavior rehearsal session. The group, which never exceeds eight children, is balanced in terms of ethnicity, nature of the presenting problem, and experience with the procedure. The more experienced children, who have already learned more adaptive responses through behavior rehearsal, are often able to teach the procedure more effectively than the therapist. The children are told that the treatment goal is for them to control themselves better and that therapy will basically be a learning process for them. Reinforcements vary, depending on the age of the child; they include candy, therapist and group approval, and checks on a score sheet. As children become proficient at the technique, their therapy sessions are spaced progressively further apart.

CASE STUDY: Brett, a thirteen-year-old boy, was referred by his school because of stealing and fighting. He said he almost always stole in a group of friends because of his fear of being thought "chicken" if he did not steal. In therapy the stealing scene was re-enacted and some of the group members played the role of "friends" trying to convince Brett to steal again. (Propaganda theory suggests that an argument has less persuasive power if one has already heard the counterarguments).

The following excerpt from a therapeutic interchange illustrates the behavior rehearsal method. In this department store scene, the parts of "friends" are played by other group members and therapist (p. 15).

Friend: Hey, Brett, dig that shirt.
Brett: Yeah, I see it.
Friend: Let's take it.
Brett: Huh, uh; you take it, not me.
Friend: You chicken?
Brett: Uh huh.
Friend: What's the matter? You afraid to get caught? You weren't afraid last week when you took the candy.
Brett: I'm reforming.
Friend: You mean you're scared; you lost your nerve.
Brett: Uh uh; I'm just beginning to think differently.

(Brett was praised by the therapist and group members when he responded appropriately in the rehearsals.)

COMMENTARY: Since his paper is on the process rather than the outcome of behavior rehearsal, Gittleman does not discuss the outcomes of most of the cases presented, including Brett. He does report that children find the procedure interesting and enjoyable. He also states that the behavior rehearsal technique has wide applicability and that he has successfully used it to remediate such childhood behavior problems as fighting, classroom disturbance, fearfulness, social withdrawal, and disobedience. It also holds promise as an "immunological" measure to prevent the development of serious problems, such as smoking, drinking, and use of drugs. The method is a creative amalgam of a variety of other techniques, including role playing, desensitization, modeling, group pressure, problem solving, and counterconditioning.

SOURCE: Gittleman, M. "Behavior Rehearsal with Children in a Community Mental Health Setting." *American Journal of Orthopsychiatry,* in press.

Additional Readings

Guidry, L. S. "Use of a Covert Punishing Contingency in Compulsive Stealing." *Journal of Behavior Therapy and Experimental Psychiatry,* 1975, *6,* 169.

A young man with a stealing compulsion of ten years' duration was treated by using covert behavior modification techniques. First the man was instructed to imagine punishing consequences to stealing, that is, being in a store having the urge to steal and then imagining the manager was watching him or that he was caught. He was to go into stores and practice imagining the managers were watching him as he shopped. To increase the power of the aversive consequences, he was instructed to systematically imagine a list of negative repercussions of stealing, such as being caught, the police being called, being handcuffed, being put in the police car, being booked, standing before the judge, and his parents being called.

Reid, J. B., and Patterson, G. R. "The Modification of Aggression and Stealing Behavior of Boys in the Home Setting." In E. Ribes-Inesta and A. Bandura (Eds.), *Analysis of Delinquency and Aggression.* New York: Wiley, 1976.

In their experience with ten cases of childhood stealing (defined as at least one theft per two weeks), Reid and Patterson found that the parents typically denied or overlooked the stealing and lacked the motivation to continue treatment. The children were often left unsupervised for long periods each day because both parents were working. The first step in treatment involved teaching the parents to correctly identify, label, and record the incidence of stealing. Stealing was defined as the possession of an object not clearly (in the parents' perception) belonging to the child. The parents were to confront the child with each stealing incident and not to allow any explanations of how he came into possession of the object. The parents then implemented a behavioral management procedure involving close monitoring, and setting consequences (loss of privileges and time out). Daily phone calls were made to the parents to encourage their cooperation. The results with the first seven families treated were remarkably successful.

Switzer, E. B. "The Reduction of Stealing Behavior in Second Graders Using a Group Contingency," in press.

Switzer studied the effects of two types of intervention programs on stealing behavior: (1) an antistealing lecture with no specific contingency implied, and (2) a direct group contingency wherein the children in a class were rewarded with extra free time for no thefts, allowed normal free time if stolen items were returned, and punished with loss of free time if stolen items were not returned. The group contingency was found to be effective in reducing stealing behavior, while the antistealing lecture was ineffective.

Fire Setting

The juvenile who deliberately sets fires poses a serious threat to the well-being not only of his family but of the entire community as well. Because of the obvious danger, the treatment of a fire-setting syndrome must be a high priority for the therapist.

Eliminating Fire-Setting Behavior

AUTHOR: Cornelius J. Holland

PRECIS: Using behavior modification methods with a persistent and severe fire-setting habit

INTRODUCTION: Robert, a seven-year-old boy, had a habit of setting fires in his home. He would set fires whenever he found matches and his parents were in bed or out of the house. Punishments such as being slapped, locked in his room, and touched with a smoldering object were only successful for a short period. Feeling helpless and enraged, his parents avoided him as much as possible and showed him very little affection. Holland met with the parents alone for five sessions to implement the following treatment plan.

BEHAVIORAL INTERVENTION: Since the mother was skeptical and would not participate initially, Robert's father carried out the plan. He told Robert that if he set any more fires he would permanently lose his highly prized baseball glove. Robert was also told to immediately bring to the father any matches or matchbook covers he found around the house. When Robert brought an empty matchbook cover the father had conspicuously placed on a table, he was immediately given five cents and urged to go to the store to spend it, which he did. For the next few evenings, his father continued to leave packets containing matches around the house, which Robert promptly brought to him. The continuous reinforcement given to Robert at this stage ranged from one to ten cents. Matches or covers found outside during the day were saved by the boy and given to the father at night. His mother became interested in the program at this point and began to reinforce Robert when he brought matches to her.

Since the possibility remained that Robert was striking some matches he found outside the home, a situation was contrived at home to strengthen nonstriking behavior. One night about a week after the program started, Robert's father informed him that he could strike a full packet of matches if he liked under the father's supervision. Twenty pennies were placed next to the pack and

Robert was told that for every match left unstruck he would receive one penny. On the other hand, one penny would be removed for every match he used. During the first session, Robert struck ten matches and received ten pennies. The next evening he earned seventeen pennies and the third evening twenty pennies. In further sessions, he consistently decided not to strike any matches. The rewards Robert received during these sessions varied, ranging up to ten cents. Throughout the entire program, the father gave social reinforcers along with the material rewards. By the end of four weeks, the boy's fire-setting habit had been eliminated. An eight-month follow-up revealed no recurrence of the habit. During these eight months, the father continued using a variable-ratio schedule of money reinforcers with the boy.

COMMENTARY: This study supports the growing evidence that the systematic use of operant methods by parents can bring deviant behaviors by children under control in a short period of time. Because of the serious nature of fire-setting behavior, it would seem most prudent to use therapeutic techniques that can eliminate the behavior in the least amount of time.

SOURCE: Holland, C. J. "Elimination by the Parents of Fire-setting Behaviour in a Seven-Year-Old Boy." *Behaviour Research and Therapy*, 1969, 7, 135–137.

Therapy for the Family of a Fire Setter

AUTHOR: Richard M. Eisler

PRECIS: Intensive, family-oriented intervention with a case of fire setting

INTRODUCTION: Eisler describes a family therapy approach for a fourteen-year-old boy referred by the courts for fire setting. J. J. expressed regret at having set several large grass fires that had endangered houses, but he could offer no explanation for his behavior. His parents were shocked at this antisocial act, because he had always been a model of responsible behavior at home.

The family history revealed that the father had lost his business five years ago and for the next four years worked out of state on various jobs. He was only able to visit the family occasionally. His wife worked as a secretary and a year prior to the intervention the father had secured a job at his wife's company and moved back home. Since his parents both worked, J. J. was responsible for caring for his two younger siblings after school and preparing supper. At the initial interview, the father and boy were quite passive and the mother tended to do most of the talking. She seemed to dominate both the father and the son. At the end of the interview, the family was asked to come to further meetings, because the fire setting appeared to be a nonverbal message from the boy that all was not well at home. The family agreed to come twice a week for three weeks to discuss their relationships.

CRISIS-ORIENTED FAMILY THERAPY: The basic rationale of family therapy is that one member's deviant behavior is a reflection of disturbed family relationships; therefore, therapy should focus on the family interactions rather than on the disturbed behavior of the individual. The family therapy in this study was offered by a crisis intervention service at a mental health center and was designed to be immediately available and short-term in nature. Typically, families were seen together from four to eight sessions over a period lasting one to six weeks. In this case, two cotherapists worked with the family on an outpatient basis. The family meetings lasted from two to three hours, in order to allow time to discuss an issue thoroughly. The therapists established three goals for the family work: to explore communication patterns, role assignments, and unresolved crises in the family.

Rather than discuss interpersonal conflicts openly, the family tended to communicate hurt feelings nonverbally; for example, the boy would set fires, while the father would withdraw from the home by joining numerous civic organizations. The therapists pointed out that there seemed to be a family rule that prohibited any direct expression of dissatisfaction or angry feelings. An assignment to make independent lists of their grievances toward one another seemed to break this barrier against open communication. The father stated that he had been feeling an outsider to the family ever since he had returned home, while J. J. related that he was very annoyed with his father for leaving home and quite disappointed in not having a closer relationship with his father since his return.

An exploration of roles revealed that the mother was disappointed in the father for not playing a more active and responsible role at home. The father, on the other hand, stated that he feared being dominated by his wife, who was quick to make family decisions. As the sessions continued, it was evident that Mr. J. was taking a much more active and assertive role in the family, which was greatly appreciated by mother and son. Also, J. J. was able to express his resentment about having to be a substitute father for his siblings even though he was not deemed responsible enough to earn spending money through a part-time job. Mr. J. then surprised the family by agreeing strongly with J. J. that too much responsibility had been placed on him.

At the end of the agreed-on six sessions, the family felt that they were doing well and decided to terminate treatment. Based on the recommendations of the therapists, the court agreed to place J. J. on probation in the custody of his parents. A follow-up meeting four months later indicated that the family seemed to be functioning better, with more open communication. One year after cessation of treatment, telephone contact revealed that there had been no further incidents of fire setting and the family felt they were doing well.

COMMENTARY: In the present approach, the goal of therapy was not to discuss the boy's fire setting but rather to explore the hypothesized underlying causes in the family, such as role confusion and faulty communication patterns. According to Eisler, crisis-oriented family therapy is indicated when:

1. Family members value each other and seem motivated to work toward a better relationship.
2. The family members seem capable of offering one another emotional support while discussing painful conflict areas.
3. Precipitant crises in the family history are readily identifiable.

SOURCE: Eisler, R. M. "Crisis Intervention in the Family of a Fire-setter." *Psychotherapy: Theory, Research and Practice,* 1972, *9,* 76–79.

Additional Readings

Kaufman, I., Heims, L. W., and Reimer, D. E. "A Re-Evaluation of the Psychodynamics of Firesetting." *American Journal of Orthopsychiatry,* 1961, *31,* 123–136.

A study of thirty fire-setting boys revealed that none of them functioned at the relatively advanced phallic level of development often described in association with fire setting. Eight of the children were diagnosed as "primary conduct disorders," eleven were borderline psychotics, and the other eleven were overtly psychotic. Most were fixated at the oral level. They felt deserted and abandoned by their parents, whom they perceived to be aggressive. While they longed for a close relationship with an adult, they feared being destroyed by adults. The authors view residential treatment as the method of choice for these children until they can develop the ego strengths necessary to cope with their overwhelming destructive drives.

Koret, S. "Family Therapy as a Therapeutic Technique in Residential Treatment." *Child Welfare,* 1973, *52,* 235–246.

A five-year-old fire-setting boy was in residential treatment for three years. The turning point in his treatment occurred a year before discharge, when his family finally entered therapy because of a crisis in the boy's life. The boy's intense loneliness, psychological self-flagellation, and despair became evident in these sessions and the family was able to extend some support to the boy. The parents were also helped to set firm and consistent limits with the children.

Macht, L. B., and Mack, J. E. "The Firesetter Syndrome." *Psychiatry*, 1968, *31*, 277–288.

Clinical interviews with four adolescent fire setters led Macht and Mack to conclude that fire setting is a complex act with multiple determinants. It is clearly not just an impulsive act. It was found that the fathers of the boys were absent when the behavior occurred so that the act seemed to represent a call from the overburdened adolescent to the absent father so as to bring him to the rescue. Also, the absence of the father clearly served to intensify sexual feelings between the adolescent and his mother. It was also noted that the father of all the boys had some significant involvement in fires themselves, such as having been firemen or themselves having a history of fire setting.

Vandersall, T. A., and Wiener, J. M. "Children Who Set Fires." *Archives of General Psychiatry*, 1970, *22*, 63–71.

A study of twenty fire setters, ages four to eleven, revealed that all but one were boys. The fire setting was found to be but one of many symptoms of poor impulse control and a generalized behavior disturbance. There was no characteristic personality type or "typical" patient. Although many of the children expressed a sense of curiosity about fires and an impatience (could not wait to start a fire at a safe place), they were generally unproductive in discussing their reasons for setting fires or their feelings about the fire. A sense of exclusion, loneliness, and unfulfilled dependency needs were prominent. Immediate intervention demands not so much insight of underlying dynamics by the child but rather support and reinstitution of appropriate controls. All the children seemed to be experiencing at least a temporary breakdown of ego controls. Thus the fire setter seems to be a child with tenuous controls of his aggressive impulses rather than a child with sexual conflicts.

Welsh, R. S. "Stimulus Satiation as a Technique for the Elimination of Juvenile Fire-Setting Behavior." Paper presented at Eastern Psychological Association Convention, Washington, D.C., April 1968.

Welsh reports the use of stimulus satiation to remove the fire-setting behavior in a seven-year-old boy. The therapist brought in twenty boxes full of small wooden matches and asked the boy if he would like to learn how to properly light them. The boy agreed and was told how to close the cover before striking, how to hold it over an ashtray, and how to hold it until he felt its heat on his fingertips and then to blow it out. In the first forty-minute session, the boy went through a box and a half of matches. In the next session, the boy soon became restless and was allowed to do something else at the end of the session. The boy showed no interest in striking the matches at the next session and was allowed to play after striking ten matches. At home, the parents reported that the boy no longer seemed fascinated with fire play. The boy was seen in traditional play therapy for several more months, during which time the fire-setting behavior did not return.

Winget, C. N., and Whitman, R. M. "Coping with Problems: Attitudes Toward Children Who Set Fires." *American Journal of Psychiatry,* 1973, *130,* 442–445.

As part of an environmental health survey, 300 urban adults were asked how they would deal with a child who repeatedly set fires. Respondents who were young, of upper socioeconomic status, and with numerous interpersonal relationships and low degrees of alienation most frequently gave positive-constructive responses indicating the use of outside resources. However, only about one third specified mental health professionals. The authors note that, by and large, children are referred for treatment by the school or by the court, which, unlike the parents, see the fire setting as a serious presenting symptom.

Runaway Reaction

The "runaway reaction" is a fairly new diagnostic category. It is described as follows. "Individuals with this disorder characteristically escape from threatening situations by running away from home for a day or more without permission. Typically they are immature and timid, and feel rejected at home, inadequate, and friendless. They often steal furtively" (American Psychiatric Association. *Diagnostic and Statistical Manual of Mental Disorders.* (2nd ed.) Washington, D.C.: American Psychiatric Association, 1968).

Each year between 600,000 and 1,000,000 teen-agers run away from their American homes. Most of these youth are from white suburbs, at least half are females, and many are no older than thirteen or fourteen. Only drug abuse rivals the runaway reaction in importance as a mental health issue for teen-age Americans. Like drug abuse, running away has proven extremely difficult to understand and treat.

The Runaway Reaction

AUTHOR: Richard L. Jenkins

PRECIS: Attempts both to characterize the psychiatric diagnosis of runaway reaction and to suggest general treatment strategies

INTRODUCTION: According to Jenkins' research, the runaway reaction tends to be a frustration response of a hurt child who is convinced that he or she is not wanted at home. Parental rejection is a common background factor; these children tend to live with one or more foster parents or stepparents. Runaway children typically have a poor self-image and sense of worthlessness.

TREATMENT: Effective treatment involves extensive work with the family to modify the home environment. The parents must recognize and alter their continuing message to the child that he or she is not wanted. If family therapy fails, then removal from the home is indicated. These children need an extended period of resocialization in an accepting atmosphere. Gradually the child should receive increasing pressure for more responsible and mature behavior. In addition, the child's low self-esteem needs to be rebuilt through the feeling that he or she is valued and cherished by others. Once the child's fears diminish, one can expect an increase in hostile acting out. This aggressiveness must be controlled while the angry feelings are openly discussed.

COMMENTARY: Jenkins describes the distinctive personality and life history factors of three types of behavior disorders: runaway reaction, group delinquent reaction, and unsocialized aggressive reaction. His data clearly indicate that the runaway child has experienced more parental rejection than children with the other two disorders. Treatment is very difficult with the runaway child and involves extensive family work or a long period away from home for socialization in an accepting but firm environment. Unfortunately, Jenkins gives us a general rather than specific approach to treatment.

SOURCE: Jenkins, R. L. "The Runaway Reaction." *American Journal of Psychiatry,* 1971, *128,* 168–173.

A Family Perspective on Adolescent Runaways

AUTHOR: Helm Stierlin

PRECIS: Emphasizes the importance of understanding underlying family dynamics, especially covert parent-child interactions

INTRODUCTION: Stierlin states that to understand differing patterns of running away, one has to understand differing family dynamics. He finds the concept of "transactional modes" helpful in understanding family dynamics. These modes reflect the "interplay and/or relative dominance of centripetal and centrifugal pushes and pulls between generations" (p. 58). Transactional modes act as covert organizing factors to the more overt and specific child-parent interactions. The three major modes are binding, expelling, and delegating.

In the binding mode, parents try to keep their children bound to themselves. There are three ways to do this. In id-binding, the child's dependency needs are exploited and he is offered infantile gratifications by the parents. In ego-binding or cognitive binding, the parent forces the child to rely on distorted messages rather than allowing the child to think things through for himself. The superego-bound child, on the other hand, is kept on a chain by parental appeals to guilt and loyalty: These children are made to feel that separation from home is the number one crime, for which only the harshest of punishments will do.

The expelling mode prevails for neglected and rejected children who are perceived as nuisances and hindrances by their parents. Often the parents give their children material things but little investment of their own time. These children are forced into a premature separation.

The delegating mode represents a combination of binding and expelling pressures. The child is encouraged to move out of the parental orbit, but only to a limited degree. He is kept on a long leash. He is typically sent out to fulfill a parental ambition, such as becoming a famous artist.

TREATMENT: Since running away is only the surface manifestation of a family problem, treatment must focus on the underlying family relationships. With teenagers who are severely bound, that is, do not run away or else run away abortively, the main therapeutic task is to unbind them and their families. The therapist must try to understand and help loosen the psychological ties that keep these children in bondage. Often an adolescent's successful running away can signal progress rather than setback; that is, it reflects an increasing ability to live independently of the parents.

The expelled adolescent, on the contrary, needs to be held back or tamed by enduring concern and affection and the consistent setting of limits. Only by such long-term care will the runaway develop a sense of family loyalty.

When a delegating mode is present, the conflicting parental messages and missions need to be explored in depth with the family. The main therapeutic task here is to reconcile conflicts and obligations within the family. Typically, many of these runaways and their families respond well to therapeutic intervention.

COMMENTARY: In working with the families of runaways, one often uncovers and has to treat the underlying causes of unsuccessful separation by the children, such as mid-life crises of parents who are suddenly confronted with old age and approaching death; maladaptive marriage relationships that force parents to desperately cling to their children for love and support; and finally, unresolved conflicts between the child's parents and their own parents (a three-generation perspective is often needed to understand this problem).

SOURCE: Stierlin, H. "A Family Perspective on Adolescent Runaways." *Archives of General Psychiatry,* 1973, *29,* 56–62.

Additional Readings

Beyer, M., Holt, S. A., Reid, T. A., and Quinlan, D. M. "Runaway Youths: Families in Conflict." Paper presented at convention of the Eastern Psychological Association, Washington, D.C., May 1973.

An intensive study of a small group of runaways revealed that most of these youths came from broken homes and many were experiencing difficulty with their stepparents. About half the parents reported that they had had strong disagreements with the child for two years or longer. Conflict areas included number of nights allowed out and hours for returning home. Many of the runaways had a recent history of poor grades and absenteeism in school. In general, there was a strong suggestion that running away is a symptom of unstable and conflict-ridden family environments. Solutions lie in greater communication and understanding between parents and children, a willingness by both sides to accept some responsibility for the problem, and the development of a closer, more caring relationship between parents and child.

On the average, the runaways thought that the experience had been helpful, while their parents did not. The personality of the runaways was found to be impulsive (tended to do things on spur of the moment) and depressed (frequent feelings of unhappiness). Many adolescents run away primarily to escape from the home, while others leave to experiment with independence or to manipulate their parents into changes that would make the relationship more satisfactory.

Riemer, M. D. "Runaway Children." *American Journal of Orthopsychiatry*, 1940, *10*, 522–526.

Riemer reports that his experiences with runaway youth indicate that their most pressing need is to be loved by their parents. When thwarted in this need, many seek to "get even" by running away and thereby causing parental anguish and guilt.

4

Hyperkinetic Behavior

The word *hyperkinetic* literally means abnormally increased and usually uncontrolled, purposeless movement. This chapter divides hyperkinesia into three types of behaviors. Restless, hyperactive behavior clearly fits the literal description of hyperkinesia. Short attention span and impulsiveness and low frustration tolerance are related problems, but do not necessarily include excessive movement. These three categories of behavior have been linked together under many different labels. In a nationally sponsored definition of minimal brain dysfunction ten characteristics most cited in the literature were listed in order of frequency. Hyperactivity was first,

321

disorders of attention fifth, and impulsiveness sixth (S. D. Clements, *Minimal Brain Dysfunction in Children—Terminology and Identification,* Washington, D.C.: U.S. Department of Health, Education and Welfare, 1966). In the recent literature, children showing some combination of behaviors covered here have increasingly been :alled *learning disabled.* A continuing focus has been on the inferred physiological (neurological, biochemical, and so on) cause of learning disabilities or brain dysfunction. Many professionals believe that accepting the neurological basis of hyperkinetic behavior leads to tolerance and improves the attitudes of the children and adults around them. There is still a difference of opinion whether or not it is possible to diagnose a child's difficulty as caused by a central processing dysfunction (J. C. Chalfont and M. A. Scheffelin, *Central Processing Dysfunctions in Children: A Review of Research,* Washington, D.C.: U.S. Department of Health, Education and Welfare, 1969). The evidence points to the feasibility and desirability of fully evaluating children to pinpoint deficits in processing information and responding appropriately. Further research may greatly modify and improve our present methods of helping hyperkinetic children.

As in the rest of this book, the articles in this chapter arrange problematic behaviors and alternative approaches. The techniques employed may well diminish the behaviors in question and promote more adaptive, satisfying behavior. Most therapists would agree that even if the cause of the difficulty is physiological, treatment (behavior modification, counseling, drugs, hypnosis, and so forth) can still be effective.

The following articles report considerable success in improving hyperkinetic behavior, using very different methods. Although stimulant drugs have been used for many years, the evidence suggests that other approaches should be tried first. In many cases, drugs are not necessary, because the behavior can be controlled. Many different procedures based on learning theory principles are found to reduce hyperkinetic behavior (also see W. I. Gardner, *Children with Learning and Behavior Problems: A Behavior Management Approach,* Boston: Allyn & Bacon, 1974). There is general consensus that the teaching and maintaining of adaptive behavior and reduction of problem behavior are essential. Adaptive behavior is defined as purposeful, calm, attentive, reflective, and tolerant. Hypnosis, psychotherapy, and drugs are also reported to be effective. When behavior is not affected, although methods are well planned and followed through, drugs may be an invaluable asset, by helping the child respond to treatment procedures. The present consensus appears to be that when drugs are used, other psychological and educational methods should also be employed at the same time.

A recent study (see Stableford, Butz, Hasazi, Leitenberg, and Peyser, 1976) found that placebos were as effective as stimulant drugs in maintaining behavior that was not hyperactive. This indicates that the drug itself did not produce appropriate, controlled behavior. Therefore, even when drugs are used to reduce extreme behavior, natural consequences may soon maintain controlled behavior. Drugs might then be successfully discontinued in a very short time (rather than being administered for many years), by substituting placebos. Careful, thorough counseling might also be effective in preventing and/or reducing psychological dependency on drugs.

Because of the specificity required by article selection, the reader may gain the impression that individual or family psychotherapy is relatively ineffective. We would like to suggest that appropriate family discussions of a child's hyperkinetic behavior (and possible causes) may often improve the family atmosphere. More tolerant and accepting parental attitudes alone may lead to some improvement in behavior. We believe that better attitudes improve receptivity and use of the methods presented here. In addition, the many school-based approaches appear quite applicable to home use. Parents can employ many of the individual techniques with their child and can use the group approaches with siblings. We strongly urge that parents use methods similar to those being employed by the child's school. This type of consistency and coordination leads to quicker, more enduring improvement in hyperkinetic behavior. A simple and effective procedure is for parents to use some reinforcement system at home when the child shows improved behavioral control in school.

Restless, Hyperactive Behavior

The word restless *literally means "without rest" or "continuously moving." Whether or not restlessness is under a child's control has long been an issue. Restlessness has often been interpreted as caused by diffuse anxiety or an attempt to feel more at ease. Hyperactivity is excessive movement, going beyond a normal or acceptable limit. Excessive activity may either be caused by physiological factors or by learning (purposeful or inadvertent reinforcement). A child's avoidance behavior and attempt to reduce anxiety may contribute to hyperactivity. Recent research confirms that, regardless of cause of hyperactivity or restlessness, children can learn to slow down. Psychotropic drugs have long played a role in the treatment of these behaviors.*

Etiology and Intervention in Hyperactivity

AUTHORS: K. Bruce Bower and Cecil D. Mercer

PRECIS: Decreasing hyperactivity by reducing distractions, training verbal mediation skills, behavior modification, observational learning, and drugs

INTRODUCTION: In this article, Bower and Mercer consider various descriptions of the hyperkinetic syndrome—hyperactive, distractible, uninhibited, impulsive, erratic, and uncoordinated behavior. Developmentally hyperactive children show a level of usual motor activity clearly greater than normal. A central nervous system dysfunction or psychosis has not been present since infancy.

Drugs are recommended to reduce the energy level of children described as being constantly stimulated, having limited sustained effort, lacking common sense, and having biologically based hyperactivity. An environmental approach is needed for children who have developed a life-style of hyperkinesis in order to cope with their life situation. These children have a hyperreaction to an unstructured, unorganized environment of instability, inconsistency, and inappropriate rearing. When these children are motivated, they can display self-control and sustained effort.

ETIOLOGY: According to one physiological approach, malfunctioning of the ascending and descending reticular formation may cause hyperactivity. Sophisticated inner speech appears to be the regulator of inhibition and excitation. Another view is that immature cortical development may cause hyperactivity. Poor reality testing, poor control, and inadequate physical abilities are construed as subcortical behavior. The drug methylphenidate may stimulate the cortex and either increase cortical resistance to subcortical impulses or increase cortical control. Presumed storms of impulses caused by diencephalic dysfunction may be controlled by amphetamines, which reportedly increase synaptic resistance and normalize diencephalic functioning.

Another set of theories center on attention and motivation. Dextroamphetamine may energize children so that they are able to adequately observe and examine their environment. Increased ability to pay attention leads to decreased hyperactivity, distractibility, and impulsiveness. Several researchers feel that psychostimulants lengthen attention span and therefore diminish hyperactivity. Stimulants improve the quality of activity, not the amount of activity, which may actually increase. In early childhood, overactivity is considered a probable predictor of later concentration and attention difficulties.

According to reinforcement theory, hyperactive behavior is a result of environmental contingencies. Educational approaches are therefore appropriate to help the child unlearn this behavior. Hyperactive children should be taught to work persistently and stick to tasks.

ENVIRONMENTAL INTERVENTION: The environmental approach to intervention suggests, first, that the interest of the instructional material be enhanced and distracting stimuli reduced. Working in cubicles reportedly improves attention and academic performance. Secondly, verbal mediation helps decrease hyperactivity by training a child to say "stop, listen, look and think *before* I answer." By using this technique, the child achieves more and reduces errors.

Third, operant conditioning has been found to be effective in lowering hyperactivity. One study used a variety of reinforcers contingent on at least twenty seconds of appropriate behavior. Destructive behavior of a six-year-old child was significantly diminished. Highly distractible, disruptive ten- to thirteen-year-olds earned incentives of recess, free time activities, special privileges, group lunch, and teacher attention. Arithmetic and reading improved, especially with the addition of payment for weekly grades. Successful operant conditioning is reported for not remaining seated, temper tantrums, uncontrolled laughter, moving out of location, and so on. These reports suggest that environmental manipulation be tried before drug therapy is employed.

Fourth, reflective teacher models have been successfully used to reduce impulsiveness in first-graders. A reflective model shown on film resulted in lower impulsiveness with fourth-graders. Peer models have been successfully used to influence various inappropriate behaviors. The models gave tokens for appropriate behavior to the child with whom they had been paired.

MEDICAL INTERVENTION: Stimulants reportedly have an alerting effect on the central nervous system, enabling the child to control his behavior and benefit from learning experiences. Inattentive behavior and number of punishments for disruption are reduced and more positive interaction occurs with the teacher. Dextroamphetamine, methylphenidate, and magnesium pemoline have led to positive changes in classroom behavior. Amphetamine sulfate is said to be more effective in many cases than dextroamphetamine sulfate. Reduced motor activity caused by administration of stimultants is reported in many studies.

Reports on the use of tranquilizers indicate that improved behavior is often accompanied by a deterioration in performance. Phenothiazines, for example, have led to impaired ability to attend and plan.

COMMENTARY: Drug intervention is clearly recommended only when other interventions have failed (it is incumbent on the therapist to ensure that real, not half-hearted or inadequately thought out, intervention has occurred). The environmental interventions described in the article may be effective, depending on the sophistication and coordination of efforts. Drugs or the four environmental interventions, with some modification, have been used for restlessness, short attention span, impulsiveness, and low frustration tolerance; with some modification, have been used with habit disorders, antisocial behaviors, and disturbed relations with peers and adults.

SOURCE: Bower, K. B., and Mercer, C. D. "Hyperactivity: Etiology and Intervention Techniques." *The Journal of School Health*, 1975, *45*, 195–202.

Methods in Child Psychotherapy and Restlessness in an Eleven-Year-Old Boy

AUTHOR: Sylvia Brody

PRECIS: Psychoanalytically oriented psychotherapy for increasing reality testing and reducing restlessness

INTRODUCTION: Brody defines child psychotherapy as psychoanalytically oriented treatment of neurotic symptoms, emotional distress, and anxiety. In such therapy, the most relevant unconscious conflicts are interpreted. The usual duration of treatment is two to three years, with sessions one to three times per week. Brody contrasts this approach to long-term psychoanalysis.

PSYCHOTHERAPY PRINCIPLES: Brody considers the applicability to children of the following adult psychotherapy principles.

1. *The therapist is a "real object" and deals with present realities.* The therapist may become "real" to a child by occasionally allowing himself to be childlike. At the same time, the therapist must be more accepting and stronger than other adults. The child is often not interested in insight into his own behavioral patterns; dealing with present realities requires much tact or the child may oppose treatment.

2. *The therapist relies on direct speech and responds actively. Expression of thought and feeling is supported, encouraged, and clarified.* The therapist learns from the child's indirect expressive behavior. The child is encouraged to verbalize his thoughts. Brody suggests caution against premature interpretations of play behavior. Transference reactions that occur must be dealt with delicately. Compared with adults, however, children's transference reactions are milder, irregular, and transient. Brody feels that support, advice, and reassurance are valid techniques, but warns that the child often distorts or misuses the information thus given. A direct verbal relationship and supportive help are therefore unreliable with children.

3. *The therapist does not interfere with useful defenses.* The therapist must employ educative efforts carefully, because it is tempting

to avoid a defense analysis with children. The child's weak defenses must be fortified, while rigid defenses are eased. The therapist does not tamper with strong, useful defenses, but does work on pathological defenses (identification with an aggressor, isolation, destructive projection, and paralyzing reaction formations).

4. *The therapist deals with the dynamic, not genetic, material.* Past, causative experiences are not probed or dwelled on. Yet the genetic determinants (the origin of the unconscious conflicts) must be understood if dynamic progress is to be made without resistances repeatedly interfering.

Brody feels that adult psychotherapy principles are awkward in applications to children, with whom the essential aim is to make more psychic energy available, by systematic interpretations of unconscious ideas and conflicts. It is a significant achievement when a child gains insight into patterns of reacting and feeling that have been ineffective. Brody discusses three psychotherapeutic goals: increasing the child's capacity for reality testing, strengthening object relations, and loosening fixations.

One of Brody's cases is presented here to illustrate the first goal, increasing the capacity for reality testing. The therapist encourages the child to examine his responses to the environment. Concrete demonstrations are used to help him perceive his distorted views, misperceptions, and unfounded ideas. The child may make better judgments and see his own role in his difficulties.

CASE STUDY: Physical restlessness caused serious school failure in an intelligent, agreeable, eleven-year-old boy, who sat still only when eating or reading science fiction. In therapy, he often talked about his satisfying fantasies about outer space and mysterious journeys, revealing his dread of reality. Brody describes his family difficulties in detail. He was worried about possibly having to take sides with one of his divorced parents and worried about a possible breakup of his father's second marriage. The therapist made several interpretations regarding his anger, fear, and worry about his parents' behavior. Reportedly, his restlessness was related to sexual fantasies. The insight he thus gained was seen as helping him to give up a dependent relationship to classmates and to have valid criti-

cisms of them. After twelve months, treatment was terminated. He
was then near the top of his class in grades.

COMMENTARY: It is difficult to adequately review articles based
on psychoanalytic psychotherapy, because specific interpretations
are often not given in detail. Brody believes that poor school performance caused by restlessness can be improved by using general
psychotherapeutic principles. The concept of increasing reality
testing was the aim of treatment used in the case presented. While
other approaches reported in this book deal more directly with reducing restless behavior, Brody reports that psychoanalytic psychotherapy is applicable to all behavior disorders covered here.

SOURCE: Brody, S. "Aims and Methods in Child Psychotherapy."
   Journal of the American Academy of Child Psychiatry, 1964, *3,*
   385–412.

Reducing Overactive Behavior

AUTHORS: Steve G. Doubros and Gary J. Daniels

PRECIS: Reducing hyperactivity by using tokens (exchangeable for toys) as differential reinforcers

INTRODUCTION: Retarded children are often overactive—especially those with a central nervous system defect. The children are behaviorally erratic, driven, uninhibited, catastrophically anxious, and perseverative. Their motor or verbal overactivity leads to poor social discriminations and inappropriate and disruptive behavior. Doubros and Daniels conducted a study with six hyperactive, retarded eight- to thirteen-year-old boys.

DIFFERENTIAL REINFORCEMENT: Conditioning sessions lasted ten minutes. Instructions to the children included a statement that they could play with any of the toys available in the therapy room and that when they heard a clanking noise they would get a token for doing well. Tokens were to be exchanged for candy at the end of each session. The experimenter then left, saying to the boys that the more tokens they received the more candy they would get (the experimenter observed from behind a one-way screen). Toys consisted of quiet-type and noisy playthings, puzzles, and drawing materials. Hyperactive behavior was recorded in order to assess effectiveness of the program. Four categories of hyperactivity were used: stationary (scratching, shuffling feet, and so on); locomotive (walking, climbing, crawling, and so on); destructive (kicking, throwing, pounding, and so on); and communication (shouting, whistling, and so on).

Reinforcement was given on a differential reinforcement schedule of other behavior, requiring thirty seconds of continued absence of any hyperactive behavior. The first interval during a session required only fifteen seconds to receive a token. The intervals later in a session increased to forty-five, sixty, seventy-five, then ninety seconds (at the forty-second session). Constructive use of time during the absence of hyperactive behavior was reinforced.

During all ten-minute sessions, there was no one in the room with the child. When the token dispenser emitted a token, a buzzer and a light were activated.

The boys' continuous use of many toys one after another was considerably reduced after conditioning. Follow-up revealed less than one-third the number of hyperactive responses present before conditioning. Verbal and motor overactivity were similarly reduced. The most hyperactive boys showed the most dramatic improvement in behavior.

COMMENTARY: Although retarded children participated in this study, the procedure described by Doubros and Daniels has been used with nonretarded children (especially children with "learning disabilities"). Traditional play therapy does not provide for a systematic reinforcement of nonhyperactive and constructive play, although many therapists have naturally employed social praise for constructive behavior. The technique used (tokens and toy exchange) could be used in individual or group sessions. Groups could be reinforced for nonhyperactive, socially cooperative behavior. Systematic differential reinforcement appears applicable for habit disorders, antisocial behaviors, and disturbed relationships with peers and adults. This article presents a simple, effective means of reducing hyperactive behavior. With imagination and modification, the approach may be used to diminish a wide range of specific, inappropriate behavior and to promote constructive, more personally satisfying behavior.

SOURCE: Doubros, S. G., and Daniels, G. J. "An Experimental Approach to the Reduction of Overactive Behavior." *Behaviour Research and Therapy*, 1966, *4*, 251–258.

Overcorrection of Inappropriate Behavior in Hyperactive Children

AUTHORS: Leonard H. Epstein, Larry A. Doke, Thomas E. Sajwaj, Sue Sorrell, and Betty Rimmer

PRECIS: Correcting inappropriate, annoying bodily movements by practicing voluntary movement

INTRODUCTION: The authors feel that overcorrection produces lasting behavioral change, is applicable in many situations, and is convenient and acceptable to most adults. They distinguish between two types of overcorrection. Restitutional overcorrection requires correcting consequences of misbehavior to a better-than-usual state. Thus a child who marks a wall would have to wash all of the walls in the room. Positive practice overcorrection requires performing correct behaviors in the same area of misbehavior. A child marking a wall would have to perform appropriate pencil-and-paper tasks requiring marking. The two forms of overcorrection may be combined. With behaviors that do not disrupt others (self-stimulation), positive practice overcorrection alone may be used. The authors feel this punishment method is quite beneficial and demonstrate that positive side effects occur.

POSITIVE PRACTICE OVERCORRECTION: Two overly active boys (five and eight years) (both diagnosed as schizophrenic) were treated with overcorrection methods. The five-year-old was hyperactive and had motor, verbal, and self-help deficits. Repetitive vocal and motor behaviors interfered with his progress. Time out and instructions had not helped. The authors categorized pounding objects with his hands as inappropriate hand movement and kicking the floor or any objects as inappropriate foot movements.

The eight-year-old made many self-stimulating, interfering hand movements and made disruptive verbal noises. Instructions and time out when these behaviors occurred had not been successful. Baseline behavior and posttreatment behavior were recorded by observers, using the categories of inappropriate hand movements, inappropriate foot movements and positions, inappropriate vocalizations, and appropriate play with toys.

For hand overcorrection, the misbehavior was described to the child and overcorrecting followed. For example, the child was told he was rubbing his face and was then asked to put his hands at his sides, over his head, in front, together, and behind his back. If the child did not respond, the adult physically aided the child to perform. Each behavior was held for fifteen seconds. The same type of overcorrection was used for inappropriate vocalization.

For foot overcorrection, the boy was seated and instructed to lift his feet and hold his legs parallel to the floor for five seconds. In this study, this procedure was used for two minutes on each occasion.

Significant improvement for both boys was observed in the categories of inappropriate hand and foot movements and vocalizations. As inappropriate behavior decreased, appropriate play with toys increased. Procedures used included telling the child about his misbehavior (feedback), stopping his activity (time out), giving instructions, forcing practice of desirable behavior, and returning the child to his activity. The improvements generalized to more appropriate behavior during free play periods.

COMMENTARY: Overcorrection appears to be a simple, effective means of modifying inappropriate behavior. For many therapists, restitutional overcorrection may have negative connotations, particularly in appearing overly punitive and in using children to do work such as cleaning. Positive practive overcorrection has the advantage of being both self-correction and self-improvement. The child learns to perform a task related to his misbehavior, but to do so in a volitional manner. This is in keeping with the goals of developing self-control and helping the child be more concretely aware of both inappropriate and appropriate behavior. Increasingly, practice and rehearsal play key roles in increasing volitional (non-helpless) behavior in children. Used in a creative manner, overcorrection may be applicable to a wide range of dysfunctional, ineffective behaviors.

SOURCE: Epstein, L. H., Doke, L. A., Sajwaj, T. E., Sorrell, S., and Rimmer, B. "Generality and Side Effects of Overcorrection." *Journal of Applied Behavior Analysis,* 1974, 7, 385–390.

Hypnotic Suggestions with Hyperactive Children

AUTHORS: Joseph Illovsky and Norman Fredman

PRECIS: Use of audiotaped group hypnotic suggestions to enhance concentration, academic motivation, and concern for others in six- to eight-year-olds

INTRODUCTION: Learning to read can be impeded by hyperactivity, short attention span, difficulty in following instructions, and low self-confidence. Illovsky and Fredman report that hypnosis has been successfully used with older children and young adults to improve relaxation, grades, study habits, motivation, and concentration. For this study, forty-eight hyperactive children, ages six to eight, were selected to receive hypnotic training. Children with perceptual distortions, thought disorders, and serious visual or auditory problems were not included. Criteria for inclusion consisted of short attention span, distractibility, and acting-out behavior.

HYPNOTIC TRAINING: A tape was prepared using two types of suggestions—learning and coping with emotional problems (Illovsky and Fredman present a verbatim description of the tape). The group hypnotic methods were intended to increase motivation and concentration. On each of fifty-five mornings, the children listened to the tape for fifteen minutes. They were told that they would learn to relax so they would be more able to learn. A large dot was placed on the wall. A monotonous voice told them to lean back and look at the dot. Instructions included eyelids getting heavier and heavier and finally closing. A feeling of relaxation was suggested, including a deepening by counting. They were asked to visualize pleasant scenes (watching clouds and so on). Suggestions for nice feelings and deeper relaxation were frequently made.

The children were also asked to think of bad things that have happened and to imagine better ways of coping. It was suggested that people often do not do things to hurt the children, but for other motivations. At various points in the tape, the children were encouraged to talk to, learn from, and be nice to others. It was suggested that sadness and anger leave when good things are thought about.

A suggestion was made that the children would think and dream about the advantages of learning in school and at home. Learning was said to make one feel good—while reading, they would feel nice and calm and would want to read and learn more. Concentration was enhanced by stressing the need to think about the material in front of them. They were then told that they would feel more and more awake as the voice counted from one to five.

Illovsky and Fredman are cautious about many variables that could affect this study. However, they report significant improvement on teacher evaluations for desire to learn, self-confidence, attention span, following directions, and reading. Restlessness was the only area not significantly improved. Students who attained a greater number of relaxations or a higher percentage of relaxations showed increased attention span.

COMMENTARY: This article demonstrates the feasibility of using group hypnotic techniques with children in primary grades. Efficiency was achieved by being able to use tapes with groups of children, so costs are low. Therapists might consider using tapes in individual therapy and devising their own suggestions tailored to their patient. Suggestions, while in relaxed states or not, have been successfully used with children. It is noteworthy that the content of the tape presented clearly focuses on the positive aspects of learning and social interaction. Many therapists suggest to children that more positive attitudes and behavior can lead to being liked more and to more personal happiness. Cognitively oriented approaches specifically emphasize a more logical, positive approach to learning, attitudes, and general behavior.

SOURCE: Illovsky, J., and Fredman, N. "Group Suggestion in Learning Disabilities of Primary Grade Children: A Feasibility Study." *The International Journal of Clinical and Experimental Hypnosis,* 1976, *24,* 87–97.

Controlling Hyperactivity

AUTHOR: Walter A. Luszki

PRECIS: Reducing hyperactivity by restraint, providing a safe retreat, and arranging appropriate school and outdoor activities

INTRODUCTION: Luszki discusses practical methods that parents and teachers can use with brain-damaged hyperactive children. Hyperactive children are characterized by demandingness, unpredictability, short attention span, distractibility, impulsiveness, difficulty with unstructured situations, perseveration, aggression, absence of fear, unresponsiveness to punishment, and lack of empathy. In school, the hyperactive child rarely sits still or finishes assignments.

CONTROL METHODS: Control is achieved by rewarding desirable behaviors and punishing undesirable behaviors. Punishments discussed by Luszki are removal of privileges and spanking immediately after every inappropriate behavior. Parental tolerance is called for, because hyperactive children lag in developing the usual skills and controls of childhood.

Restraint. For extremely hyperactive children, Luszki recommends methods that, he warns, may appear harsh or punitive. Using a seat belt at a stationary desk is one means of control. When restrained, the child is told that the purpose is to help him, not harm him. Luszki suggests that a seat belt be introduced positively, as something used by pilots and race car drivers.

A Retreat. Since parents may react with aggression to uncontrolled, overly active, annoying destructive behavior on the part of their child, Luszki suggests methods to prevent the escalating of anger. He recommends establishing a protected area at home and in school and describes details of such a "retreat" area. When overly active or under stress, the child can go to the retreat room to play undisturbed. Luszki suggests inside screens to protect windows, a blackboard attached to a wall, and colored chalk. The floor should be covered with thick matting.

The retreat room should have a positive, not punitive, conno-
tation. Parents should spend time there playing with the child. Toys
selected for the room ought to be rugged and provide for motor
release. Mechanical toys are not recommended. Water colors, clay,
crayons, charcoal, sand, large block sets, a sturdy dollhouse, and
wooden trains are suggested. Discarded pans and other kitchen
equipment may be used.

Outdoor Activities at Home. Relaxing long walks with the child
can be calming. A fenced yard with sandbox, swings, slide, and
ladder is conducive to active play. In warm weather, a hose, sprin-
kler, wading pool, and sand provide outlets. Digging and pounding
with a rubber hammer are highly recommended. Appropriate
chores include watering, raking leaves, shoveling snow, sweeping,
and washing the family car.

School Activities. In classrooms, order is often provided by
cubicles. Routines are spelled out and structure is clearly set and
adhered to. Luszki suggests a "retreat" room at school, where children may spend time appropriately. Children may also be sent to
spend time with a physical education teacher in the gym. Appropriate chores at school include cleaning with large sponges and sand-
ing wooden surfaces. Coordination games can be used, in which
children throw crumpled paper or bean bags into a wastepaper
basket.

COMMENTARY: Luszki makes many specific suggestions for practical approaches to coping with very hyperactive children. Therapists who provide parent counseling should become familiar with
a variety of specific child-rearing activities. Some readers may dis-
agree with the methods presented here (however, see the article
for other suggestions). Control techniques are often controversial,
especially when coping with hyperactive children. In our experience, some of the control techniques have been positively accepted
and have surprisingly improved behavior and lessened hyperactivity. Use of a retreat for letting off steam has been particularly
effective.

SOURCE: Luszki, W. A. "Controlling the Brain-Damaged Hyperactive Child." *Journal of Learning Disabilities,* 1968, *1,* 672–680.

Drugs for Hyperkinetic and Perceptually Handicapped Children

AUTHOR: J. Gordon Millichap

PRECIS: Assessing hyperkinesis by using an actometer, electro-encephalogram, and treatment with stimulant, antianxiety, antipsychotic, and anticonvulsant drugs

INTRODUCTION: Hyperactivity is estimated to affect 4 percent of school children and 40 percent of children referred to mental health clinics for behavior problems. Hyperkinetic children have short attention and concentration spans and often engage in unfocused, irrelevant activity. The problems are caused by their impulsiveness and restlessness. They are often seen as spoiled, impolite, and odd. Approximately 50 percent of hyperkinetic children have abnormal electroencephalograms and some have identifiable convulsive disorders. Inability to concentrate may be related to petit mal seizures. Motor hyperactivity and learning difficulties may be improved by drugs. When hyperactivity is reduced, attention, memory, perception, and coordination should improve. Hyperkinetic behavior either may be identified in infancy or may only become noticed when school begins.

EVALUATION: Excessive motor activity can be readily reported by parents and school and observed in the examining room. An actometer can be easily used to measure amount of movement (the child wears the device on the ankle or wrist). Millichap recommends standard intelligence tests, achievement tests, various psychometric tests, and completion of a behavior rating scale. Unevenness of performance may reflect a specific learning disability or distractibility and impulsiveness. A neurological examination (including an electroencephalogram) is required, often in consultation with a pediatric neurologist. Common abnormalities include inability to maintain posture or gaze, poor finger-to-nose coordination, poor alternate arm movements, gait ataxia, and poor hopping skills. In addition, the child may exhibit Babinski responses, involuntary movement of outstretched arms, and speech disorders.

Stimulant Drugs. Methylphenidate is the treatment of choice, followed by dextroamphetamine sulfate in degree of success. Millichap considers deanol acetamidobenzoate of dubious value. The initial dose of methylphenidate is .25 mg per kg of body weight daily, half before breakfast and half before lunch. Each succeeding week, the dosage is doubled up to 2 mg per kg of body weight daily. Responses should be carefully monitored by parents and teachers and by reexamination of the child after two to four weeks. Short-term trials (four to eight weeks) are suggested. Recommended dextroamphetamine daily dosages are .25 mg/kg initially, to 1.0 mg/kg.

Antianxiety and Antipsychotic Agents. In studies reported by Millichap, hyperkinetic behavior was improved in 60 percent of children with chlordiazepoxide or chlorpromazine. Less effective was reserpine (34 percent improved). Promazine hydrochloride was not found to be effective. Chlordiazepoxide (.25 to 1.0 mg/kg daily) is recommended if a stimulant causes increased activity.

Anticonvulsants. The effects of anticonvulsants are difficult to judge, because they are primarily used with hyperkinetic children who also have convulsive seizures. Primidone has been effective, but phenobarbital has variable effects and may increase hyperactivity. More studies are called for to evaluate diphenylhydantoin sodium.

COMMENTARY: In contrast to other views, Millichap considers an electroencephalogram to be a necessary part of a medical examination, stating that 50 percent of all hyperkinetic children have abnormal electroencephalograms. He views drugs as adjuncts to remedial education and carefully and clearly recommends only short-term use of drugs. If behavior rating scales were not only used as part of the evaluative procedure, but were also used in assessing effectiveness of drugs, parents and teachers would then have a formal method of recording their behavioral observations and providing feedback to the physician. A device, such as the actometer, to measure the amount of activity to provide feedback should be widely used.

SOURCE: Millichap, J. G. "Drugs in Management of Hyperkinetic and Perceptually Handicapped Children." *Journal of the American Medical Association,* 1968, *206,* 1527–1530.

Individual and Group Consequences for Hyperactive Children

AUTHORS: Alan Rosenbaum, K. Daniel O'Leary, and Rolf G. Jacob

PRECIS: Reducing hyperactivity in eight- to twelve-year-old boys with individual or group rewards of candy

INTRODUCTION: The authors note that, because the symptoms are ambiguous, reports by parents and teachers (without a necessary evaluation of the child) have been used in diagnosing a child as hyperactive. Stimulant drugs have been used successfully but entail some negative physical and psychological side effects. One study indicated that combining drugs and behavior modification resulted in more effective treatment than obtained by using drugs alone. Rosenbaum, O'Leary, and Jacob discuss and cite studies concerning group rewards and group contingencies. Group rewards provide peer approval of appropriate behavior and may lead to peer reinforcement after group rewards are withdrawn. Ten hyperactive boys (ages eight to twelve) were carefully selected to participate in this study of the effectiveness of behavioral intervention, comparing group and individual rewards.

METHODS: Rosenbaum, O'Leary, and Jacob explained the principles of the two programs to the teachers and gave them a package including a manual, materials, and suggestions for proceeding. Back-up reinforcers were to be penny candies. One experimenter met with each teacher to select an appropriate target behavior for each boy, such as completing work, staying in seat, and no fighting.

In the individual reward group, the teacher explained the program privately to each boy; no one else knew about the arrangement. For example, a teacher told a boy that he had trouble sitting still and concentrating and that he had been selected for a special program that would help him to do better. The teacher explained the rules to the boy and gave him a reward card at the end of each hour, which showed whether or not the rules were followed. Each reward card was exchanged for candy at the end of the school day.

In the group reward format, the teacher discussed the program with the boy and his class together. For example, it was announced that all present knew that the boy in question was having trouble sitting still and completing his work and that a special program would be used to help him work better. The teacher read the rules and explained that if he followed the rules he would receive a reward card at the end of each hour. For each card he received, everyone would receive a piece of candy at the end of the day. The class was told that they could help by ignoring his bad behavior and by telling him when he was working or behaving well. A chart was drawn on the blackboard and rewards were recorded for all to see.

For both individual or group reward formats, the teacher repeated the rules each morning. After each four-hour day, the child received a reward card if the rating was positive. If the child did not receive a card, the teacher verbally emphasized any positive behavior and told the boys that they could earn cards in the future. Teachers used their judgment in awarding cards regarding progress and effort and gradually raised the criteria. After cards had been given for four weeks, the boys were told that they were doing well and were expected to continue to behave well, even though there was no more candy left.

Various measures were used to assess program effectiveness. The teachers were significantly more pleased with the group method. Group reward was considered moderately more effective than individual award, but statistical significance was not reached. Both methods led to significant reduction in hyperactivity, which was maintained for four weeks after reinforcement was discontinued.

COMMENTARY: Both group and individual rewards offer alternatives to drug therapy for hyperactive children. Many behaviors involved in hyperactivity are annoying (and can lead to negative feedback) to peers as well as to adults. In addition to providing reinforcement, peer pressure may aid the child to control his behavior. However, the group may have to be prevented from ostracizing or punishing the child if he does not succeed. The classroom climate can be very positively influenced by the emphasis on having the group ignore bad behavior and praise appropriate behavior. Reducing negative feedback helps the child feel less negative about himself. The teacher's open statement that "we are all trying to help a student with difficulties" may in itself promote a helping, more positive atmosphere.

SOURCE: Rosenbaum, A., O'Leary, K. D., and Jacob, R. G. "Behavioral Intervention with Hyperactive Children: Group Consequences as a Supplement to Individual Contingencies." *Behavior Therapy*, 1975, *6*, 315–323.

Reducing Hyperactivity by Music

AUTHOR: Thomas J. Scott

PRECIS: Background music to promote calmness and enhance academic functioning of seven- to eleven-year-old boys

INTRODUCTION: Scott describes hyperactive children as frenzied and directionless—characteristics that prevent purposeful exploration and repetitive acts. Drugs, operant conditioning, and control of stimulus level have been used to reduce hyperactivity and enhance learning. Reducing extraneous stimulation has promoted learning and diminished hyperactivity. Working in a small booth has helped many children. In this study, Scott reports that background music had a calming effect on four seven- to eleven-year-old boys in a special classroom. The boys were disruptive, provocative, and mildly to moderately hyperactive.

METHOD: Four different conditions were used in a standardly equipped room that also contained three-sided booths. When seated in the booths, the children could not see, but could hear, each other. The conditions were (1) normal seating in the open area, (2) normal, with background music, (3) working in booths, (4) working in booths, with background music. The music was played at a normal listening level and consisted of music the boys liked—The Beatles' albums *Sergeant Pepper's Lonely Hearts Club Band* and *Magical Mystery Tour.*

The dependent variable described was completion of arithmetic problems within the ability of each child, in a ten-minute period. The three special conditions resulted in better functioning than did the normal situation; three boys did best under the normal condition with music. Scott notes the need to further analyze effects of music, but concludes that activity is not just a function of stimulus level. The teacher involved in the study continued to use background music because she thought it useful; moreover, the boys requested music.

COMMENTARY: Although his findings are far from thoroughly verified, Scott's article is presented here because of the provocative nature of those findings. Many professionals have been dissatisfied with having only an option of reducing stimuli for hyperactive children. Some theorists have even called for increasing stimuli in a controlled manner. Music may provide pleasing additional stimuli that helps hyperactive children apply their skills better. Others may need lowered stimulation or enhanced stimulation of a different type. Background music for brief periods may also have a calming effect for children with other behavior problems.

SOURCE: Scott, T. J. "The Use of Music to Reduce Hyperactivity in Children." *American Journal of Orthopsychiatry,* 1970, *40,* 677–680.

Behavior Therapy or Stimulant Drugs for Hyperactivity

AUTHORS: William Stableford, Robert Butz, Joseph Hasazi, Harold Leitenberg, and Janis Peyser

PRECIS: Maintaining nonhyperactive behavior by using positive reinforcement and substituting placebos for stimulant drugs

INTRODUCTION: Stimulant drugs (mainly methylphenidate and dextroamphetamine) have often not been effective with a segment of the hyperactive child population. The authors of this study discuss the negative side effects of some drugs, such as anorexia, insomnia, suppression of growth rate, increased activity, and psychosis. Moreover, placebos have been found to be effective in controlling hyperactivity in some children. The authors state that group studies mask effects on individual children. They discuss positive reports of reducing hyperactivity with conditioning techniques and by combining conditioning and drugs. Two hyperactive boys (eight and eleven years old) were treated by using a design permitting analysis of interactive effects of drugs, placebo, and behavior therapy.

CASE STUDY 1: An eight-year-old boy had been taking methylphenidate for several months (10 mg at breakfast and 5 mg in the afternoon). The goal of treatment was to reduce dosage because he behaved well at school but was dreamy and lacked his usual vitality. Expectations that he was calm when taking the drug and hyperactive when not had developed by teachers and the boy. When not taking the drug, the boy was considered disruptive, uncooperative, and overactive.

An observer periodically rated his behavior, using the categories of out-of-seat, on-task, appropriate, and inappropriate behavior. The boy and his teachers were unaware of the gradual substitution of placebos at the rate of a reduction of 5 mg/week. After five weeks, all pills were terminated and a behavior therapy program implemented. The boy now carried a "behavior rating card" that listed five specific satisfactory and five unsatisfactory behaviors. The teacher placed a star for satisfactory behavior or an X for unsatisfactory behavior on the card. Two out of three satisfactory ratings resulted in a selected treat (free time, candy, and so on) for the whole class at the end of the day. The boy voluntarily changed the criterion to three out of three satisfactory ratings. In addition, teachers were instructed to ignore inappropriate behavior and to socially reinforce on-task and appropriate behavior.

A high percentage of on-task and appropriate behavior continued throughout the substitution of placebos. During the fifth week, when all pills were terminated, a significant worsening of behavior occurred, suggesting that the placebo effect had occurred and that appropriate behavior may have been a function of taking pills. Institution of the behavior modification program during the sixth week resulted in the same high rate of appropriate behavior as previously recorded.

CASE STUDY 2: A hyperactive eleven-year-old boy was taking 25 mg of dextroamphetamine/day for three years (15 mg at breakfast and 10 mg after school). Reduction in dosage was desired. Observations made were relatively similar to the first study, with the addition of a home-based behavioral program and observations by the mother. His mother awarded points each day for specified helpful or calm behavior. Points were subtracted for specific negative behaviors. Each morning, the points were exchanged for money at a set rate. After twenty-five days of the home behavior program, drug dosage was reduced by 5 mg/week, placebos being substituted. In school, behavior remained much the same through placebo substitution; some variability was reported, but behavior returned to usual by the end of the week. At home, the point system was effective and drug reduction did not affect improved home behavior.

COMMENTARY: The authors conclude that neither boys needed drugs to control hyperactive behavior. Both the children and significant adults appeared to have become dependent on pill taking. The authors acknowledge the possibility that drugs may be necessary in specific cases, but feel that each case must be considered individually. Behavior therapy should be considered where applicable and where adult cooperation exists. Recently, more professionals are advocating the use of behavioral methods before drugs are administered. Success with such methods would then obviate the need for drugs and the possible negative side effects. The use of placebos to gradually reduce dosage, with or without instituting a behavioral reinforcement program, is promising. When children or adults have come to rely on drugs, placebo substitution may be used to reduce or eliminate drugs while the effects are assessed. It cannot be stressed too strongly that one key to successful use of this method is an accurate, reliable assessment of behavioral change. Independent observers, such as parents or high school or college students, can be successfully employed to sample behavior. Volunteers are usually readily available to help.

SOURCE: Stableford, W., Butz, R., Hasazi, J., Leitenberg, H., and Peyser, J. "Sequential Withdrawal of Stimulant Drugs and Use of Behavior Therapy with Two Hyperactive Boys." *American Journal of Orthopsychiatry*, 1976, *46*, 302–312.

Additional Readings

Ayllon, T., Layman, D., and Kandel, H. "A Behavioral-Educational Alternative to Drug Control of Hyperactive Children." *Journal of Applied Behavior Analysis*, 1975, *8*, 137–146.

The authors replaced drugs with contingency management techniques to control hyperactivity and improve academic performance. Token reinforcement was used for correct responses of three children (ages eight, nine, and ten) in math and reading. Check marks on an index card were exchanged for items priced at from one to seventy-five check marks. Items and activities used as back-up reinforcers included candy, school supplies, free time, lunch in the teacher's room, and picnics in the park. Reinforcing academic performance helped suppress hyperactivity. The academic gains produced by the reinforcement contrasted dramatically with the children's lack of academic progress when receiving medication.

Christensen, D. E. "Effects of Combining Methylphendiate and a Classroom Token System in Modifying Hyperactive Behavior." *American Journal of Mental Deficiency*, 1975, *80*, 266–276.

Sixteen hyperactive, institutionalized retarded children (nine to fifteen years old) were studied, using a combination of a drug (ritalin) and a behavioral management program. Management procedures included a token reinforcement system, contingent teacher attention and praise, rules, and educational class structure. Checks were marked on a sheet taped to each desk. Target behaviors included paying attention during group lesson, working hard, completing assigned work, and doing work correctly. The attained goal was reduction of hyperactive and deviant behavior by strengthening work-oriented, prosocial behavior. Addition of the drug did *not* enhance the effects of the management procedures.

Douglas, V. I. "Are Drugs Enough? To Treat or To Train the Hyperactive Child." *International Journal of Mental Health,* 1975, *41*, 199–212.

Douglas cites evidence for the short-term effectiveness of methylphenidate on problems of attention and impulsiveness. She feels that drugs may give a child the experience of being controlled and may enhance the learning of self-control. Douglas considers various behavioral methods effective and quite promising— for example, (1) verbalizing effective problem-solving strategies to oneself (planning, stopping to think, being careful); (2) film models who verbalize and demonstrate scanning strategies; (3) teaching selective attention with cutouts; and (4) training children to stop and take into account the intentions of others (and therefore to make better judgments).

Eisenberg, L. "The Management of the Hyperkinetic Child." *Developmental Medicine and Child Neurology,* 1966, *8*, 593–598.

Eisenberg considers essential a thorough pediatric, neurological, and psychological examination of the overactive child, as well as an assessment of the child's personality, family dynamics, and community resources. Drug therapy is appropriate, especially the use of the stimulants dextroamphetamine and methylphenidate. Somewhat less effective are diphenydramine and chlorpromazine. The environment should be reordered to permit external behavioral control, which allows the child to internalize what is learned. Eisenberg gives examples of parent counseling, in which persistent, consistent reinforcement is suggested.

Gerstein, A. I. "Variations in Treatment Technique in Group Activity Therapy." *Psychotherapy: Theory, Research and Practice,* 1974, *11*, 343–345.

Gerstein discusses activity groups for "ego-impaired" boys from eleven to thirteen years of age. Such boys may or may not be diagnosed as having organic brain damage, but they are frequently hyperkinetic and have poor fine and gross motor coordination and visual-motor impairments. Sessions are divided into group discussion and a physical activity or woodworking. The therapist promotes understanding of social responsibility and causal relationships. He aids boys who have difficulty with planning ahead or with self-control. Neatness and control are emphasized. The rules of any game or activity that is played are discussed with the therapist acting as referee.

Lambert, N. M., Windmiller, M., Sandoval, J., and Moore, B. "Hyperactive Children and the Efficacy of Psychoactive Drugs as a Treatment Intervention." *American Journal of Orthopsychiatry,* 1976, *46*, 336–352.

This article discusses genetic, biochemical, physical trauma, or emotional disturbance as possible causes of hyperactivity. Reviewing thirty-nine drug studies, the authors conclude that, rather than a single category of hyperactivity, there should be differential diagnoses, multiple etiologies, and differential treatment. For example, one hypothesis is that there are three categories leading to three different approaches: (1) neurological impairment indicates drug therapy; (2) inability to process information due to overactivity indicates behavior modification; and (3) impulsiveness (as opposed to reflectiveness) indicates reinforcement and slow-down techniques.

Loney, J., and Ordona, T. T. "Using Cerebral Stimulants to Treat MBD." *American Journal of Orthopsychiatry,* 1975, *45*, 564–572.

In studying 135 case records of six- to twelve-year-old boys with minimal brain dysfunction, Loney and Ordona found that approximately 60 percent were improved with the use of ritalin. They discuss methodological problems, but, in general, they feel that stimulant medication produces more energetic, less withdrawn, and more competent children. Loss of appetite and sleep disturbances occurred, but side effects of ritalin were minimal and of short duration. Loney and Ordona suggest administering drugs only after trying educational tutoring, psychotherapy, family counseling, and so on, or only in cases where hyperactivity is extreme or where symptoms are numerous.

Mattos, R. L., Mattson, R. H., Walker, H. M., and Buckley, N. K. "Reinforcement and Aversive Control in the Modification of Behavior." *Academic Therapy,* 1969, *5,* 37–52.

The deviant behavior and distractibility of boys studied (in fourth, fifth, and sixth grades) were so great that task-oriented behavior in class occurred only 50 percent of the time. The boys were frequently hyperactive, defiant, and physically and verbally abusive. A token economy was effectively used; students received points for appropriate social and academic behavior. Points were traded in for free time or tangible objects. Using the aversive consequences of a time-out room for not completing academic assignments was more effective than positive reinforcement alone, in increasing task-oriented behavior. Group reinforcement was effective when positive reinforcers (trips) and aversive consequences (peer disapproval) were combined.

Miklich, D. R. "Operant Conditioning Procedures with Systematic Desensitization in a Hyperkinetic Asthmatic Boy." *Journal of Behavior Therapy and Experimental Psychiatry,* 1973, *4,* 177–182.

The panic reactions of a six-year-old hyperkinetic boy were interfering with medical treatment of his asthma. The boy's hyperkinesis and denial of fears or anxiety made the usual systematic desensitization procedures impossible. Therapy consisted of operant conditioning to shape quiet, relaxed sitting and then vividly describing progressively worse asthma while he relaxed. Rewards used for relaxing were playing with a stopwatch, receiving a pad of drawing paper, visiting a computer, and seeing himself on closed-circuit television. After nine trials of descriptions of asthma (the last one being death from status asthmaticus), the boy used accumulated points to purchase two toys in a store.

Millichap, J. G. "Drugs in the Management of Minimal Brain Dysfunction." *International Journal of Child Psychotherapy,* 1972, *1,* 65–81.

Millichap considers methylphenidate and dextroamphetamine to be most effective in controlling hyperactivity, increasing attention span, reducing impulsiveness, and reducing aggressive behavior. He recommends short-term trials of these stimulants in conjunction with remedial education. The most effective results are seen with a high degree of hyperkinesis and/or a number of neurological abnormalities. In cases where stimulants are not effective, Millichap recommends thioridazine, chlordiazepoxide, chlorpromazine, and imipramine. Auditory perception, self-control, and personality disorder may improve with diphenylhydantoin (indicated in cases of electroencephalogram abnormalities). Contraindicated are barbiturates, which usually increase hyperactivity.

Millman, H. L. "Psychoneurological Learning and Behavior Problems: The Importance of Treatment Coordination." *Journal of Clinical Child Psychology*, 1974, *3*, 26–30.

Millman considers ineffective treatment based on a belief in psychogenic causation of cases where psychoneurological inefficiency is present. He recommends coordination of efforts to treat hyperactivity, perceptual-motor impairments, and emotional lability and discusses applications of learning theory, counseling for the child, parent counseling, education, recreation, medication, vision, speech, and audition. The professional explains hyperactivity to the parents. Concrete methods should be used with the child so that he will no longer feel helpless under stress.

O'Leary, K. D., Pelham, W. E., Rosenbaum, A., and Price, G. H. "Behavioral Treatment of Hyperkinetic Children: An Experimental Evaluation of Its Usefulness." *Clinical Pediatrics*, 1976, *15*, 510–515.

This article gives reasons for the need of approaches to hyperkinesis other than or in addition to drugs. The authors report a successful treatment program for eight- to ten-year-old children, consisting of (1) specification of daily classroom goals; (2) praise for effort to achieve these goals; (3) daily evaluation; (4) daily progress report to parents; and (5) parental rewards to child for progress. Rewards were carefully selected, such as extra television, special dessert, playing a game with a parent, and spending money. Weekly rewards (such as a fishing trip or special dinner at relatives or restaurant) were also used. Four out of five children achieved improved daily reports.

Patterson, G. R., Jones, R., Whittier, J., and Wrights, M. A. "A Behavior Modification Technique for the Hyperactive Child." *Behaviour Research and Therapy*, 1965, *2*, 217–226.

The authors describe conditioning procedures for a ten-year-old brain-injured hyperactive boy. An apparatus was used to teach him to sit still so he could study better. A buzz on his earphone indicated candy earned, which he received at the end of each ten-minute trial. Rewards were earned for each ten-second period in which there were no nonattentive behaviors. Conditioning was also conducted in the classroom for five- to eighteen-minute intervals. Sitting still earned candy both for him and for the rest of the class.

Quinn, P. O., and Rapoport, J. L. "One-Year Follow-Up of Hyperactive Boys Treated with Imipramine or Methylphenidate." *American Journal of Psychiatry*, 1975, *132*, 241–245.

Quinn and Rapoport found that imipramine and methylphenidate decreased the rate of weight gain in seventy-six hyperactive boys. Methylphenidate was found to be more generally effective in reducing hyperactivity, especially with the more aggressive boys. However, both drugs led to significant and similar decreases in classroom ratings of hyperactivity and conduct disorder. Quinn and Rapoport feel that, for selected children, imipramine is a useful alternative to stimulant drugs.

Sandoval, J., Lambert, N. M., and Yandell, W. "Current Medical Practice and Hyperactive Children." *American Journal of Orthopsychiatry*, 1976, *46*, 323–334.

Physical trauma and diseases are not judged by physicians as consistently related to hyperactivity in children. The authors report that evidence from laboratory findings or physical examination and positive neurological findings is not viewed as important in diagnosis. The most important indicators used are behavior, the child's history, and family history. Although cerebral stimulants are used, physicians frequently recommend interventions that alter home and school environments.

Solomons, G. "The Hyperactive Child." *Journal of Iowa Medical Society*, 1965, *55*, 464–469.

Solomons defines hyperkinesis and notes that a change of visual fixation in the hyperactive brain-damaged child is accompanied by a change in his activity. In contrast, hyperactive children who are not brain damaged can continue present activity while looking away from the task. Solomons reviews drug therapy, including dextroamphetamine, methylphenidate, thioridazine, chlorpromazine, prochlorperazine, and diphenhydramine. He suggests methylphenidate is used for unusually anxious and jittery children and chlorpromazine and prochlorperazine for mentally retarded children with temper tantrums and destructive behavior. Dextroamphetamine is Solomons' first choice; the parents should be warned that the child may lose his appetite, develop sleep problems, and alter facial appearance and told that the drug is not habit-forming. Parents are told to reduce their pressure on their child.

Stine, J.J. "Symptom Alleviation in the Hyperactive Child by Dietary Modification: A Report of Two Cases." *American Journal of Orthopsychiatry*, 1976, *46*, 637–645.

Two hyperactive boys (four and five years old) were placed on the Feingold-Kaiser-Permanente (K-P) elimination diet. The hypothesis underlying this treatment is that hyperactivity is caused by a genetically determined central nervous system hyperreactivity to chemicals of low molecular weight used as food additives. Stine reports that gradual improvement of motor overactivity and extreme impulsiveness occurred, in contrast to the rapid improvement reported by Feingold and by users of stimulant drugs. Stine calls for further study and speculates that the diet might be very suitable for young children.

Weithorn, C. J., and Ross, R. "Stimulant Drugs for Hyperactivity: Some Additional Disturbing Questions." *American Journal of Orthopsychiatry*, 1976, *46*, 168–173.

Weithorn and Ross report that an increasing number of children (200,000 in 1970) are receiving stimulant drugs for hyperactivity. Rigorous critieria are called for, because a heterogeneous population is thus being treated by medication that has variable and idiosyncratic effects. Issues discussed are the need to know the characteristics of the treated population, the criteria for using cerebral stimulants, and the possible overuse of drugs when educational and other services would be more appropriate. Weithorn and Ross also discuss the need to assess and inform physicians and parents of the variable, idiosyncratic drug effects.

Whitman, T. L., Caponigri, V., and Mercurio, J. "Reducing Hyperactive Behavior in a Severely Retarded Child." *Mental Retardation*, 1971, *9*, 17–19.

Hyperactivity in a six-year-old retarded female was reduced by periodic reinforcement. Reinforcement was given for sitting down, which was incompatible with her hyperactive behavior. If the command "sit down" did not work, she was led to the chair and guided gently into it. Immediate food reinforcers (chocolate, raisins, and cheese crackers) and verbal praise were used. Then she was encouraged to sit while receiving auditory, visual, or tactile stimulation. Progressively longer intervals were reinforced and then ten fifteen-minute training sessions with no reinforcement were added.

Wright, L. S., and McKenzie, C. D. "A Talking Group Therapy for Hyperactive Eleven-Year-Old Boys." *Devereux Forum*, 1973, *8*, 1–24.

Wright and McKenzie describe thirty separate sessions and discuss the progress of every boy. The boys were asked to suggest rules to enhance a talking group. The group was put under group control so that the therapist could function as a therapist rather than as a disciplinarian. As the boys were in residential treatment, feelings about separation were often the focus of discussion. Because the boys had developmental problems, discussion of overwhelming stimuli was discouraged. Sitting and talking was an achieved goal. Wright and McKenzie present group dynamics and each boy's difficulties in detail.

Zentall, S. S., and Zentall, T. R. "Activity and Task Performance of Hyperactive Children as a Function of Environmental Stimulation." *Journal of Consulting and Clinical Psychology*, 1976, *44*, 693–697.

The Zentalls report that high stimulation lowered activity and did not reduce task performance of hyperactive seven- to eleven-year-old children. High stimulation was provided by brightly colored pictures and posters, hanging objects, a screen decorated with a brightly colored three-dimensional papier-mâché scene, flashing Christmas lights, and rock music. The tasks selected were sitting still and academic performance. The Zentalls feel that understimulation precipitates hyperactive behavior and consider their findings compatible with other studies showing stimulant drugs leading to decreased activity, increased attention, and better performance in many hyperactive children.

Short Attention Span

The term attention span *refers to the amount of time a person is able to concentrate. Attending is the application of the mind to a thought or object. Attention requires narrowing or focusing awareness and receptiveness, selecting relevant stimuli and ignoring extraneous, irrelevant stimuli (a filtering mechanism). Effective learning requires focusing attention on different aspects of a task. Hyperactivity and distractibility can impair concentration and perseverance and can therefore shorten attention span. Disorders of attention are often characterized by short attention span, distractibility, and perseveration. In children, even in those with a usually extremely short attention span, length of attention span may vary widely at different times and in different situations.*

Effects of Behavioral Treatment on On-Task Behavior and Peer Interaction

AUTHORS: Loren E. Acker, Peter R. Oliver, John A. Carmichael, and Michael J. Ozerkevich

PRECIS: Increasing attention span of a ten-year-old boy by rewarding his classmates for his on-task behavior

INTRODUCTION: Extrinsic and intrinsic reinforcers have been successfully used to increase time of on-task behavior, to reduce disruptive behavior, and to improve writing, spelling, and arithmetic skills. Peers have been used to aid in improving a designated child's behavior. When the child shows appropriate behavior, the entire class receives some reinforcement (individual-contingent, group reinforcement). This study was concerned with improving a child's on-task behavior and assessing his social interaction and popularity as a result of an individual and group reinforcement program.

METHOD: The authors present the case of a ten-year-old boy who spent very little time on appropriate tasks in a regular, combined fifth- and sixth-grade class of thirty-five students. He wandered around the room and engaged in many irrelevant activities. Sociometric ratings for all class members ($+4$ to -4) were obtained for the child's most and least favorite classmate with whom to sit, play, study, and have lunch. The authors explain in detail how to observe and record on- or off-task behavior and type of social interaction occurring. Baseline observations were recorded.

The class and the boy were told separately about the new program, described as follows. After five minutes of the boy's on-task behavior, a point (accumulated to earn free time) was recorded by an observer on the blackboard. When an observer was not present, the teacher observed and put points on the board at specified intervals. During the day, a point could be traded for three minutes of special group activity. The activity was selected in a discussion between the boy and his classmates. At first, additional gymnasium time was often selected. Later, events such as museum visits were selected.

The program was successful in dramatically increasing on-task behavior. However, there was a decline in the on-task behavior of three "control" children. The results of the peer interaction are not made entirely clear, but the implication is that peers appeared to ignore off-task behavior rather than to encourage on-task behavior. After one week, a dramatic decrease in the boy's popularity occurred, followed by a return (which was maintained) to his previous level. The authors point out that the program was effective in spite of the fact that an unplanned change in teachers occurred.

COMMENTARY: The focus on on-task behavior increases attention span. Rather than wandering and being distracted by a variety of stimuli, the child is reinforced for paying attention to appropriate tasks. Reinforcement by using selection of free-time activities has become increasingly popular in classrooms. Parents have also successfully used child-selected rewards for improving a variety of behaviors. Improved attention might be even more rapidly and more enduringly attained by using both a classroom and a home contingency program. Parents could praise more attentive behavior at home and could provide praise or rewards when informed of successful attentiveness in school. Peer popularity would have to be addressed by other means, such as reinforcing play and talk with others or pairing the child with a more popular classmate on different tasks. Although in this study peers appeared only to ignore off-task behavior, they could be asked to encourage and praise on-task behavior. Having siblings do this at home might lead to more attentive behavior and a more positive, less hostile, home atmosphere.

SOURCE: Acker, L. E., Oliver, P. R., Carmichael, J. A., and Ozerkevich, M. J. "Interpersonal Attractiveness and Peer Interactions During Behavioural Treatment of the Target Child." *Canadian Journal of Behavioural Science,* 1975, 7, 262–273.

Decreasing Inattentiveness and Impulsiveness in Hyperactive Children

AUTHOR: Virginia I. Douglas

PRECIS: Training hyperactive children to stop, look, and listen in order to be more reflective, consider alternatives, and focus on essentials

INTRODUCTION: Hyperactive children are described as always on the move, unable to concentrate, and overly impulsive. Frequently, these behaviors have been present from infancy or early childhood. Douglas contends that sustaining attention and controlling impulses may be more important than curtailing overactivity. Short attention span leads to shifting goals and the resulting disorganized behavior may exaggerate the impression of hyperactivity. Douglas and her colleagues conducted various studies with hyperactive children (excluding brain damaged, retarded, neurotic, and psychotic) and controls from ages six to fourteen. Approximately 85 percent of the total of fifty hyperactive children referred were male.

Performance. Douglas noted a very high incidence of failing grades, including significantly lower grades for hyperactives than for the control group. The children showed low frustration tolerance and poor concentration and organization. They achieved lower scores on group intelligence tests than on individually administered tests. A striking finding was that hyperactive children often engaged in purposeful activity that was unrelated to ongoing classroom activity. The child's goals and the teacher's goals appeared to differ.

Hyperactive children did not show a consistent pattern on subtests of the Wechsler Intelligence Scale for Children, but did show more subtest variability. Serious difficulties appeared on psychological tests measuring visual-motor skills and fine and gross motor coordination (tasks requiring care and concentration). Hyperactive children learned best using a "concept learning apparatus" under continuous reinforcement conditions. The machine provided immediate feedback and reinforcement for correct responses. Severe learning impairment occurred for the hyperactives under 50 percent partial reinforcement.

Studies of Attention. Douglas presents an extensive review of literature, from which selected conclusions are presented here. Hyperactive children were found to be able to react as quickly as normals, but erratic performance lowered their average. Other studies conclude that hyperactive children should be trained to concentrate on the critical aspects of a learning situation. Increasing general motivation was not sufficient to improve performance. Significantly, other findings have found worse performance under general, noncontingent praise. Attention problems have been found even when hyperactive children have worked alone in an empty, sound-proofed room. Impulsive children have been found to decide too quickly, frequently making errors. Reflective children take their time and make few errors. One study advocates training the child to delay his response until he has examined various alternatives (progressing from simpler to more complex alternatives). He could be taught to focus on the essential features of a task. Certain games can be used, in which success is only possible when the child shows impulse control. Reflective strategies can be taught; the child is encouraged to verbally describe the strategies and then to follow them. In hyperactive children, maturation alone does not lead to improvement in impulsiveness and attentiveness, even if they become relatively less active.

Stimulant Drugs. Douglas reports that chlorpromazine was not found to improve cognitive functioning, while methylphenidate did produce positive changes (5 mg/day to maximum 100 mg/day—average dose, 60 mg/day). Improvement in many specific tests are detailed. The conclusion is that methylphenidate helps the hyperactive child sustain attention and control impulsiveness. Douglas believes that drugs should be used only if the behavioral problems are extremely debilitating and cites possible negative side effects. Appropriate training of attention and impulse control is seen as diminishing the need for drug usage.

Stop, Look, and Listen. Hyperactive children have difficulty controlling impulses and coping with situations requiring care, concentration, or organized planning. They react with their first thought or to obvious aspects of a situation. This "inability to stop, look, and listen" also affects social behavior. A study of normal children concluded that the ability to stop, look, and listen is an important factor in effectively coping with many situations. Also, attentional behavior is discussed as being linked to the development of moral behavior (such as judgment and cheating).

COMMENTARY: Douglas makes an impressive case for the need to train hyperactive children to stop, look, and listen. She links short attention span to impulsiveness and describes various methods to decrease impulsiveness and improve attentiveness. If children became more reflective, considered alternatives, and learned to focus on essentials, they would become (or appear to be) less hyperactive. Douglas makes an important point in noting that the child often engages in purposeful activity that is unrelated to the teacher's goals. This implies a need to engage the child in such a manner that his goals become congruent with the teacher's goals. Particularly promising techniques appear to be the teaching of reflective strategies and the use of games in which children must control impulses in order to be successful. The approaches described in this article are applicable to all hyperkinetic behaviors.

SOURCE: Douglas, V. I. "Stop, Look, and Listen: The Problem of Sustained Attention and Impulse Control in Hyperactive and Normal Children." *Canadian Journal of Behavioural Science,* 1972, *4,* 259–282.

Increasing Attentive Behavior in a Hyperactive Child

AUTHORS: Gerald R. Patterson, Richard Jones, James Whittier, and Mary A. Wright

PRECIS: Conditioning attentiveness by reinforcing on-task behavior (while doing homework assignments) during ten-minute intervals

INTRODUCTION: Hyperactivity is one of the most frequent causes for referral to mental health clinics. Although causes of hyperactivity are varied, control appears essential, because overactivity can interfere with the development of socially appropriate behavior. Extreme overactivity often leads to negative reactions from others and punishment may result even when the child is acting in a socially appropriate manner. The procedure described in this study was based on prior studies of conditioning that produced more attentive behavior. Effects persist because peers and adults become more positively socially reinforcing to the more attentive child.

A ten-year-old, brain-injured, hyperactive, aggressive boy with a short attention span was conditioned to be more attentive in class. The positive effects generalized and continued. Because many nonattending behaviors are possible in the classroom (looking out of the window, walking around, and so on), the boy was given immediate reinforcement only when attending behavior occurred in brief, preset intervals.

METHOD: The authors observed the boy and a comparable control and recorded seven categories of nonattending behaviors. Details of the checklist and the procedure are described.

Conditioning. Each day the boy was taken out of class for ten minutes. It was explained that the equipment used would help teach him to sit still so he could study better. A small radio receiving unit was snapped onto his back. He wore earphones and was informed that each buzz signified that he earned a piece of candy. He then worked on a homework assignment. For each ten-second attentive period, the experimenter placed a candy in a cup. After the session, the boy took the candy with him back to class.

The next step took place in class for five- to eighteen-minute intervals. The class was told that he had trouble sitting still, which made it hard for him to learn. It was explained that the earphones told him when he was sitting still, which would earn candy for him and for the rest of the class. A signal for each ten-second attentive interval was transmitted by the experimenter, who sat behind a one-way mirror. Reinforcement was later changed to pennies and plastic soldiers (a special preference of his).

Conditioning increased the boy's attentive behavior in class. There are implications in this study, as well as in the literature, that the procedure also increases the attentiveness of other children in the classroom. The authors noted the differential effect on different categories of nonattentive behavior. Fiddling and distraction were most consistently reduced. Various motor movements were only temporarily reduced and walking was not affected at all. In a different study, loud cheers and clapping by the class had beneficial effects and appeared to enhance the target child's status. The authors consider peer group reactions as important and very amenable to reinforcement procedures.

COMMENTARY: The authors believe that reducing negative behavior leads to a naturally occurring higher frequency of positive social reinforcement from others. One implication is that changing one behavior may lead to changes in other behaviors. Aside from behavioral change, a child may well begin to feel an increased sense of worth, because he receives more social approval, and may feel responsible for (and proud of) his enhanced self-control. It may be well worth the effort to deliberately enhance the child's feelings of participation in any behavioral change (some programs may only assume that the child feels proud of himself). All concerned, especially the parents, could congratulate the child and verbally emphasize his or her improved behavior and increased self-control.

SOURCE: Patterson, G. R., Jones, R., Whittier, J., and Wright, M. A. "A Behavior Modification Technique for the Hyperactive Child." *Behaviour Research and Therapy*, 1965, 2, 217–226.

Teaching Attentiveness With a Workbox

AUTHORS: Roberta S. Ray, David A. Shaw, and Joseph A. Cobb

PRECIS: Individual and group reinforcement based on number of light flashes earned for attentive time intervals

INTRODUCTION: Ray, Shaw, and Cobb present a rationale for the need to increase attention and adaptive classroom behavior while decreasing maladaptive behavior. This is contrasted with the traditional treatment approach of talking and verbal insight. It is pointed out that labeling a child is less important than lowering the rate of maladaptive behavior. Consistency, contingency, immediate consequences, and small steps—stressed as important behavior modification techniques—are described in detail. The authors consider social consequences critical in maintaining desirable or undesirable behavior. They note that attention should be paid to ensure transfer of learning to other situations. Counselors therefore should be urged to influence peers' and teachers' responses to a child's behavior.

PROCEDURE: The procedure described was designed for children who are inattentive, talk inappropriately, move around inappropriately, move while seated (which impairs concentration), and make disruptive noise. Specific problem behaviors are identified and then objectively observed and counted. It is essential that the counselor discover what the teacher considers appropriate or inappropriate and in what situations. The behaviors should then be made clear to the class.

In private, the counselor explains to the child that the workbox will be used to help him learn better. The class is told that he has trouble sitting still, which makes it hard to learn. Each time the light flashes on the workbox, he will know he has been sitting still and working and that he has earned candy for himself and the rest of the class. A counter on the workbox indicates how much candy he can give to the class. It is explained that the class can help by ignoring his inappropriate behaviors. Other rewards might be substituted for candy.

A point is given for every five-second period during which there is no inappropriate behavior. The time interval is restarted if the child exhibits any prohibited behavior. Time periods are gradually increased. However, shorter intervals are used if the child does not succeed on three consecutive intervals. If shorter intervals do not work, then the reward might be too weak, too distant, or require too many points. Careful and slow progression often results in no missed intervals. The counselor is encouraged to involve children in the choice of rewards, examples of which are extra recess time, candy, films, parties, and music. The authors describe detailed formulas and use of point systems. Plans are always made to phase out the use of the workbox. Behaving appropriately without the box is rewarded. Other uses of radio-controlled boxes are described, such as increasing unaggressive playground behavior.

For extremely disruptive or aggressive children, time-out procedures are recommended. Time out is a period in which rewards cannot be earned. Usually the child is briefly sent by himself to another room where there is little to do. Time out is explained positively to the child and carried through in a consistent, matter-of-fact manner.

Programs for two boys (eight and ten years old) are described in detail. In both cases, a workbox was used to increase attention behavior and then to reward academic performance. The authors present detailed observations and diagrams to illustrate the effectiveness of the programs. They also discuss different rewards and ongoing modifications of the program and note that adaptive behaviors are said to continue, because significant others have learned to reward them appropriately.

COMMENTARY: This article provides an unusually detailed description of instituting and modifying behavioral change programs. It is worth studying for the principles stated and the translation into practical suggestions. Many might find the use of a workbox acceptable and useful. There are other ways that a method of counting could be devised without the child having to wear earphones or having a box on the table. The important aspects appear to be the accountability feature and the feedback to the child (and the group) regarding improved behavior. Many techniques that have been successfully reported by others are incorporated here, such as time out and asking the group to help by ignoring inappropriate behavior. For those interested in the workbox format, applicability is feasible for any observable behavior.

SOURCE: Ray, R. S., Shaw, D. A., and Cobb, J. A. "The Work Box: An Innovation in Teaching Attentional Behavior." *The School Counselor*, 1970, *18*, 15–35.

Modifying Attention and Hyperactivity Through Breathing Control

AUTHORS: D. Dwayne Simpson and Arnold E. Nelson

PRECIS: Increasing regulated breathing by providing feedback and positive reinforcement

INTRODUCTION: Simpson and Nelson note that excessive motor behavior, lack of attention, and distractibility interfere with academic progress of hyperactive children. Overactivity drives the child to go from one interest to another without focusing attention. The child has family and social problems caused by the situational inappropriateness of his overactivity. Simpson and Nelson discuss drug therapy in the light of frequent ineffectiveness and negative or questionable side effects. Behavior modification has been quite successful, except that target behavior has often been only reduction of activity, rather than the establishment of appropriate behavior, such as attending.

The authors suggest that it would be helpful to identify a higher-order variable, so that numerous problem behaviors do not have to be identified, counted, and selectively reinforced. They propose respiration control as a behavior that indirectly affects a group of other problem behaviors. Breathing plays a role both in yoga and Zen meditation and is used in physical relaxation training. Gross body movements are related to control of breathing. Regular and even breathing is assumed to be related to self-control in general and disruptive motor behaviors in particular. The child thus only has to focus on one behavior. Visual feedback is an easy matter since respiration can be recorded and displayed for the child to see. Regular, more shallow and quickened respiration has been found to characterize attentiveness.

METHOD: Six (six- to eight-year-old) hyperactive boys participated, three as controls and three in the experiment. Simpson and Nelson describe the training room which contains an oscilloscope (that visually displays respiration rate) and other equipment. Pretesting, training, and posttesting lasted three and one half months, usually for one hour twice a week. In pretesting, four attention and vigilance tests were individually administered. Respiration recordings were performed during each test.

The training phase lasted for eleven weeks. The experimental group was trained to attend and to exert control of respiration by the use of feedback and operant conditioning. Regulated breathing was reinforced with tokens that were later exchanged for candy or money. An idealized pattern was projected on the oscilloscope and tokens were given for approximating the pattern. Length of training periods and schedules of reinforcement were individually determined. The control group performed a vigilance task and were rewarded for correctly identifying two similar patterns on the oscilloscope.

Generalization training was used to extend breathing practice to other situations approximating school situations. Training in regulating breathing was given without a target pattern present. Various slide shows and academic lessons took place in order to generalize regulated breathing to academic tasks requiring attentiveness. All six boys were placed together for these sessions. To increase social awareness, rewards were given to individuals based on tokens earned by all the boys. Posttesting was performed after this training was completed.

Simpson and Nelson present their results in detail. Compared to controls, children who received breathing control and attention training showed more favorable changes in posttesting. Irregularities of breathing were reduced. Differences did occur in speed of acquisition and level of breathing control. In general, transfer of training to the classroom was limited. The authors state that generalization should be enhanced by reinforced training in the classroom and other situations.

COMMENTARY: Breathing control may combine increased attention and relaxation. Many adults and children have experienced relaxation and a "feeling of happiness" through meditation involving focus on breathing. The idea of using respiration feedback appears promising, even when done informally in an office, as are recent reports regarding a variety of biofeedback approaches, especially the use of feedback regarding electrical muscle activity for relaxation. It is possible that regular relaxed breathing practice in itself might enhance a child's perception of self-control and of his ability to influence his own bodily functions. From reports and observations, a greater sense of self-control has been reported in hyperactive children who have been taught to employ muscle relaxation when experiencing stress.

SOURCE: Simpson, D. D., and Nelson, A. E. "Attention Training Through Breathing Control to Modify Hyperactivity." *Journal of Learning Disabilities*, 1974, 7, 274–283.

Additional Readings

Alabiso, F. "Operant Control of Attention Behavior: A Treatment for Hyperactivity." *Behavior Therapy*, 1975, 6, 39–42.

Longer attention span, focusing, and selective attention were reinforced in eight, hyperactive retarded children from eight to twelve years of age. Increased focused attention reduced distractibility, increased selective attention, and improved discriminative ability. Token and social reinforcement were contingent on remaining seated (span training). Focused training consisted of being reinforced for copying digits and symbols in sequence. Laboratory training did generalize to the classroom.

Blyth, Z. "Group Treatment for Handicapped Children." *Journal of Psychiatric Nursing and Mental Health Services*, 1969, 7, 172–173.

Moderately brain-damaged hyperactive and distractible children were involved in group treatment over a six-month period. They earned poker chips that were exchangeable for items selected jointly by parents and child. Parents were aided in establishing realistic, consistent limits, minimizing distracting stimuli, and providing outlets for energy and creativity. Distractibility decreased and social skills improved markedly.

Kennedy, D. A., and Thompson, I. "Use of Reinforcement Technique with a First-Grade Boy." *Personnel and Guidance Journal*, 1967, 46, 366–370.

In counseling, a reinforcement method was used to modify

attending behavior in a six-year-old boy. He was inattentive in class, did not follow directions, often did not complete assignments, and rarely made eye contact with others. During sessions, he was quite inattentive. A stopwatch was used to measure behavior; he was given candy for each minute of paying attention (eye contact or sitting and looking in the direction of the counselor). At first, candy was given after each minute; later, at the end of the session. Attention increased both in counseling and in the classroom. Marked improvement occurred in completion of academic assignments.

Maggs, A. "Attention and Motivation Management Techniques with the Mentally Retarded." *Australian Journal of Mental Retardation,* 1974, *4,* 97–101.

Maggs describes specific techniques to increase attention and motivation in mentally retarded children. Contingency between behavior and reinforcer is discussed in terms of relevance and immediacy, as well as continuous and intermittent reinforcement. Maggs feels that reinforcement moves from concrete extrinsic to abstract intrinsic. For example, reinforcement can move up a hierarchy from edibles, tokens, social praise, being correct, to being competent (abstract intrinsic). Maggs stresses that the child's attention must be focused on the relevant aspects of a problem; correct attention must be immediately reinforced; and overlearning must occur to facilitate transfer of attention.

Millman, H. L. "Treatment of Problems Associated with Cognitive and Perceptual-Motor Deficits." *Child Welfare,* 1972, *51,* 447–451.

Millman reports that appreciating subtle intellectual or perceptual-motor weaknesses can suggest specific techniques for improving children's behavior. He discusses figure-ground deficits in terms of visual, auditory, and social situations. A child's understanding of instructions (figure) may require additional special instructions. Millman recommends exercises in focusing in order to strengthen the child's ability to attend to tasks; suggests practice in looking and listening for longer time intervals; and discusses how to strengthen deficient functioning and teach specific compensatory behavior.

Okovita, H. W., and Bucher, B. "Attending Behavior of Children Near a Child Who Is Reinforced for Attending." *Psychology in the Schools,* 1976, *13,* 205–211.

Okovita and Bucher report a study to assess what happens to the behavior of nursery school children when one child is reinforced for attention. The rewarded pupil and two other target children showed increased attention. Back-up reinforcers (toys and candy) were contingent on points obtained for attending (appropriate quiet, sitting, looking, and copying behavior). No disturbing effects on nonrewarded children were reported when one child was rewarded. The authors interpret the data as supporting a modeling effect.

Patterson, C. J., and Mischel, W. "Plans to Resist Distraction." *Developmental Psychology,* 1975, *11,* 369–378.

Patterson and Mischel conducted two experiments with preschool children in order to increase their resistance to distraction. A clown box was used to provide distractions and verbal invitations to play. Three plans of resistance were taught to one group and only one plan was taught to the other groups. Plan One urged the child to not look at the clown and to say that he could not play because he was working. Plan Two suggested saying to himself that he was going to keep working so he could play later. Plan Three stated that the child could pretend that there was a brick wall so he could not see the clown. Rehearsal was not required for adequate task performance. Giving only one plan was at least as effective as suggesting three alternative plans to resist distraction. The two experimental groups worked significantly longer at a task than did the no-plan control group.

Rapoport, J. "Childhood Behavior and Learning Problems Treated with Imipramine." *International Journal of Neuropsychiatry,* 1965, *1,* 635–642.

Imipramine was used with forty-one patients, ages five through twenty-one. Duration of treatment was six months to two years, usually not exceeding one year. Excessive energy, outbursts, short attention span, and various learning problems were typical and were considered to have been caused by physiological cerebral dysfunction. Imipramine influences the reticular formation and has an antidepressant and tranquilizing effect. Rapoport presents details on appropriate steps leading to optimum dosage. A typical case summary of a nine-year-old boy is reviewed. The drug markedly improved behavior and learning in thirty-three children (80 percent). Dosage varied from 10 mg to 40 mg, most patients receiving 20 mg/daily. Sleep was more restful and compulsive behavior disappeared. Handwriting, arithmetic, and reading improved. Both school reports and psychological tests indicated marked improvement in attention span and general alertness.

Salzinger, K., Feldman, R. S., and Portnoy, S. "Training Parents of Brain-Injured Children in the Use of Operant Conditioning Procedures." *Behavior Therapy*, 1970, *1*, 4–32.

Operant conditioning principles were taught to parents of brain-injured children. Objective observing and recording were stressed. Daily records revealed antecedents and consequences of disturbing behavior. Educated parents all succeeded in effectively changing their child's behavior. Different approaches are suggested for less-educated parents with lower comprehension skills. A detailed operant conditioning manual was given to the parents and detailed instruction was given in developing specific behavior modification programs. General procedures for a behavioral program included shaping new behavior, introducing new behavior by reinforcing imitation, reinforcing desired behavior positively or by removing negative reinforcement, reinforcing incompatible behavior positively or by removing negative reinforcement, extinction, satiation, reinforcing undesirable behavior negatively, eliminating undesirable behavior by removing positive reinforcement, and eliminating the discriminative stimulus for undesirable behavior. Many deviant behaviors were addressed, including short attention span, hyperactivity, tantrums, low frustration tolerance, and social difficulties.

Santostefano, S., and Stayton, S. "Training the Preschool Retarded Child in Focusing Attention: A Program for Parents." *American Journal of Orthopsychiatry*, 1967, *37*, 732–743.

Retarded children were trained by their mothers to pay selective, active attention. Gains were made in several cognitive variables, tested by trail maze, picture discrimination, buttons, object sort, and body imitation tests. Results supported the hypothesis that training focal attention generalizes and facilitates higher level functioning. A manual, training materials, and daily record forms were given to the mothers. Home training proceeded for four months for ten to twenty minutes daily. Magnetic cutouts were used; the child had to remove particular, progressively more difficult ones.

Surratt, P. R., Ulrich, R. E., and Hawkins, R. P. "An Elementary Student as a Behavioral Engineer." *Journal of Applied Behavior Analysis,* 1969, *2,* 85–92.

A fifth-grade "behavioral engineer" modified non-study behaviors of four first-graders, who talked, walked around the room, and daydreamed instead of completing study assignments. The engineer used an electronic apparatus that controlled four timers. A timer was turned on when a student was working—counting, writing, looking at the blackboard, and so on. A switch was turned to off for any other behavior. The percent of time working was computed for each session. For a specified amount of working, a ticket was given on which the student specified his own reward (going to gym, playground, helping janitor, and so on). The authors added other variables and discuss the resulting interactions. They report significant improvement in working and follow-up behavior.

Impulsiveness and Low Frustration Tolerance

An impulse is a spontaneous inclination to perform a (usually) unpremeditated action. The action usually has a sudden, forceful, compelling quality. Action is taken without the consequences being considered. Impulse disorders are associated with central nervous system impairment and have also been described in impulse neuroses (such as addiction, kleptomania, and pyromania) and perversions (such as voyeurism and exhibitionism). Frustration involves a sense of dissatisfaction stemming from unfulfilled needs or desires or from unresolved problems. Tolerating frustration requires enduring or putting up with dissatisfaction. The need for immediate gratification of an impulse is the equivalent of having very little frustration tolerance. With age, children increase in patience and ability to function in spite of increasing amounts of frustration. Tolerance is necessary for new tasks that may involve attention, persistence, delay of gratification, failure, and less individual attention.

Operant Conditioning of Self-Control

AUTHOR: Ralph O. Blackwood

PRECIS: Teaching children to anticipate consequences and to think of a warning that prevents misbehavior

INTRODUCTION: Blackwood notes that while operant conditioning reduces undesirable behavior in social groups, it does not eliminate such behavior, which can still interfere with programs in various areas. He presents a theoretical discussion of operantly conditioned, verbally mediated control (traditional behavior modification is unmediated). The teacher's verbal control does not lead to the child's self-control unless the child can produce his own verbal self-warning when tempted. The conditioned reinforcers of the child's verbal behavior cancels opposing, immediate reinforcers.

VERBAL MEDIATION TRAINING: In the study described by Blackwood, procedures were developed for training children to think of the consequences of their behavior. By interviewing children, it was discovered that self-controlled children verbalized the consequences of disruptive and acceptable behavior. They described immediate and delayed consequences, valuing small immediate rewards more than strong, delayed consequences. None of the misbehaving children verbalized consequences or understood delayed rewards and punishments. A pilot study clarified the hypothesis that operant verbal mediation training reduces the misbehavior of children who have continued to misbehave after traditional behavior modification has been employed. They were given a typed paragraph describing misbehavior and negative consequences, as well as desired behavior and reinforcing consequences. The paragraph was to be copied, paraphrased, recited from memory, and role played. Practice conditions the descriptions as strong verbal response chains elicited by the tempting situations.

Blackwood also describes an experiment in which eighth- and ninth-grade children were given mediation essays or essays that did not discuss the consequences of misbehavior (the latter were for the control group). Observation indicated significant reduction of misbehavior for the experimental group.

METHOD FOR TRAINING: Blackwood gives a detailed description of his method, as follows.

Essays. Each mediation essay consisted of four questions and answers for each child.

1. "What did I do wrong?" (example: "I was talking without permission").

2. A question concerning the inappropriateness of the behavior (example: "Why should I not blurt out whatever comes into my head?"). A paragraph follows describing the various negative consequences of the behavior (example: "Time will drag"; "I may miss important things"; "I may have to stay after school").

3. A question asking what the child should have been doing, followed by a concrete description of the desirable behavior.

4. A question concerning the reasons for desirable behavior, followed by a concrete description of reinforcing consequences of desirable behavior. This description contained a reference to the tempting situations (example: "Even if I have an interesting idea, I should get permission to speak").

Procedure. If a child misbehaved, an essay was placed on his desk. Not cooperating in copying the essays led to greater punishments: If the work was not submitted the next day, the assignment was doubled; then detention was used; then the child was sent to the principal's office; and so on. Acceptance of the essay assignment was verbally praised. Detention was made highly aversive by not permitting the children's usual behaviors, such as erasing boards, lining up chairs, and engaging in group discussions (which would be inadvertent positive reinforcement). Release from detention was earned by cooperating and working on the essay.

The first two misbehaviors led to copying essays at home. A third misbehavior resulted in detention after school and paraphrasing the essay. Continued misbehavior required further paraphrasing each time. Eighth, ninth, and tenth misbehaviors required detention and writing the essay in the child's own words from memory. Further misbehavior required verbal descriptions of situations that led to misbehavior and what the child thought when tempted. At times, the child was told to act out misbehavior as well as the desired behavior and to describe the consequences.

COMMENTARY: Although the experiment yielded positive results, Blackwood suggests further study. However, combining mediation training with escape-avoidance conditioning appears very promising with impulsive children who show poor self-control. It provides a concrete method in an area where few specific methods have been offered. The method appears promising for other behavior disorders as well. The techniques may be used in a progressive hierarchical fashion. The mediation training without the escape-avoidance conditioning may still produce positive results.

SOURCE: Blackwood, R. O. "The Operant Conditioning of Verbally Mediated Self-Control in the Classroom." *Journal of School Psychology,* 1970, *8,* 251–258.

Modifying Aggression and Impulsiveness Through Modeling

AUTHORS: Sally E. Goodwin and Michael J. Mahoney

PRECIS: Increasing frustration tolerance by having children view a videotape of a model who uses covert self-instructions in successfully coping with peer taunting

INTRODUCTION: Modeling techniques have been used to modify observable motor responses. Because thoughts influence all behavior, internal responses are receptive to modeling procedures. In this study, behavioral modeling was combined with thoughts about adaptive coping; the therapist verbally emphasized the behavior. Rehearsed practice was also employed.

CASE STUDIES: Three impulsive and hyperactive boys were selected for the study. Observers time-sampled classroom behavior, rating boys as disruptive or nondisruptive regarding aggression, destructiveness, and hyperactivity.

Procedures. The boys were taught a verbal taunting game. Each boy stood for a while in the inner of two concentric circles, while the others taunted him. The taunters had been told: "The object of this circle is for you to make [John] mad. You are going to try to make him 'lose his cool' in the next two minutes. You may use any gestures or words you wish, any language or tricks you think will make him lose his temper. You can move around, jump, yell, or scream. However, you must stay outside the outer circle, and may not touch or spit on [John] in any way" (p. 200). Tokens were awarded for successful taunting. Prizes were purchased with the tokens.

The tauntee was told: "These kids are going to try to make you mad. You are going to try to stay calm. They cannot touch or spit on you and they must stay outside the outer circle. You must stay inside your inner circle. You may answer their comments in any way you wish. If at any time you want to turn off their taunts, turn on this flashlight as a signal and taunters will stop" (pp. 200, 201). Regardless of performance, tauntees were given tokens.

Two modeling sessions were conducted. The first had the boys observe a videotape of a nine-year-old boy being taunted by five children. The model remained calm and dealt with taunts by the use of "covert self-instructions." The thoughts were added to the tape after it was made. Comments were added such as "I won't get mad" and "I'm not going to let them bug me." After observing, a taunting session took place. A week later, the videotape was observed again. The thoughts and actions of the model were discussed by the group leader. He emphasized that this approach was an effective way of coping with verbal aggression. Each boy was asked to repeat as many coping responses as he could recall and then a taunting session was held. One week later, a final taunting session took place, with no observation or discussion of coping responses. Observation of classroom behavior occurred one day later.

The boys' coping responses increased from baseline and during the two modeling sessions. Nondisruptive classroom behavior improved. The three boys' nondisruptive classroom behavior went from approximately 60 percent (pretest) to approximately 90 percent (posttest).

COMMENTARY: As Goodwin and Mahoney point out, their approach is experimental and needing of further study and validation. It is presented here because it is an example of an "experimental" approach to modifying resistant disruptive behavior. Impulsive reaction and tolerance of aggression are difficult to influence. Learning theory (especially modeling) has led to a variety of approaches that influence impulsive, disruptive behavior. By helping children develop concrete methods of self-control, impulsiveness may be directly influenced. Observing and rehearsing specific behaviors may enable a child to cope better with a stressful environment.

SOURCE: Goodwin, S. E., and Mahoney, M. J. "Modification of Aggression Through Modeling: An Experimental Probe." *Journal of Behavior Therapy and Experimental Psychiatry*, 1975, *6*, 200–202.

The Changing Role of the Psychotherapist: Modifying Impulsiveness

AUTHOR: Stanley Kissel

PRECIS: Developing skills and frustration tolerance by using model building with an impulsive nine-year-old boy

INTRODUCTION: Recent social conditions have required changes in the conception of time, emphasized limited resources and pointed up a need for therapists to work with a wider range of clients. Traditional therapy has not been effective with children who have developmental difficulties (hyperkinesia, communication disorder, and minimal brain dysfunction). Psychotherapy with children has become more structured and goal-directed. The therapist has had to become more active, directive, and educationally oriented. At times, the therapist may be seen as a master strategist who formulates a plan to get the child back in school or to begin eating again. Behavior modification is usually associated with the approach Kissel describes, but Kissel himself considers his interventions to fall within the framework of cognitively oriented ego psychology.

LEARNING DISABILITIES THERAPY: Kissel notes that children are frequently brought to mental health clinics for school difficulties. Instead of having family or emotional conflict, some of these children have deficiencies in motor functioning, perception, and ability to conceptualize. They are overly active, easily frustrated, and having a short attention span. School failure has lowered their self-esteem and they therefore avoid academic learning experiences. Play therapy for dealing with anxiety and psychological conflicts is therefore not appropriate, play therapy should teach frustration tolerance, ability to think and act in sequence, and orderliness. Model building has been used to teach children these skills.

CASE STUDY: Kissel describes the case of a nine-year-old of average intelligence, referred because of disruptive class behavior and poor academic achievement. He was impulsive, perceptually impaired, and poorly coordinated. At first he was belligerent and often refused to talk. Three relatively simple models were offered to him. They contained medium-sized pieces with mostly picture instructions. Impulsively, he glued the largest pieces together. This worked for simple models, but not for more difficult ones. He thus learned that it is better to work slower. Experience forced him to see that careful work leads to quicker results than impulsive behavior aimed at an immediate reward. Through his own efforts, the boy learned that attention to details and orderliness were important. More difficult models, taking two to three weeks to construct, helped him develop higher frustration tolerance. Later, reading instructions, relating words to numbers, and keeping records of the sequence of events were added. Model building provided positive feedback, enhanced the boy's self-esteem, and improved his fine motor coordination.

COMMENTARY: Kissel's focus is on developing skills that are relevant to academic deficits, not on revealing neurotic conflicts. He also discusses direct intervention through short-term family therapy and mutual storytelling with children with varous behavior problems. Kissel stresses the need for flexibility of approach and for using more than one theoretical model. Recent research and clinical case studies support Kissel's emphasis on more directive approaches with behavior-disordered children. The case presented fits current descriptions of children with developmental learning disabilities or minimal brain dysfunction. With such children, cognitively oriented methods to strengthen deficits are increasingly used by therapists from diverse orientations.

SOURCE: Kissel, S. "The Child Psychotherapist's Changing Role." *Professional Psychology,* 1975, *6,* 261–266.

Developing Self-Control in Impulsive Children

AUTHORS: Donald H. Meichenbaum and Joseph Goodman

PRECIS: Teaching children to talk to themselves in order to decrease impulsiveness and enhance performance

INTRODUCTION: Meichenbaum and Goodman discuss the interaction between self-verbalizaton and nonverbal behavior. They believe that problem solving consists of comprehension, production, and mediation. Improving performance and self-control requires training in task comprehension, spontaneously producing mediators, and using mediators to control nonverbal behavior. Two studies produced data that demonstrated the efficacy of the methods used. Impulsive children (ages five to nine) were trained to use self-instructions, which strengthened their own verbal control and overcame comprehension, production, or mediational deficits. The children were trained to reinforce their own behavior.

COGNITIVE TRAINING: Four half-hour sessions took place over a two-week period. First the trainer performed a task while talking aloud, the child observed. Then the child performed the task in response to verbal instructions. The child next performed the task while instructing himself verbally; then while whispering to himself; and finally with no lip movements. The verbalizations used concerned (1) the nature and demands of the task (to enhance comprehension); (2) rehearsal and planning (to overcome production deficiency); (3) self-instructions (to overcome mediation weakness); and (4) self-reinforcement.

An example of a modeled verbalization follows. "Okay, what is it I have to do? You want me to copy the picture with the different lines. I have to go slow and be careful. Okay, draw the line down, down, good; then to the right, that's it; now down some more and to the left. Good, I'm doing fine so far. Remember go slow. Now back up again. No, I was supposed to go down. That's okay. Just erase the line carefully. . . . Good. Even if I make an error I can go on slowly and carefully. Okay, I have to go down now. Finished, I did it" (p. 117). Meichenbaum and Goodman note that it is important to include an appropriate response to an error.

Different tasks were used, ranging from simple sensori-motor to problem-solving tasks. The trainer modeled the self-verbalizations and then used a fading procedure to promote covert self-instructions.

In another study, the group that used cognitive modeling and self-instructional training group did significantly better than a cognitive modeling group that did not receive specific training. The following monolog is an example of cognitive modeling in a picture-matching task. "I have to remember to go slowly to get it right. Look carefully at this one . . . now look at these carefully. . . . Is this one different? Yes, it has an extra leaf. Good, I can eliminate this one. Now, let's look at this one. . . . I think it's this one, but let me first check the others. Good, I'm going slow and carefully. Okay, I think it's this one." When an error was made, coping skills were modeled. "It's okay, just be careful. I should have looked more carefully. Follow the plan to check each one. Good, I'm going slowly" (p. 121). For the group that improved most, explicit self-instruction training was added to cognitive modeling. The child practiced the task and was told to talk aloud to himself in the manner shown. Fading to covert instructions was employed.

The two studies showed that impulsive children could learn to talk to themselves and could thus improve their performance on psychometric tests assessing cognitive impulsiveness and performance and motor skills.

COMMENTARY: Meichenbaum and Goodman feel that cognitive self-instructional training is applicable to many problems, including cultural deprivation complicated by central language deficits, schizophrenia with attentional deficits, and psychophysiological reactions. Greater self-control might be seen as advantageous in any situation. Improvement in test taking is certainly a worthwhile goal in itself. Meichenbaum and Goodman offer a specific, rather than a general approach, to behavioral disorder and make a significant contribution in the use of an individualized self-instructional method. Using this method, the therapist can select an inappropriate behavior, such as impulsive talking, hitting, and shouting, and teach the child self-control in thought and behavior.

SOURCE: Meichenbaum, D. H., and Goodman, J. "Training Impulsive Children to Talk to Themselves: A Means of Developing Self-Control." *Journal of Abnormal Psychology*, 1971, *77*, 115–126.

Controlling Frustration by Conditioning

AUTHOR: Cecilia Pollack

PRECIS: Inhibiting explosive behavior by reinforcing children for finger-signing the letter *C* (symbolizing "control") in frustrating situations

INTRODUCTION: Pollack presents a theoretical discussion of how internal speech (verbally formulated rules) can help the child orient himself. Six "minimally brain-injured" boys, ages eight to twelve years, were used in this study. The boys characteristically showed low frustration tolerance and frequent emotional outbursts.

CONDITIONING FRUSTRATION: The six boys engaged in discussion with the experimenter. Pollack reproduces verbatim a conversation wherein she explained the meaning of frustration. Using the boys' examples, anger was explained as being a result of frustration. Feeling frustrated was described as leading to anger, tantrums, crying, and so on. One boy in the group was used as an example of someone who could feel frustrated but who could control anger. Pollack associated the word *frustration* with concrete behavioral acts of each boy. Then she told the boys that there was an easy way of controlling their frustration reactions. When they felt angry, they were to make the letter *C* with their fingers; *C* meant "control." This behavior would prevent outbursts. To practice, while finger-signing *C,* the boys said the word *control.* This behavior was to be the stimulus for initiating the inhibitory process that counteracts explosive behavior.

Pollack went on to provide motivation for the boys to control their frustration reactions. She stressed that children in regular classes had learned to control their anger when frustrated. Possibly being placed in a regular class would increase the boys' motivation to control their anger. She then stated that she would help them achieve that goal. A behavior control chart indicated each time a boy controlled an expression of frustration. Stars were awarded; twenty-five could be exchanged for a prize. Another reward was being closer to being able to attend a regular class.

Twenty-five boxes were drawn after each name on the "Control Chart." Each boy pasted his star up by himself. A large box at the end of the row was for the gold star signifying that the boy had reached his goal. The one boy who already could control his anger was awarded the gold star and prize immediately by agreement of the group.

Pollack describes each boy's response to the procedure. Varying levels of understanding of "frustration" were achieved. Four of the five boys made considerable progress in self-control. One went to a regular class next semester. This boy, who had the best language skills, presumably understood the abstract concept of frustration reaction and had thus learned to control his own behavior. One boy, who did not appear to understand the concept, applied it to all types of misbehavior and had to be taught the concept more concretely. The boy who made no progress was seen as having virtually no abstract ability. His only learning appeared to be that he should not cry when he received a bad grade. In addition, his retention was extremely poor.

The three steps Pollack used were verbal analysis of the concept of frustration and its concrete expression, developing motivation for change, and selective positive reinforcement. Continued reinforcement by stars developed a pattern of inhibiting explosive behavior. Furthermore, the pattern of control generalized to adaptive behavior in other situations.

COMMENTARY: Pollack believes that counterconditioning holds great promise for children who are not brain injured. Children without language deficits would have little difficulty understanding concepts and being able to generalize. The basic method of providing a means for self-control appears to be practical and widely applicable. Reversing negative behavioral habits is very frequently stated as an important goal by children, parents, teachers, and therapists. The child often feels helpless and depends on adults to change such habits. Providing a method for children to employ offers them a clear message that they are not helpless. Decreasing anger, depression, anxiety, and so on may be possible by having the child decondition himself while being rewarded by adults. Another possibility would be to teach the child to say congratulatory sentences to himself as he improves.

SOURCE: Pollack, C. "A Conditioning Approach to Frustration Reaction in Minimally Brain-Injured Children." *Journal of Learning Disabilities,* 1968, *1,* 681–688.

Additional Readings

Ayllon, T., Layman, D., and Burke, S. "Disruptive Behavior and Reinforcement of Academic Performance." *Psychological Record,* 1972, *22,* 315–323.

Disruptive, educable, retarded, twelve- to thirteen-year-old boys were contingently reinforced for academic performance. Disruptive behavior was defined as gross motor, verbalizing, and noise. Impulsive, out-of-seat, throwing, calling out, and pounding behaviors were typical. Reading and arithmetic progress resulted in tokens, exchangeable for reinforcers (candy, playing with perceptual games, listening to records, playing with puzzles, talking to a friend, and selection of academic materials). Reinforcers cost from one to five tokens. Both academic performance and disruptive behaviors improved significantly.

Finch, A. J., Wilkinson, M. D., Nelson, W. M., and Montgomery, L. E. "Modification of an Impulsive Cognitive Tempo in Emotionally Disturbed Boys." *Journal of Abnormal Child Psychology,* 1975, *3,* 49–52.

Cognitive training was effective in modifying impulsiveness in fifteen boys (average age, eleven years). They were seen individually for six half-hour sessions over a three-week period. The experimenter performed a task while repeating specific instructions to herself aloud. When she made an error (deliberately), she said that she should have been more careful and should have gone slower. The boy then performed the task while giving himself verbal instructions. When necessary, assistance in self-instruction was given. Silent self-instruction was used during the last two sessions. Latency time was increased and number of errors were decreased, both significantly.

Kendall, P. C., and Finch, A. J. "A Cognitive-Behavioral Treatment for Impulse Control: A Case Study." *Journal of Consulting and Clinical Psychology,* 1976, *44,* 852–857.

Impulse control was significantly improved in an aggressive, very active, uncooperative nine-year-old boy. Six sessions were held, consisting of verbal self-instructions and a response cost procedure. The behaviors focused on were inappropriate and untimely changes in behavior (incomplete action). Verbal self-instructions were modeled by the therapist, first aloud and later by whispering. Self-instructions were step-by-step definitions of the problem (mazes), approach to be used, and focusing and coping statements. Covert (talk to himself) instructions were used by the boy. Response cost consisted of a loss of one dime (of five dimes he had been given) if he inappropriately changed behavior before completion. Generalization sessions were held in a different room, with different games, and with a different therapist.

Lourie, R. S. "Psychoactive Drugs in Pediatrics." *Pediatrics,* 1964, *34,* 691–693.

Stimulants (amphetamines and methylphenidate) have calming effects on impulsive and acting-out children. Lourie reports striking results with constitutionally hyperactive, impulsive, distractible children. Very small doses (2.5 mg) of amphetamine or d-amphetamine, twice a day, can significantly diminish impulsiveness and hyperactivity. Larger doses have been effective with severely acting-out, impulsive children. Lourie calls for short-term trials to assess drug effectiveness.

Shure, M. B., Newman, S., and Silver, S. "Problem-Solving Thinking Among Adjusted, Impulsive, and Inhibited Head Start Children." Paper presented at the meeting of the Eastern Psychological Association, Washington, D.C., April 1973.

Theoretically, healthy functioning is related to the ability to think through and solve everyday problems. Less frustration results from successful problem solving. Children often become preoccupied with the end goal, rather than keeping aware of the means to attainment and of the interfering obstacles. Impulsive children give very few problem solutions. Also, consequential thinking is related to behavioral adjustment. The authors discuss the need for a training program to teach the conceptualization of alternative solutions and consequences. They predict that more options and the ability to evaluate consequences should lead to less frustration and more adaptive functioning.

5

Disturbed Relationship with Children

Social ineffectiveness with age mates represents a serious obstacle to the psychological adjustment of school-age children. Social difficulties correlate highly with emotional problems, school maladjustment, and general psychological deviance. Moreover, social problems with peers are highly predictive of later emotional difficulties in adulthood. This chapter is concerned with children who clearly have a deficiency in the skills and/or motivation necessary to engage in cooperative, mutually satisfying transactions with other children. Characteristically, these deficits are manifested in either fight (hostility) or flight (withdrawal) reactions to peers and/or siblings. Prolonged use of either reaction inevitably results in social isolation or rejection. The underlying causes of maladaptive peer relations are numerous, including parental rejection or overdependency, martial conflict, minimal brain dysfunction, reactions to trauma or stress, and poor self-esteem. Parental modeling also seems to be a factor, because individualism and competition are highly valued behaviors in our culture. Alienation and mistrust of others are becoming increasingly prevalent, especially in our larger urban centers.

Specific techniques for achieving group acceptance for socially inept children are presented in this chapter. Since the problem lies in peer transactions, the treatment of choice in recent years has been to involve peers in the treatment by means of group or dyadic therapy. Typically, behavioral methods are used to motivate the peers to exert group pressure on a child so that he or she will engage in more cooperative social interactions. Often a child's parents and/or teachers are trained to administer the behavioral contingencies in the natural environment.

The use of group methods for socialization problems reflects the fact that the peer and sibling subcultures exert a strong influence on preadolescents to conform to group norms. In adolescence, these group pressures become even more powerful. For instance, one study revealed that when high school students' friends encouraged or approved of drug use, 73 percent used drugs. When friends disapproved, only 27 percent reported using drugs.

A major problem in the use of groups with preadolescent children is control, that is, the handling of aggressive behavior. Almost immediately on entering a group situation, children will test its limits. The most difficult aspect of child group therapy is the management of disruptive behavior, which tends to be present in most such groups. For this reason, therapists have turned to the following procedures: setting and enforcing clear limits, providing physical activities to drain off excess energy, and employing heterogeneous grouping (aggressive children mixed with shy, withdrawn children). A major advantage of the group approach is that it tends to be slightly more efficient than individual methods—more children can be treated with the same resources.

It appears, then, that peer and sibling subsystems are finally getting the attention from therapists that they deserve. It remains to be seen whether this is a current fad or a therapeutic breakthrough.

Social Isolation

An earlier section of this book discussed the treatment of shy, withdrawn children whose low level of social interaction was caused, in general, by a passive failure to approach others because of inexperience, lack of confidence, or a pleasurable absorption in solitary activities. In this section, the focus is on the severely withdrawn child who not only has no friends, but shows an active avoidance of peers because of intense anxiety and fearfulness. (Also see section on Shy, Withdrawn Behavior.*)*

Modifying Extreme Social Withdrawal by Modeling with Guided Participation

AUTHORS: Dorothea M. Ross, Sheila A. Ross, and Thomas A. Evans

PRECIS: Reduction of young boy's fear of peer relations by the use of adult modeling and joint participation in social interactions

INTRODUCTION: In modeling with guided participation, a model leads a child through a hierarchy of increasingly difficult tasks, by means of demonstrations, practice, and joint participation, until the child can perform the previously feared response. In this study a six-year-old boy showed such intense fear and avoidance of interactions with his peers that the usual modeling techniques were not applicable. The boy even resisted watching movies and television programs that showed young children. The goal of treatment was to reduce the boy's fear of interacting with his peers while building his social coping skills.

TREATMENT PROGRAM: A female psychologist and a male psychology student who acted as a model conducted the seven-week treatment program. Each week the boy received three ninety-minute sessions, one each with the psychologist and the student, and a joint third session.

During the first phase of the program, which lasted four sessions, the student tried to establish a relationship so that the boy would imitate him. To this end, the student gave a variety of tangible and social reinforcers, rewarded the boy for imitative acts, and was immediately responsive to the boy's requests for attention, help, and approval. During her sessions, the psychologist encouraged the boy to imitate the student's behaviors and rewarded him when he did so. By the end of this phase, the boy had become strongly attached to the student model and talked about him constantly.

The final stage of treatment involved reducing the boy's fear of peers and teaching him positive social interaction skills. The following seven techniques were often employed during the seventeen sessions in this phase:

1. *Graduated series of social interactions.* The boy was given the opportunity to watch the student interacting positively with other children. Because the boy at first refused to watch, either the psychologist provided a running commentary or the student would recount what had happened.

2. *Symbolic modeling presentations.* Both adults briefly presented pictures, stories, or movies involving children and discussed the positive aspects of social interactions.

3. *Providing information.* While the boy watched, the student modeled fear of peer interactions. For example, he asked the psychologist funny but fearful questions, such as "What if he calls me a slippery banana?" This gave the psychologist the opportunity to provide specific reassurance and information.

4. *Role play.* Both adults exhibited appropriate social behaviors within a context of prearranged arguments about humorous, hypothetical social transactions. The boy was drawn into the arguments on the pretext that his help was needed to win the argument.

5. *Graduated series of joint participations in social interactions.* The student model interacted with other children while the boy accompanied him. At first, the boy assisted by carrying materials. To show that other children had rewarding value, situations were set up in which another child was essential to the success of an activity, such as a game that required more than two players.

6. *Modeling.* Both adults first demonstrated and then gave the boy practice in game skills, tricks, slang, and other behaviors designed to promote effective peer interactions.

7. *Situational tests.* With one adult observing, the boy was required to go to a park and just play near the other children. As he gained confidence, he was encouraged to engage in social interactions. Problems were handled by subsequent role play and modeling sessions.

Pretests and posttests revealed that the seven-week treatment program was effective in increasing the boy's social interactions so that they approximated those of normal children. In addition, the frequency of his avoidance behaviors was drastically reduced. A two-month follow-up revealed that his improvement not only had endured but also had generalized to a variety of settings. The child was now able to approach groups of children and engage them in both verbal and play behaviors.

COMMENTARY: The results of this study support previous investigations that have indicated that the technique of modeling with guided participation, developed by Bandura and his colleagues, is a highly successful way of eliminating severe fears or phobias (Bandura, A. "Modeling Approaches to the Modification of Phobic Disorders." In, *CIBA Foundation Symposium: The Role of Learning in Psychotherapy.* Churchill: London, 1968). Although more complex and intensive than general modeling procedures, the guided participation method seems to be the treatment of choice with a really fearful child who will not attend when simply exposed to a positive model. This procedure appears to be widely applicable to problems involving intense anxiety—including both primary and secondary reactions.

SOURCE: Ross, D. M., Ross, S. A., and Evans, T. A. "The Modification of Extreme Social Withdrawal by Modeling with Guided Participation." *Journal of Behavior Therapy and Experimental Psychiatry,* 1971, *2,* 275–279.

Multimedia Group Treatment

AUTHOR: Howard A. Savin

PRECIS: Videotape feedback and social skills training to treat a group of socially inept adolescents in a residential setting

INTRODUCTION: Savin experimented with a group treatment strategy to build social skills in a group of severely withdrawn and passive male adolescents (ages twelve to nineteen) in residential treatment. The goal of this intervention was to develop four specific social behaviors: eye contact, physical posture, verbal responsiveness, and expression of feeling. Training for the seven members of the experimental group consisted of relationship-building interactions with two cotherapists and using videotape equipment to record and play back interactional sequences.

TREATMENT: Following a microcounseling paradigm, training consisted of direct skills training in a group context. First the group was instructed in the component skills of attending and self-expression by means of didactic instruction, modeled demonstrations via videotape, live rehearsals, and coaching. Then the group members practiced discussing real-life problems and received videotape feedback of their interactions. The modeling videotapes had been prepared by two psychological trainees, who had filmed five-minute sequences depicting negative and positive examples of specific communication skills.

Situation tests—dyadic interviews that were rated by observers—were used to evaluate the pretest and posttest interpersonal skills of the experimental and a control group. The analysis revealed that the experimental group developed greater skill proficiency. Additional unsolicited reports from other staff members and parents revealed that many of the boys in the experimental group were exhibiting better conversational abilities, that is, seemed more talkative and attentive with others.

COMMENTARY: This study effectively combines two highly regarded approaches for developing interpersonal relations: skills-specific training and focused videotape feedback. Although the videotape feedback initially provoked anxiety, the group members soon adapted to seeing their faces on the screen and began to focus on their interpersonal functioning. Videotape technology not only can be highly motivating to adolescents, but also can offer them a more objective perspective on their social transactions. Further replications of this study with larger groups are needed, because the sample was small. The use of a structured group learning experience with videotape feedback clearly requires the expenditure of considerable time and money.

SOURCE: Savin, H. A. "Multi-Media Group Treatment with Socially Inept Adolescents." *The Clinical Psychologist*, 1976, *29*, 14–17.

Peer Pair Therapy for Withdrawn Children

AUTHOR: Morton P. Birnbaum

PRECIS: Developing social interaction skills in pairs of extremely withdrawn children

INTRODUCTION: Birnbaum notes that the traditional therapeutic approach to withdrawn children has been group therapy, which is frequently unsuccessful because these children, due to the nature of their problem, tend to be overlooked or to retreat inward even further in a group situation involving three, four, or more children. In individual therapy, social isolates tend to throw up rigid defenses because of the pressure they feel to relate. Birnbaum therefore proposes a new approach to withdrawn children: "peer pair psychotherapy."

Seeing children in pairs, Birnbaum states, reduces the intensity of the therapist-child relationship to levels more acceptable to the child. Also, the shy child tends to find the limited relationship offered by another withdrawn child easier to manage. Furthermore, learning theory suggests the advantage of vicarious reinforcement—the reinforcement effect on one child of merely watching behaviors of a model who receives positive reinforcement. In this connection, studies have shown that withdrawn children who simply observed a film where children were reinforced for social interaction increased their own social responsiveness. The peer-pair situation offers the therapist increased control over reinforcement contingencies for positive social interactions.

PEER PAIR PSYCHOTHERAPY: Birnbaum describes a number of case studies in which he treated pairs of withdrawn children in his office. Typically, the children begin therapy by engaging in parallel play while largely ignoring both the peer and the therapist. The children generally do not find the situation threatening and little or no prodding is required to get them to attend weekly meetings.

Because withdrawn children tend to relate better to things (such as books, toys, and mechanical objects) than to people, the therapeutic goal is to promote positive social interactions between the pair. To this end, the therapist employs a variety of techniques. The beginning of a relationship between the children is fostered by counseling techniques such as praising "feeling" statements in the children (for example, "I feel embarrassed to look at Johnny when I say I like kidding around with him" and "I would feel upset if *my* parents sold my bike without telling me"); commenting favorably on supportive statements between the pair ("I believe you, David; I think you are telling the truth"); approving feedback statements between children ("You don't take care of the toys I lend you"); and promoting acts of caring such as exchanging Christmas presents and visiting one another when sick.

Other therapeutic strategies include presenting games (for example, checkers) and activities (for example, parties) that require social interactions and using behavioral methods such as giving tokens exchangeable for candy for verbal communications between the pair. On occasion, the therapist may offer the children interpretations of their defensive actions. With some pairs, Birnbaum has found it helpful to schedule periodic individual sessions with each child in the pair.

In general, Birnbaum reports, peer pair therapy produces limited but positive social interactions between participating pairs of preadolescent children (ages six to twelve). His conclusion is based on the children's increased communication during the therapy sessions and reports of improvement at home and in school.

COMMENTARY: Peer pair psychotherapy seems most suited for situations where social withdrawal is rather extreme in both children. Birnbaum has found that the optimal pairing of children for this approach requires a fairly close match in degree of interpersonal withdrawal, because a socially outgoing or aggressive child would probably be too threatening for a severely withdrawn child.

SOURCE: Birnbaum, M. P. "Peer Pair Psychotherapy: A New Approach to Withdrawn Children." *Journal of Clinical Child Psychology,* 1975, Spring, 13–16.

Eliminating Isolate Behavior in the Classroom

AUTHOR: Phyllis Perelman

PRECIS: Teacher use of applied behavior analysis to modify isolate behavior in a seven-year-old girl

INTRODUCTION: Julie, a seven-year-old girl in a learning disability class, was an extreme isolate in school. Perelman defines isolate behavior as being outside the group area where the rest of the class was interacting with the teacher. The following study was conducted by Julie's teacher, who was enrolled in an applied behavior analysis course.

APPLIED BEHAVIOR ANALYSIS: First, the teacher recorded the number of minutes Julie spent in the group during the morning language period and afternoon arithmetic session. Then Julie was told that for every minute she stayed in the group during the language and math lessons she would earn a minute to play with her jumprope during recess. The teacher had previously observed that Julie was strongly attached to her jumprope, which she carried to school every day.

After the jumprope contingency was instituted, Julie immediately began to spend time in both the morning and afternoon groups. Soon she was spending the entire twenty-minute periods in the group. The teacher also noted that Julie not only improved her participation in classroom discussions, but, even more importantly, had become much more open and willing to interact with her classmates.

COMMENTARY: This study illustrates that, with proper instruction, regular classroom teachers can design and implement programs involving applied behavior analysis. Perelman reports that the state of Vermont is now working toward the goal of supplying consultants in applied behavior analysis to each of its fifty-three school districts.

SOURCE: Perelman, P. "Elimination of Isolate Behavior of a Girl in a Learning Disability Class." Paper presented at the 50th Annual International Convention of the Council for Exceptional Children, Washington,D.C., March 1972.

Play Therapy

AUTHOR: Virginia Axline

PRECIS: Using nondirective play techniques to overcome social inhibition in a five-year-old boy

INTRODUCTION: According to Axline, play therapy is not just another play activity for the child but a uniquely different experience. Based on the principles of nondirective counseling, her approach is to be generally accepting of children in the playroom while giving them freedom to be themselves. By experiencing their real self more completely in the playroom, troubled children begin to know and accept themselves a little better. Thus, rather than planning activities for the children, Axline lays out play materials and asks the child to decide what he or she would like to do. With so few restrictions on their behavior, children tend to become more relaxed and spontaneous. Negative feelings and behaviors are accepted and allowed release. With time, the negative feelings tend to lessen in frequency and intensity so that more positive feelings toward self and others can emerge. The focus of nondirective play therapy is always on here-and-now behavior rather than on possible etiological factors or past misdeeds.

CASE STUDY: Billy, a five-year-old boy who was in danger of being expelled from his kindergarten class, was referred because he refused to talk to anyone and would crawl around the classroom like a baby. Whenever another child approached him, he hid his face in his arms and rolled up into a ball. Because a recent IQ score had been only 68, his mother was worried that he might be mentally defective.

Billy entered the playroom for his first session with a drooping figure and dragging gait. He completely ignored the therapist and stood for a long time in the center of the room. The therapist explained to him that he could play with any of the toys in the room if he so desired. Finally Billy went to the sandbox and just sifted sand through his hands for the rest of the forty-five-minute session. The second week, he seemed more alert and would look silently at the therapist. He also played with toy cars in the sandbox. During the third session, he made a few comments to the therapist about his sandbox play and she replied each time he spoke. By the fourth session he no longer dragged his feet, his eyes were alert, and he talked more with the therapist. His mother noted that he was more talkative at home, seemed less tense, and his regressive, infantile behavior was disappearing. The school observed similar changes. Billy continued to become more spontaneous and talkative during the ensuing sessions and his play became more complex and imaginative. He became more assertive at home; even stubborn at times when he wanted to do things *his* way. A series of group play experiences ended Billy's treatment. He accepted the other children quite graciously and interacted with them well. Billy seemed more confident in himself and his IQ score was now in the average range. A follow-up one year after termination of treatment revealed that Billy was adjusting well at home and in school. His mother reported that he was a happy, relaxed child who was still a little shy in a large group.

COMMENTARY: Axline has successfully employed nondirective play therapy with a wide variety of cases, including both aggressive, acting-out youngsters and shy, withdrawn children. This approach seems most effective with overly inhibited, young children (ages three to eight) who come from very restrictive home environments. Such children tend to grow in self-confidence from the new experience of complete acceptance and freedom to do things their own way.

SOURCE: Axline, V. "Some Observations on Play Therapy." *Journal of Consulting Psychology*, 1948, *12*, 209–216.

Additional Readings

Allen, K. E., Hart, B., Buell, J. S., Harris, F. R., and Wolf, M. M. "Effects of Social Reinforcement on Isolate Behavior of a Nursery School Child." *Child Development*, 1964, *35*, 511–518.

A four-year-old girl who exhibited a low rate of social interaction with her peers was helped to obtain sustained play relations by the use of behavioral principles. The positive reinforcer was teacher attention given contingent on interaction with another child and withheld consequent on solitary play or attempted interactions solely with an adult. The reinforcement frequencies were thinned as peer interactions became firmly established.

Allen, R. P., Safer, D. J., Heaton, R., Ward, A., and Barrell, M. "Behavior Therapy for Socially Ineffective Children." *Journal of Child Psychiatry*, 1975, *14*, 500–509.

In the school, a group treatment program was set up that stressed the tangible reinforcement of graduated social tasks. Social ineffectiveness was determined by the teacher's judgment and the child's failure to receive peer sociogram selections. Tokens, exchangeable for toys and candy, were given to the fourth- and fifth-graders in the experimental groups for a variety of prosocial behaviors, such as playing simple interactive games, setting rules for group interaction, and showing consideration for others. The tokens were given on a variable interval schedule (ranging from two to nine minutes) using a simple bell timer. Each child who was participating in present target behaviors when the bell rang was given a token. In the final phase of treatment, prosocial behaviors on the playground were rewarded with tokens by the classroom teachers. Results indicated that about 75 percent of children receiving this reinforcement improved.

Levison, C. A. "Use of the Peer Group in the Socialization of the Isolate Child." Mimeographed report. Chicago: Department of Psychiatry, University of Chicago, 1967.

Work with isolated children in Head Start classrooms has indicated that, as the child receives positive reinforcement from his peers, his classroom verbal interaction and cooperative play increases. Levison paired social isolates in dyadic play sessions with peers who exhibited a high rate of social rewards (spontaneously shared toys and candy, smiled, praised, and laughed). Opportunities to participate in these dramatic play sessions (involving housekeeping, trucks, and puppets) resulted in improved social interaction by the isolated preschooler.

Overt Hostility Toward Peers

This section deals with overt, frequent, intense fighting (verbal and physical) between peers. Other sections in this book relate to hostility directed at parents or siblings, as well as to a more diffuse type of aggressiveness that spills over onto everybody. (Also see sections on Aggressiveness *and* Sibling Rivalry.*)*

A Group Play Technique for Rewarding Social Responsibility

AUTHORS: Albert S. Carlin and Hubert E. Armstrong

PRECIS: Utilizing social learning theory to reduce hostility in four severely disturbed boys

INTRODUCTION: It came to the authors' attention that a crisis had developed with a group of boys on a children's day-care unit. The physical fighting and teasing among four boys had become sufficiently intense that it was interfering with treatment, not only for the boys concerned but also for the rest of the children on the unit. Drawing on social learning theory and operant techniques, Carlin and Armstrong devised a group treatment program with two main characteristics: (1) the encouragement of social responsibility—that is, teaching children that the behavior of other group members is partially their own responsibility—and (2) a token reinforcement of social participation in a natural setting.

GROUP PLAY: Four days a week for five weeks, the four boys were brought together in a group for a ninety-minute period of cooperative play. Carlin and Armstrong, together with the two nurses regularly assigned to the boys at this time, acted as therapists. The boys, ages seven to twelve, were severely disturbed children (several diagnosed as schizophrenic and minimally brain damaged) who exhibited explosive, hostile, acting-out behavior. When brought together for several days of observation, the boys would typically interact by teasing and physically attacking one another. At this point, Carlin and Armstrong described the new treatment plan to the boys:

> We notice that you guys have a terrible time playing together and you don't seem to be having as much fun as you might because you are always fighting. We have decided that we are going to pay you to play together. When at least three of you are playing together and seem to be having a good time, we're going to give you five dollars

[the dollars were obsolete state tax tokens that had an
official look and were unobtainable elsewhere]. When
one of you is extra helpful to another, you're going to
get paid a bonus of a couple of dollars more. But when
you start fighting together or have trouble getting along
in a way that you can't handle yourselves and one of
us has to come in and settle it for you, then it's going to
cost you money. Everytime one of you hits another for
no reason or hits the other guy when there is a better
way to settle the problem, it's going to cost you six dollars.
All the money you earn will go into this box and at the
end of the time that you play each day, we will split up
the money among you. The money you earn out here
can buy the things in the store [a large tray heaped high
with candies, toy soldiers, marbles, and other objects
attractive to boys this age] [p. 171].

The boys were reminded about the specifics of the plan each
day before they began their group session.

The boys seemed enthusiastic about the plan and the first day
produced a remarkable change in their behavior. Rather than provoking each other as usual, they worked together in harmony to
build a spaceship out of blocks. When tokens were paid to the boys
during the session, there was a simultaneous announcement of the
amount and reason for payment. When a fine was levied near the
end of the session, because of the misbehavior of one of the boys,
the group members were told it was their responsibility to stop the
boy from throwing things at the adults. With the help of adult suggestions, the group was able to engage the deviant boy in a constructive activity, which meant that the rest of the earnings was preserved.

After several sessions, it became obvious that the system of
fines was not sufficient to halt all the disruptive behaviors. The
group was just not able to cope with certain of its members. Thus,
a "penalty box" was initiated, that is, an out-of-control child was
physically placed in a penalty box by the adults. During this period,
the child could not receive rewards earned by the rest of the group
nor could any of his behaviors while in the box penalize the rest of
the group. The penalty system proved effective in controlling the

behavior of one of the most disturbed boys. Subsequently, one of the group members was discharged, while two of the remaining boys seemed to derive more satisfaction from their positive relationship than from the rewards of including the third boy in their play. At this point, the fining procedure was eliminated and the boys were just rewarded for appropriate behaviors. All misbehaviors were simply ignored. During the remaining sessions, a genuine warmth seemed to be developing among the three group members. There was also far less acting-out behavior during the sessions. The program was terminated on the discharge of a second group member.

COMMENTARY: Although there was no formal evaluation of this program, Carlin and Armstrong stated that it successfully inhibited the aggressive acting out of the children, who were then able to work together in reasonable harmony. By the time the program was over, the staff on the boys' wards also reported that the boys' destructive behavior had markedly diminished. During the play sessions, the children were observed to be helping one another behave properly by the use of such techniques as distraction, avoidance, and reminders. Through the flexible use of operant and group techniques, Carlin and Armstrong were able to instill a sense of social responsibility in the boys and some of the boys even began to develop mutually gratifying friendships.

SOURCE: Carlin, A. S., and Armstrong, H. E. "Rewarding Social Responsibility in Disturbed Children: A Group Play Technique." *Psychotherapy: Theory, Research and Practice,* 1968, *5,* 169–174.

Control of Aggression in a Nursery School Class

AUTHORS: Paul Brown and Rogers Elliott

PRECIS: Having teachers systematically ignore aggression and attend to acts incompatible with aggression

INTRODUCTION: Traditionally, most adults inhibit aggression in children by developing anxiety through the use of punishment and/or by developing guilt through the inculcation of moral values. Brown and Elliott, on the other hand, attempted to inhibit the aggressive behavior of all the boys in a nursery school class by strengthening incompatible positive responses. The subjects were twenty-seven boys ages three and four. The goal of the study was to control both verbal aggression (hitting, pushing and holding) and verbal hostility (disparaging and threatening). From social learning theory, Brown and Elliott hypothesized that adult attention had served as a prime reinforcer for the aggressive behaviors.

TREATMENT: During the one week of this experiment, the classroom teachers were instructed to ignore the aggressive acts of the boys while making a concerted effort to attend to and praise non-aggressive, cooperative, and peaceful behavior. If there was danger of physical injury (for example, one boy hammering on another boy's head), the teachers were instructed to separate the two and then leave. A comparison of pretest and posttest observations revealed that significant reductions in both kinds of aggressive acts were achieved.

COMMENTARY: One of the authors actually stayed in the classroom during the intervention week to ensure that the experimental procedure was followed. This undoubtedly contributed to the success of the study, as the teachers reported that it was very difficult for them not to attend to the aggressive behaviors of children. Although skeptical of the success of the procedures, the teachers later became convinced of the efficacy of the method.

SOURCE: Brown, P., and Elliott, R. "Control of Aggression in a Nursery School Class." *Journal of Experimental Child Psychology,* 1965, *2,* 103–107.

A Sensitivity Training Approach
to Group Therapy

AUTHOR: Uri Rueveni

PRECIS: Modifying classroom disturbance by sensitivity training with junior high school students

INTRODUCTION: Acting as a consultant to a junior high school located in a ghetto neighborhood, Rueveni helped the school organize a sensitivity training program. Teachers were asked to submit names of students whose aggressive behavior (fighting, destructiveness) was currently unmanageable. After receiving a personal explanation of the purpose of the training, twenty of the thirty students on the list volunteered to participate. Five students dropped out after the first two weeks; the continuing group included ten black and five Puerto Rican students from thirteen to fifteen years of age—eight boys and seven girls. The group met with the two therapists in a school classroom for two hours once a week until the end of the school year—a period of five months.

SENSITIVITY TRAINING: The objectives of the group were to help the students increase: (1) their social sensitivity (perceptions and feelings about the personalities and emotions of other children and school personnel) and (2) their behavioral flexibility (ability to behave appropriately in interpersonal situations). A variety of techniques were employed to help the students create some common bonds, share mutual concerns, and become more aware of their own needs and needs of others. The following is a brief description of some of the group exercises:

1. *Grab Bag.* A paper bag filled with slips of paper was passed around the group. Each slip contained a familiar word, such as *school, teachers, anger, fight, hate,* and *cool.* Each group member was asked to read the word on his slip and describe his feelings about the word to the others. Initially, the students revealed many negative feelings about school and their teachers. The therapists just listened

and tried to really understand the students' deep-seated feelings. As the sessions continued, the associations of the students became more positive; for example, *fight*—"we don't have to fight."

2. *Strength Bombardment.* The teen-ager who was "it" sat in the center of the circle. Each group member in turn was asked to describe what he liked about the designated person and to express all of the positive feelings he had toward him. Most of the students were obviously delighted to receive positive feedback.

3. *Blind Walk.* The students split into two-member teams, with one member playing the role of leader and the other of blind follower. With his eyes closed, the follower relied on the leader to take his arm and guide him on a walk around the classroom. After five minutes, the students reversed roles. This exercise made the students more aware of the feelings of interpersonal trust and dependency.

4. *Free Time.* The students split up into two-member teams to plan and engage in a ten-minute activity. Among the mutually enjoyable activities engaged in by the dyads were singing "soul" songs, dictating into a tape recorder, and planning a party.

5. *Expressing Negative Feelings.* The members of the group selected a "speaker" to sit in the center of a circle and express his negative feelings toward school personnel and other students. As expected, it was much harder for students to express negative as opposed to positive feelings. It was particularly difficult for them to direct angry feelings to one another, because doing so tended to provoke considerable guilt in the confronter and tension among members. Most students, however, could accept criticism and deal with it constructively. One fight did break out as a result of this exercise, but the two male students involved later made up and eventually became close friends.

Reports from teachers and students about this sensitivity program were generally enthusiastic. Some teacchers did complain that their students were now expressing unfair criticisms toward them. These teachers were invited to the group sessions to observe the purpose and nature of the sensitivity interactions. Incidents of aggression among students who participated in the group training were lower at the end of the program than at the beginning.

COMMENTARY: Although quite popular in the late 1960s, the use of encounter group techniques seems to be on the decline in recent years. A major criticism of encounter process is that, without extensive training of group leaders and careful screening of participants, the tensions inherent in the encounter sessions can trigger off serious emotional upheavals in the group members. On the other hand, encounter and sensitivity methods have been reported to be dramatically successful in some cases, particularly with drug addicts.

SOURCE: Rueveni, U. "Using Sensitivity Training with Junior High School Students." *Children*, 1971, *18*, 69–72.

Tailormade Peer Therapy Groups

AUTHOR: Paul W. Clement

PRECIS: Applying social learning theory in a group context

INTRODUCTION: Whenever a child experiences a behavior problem related to his peers, such as impulsive aggressive behavior, Clement suggests tailormade peer therapy groups can be helpful. Clement presents a detailed case study involving Jeff, a five-year-old boy who had no friends in his kindergarten class because he frequently teased and pinched his peers. Typically, the peer therapy group is formed by the child's parents or teacher, who recruit three to five peers from the local neighborhood or the classroom. The parents generally invite the parents of the other children over to their house for coffee and an explanation of the procedure is given by the therapist. The parents are told that their children are not to receive therapy themselves but to act as therapeutic agents for the target child.

TREATMENT: The tailormade peer group usually meets for an hour a week in the large playroom at a mental health clinic. In a gamelike atmosphere, one child is chosen at random to be "chief" and to wear the headdress that contains a bug-in-the-ear device. The therapist observes through a one-way mirror and coaches the "chief" as to when to give tokens to the other children. These tokens are redeemed at the end of the session for material rewards from the therapist's "store." Tokens are awarded whenever the children play cooperatively with one another. The "chief" receives the same number of tokens as the child earning the most tokens for that day.

Another procedure involves having the "chief" record points for the group on a Lehigh Valley Electronics points counter whenever the therapist's pocket programer goes "beep." The therapist actuates the "beep" whenever the target child is playing cooperatively with one or more of the other children. Videotape feedback, live modeling, and behavioral rehearsal are also common techniques used in these group sessions. At the end of a session, the therapist often asks the children to practice their group behaviors during the coming week in the natural environment. Teachers and parents are also often given behavioral prescriptions for the next week.

COMMENTARY: This procedure illustrates the use of group contingencies with peers recruited from the child's class or neighborhood. Clement has found that, with a little persuasion and explanation, parents are generally willing to "loan" their children for such a purpose. The approach can be used to modify the behavior of hostile/aggressive, bizarre/psychotic, shy/withdrawn, and immature/scapegoated children. Clement also reports success with tailormade groups formed with siblings rather than peers. The major rationale for using peers or siblings as therapeutic agents is to enhance the generalization of treatment effects from the treatment setting to the home and/or classroom environments.

SOURCE: Clement, P. W. "Tailor-Made Peer Therapy Groups for Children." In B. Lubin (chairman), "Parents and Psychologists: The New Team." Symposium presented at the American Psychological Association Convention, Washington, D.C., September 1976.

Additional Readings

Dannefer, E., Brown, R., and Epstein, N. "Experience in Developing a Combined Activity and Verbal Group Therapy Program with Latency-Age Boys." *International Journal of Group Psychotherapy,* 1975, *25,* 331–337.

After experimenting with different models, the authors decided to combine both activities and verbal interactions in one group session. During the activity session, a short discussion session was held that maximized the effectiveness of both verbal and active group therapy. The group assigned each boy specific tasks related to his problem. An aggressive boy, for example, would be assigned the task of playing cooperatively with another boy. If he did well at his task, the boy would receive a gold star; if he did not do well, he was given a blue star; and if he lied to the group, he would be assigned a red star. Whenever a boy forgot his task, he not only received no star but was also given rebukes from the group, such as

"This group is only for guys who want to change." At the end of each month, the boy with the most gold stars was given the "Most Improved Player" trophy. To uncover a boy who was lying, the group played a "detective" game, in which they looked for missing facts in a boy's story or a logically incoherent report. Once a month, the boy's parents were invited to observe the group through a one-way mirror.

Henderson, W. E., and Silber, L. "The Behavioral Contracting Group: A Group Approach to Treating Children in an Outpatient Setting." Unpublished manuscript. Raleigh, N.C.: W. H. Trentman Mental Health Center, 1976.

Henderson and Silber use behavioral techniques to treat five to eight preadolescent children in an open-ended group. The group meets for one-and-a-half hours a week. Sitting in a circle, for the first forty-five minutes they set up or discuss the contracts they will work on at home during the next week. Parents and/or teachers are sent a copy of the contract and asked to record daily the presence or absence of specific problem behaviors, such as not hitting a brother. Group members earn tokens not only for setting up and fulfilling their contracts but also for specific prosocial behaviors during the activity period of the session. Thus, while playing a table game, a boy might earn a token for playing by the rules of the game, or ignoring provocative teasing of others. Refreshments are served at the end of the session and then the boys go to the cotherapists' "store" either to bank their tokens or to exchange them for concrete rewards, like candy, models, and radios. Most disruptive behavior in the group is handled by ignoring it or paying attention to the desirable behavior of another child. Excessive aggressiveness, such as kicking or fighting, is handled first by placing the boy in a corner for five minutes of quiet time. If this proves unsuccessful, the boy is sent to a separate isolation room until he can remain quiet for five minutes. The parents of the boys attend separate bimonthly groups for instruction in behavioral and child management principles.

Pinkston, E. M., Reese, N. M., LeBlanc, J. M., and Baer, D. M. "Independent Control of a Preschool Child's Aggression and Peer Interaction by Contingent Teacher Attention." *Journal of Applied Behavior Analysis*, 1973, *6*, 115–124.

To handle the persistent aggression of a preschool child toward his peers, his teacher was instructed to largely ignore the child's aggressive behavior and to attend instead to whatever child he was attacking. Moreover, all positive behaviors by the aggressive child were attended to by the teacher. This decreased the aggressive behavior to an acceptable level.

Rhodes, S. L. "Short-Term Groups of Latency-Age Children in a School Setting." *International Journal of Group Psychotherapy,* 1973, *23,* 204–215.

Short-term group therapy (six to eight sessions) was carried out in a school setting with latency-age children. The therapists used a conventional verbal treatment model that emphasized interpretation of here-and-now behavior, pointing out alternative courses of action, reflection of feelings, and role playing. Group members were encouraged to set their own rules and confront one another in regard to inappropriate behavior.

Stedman, J. M., Peterson, T. L., and Cardarelle, J. "Application of a Token System in a Preadolescent Boys' Group." *Journal of Behavior Therapy and Experimental Psychiatry,* 1971, *2,* 23–29.

Operant procedures were used with a group of eight preadolescent boys whose general mode of relating was hostile and aggressive. Within an activity group format, tokens were given for a wide variety of prosocial behaviors, such as participating in group decision making, listening to others, and trying to help others with their problems. Most of the tokens were given at fixed time intervals (after ten, thirty, and forty-five minutes of the activity segment of the session). Tokens could be exchanged for the right to attend the next session, to participate in the party held during the last ten minutes of each session, and to go on field trips.

Sibling Rivalry

Sibling rivalry tends to occur when the child's need to feel worthwhile is frustrated, whereas jealousy occurs when the need to love and be loved is frustrated (M. Smart and R. Smart, An Introduction to Family Relationships, *Philadelphia: Saunders, 1953). Feelings of jealousy are more likely to be directed toward a younger sibling, and rivalrous feelings toward an older sibling. Competition and envy are also involved when a child endeavors to do as well as or better than another sibling.*

The sibling relationship is an area that has been relatively neglected in the social psychology literature. We still know very little, for example, about "normal" sibling interactions at different age levels. Consequently, it is very difficult to define disturbed sibling relations in cases that fall short of actual physical injury. We also do not know why siblings in some families generally act in a positive and supportive manner toward one another, while negative feelings and verbal putdowns among siblings tend to prevail in other households.

Excessive fighting among siblings is a common complaint among parents. A most effective intervention for reducing this fighting is time out, that is, sending all the children who are involved in the altercation to time-out areas, such as their bedrooms. No attempt is made to determine who was to blame for the fight. In this way, the siblings are discouraged from baiting one another into starting a fight. Parents should couple this time-out technique with praise and attention when the siblings are playing cooperatively together. The following articles present alternate strategies for coping with more intense expressions of hostility among siblings. (Also see section on Overt Hostility Toward Peers.*)*

Modifying a Deviant Sibling Interaction Pattern in the Home

AUTHORS: K. Daniel O'Leary, Susan O'Leary, and Wesley C. Becker

PRECIS: Modifying the destructive interpersonal relations of two brothers by the use of a token reinforcement system and time out from positive reinforcement

INTRODUCTION: This study focused on the deviant interactions of two siblings—Barry, six years old, and Jeff, three years old. The boys frequently angered their mother by yelling, hitting, and destroying each other's toys while in the basement playroom. Barry had been receiving psychotherapy for two years and was described as extremely hyperactive, aggressive, and destructive.

REINFORCEMENT TECHNIQUES: During the first two days of treatment, the cooperative behaviors emitted by either child were continually reinforced by the therapist, who put an M & M candy in the child's mouth while saying "Good." Cooperative behaviors were defined as any incidence of asking for a toy, requesting each other's help, and saying "Please" and "Thank you." For the third and fourth days, the boys' cooperative behaviors were alternately reinforced every second or fourth time. Beginning on the fifth day, the boys were explicitly told that they would receive an M & M if they asked each other for things, if they answered each other's questions, if they said "Please" and "Thank you," and if they played nicely together, that is, made things together, took turns, or carried out a request. The boys were reminded of these instructions at the start of subsequent sessions and during each session as deemed necessary.

A token reinforcement system was also introduced on the fifth day. Apart from getting M & M's, the boys were told that checks would be put on the blackboard for cooperative behavior and removed for deviant acts. Checks were redeemable for back-up reinforcers that included candy bars, bubble gum, caps, kites, comic books, puzzles, and other inexpensive toys. By the twelfth day, the M & M's were discontinued and the number of checks needed for back-up reinforcers gradually increased. If a boy threw a temper tantrum because he did not receive a back-up reward after a session, this behavior was ignored by both therapist and parent. After sixteen sessions, the mean percentage of cooperative play had increased from 46 percent to 80 percent during a session.

At this point, the administration of the token system was turned over to the mother, with two modifications. First, a punishment contingency was applied to incidents of kicking, hitting, name calling, and throwing objects at each other. The assignment of tokens alone had not proven powerful enough to eliminate these aggressive interactions. The punishment consisted of isolating the aggressor in the bathroom where there was little opportunity for amusement. The boy had to remain in the bathroom at least five minutes and had to be quiet for a three-minute period prior to being let out. Also the token system now required points to be earned over several days before payoff would occur. Although the mother at first received nonverbal signals from the therapist as to when to administer contingencies, she soon ran the program entirely on her own. The time-out procedure was employed as much as four times a day in the beginning, but only once during the last four days. By the end of the second thirteen sessions, the recordings indicated that the boys were being cooperative 90 percent of the time. At this point, the experimental procedure was discontinued, although the mother continued to use the time-out punishment with the boys for incidents of hitting, kicking, and pushing. She also gave positive rewards (a penny) to Barry for every time he made his bed.

COMMENTARY: Although the experimental procedure did not completely eliminate Barry's explosive outbursts, his parents and teachers reported that the incidence of his aggressive acts decreased markedly during the following year. It would seem, then, that the reinforcement techniques were successful in reducing the frequency of aggressive behaviors in a severely disturbed child. This was one of the first studies to demonstrate that parents can be trained to execute behavior modification systems in the home. By involving parents in the administration of treatment, one lays the groundwork for the maintenance of any behavior gains after contact with the therapist ends.

SOURCE: O'Leary, K. D., O'Leary, S., and Becker, W. C. "Modification of a Deviant Sibling Interaction Pattern in the Home." *Behaviour Research and Therapy,* 1967, *5,* 113–120.

Behavior Therapy with Children

AUTHOR: Salvatore Russo

PRECIS: Applying social learning theory to help a young boy get along with his sisters and parents

INTRODUCTION: Rather than discussing child management problems with parents in the office, Russo experimented with a different approach: direct supervision of parents as they interact with their children in the playroom. Initially, the parent is asked to observe the therapist using behavioral approaches with their child; then the parent is invited to participate and it becomes a three-way interaction. Eventually the therapist observes the parent and child interacting with each other. Often other family members are invited to participate. The goal is to help the family develop and use behavioral techniques at home.

Russo discusses the case of Mike, an eight-year-old, hyperactive boy who was referred to the outpatient clinic because of poor home adjustment, particularly with his three sisters. Mike was physically abusive to his sisters and on different occasions had pushed them off bikes, swings, and into deep swimming pools.

TREATMENT: The treatment plan initially involved seeing the mother and boy together in the office for fifteen minutes to discuss the events of the previous week. Then they were seen in operant play therapy for forty-five minutes. A final thirty-minute conference was held with the mother alone.

When the boy acted in a socially acceptable manner with the mother in the playroom, she was urged to join in the activity enthusiastically. When he broke rules, the mother was advised to immediately turn her back and completely ignore the child. She was to smoke, converse, or play a game with the therapist, or begin an activity of her own. As expected, the boy reacted to this behavior by escalating his temper tantrums, so that several stormy sessions ensued. The therapist often offered immediate comments on the meaning of the boy's behavior. Mike soon found he could no longer cheat, change the rules, or make his mother do his bidding in the playroom. He gradually learned he could not get his own way any more, so he became more cooperative with his mother in the sessions. Soon he seemed to enjoy her company and the play sessions thoroughly. At this point, his sisters were brought into the playroom on an individual basis. It became obvious that they viewed Mike as the black sheep of the family. Their provocative behavior served to aggravate his deviant behavior both in the playroom and at home.

After twenty sessions, Mike was considered much improved. He was less hostile and asserted himself in a more socially acceptable way. He was more relaxed at home and even the teasing of his sisters had become more playful and benevolent. His parents were much relieved to discover that his misbehavior seemed to be the result of faulty learning rather than of the "brain damage" suggested by other professionals.

COMMENTARY: This study represents a pioneering effort to supervise parents directly as they attempted to develop more effective child management skills. The therapist not only modeled the desired management techniques but also was present to offer advice and comments when a real-life problem was displayed in the playroom. The unique advantage of this approach is that the therapist is able to observe and supervise interactions of family members firsthand, rather than having to rely on secondhand reports of parents and children. Sibling rivalry tends to be a high-frequency behavior that is most amenable to the application of operant techniques, especially when on-the-spot supervision is available from the therapist.

SOURCE: Russo, S. "Adaptations in Behavioural Therapy with Children." *Behaviour Research and Therapy*, 1964, 2, 43–47.

Therapy of a Six-Year-Old Who Committed Fratricide

AUTHORS: Maria Paluszny and Marie McNabb

PRECIS: Dynamically oriented case study of a girl who had killed her four-month-old brother

INTRODUCTION: Although hostility between siblings tends to be quite intense at times, it seldom reaches the point of a murderous act. Siblings undoubtedly think about killing one another but they seldom act it out. In this article, Paluszny and McNabb recount the underlying dynamics and psychoanalytic treatment of a case of fratricide. Maggie, an appealing six-year-old girl, was brought to treatment because she had killed her four-month-old brother two days before.

DYNAMICS: The oldest of three children in a one-parent family, Maggie had experienced her alcoholic father becoming physically violent toward both her and her mother. The mother had separated from the father when Maggie was three. The younger siblings, Sally, age two and a half, and John, four months, had two different fathers who did not become involved with the family. After rebelling against a strict Baptist upbringing, Maggie's twenty-three-year-old mother had found herself a high school dropout with three children to raise by herself.

The incident occurred when her mother had left Maggie alone for a half hour in charge of the two younger siblings. The mother returned to find the baby dead in his crib. Maggie stated that she had taken John from his crib and put him on the sofa. He then fell off and began crying. To quiet him, Maggie said, she had choked him. An autopsy, however, revealed numerous skull fractures that could not have been caused by a simple fall. Most probably Maggie had repeatedly hit the infant's head on the floor to stop him from crying. The mother was placed on probation for neglect charges on the understanding that she and Maggie would begin outpatient treatment. In therapy, the mother revealed that she viewed Maggie as a "bad child" who had deprived her of a son. It seems that having a son was extremely important to the mother's self-esteem at this time.

TREATMENT: Since Maggie exhibited massive repression and regression in outpatient sessions, it was decided to admit her to day treatment. Also, her mother soon became pregnant again and it was felt that more extensive work was needed to prevent the history from repeating itself.

    The first goal of therapy was to slowly undermine Maggie's rigid defenses so that she could remember and reexperience her brother's death and the concomitant feelings. Through clay and doll play, Maggie was gradually able to talk about her brother. The therapist helped her talk by using prompts ("Did you perhaps hit him?") and interpretation of resistances ("Is it hard for you to talk about babies because something unpleasant happened to yours?"). Maggie usually accepted the therapist's interpretations readily.

    After her brother's death, Maggie had become unwilling to show any anger whatsoever, even when provoked by her peers. As soon as she was able to talk a little about her brother, however, her angry feelings began to emerge. She started to hit dolls in the playroom and struck out at her therapist and teachers. Maggie responded immediately to controls and seemed to be asking for external help with these hostile impulses. Once her mother had delivered a new baby brother, Maggie's hostile acting out decreased substantially.

    In therapy, Maggie began to remember more about John's death. She recalled that he had been crying in his crib and that she had picked him up but could not remember anything thereafter— if he had fallen or if she had hit him. She did feel responsible for his death and felt she must be "bad." The therapist tried to help her intellectualize her guilt feelings by pointing out that even if she had felt like killing John she could not have known it would be forever.

    At this stage, Maggie's unconscious wish to be punished seemed to produce provocative behavior. She repeatedly stated that she was bad and that her mother called her "stupid." When the therapist disagreed with these evaluations, Maggie tried to prove their validity by attempting to hit or hurt the therapist. The therapist interpreted the reason for her hostile acts and repeated her belief that Maggie was not bad. A turning point in therapy happened at this time: Maggie repeatedly buried a small coffin in the sandbox and began to cry. The therapist verbalized what Maggie must be feeling and sat with her while she expressed her intense sadness and regret over the incident.

Feelings of depression resulting from parental loss and rejection were prominent in the final stage of therapy. Maggie would often attempt to satisfy her unmet needs for nurturance by stealing things and eating. The motives for these behaviors were pointed out to her and it was suggested that talking about her feelings would be more helpful. Fortunately, at this time Maggie and her siblings were being cared for primarily by their maternal grandmother, who was able to meet some of Maggie's needs for nurturance and attention. Whenever possible, the therapist encouraged Maggie to talk about her home life. In school, the staff tried to give extra support by expressing their feelings of liking and caring for Maggie. Maggie responded to this increased attention by taking more pride in her appearance. After one year of day treatment, Maggie was able to return to public school. Her therapy was turned over to the school social worker, who concentrated on supportive services. At home, Maggie was observed to be relating naturally to her siblings, including the new baby. A one-year follow-up indicated that Maggie was doing well at home and in school.

COMMENTARY: In this case, the roots of fratricide involved severe parental abuse and neglect. The focus of therapy was on helping the child discuss and accept her role in the death of her brother. In helping a child cope with guilt feelings in such cases, it is important for the therapist to realize that the act of killing is psychologically quite different for a child than for an adult. There is considerable evidence to support the fact that young children do not comprehend the finality of death. Another goal of therapy in this case was to help the child obtain alternate sources of nurturance and support apart from her mother.

SOURCE: Paluszny, M., and McNabb, M. "Therapy of a Six-Year-Old Who Committed Fratricide." *Journal of Child Psychiatry,* 1975, *14,* 319–336.

Additional Readings

Pfouts, J. H. "The Sibling Relationship: A Forgotten Dimension." *Social Work,* 1976, *21,* 200–204.

Pfouts reports on a study of the effects of social comparison of siblings by parents. The findings supported the hypothesis that when children differ significantly in cognitive or personality characteristics that are highly valued by parents, the less well-endowed child will show more hostility toward siblings than will the more favorably endowed. Intervention, then, should be directed toward helping the less successful child find new roles in which he can gain family recognition and self-esteem.

Shapiro, S. "Ever Do in Your Kid Brother?" *Psychiatric Quarterly,* 1973, *47,* 203–207.

Shapiro describes the intense hostility that exists at times between normal siblings—in this case, a sister and brother. Infuriated at being punished for fighting with her kid brother, the girl declared that she wished her brother were "dead and buried." She soon came to regret this remark when the brother was injured in a car accident. The boy's first gesture after recovering from a mild concussion was to stick his tongue out at his sister!

6

Disturbed Relationship
with Parents

Successful intervention in disturbed relationships between child and parents has been mainly accomplished by psychodynamic and by learning-theory methods. There is a growing trend toward combining these approaches to reduce tension, increase satisfaction, and improve communication. Behavioral and psychodynamic therapists focus on the same problems but use different language when explaining cause and treatment. However, the behavioral methods are frequently more detailed and formalized and more consistently applied. Some of the techniques used are unique to therapists operating within a learning-theory framework.

429

Many of the studies described in this chapter that concern overt hostility toward parents employ various learning theory approaches. Engeln, Knutson, Laughy and Garlington (1968) use different therapists for each family member and often see battling siblings together in order to decrease their fighting. Johnson and Brown (1969) suggest that the therapist model child-rearing techniques for parents. Parents are also involved in direct instruction and group discussion and learn to use social reinforcement. Bernal (1969) tailors behavioral approaches for parental use by analyzing videotapes of family interaction. Parents may be urged to reduce their own unproductive verbalizations, ignore abusive behavior, or use positive or negative reinforcement. Boisvert (1974) suggests time out for hostile acts, combined with social reinforcement.

Coe (1970) stresses combining family communication and learning theory approaches. Barcai and Rabkin (1972) offer a novel method of influencing family communication—the family temporarily excommunicates the hostile, uncooperative member, thus giving a clear message that unacceptable behavior will not be tolerated and interaction will only occur in the presence of acceptable behavior. Sanders (1975) approaches disturbed interaction by actually teaching the parents to express warmth to their child. And Brandzel (1965) employs a psychodynamic approach to resolving family conflicts.

Behavioral and psychodynamic approaches used with hostile children have also been employed to reduce a child's overdependency on parents. Khan (1971) notes that physical separation is dramatically effective in breaking a strong overly dependent relationship. Once parents and child are separated, both psychodynamic and behavioral approaches (token economy) are used to promote the child's independent functioning. A straightforward application of learning theory is typified by Wahler, Winkel, Peterson, and Morrison (1965), who teach parents to reinforce the child's independent behavior. Straughan (1964) desensitized a child (by counterconditioning and counseling the parents) to a tense, inhibiting mother. Kramer and Settlage (1962) foster psychological and independent growth with psychoanalytic methods.

When a family is seen together, an eclectic approach can be used to influence the behavior and attitudes of the child and the parents. Interaction patterns can be observed and destructive patterns can be pointed out and changed. More satisfying responses may occur both during therapy and at home. Focusing on and discussing each member's perceptions may lead to changes in the habitual, long-standing pattern. When family members' goals become clearer to themselves and others, their goals may become more reachable. In discussions, once individual goals (desires) are identified, specific behavioral techniques or communication exercises may be beneficially employed. For example, a therapist may see a hostile daughter and her parents, who all desire a more pleasant, calmer atmosphere. The angry girl feels that her parents are unfair and that her own belligerence is justified. It soon becomes clear that the parents expect cooperative and respectful behavior from the girl and they feel disappointed. At this point, a behavioral approach might be suggested—that all family members begin to reinforce each other positively and to ignore inappropriate behavior. This intervention may change the pattern, reduce the girl's hostile behavior, and lead to more positive interactions and the perception that their wishes are being more adequately achieved. Family members may be asked to deliberately not respond with disappointment and anger, which only lead to an increase in angry responses. The girl may be taught to control her angry responses by using muscular relaxation when aroused or by thinking about a pleasant event or key words (such as *calm down*). It can be particularly effective to arrange a situation in which the girl views her parents as being helpful by participating with her in the new control process. They might remind her, in an agreed-on manner, to employ her own self-control methods. Similarly, the girl may play a helpful role by reminding the parents when they lapse into a previously agreed-on negative mode of reacting. Some families like a formal discussion hour in which everyone has a turn to speak while others listen. This approach fosters a feeling of importance and respect, because each individual is taken seriously.

A growing trend is to analyze the family system, understand the interactive pattern, and directly influence the system. This approach has been used for all of the behavior problems in this book. It is especially applicable when the predominant problem is the disturbed parent-child relationship, manifested by a child's hostility or overdependency. An angry girl, for example, may be incorrigible when with the parents. Their inability to cope with her may be a result of their marital differences, which prevent them from taking a unified, effective position. A grandparent may be playing a contributing role by siding with the girl or interfering in some way. The analysis of the system makes for a different type of intervention than does viewing the child as a hostile individual who requires individual psychotherapy. Regardless of theoretical orientation, the therapist can then approach the identified disturbed pattern.

Overt Hostility Toward Parents

Overt hostility is the open display of antagonism, ill will, opposition, or resistance. Hostile children often act as if their parents were enemies, with whom they have frequent battles. Hostile children are often critical of others, easily annoyed, irritable, and complaining. The goal of therapy is to help the child be more friendly, cooperative, helpful, and respectful. (Also see the section on Aggressiveness.)

Excommunication in Family Therapy

AUTHORS: Avner Barcai and Leslie Rabkin

PRECIS: Parents' use of intentionally isolating hostile children in order to promote cooperative behavior

INTRODUCTION: Barcai and Rabkin note that ignoring a child can successfully diminish undesirable behavior. They suggest that active, intentional isolation (excommunication) can also be a powerful change agent, especially with rebellious and spiteful preadolescents and adolescents who have been resistant to conventional treatment and with adolescents who act out overt or covert conflicts between the parents. Such parents do not act together to set appropriate limits. Barcai and Rabkin report that "incurable" adolescents have responded to this approach, showing more normal adolescent behavior after being excommunicated.

CASE STUDY: A thirteen-year-old girl was referred for extreme misbehavior in school and refusal to follow any rules. At home, she did what she pleased or had a temper tantrum until she got what she wanted. She had been spoiled by both of her parents and was becoming more difficult to manage. During a family therapy interview, she ran out of the room. Her mother felt helpless and her father was furious. Discussion revealed their past lack of consensus and use of ineffective restrictive or permissive methods of child rearing. In summarizing the situation, the therapist noted that the girl never had learned to postpone gratification. Before the next meeting, the parents were asked to define acceptable and unacceptable behavior and decide on appropriate punishment. The mother appeared helpless and showed anger toward the father's wish to use force on his daughter. They reported an incident in which the father had spanked the girl for misbehavior and the mother had consoled her. The mother was seen as using her daughter in the conflict with her husband.

    During the next session, it was clear that marital hostility prevented any cooperation. Any move by one parent was belittled and sabotaged by the other and the children were caught between constantly changing loyalties. The therapist considered the girl to be scapegoated in the continual parental battles. When a family uproar occurred, she smiled victoriously, presumably to hide her unhappiness.

Since the parents would not cooperate and frequently distorted events, they were asked only not to respond at all to their daughter. None of the family were to respond unless she did what was specifically required of her (such as picking up her clothes). Nothing would be done for her until she demonstrated readiness to cooperate. It was stressed that this was not revenge, but a method to help her return to the family. The therapist told them he was available at any time to handle any crisis that arose. The family followed the plan and did not respond to the girl's threats. She angrily left the house but returned several hours later and cleaned her room. The father had told her that she would be welcomed back, but only on the family's terms, and the mother agreed. During the next two weeks, the excommunication method had to be employed on two other occasions—with successful results. Grudgingly, the girl began to accept school discipline.

The therapist interpreted the girl's behavior as acting out her mother's anger at the father and her mother's rebellious feelings. Instead of confronting his wife, the father became angry at his daughter. Her siblings envied and hated her. The therapist saw her as being stuck in an intensive, hostile dependent relationship with her family. Excommunication gave her a clear task, expectation to obey rules, a way to learn postponement of immediate gratification, and distance from her parents.

COMMENTARY: Barcai and Rabkin see the process as undermining the necessity for the child to be a pawn in the family conflict and review the treatment of thirty-two adolescents and their families. They note that many types of acting out may occur with this method and suggest caution, but feel that a warm, firm, experienced, available therapist is capable of handling any crisis that arises.

With rebellious, hostile children who have been resistant to change, excommunication is a provocative method to consider. Barcai and Rabkin clearly outline advantages and problems, but they make a good case for its use with parents who cannot cooperate when using usual child-rearing techniques. The approach can help a family develop clear, unambivalent messages. Not responding is a task that the parents can do together without criticizing each other. The child quickly learns that this time family members mean what they say. Excommunication is seen as an effective, efficient means of breaking a difficult, long-standing pattern of family conflict.

SOURCE: Barcai, A., and Rabkin, L. "Excommunication as a Family Therapy Technique." *Archives of General Psychiatry,* 1972, *27,* 804–808.

Training Mothers to Modify Brat Behavior

AUTHOR: Martha E. Bernal

PRECIS: Use of televised feedback in teaching parents operant learning principles to modify their child's hostile behavior

INTRODUCTION: Bernal defines brats as children who throw many tantrums, make threats, and are assaultive and defiant. She trained parents in child management by teaching them operant learning principles with the aid of televised behavioral feedback. First, interactions between parent and child are analyzed to discover patterns that maintain brat behaviors. Instructions are then designed for those particular behavioral chains. The parent watches a previous tape and is instructed as to appropriate responses for the session, which follows immediately. In order to change the child's behavior, Bernal feels, his social environment must be reprogramed.

CASE STUDY 1: An eight-and-a-half-year-old boy was referred because of his frequent temper tantrums and physical attacks on his mother, teachers, and peers. He was told that he and his mother were going to learn how to get along together. The mother was asked to keep detailed notes about daily conflicts. Observations revealed that when he made demands, his mother gave in. If she did not comply, he carried out his threats to hit her, scream, break his glasses, and so forth. No warmth was expressed between them. She was afraid of him and worried about precipitating any outbursts.

   Bernal defined the goals of training as (1) the mother should reduce verbalizing and selectively ignore abusive behavior, (2) specific maternal behavior should be established as conditioned negative reinforcers through association with physical punishment, and (3) the mother should identify acceptable behaviors and reinforce them with warmth and praise. For each session, after thirty minutes of instruction, the mother interacted with her son for fifteen minutes. A bell tone cued the mother to stop talking and turn away. If physically attacked, the mother was to ignore the behavior and walk away. If that did not work, she was to tell him she was angry and firmly tell him to stop. Finally, she was to spank him hard, without threats.

Bernal describes seven intervention sessions in detail. Graphs are used to illustrate dramatic reduction of general and physical abuse. Observers rated the incidence of general abuse (profanity, refusal to obey, sulking, rudeness, demands, whining, and threats) and physical abuse (hitting, biting, kicking, tantrums, and throwing objects). The boy's behavior during the last five weeks of the twenty-five-week period was seen as being comparable to that of an average child. Beginning with the eighteenth week and continuing through the next two years, affectionate behavior was seen and reported.

CASE STUDY 2: A five-year-old boy was disobedient, defiant, hyperactive, destructive, and physically abusive toward his three-year-old brother. He was socially appropriate with people other than his mother. Observations revealed that his mother did not discipline him effectually. She nagged and threatened, but rarely carried out her threats. She was warm and affectionate with the younger brother and sarcastic and angry with her older son. As in the case previously reported, this mother was taught management techniques, including ways to reduce favoritism. She was encouraged to be less irritable. Bernal reports on seven spaced intervention sessions, which included training in extinction, praise, and punishment procedures. The boy's behavior improved both at home and at school.

Both cases showed one week of increased abuse. Bernal feels this occurred because lower-strength behaviors emerged when high-strength abusive behaviors were no longer reinforced.

COMMENTARY: Bernal considers this approach applicable when parents are cooperative, when there is no interference from anyone at home, and when the child exhibits a high rate of problem behavior. Feedback by viewing one's own behavior in an interaction may be educational in itself. Beneficial discussions of such feedback have been used by therapists of varied theoretical backgrounds. The combination of learning theory approaches and video feedback appears applicable to problems relating to faulty child-rearing practices. This approach may make for dramatic and more efficient intervention, especially with many parents who have to "see it to believe it."

SOURCE: Bernal, M. E. "Behavioral Feedback in the Modification of Brat Behaviors." *The Journal of Nervous and Mental Disease,* 1969, *148,* 375–385.

Behavior Shaping of a Noncompliant, Hostile Boy

AUTHOR: Maurice J. Boisvert

PRECIS: Parental use of positive and negative reinforcement and time out in promoting compliant behavior in a seven-year-old boy

INTRODUCTION: When traditional techniques fail, new therapeutic tools should be used. Boisvert reviews time-out techniques for modifying behavior. The individual's normal activities are suspended for a period of isolation, ranging from two minutes to two hours. Boisvert presents a case in which time out and positive and negative reinforcement were employed. The problem behaviors to be diminished were defined by the parents.

CASE STUDY: A seven-year-old boy was brought to the clinic for suspected retardation. Testing revealed functional retardation but a potential for improvement. The parents were seen as passive, hostile people who felt insecure and frightened. Psychotherapy moved very slowly with them. In play therapy, the boy was resistant and displayed many fears and anxieties. After eighteen sessions, the parents still could not handle their son. While therapy continued with him, the parents were offered behavioral techniques to modify his behavior at home.

    The parents considered the boy's physical fighting and arguing with them and his siblings as being most disruptive. When he did not immediately get his way, he became very aggressive. Both parents were ambivalent and reacted inconsistently and inappropriately. When he refused to comply, the parents felt helpless. The parents were taught general learning theory principles, with a scientific approach to teaching new behavior. They were asked to keep a diary of difficult incidents (fighting and arguing) and to list the boy's likes (baseball, music, television, and candy) and dislikes (noise, doctors, barbers, baths, and toilets). Time out and positive and negative reinforcement were used to reduce fighting. Arguing was approached with positive and negative reinforcement.

An outline for home treatment was given to the parents and explained to them. The boy was to receive three tokens and verbal praise for no fighting or arguing for one hour. Fighting resulted in loss of two tokens and being sent to his room for ten minutes. Arguing resulted in a loss of one token. Tokens were used to pay for television viewing and candy. After four o'clock, television watching was only available by the use of tokens. The therapist stressed the need for the parents to give clear explanations, be consistent, and use a matter-of-fact tone of voice.

This method was designed to help the parents be clear, consistent, and nonambivalent. During six weeks after introducing the program, there was a significant reduction of recorded fighting incidents compared with a baseline rate. The parents felt more in control and had more positive attitudes toward their son. Arguing was still a problem and Boisvert drew the implication that only one type of behavior ought to be focused on.

COMMENTARY: Boisvert's article clearly highlights the desirability of methods tailored to clients' problems. When psychotherapy did not affect a perceived significant disruptive behavior, the parents were taught a specific behavioral approach. This was a concrete way of intervening in the pattern of helpless parents interacting with a powerful, obnoxious child. It gave the parents the choice to participate, which they enthusiastically did. Seeing the child alone while parents are using new child-rearing strategies gives the child the opportunity to express feelings and reactions to an accepting therapist.

SOURCE: Boisvert, M. J. "Behavior Shaping as an Alternative to Psychotherapy." *Social Casework,* 1974, *55,* 43–47.

Family Sessions to Resolve Oedipal Struggles

AUTHOR: Esther Brandzel

PRECIS: Using psychodynamic approaches in family sessions to resolve conflicts, reduce the child's hostility, and promote satisfactory family problem solving

INTRODUCTION: Brandzel feels that even when family therapy is not used, an initial family interview is diagnostically valuable. The therapist can thus see individual pathology in the context of family interaction and can select treatment accordingly. The therapist's intervention in the family pattern can relieve the burden on the family scapegoat and can relieve others' guilt or defensiveness. The scapegoated child often views the therapist as another adult to be resisted. Brandzel feels that family therapy is warranted even when the child has internalized a problem, because the problem is never the child's alone.

CASE STUDY: A girl thirteen and a half years old was referred because of constant friction with her parents, irresponsibility about chores, and messiness. She showed intense hostility, which frightened the mother, who felt unable to control her. The father sided with his daughter.Brandzel saw the family as unable to resolve an oedipal conflict.

The parents had a poor history of relating to each other. When Mrs. A. could not control Mr. A., she became angry and nagging. Mr. A. suppressed his anger, tried to please his wife, and became more tense and frustrated. The daughter became openly rebellious and negative and Mr. A. wound up protecting her from her mother. Mrs. A. felt rejected, while daughter and father became closer. Mrs. A. worried about becoming more domineering, as her own mother had been, and felt displaced by her daughter. Aside from this pattern of serious hostility, the family shared many interests and activities.

During the first interview, the therapist stated than when a youngster was that unhappy, everyone in the family had a part in the problem. The daughter was shocked and confused when her mother accused her of taking her husband away. Brandzel describes the attacks and counterattacks by the parents; the daughter wound up in the middle of these conflicts. She also complained that her mother was overly restrictive. By asking how they reached this confusion and unhappiness, the therapist shifted the focus from the daughter to the parental relationship, which was seen as the core conflict. The exploration of roles and responsibilities was intended to help the daughter feel and act like the child she was, rather than like an adult battling her mother for her father.

During the second session, the therapist asked a question regarding the daughter's sitting between her parents. She expressed a fear that they might hurt each other or break up the marriage. She also appeared frightened of possible violence by her parents toward her. The therapist saw this pattern as the appropriate family diagnosis. The girl admired but feared her father, placated him, and prevented her parents from killing each other. The core difficulty was their shared fear of aggression: They saw expressing anger as inappropriate, possibly meaning that they were crazy. The girl was not forming an identity of her own (identifying with peers, experimenting with boys, and so forth) and was not freeing herself from her parents.

The mother requested individual therapy in addition to family therapy because she was afraid of becoming withdrawn and depressed. The therapist agreed, noting the need for the mother to learn to respond in a manner different from her pattern of hostility and depression. She often responded to situations as if there were only a right or wrong way, with no middle ground possible. Individual therapy focused on her responding to feelings, not in terms of who was right or wrong. The therapist told the mother that she (the therapist) felt frustrated and angry at the mother's constant attempts to prove herself as being a good mother. Brandzel feels that having the same therapist do both family and individual therapy facilitated progress.

Brandzel believes that family therapy not only relieved pressures, but also uncovered suppressed, unrealistic, and unconscious factors that interfered with the family's problem solving. The family members needed to become aware of their conflicts and the girl had to develop growth-producing satisfactions. One key was the parents' demonstration that they did not need their daughter to act as a buffer zone. A practical problem involving summer plans was discussed in detail. The therapist suggested that the girl not be forced to attend summer camp. A viable solution was worked out whereby the family members would stay together and work out their difficulties. However, the girl would spend two weeks with friends away from home.

As the family resolved its fear of excessive anger, progress occurred. The parents came closer together and their daughter became more responsible and decisive. Rather than acting as a buffer, the girl began to face her own maturational problems.

COMMENTARY: Brandzel's article presents a therapeutic approach with a dynamic, family focus rather than a focus on diminishing the angry, tense relationship between parents and daughter. Theoretically, conflictual patterns are thus confronted and positive interaction and individual growth emphasized. Theoretically, three generations can benefit from family therapy if conflicting family patterns are resolved before children marry and have their own children. Clinicians who are psychoanalytically oriented would concur with Brandzel's conclusion that the resolution of the oedipal problem led to better psychological growth of all members. Psychodynamic clinicians and family system advocates may agree with Brandzel's general approach of analyzing and changing the various problematic interactions. The approach Brandzel describes has been applied to all of the disorders covered in this book. Behavioral therapists also are talking more and more about focusing on and changing inappropriate interactions. The language used would be quite different from Brandzel's, but the family would be encouraged to give up nonproductive interaction, to communicate openly, and to behave in a manner that would lead to more positive satisfaction for all.

SOURCE: Brandzel, E. "Working Through the Oedipal Struggle in Family-Unit Sessions." *Social Casework*, 1965, *46*, 414–422.

A Family Operant Program to Treat
Disturbing Child Behavior

AUTHOR: William C. Coe

PRECIS: Combining family therapy and operant conditioning to reduce destructive family interaction and promote adaptive child behavior

INTRODUCTION: Coe recommends brief therapy for latency-age and adolescent children whose behavior upsets others, such as disruption, truancy, and generally poor achievement in all areas. Family communication in such cases is often destructive and the child's self-esteem is very low. Coe describes his technique as a combination of family therapy, using nonprofessionals as therapeutic agents, behavior modification, and common sense. Faculty communication in the family is a key factor and the therapist therefore acts as a consultant to the family. Approaches based on learning theory (operant conditioning) are used to modify faulty family patterns, in conjunction with innovative ideas from any source.

FAMILY INTERVENTION: During the first session, parents are interviewed first; then the child; and then all together. This approach is indicated when (1) the parents are unable to change the clearly viewed behavioral complaints about their child; (2) the parents only employ punishment or loss of privileges in attempts to control the behavior; (3) the child feels oppressed, overly restricted, and unable to communicate with his parents; and (4) family interaction is characterized by complaints, hostility, and generally poor communication. The therapist stresses the fact that the family interactions are not satisfactory for any member and that parents do not have to continue to nag the child. Also, the child will be able to do what he wants to.

CASE STUDY: Coe treated a boy with neurological problems; he saw the boy and his parents as sharing distrust, alienation, and circular hangups—patterns of mutual mistrust and disbelief in each other. They were all told that he should do whatever he wants, which was really to behave properly. The parents would not punish him or constantly try to get him to do things, but would treat him as an adult and give him responsibility for his own actions.

Coe explained and modeled clear communication and problem solving. The family was asked to come to some agreement (problem solving) on specific and desirable and undesirable behaviors. If they could not agree, they were to use the therapist as a consultant. They were asked to make up three lists: (1) "don't"—all were to agree that the boy showed these behaviors but should not; (2) "do"—all were to agree he should show these behaviors but had trouble in doing so; and (3) reinforcers—behaviors or things he likes (even if the parents do not). Examples of each were discussed and generalities questioned until specifics were achieved. In discussing the task, key words stressed were *we, all,* and *exactly.*

Coe then discussed a plan whereby the boy would receive credit for showing behaviors on the *Do* list and would pay for all behaviors on the *Don't* or *Reinforcer* lists. Discussions at home were to define and settle payments and charges. Coe outlined general principles to follow in such discussions, such as placing more value on significant positive or negative behaviors. First, costs for items on the *Don't* and *Reinforcer* lists were to be set and then points for items on the *Do* list were to be determined, to balance the system and enable the boy to afford reinforcers. The goal was to enable the boy to earn enough also for the purchase of long-term reinforcers, such as a special outing or money. Punishment was only to be used if costs for items on the *Don't* list were not effective.

The plan worked well—the boy saved 400 points in the first two weeks. Coe reports that this program resulted in more adaptive behavior, greater responsibility, and improved self-image.

COMMENTARY: Coe feels that an important feature of the family operant program is the provision of a method on which to focus, rather than on continuing destructive family interactions. When disagreements arise, the system fosters compromises and cooperation. Rather than criticisms of each other, mutual problem solving becomes the focus of interaction. This method is an example of one attempt to combine the successful outcomes reported by psychodynamic family therapists with the empirically proven successes of behavioral techniques. The combination would be widely applicable to other behavior disorders.

SOURCE: Coe, W. C. "A Family Operant Program." Paper presented at the Western Psychological Association Annual Meeting, Los Angeles, April 1970.

Behavior Modification with the Family
of a Disobedient Boy

AUTHORS: Richard Engeln, John Knutson, Linwood Laughy, and
Warren Garlington

PRECIS: A therapist modeling appropriate behavioral methods
with a mother's previously uncontrollable six-year-old son

INTRODUCTION: This article reviews successful studies of modification of children's behavior by a parent. The study presented was
based on learning theory principles and used the entire family in the
modification process.

CASE STUDY: A six-year-old boy was referred as being uncontrollable. He refused to follow any instructions, had temper tantrums, was aggressive, and swore. In addition to his extreme
disobedience, he often provoked others. The father spent very
little time at home and interacted with his children in an irritated,
punitive manner. The mother felt totally inadequate with her
family.

Family therapy was carried out weekly for eleven months by
three therapists: One saw the mother, one saw the boy, and one
visited the father. The mother was interviewed in order to assess
home reinforcement contingencies. A brief written description and
discussions with her were used to help her understand operant
conditioning to be used with the child. In play therapy, compliance
shown by obeying adult commands was chosen as a significant behavior. Eye contact and correct responses to brief commands (for
example, "Put the blocks on the table") were recorded and reinforced with candy and social approval. The boy's inattention or lack
of compliance resulted in the therapist not responding for sixty
seconds. Later, eye contact and following commands were reinforced only if both occurred together.

The mother and her therapist observed and discussed effective techniques used in the play therapy and then entered the play-

room. The mother made several commands and ineffectively used the arranged contingencies. With discussion and practice, the mother improved and became effective in controlling her son's behavior. At home, a reward system using stars was designed and extinction of the undesirable behavior was employed.

As the boy's behavior improved, his older brother became disobedient, aggressive, and fought with him. Both boys were seen together in the playroom where working together on command and spontaneous cooperation were reinforced. Independent rewards were more effective than rewards for both working together. Two large cardboard counters were used. When both were cooperative, they each gained three points. If only one was cooperative, he would earn one point. Aggression resulted in a loss of five points. Points were used to purchase ice cream or visit an animal laboratory. The number of points required was raised each session.

The article presents details of monitoring phases of improvement at the clinic and at home. Improvement was sporadic and uneven, with time out being quite effective. The boy had to learn that unacceptable behavior would not influence the therapist's refusal to respond. Cooperation between the brothers was quickly fostered by the contingencies used and obedience and cooperation were greatly increased. With peers, the boy was rarely provocative. The mother reported that an improved relationship with her husband resulted from their working together on their children's problems.

COMMENTARY: This family study illustrates the flexible use of behavioral techniques to meet the changing problems. Applying the methods to the sibling fighting was a logical and effective step and is in keeping with recent reports of successfully using behavioral methods in offices with siblings and with groups of children. Involving the father and gaining his confidence appears well worth the professional hours spent. Since "difficult" families are unmotivated or unresponsive to traditional mental health approaches, this case suggests a valuable direction for therapy in providing separate therapists for different functions. The combination of "special" therapist interest and a consistent, clearly defined method may be especially effective with "difficult" families, although one therapist might also perform the same functions.

SOURCE: Engeln, R., Knutson, J., Laughy, L., and Garlington, W. "Behaviour Modification Techniques Applied to a Family Unit: A Case Study." *Journal of Child Psychology and Psychiatry,* 1968, 9, 245–252.

Individual Treatment of a Defiant Child in the Context of Family Therapy

AUTHOR: David Hallowitz

PRECIS: Combining individual and family therapy to reduce defiance and change destructive parent-child relationships

INTRODUCTION: Hallowitz experimented with adding individual therapy to the usual flexible format of family sessions and separate individual interviews when families were not progressing. This article is based on Hallowitz's experiences with children and adolescents characterized by reactive emotional disorders. Typically, the parent-child relationships followed vicious cycles of destructive behavior. The following sections describe situations in which Hallowitz feels individual therapy is required.

EXTREMELY INTENSE VICIOUS CYCLE: Hallowitz feels that oedipal conflicts are quite amenable to family therapy. The child learns that his or her fears and hatred are not necessary. However, intense mutual hostility between child and parent of the same sex may not be resolvable in family therapy because mutually positive feelings have not developed. Switching to individual therapy with the child enables him to resolve hostility through the transference relationship with the therapist.

To illustrate this process, Hallowitz discusses the case of a defiant, hostile nine-year-old boy. Blatant oedipal conflict was present; he was jealous of his father and inappropriately and overly affectionate with his mother. Various problems related to the oedipal difficulties were discussed and interpreted in family sessions to no avail. The parents were briefly seen together with the boy and then he was seen individually. With toys he expressed hostile feelings, "killing" and "attacking" the therapist. He thus (theoretically) learned that the therapist would not destroy him but would still accept and like him. After four months of individual therapy, family sessions were resumed. Improvement in family interactions was rapidly seen.

Hallowitz also discusses the case of a sullen, provocative eight-year-old boy. In family sessions, he expressed anger and feelings that he lacked parental love. The parents discussed his impossible, negativistic behavior. Interpretations and open discussion did not lead to progress and the boy's behavior appeared to get worse. He was seen weekly and family sessions were held monthly. In individual therapy, he was provocative and hostile to the therapist. This behavior was used to help him understand the angry reactions of others toward him. His anger diminished and he became more affectionate. Progress was considerable and the usual family sessions were resumed.

NEED FOR NURTURE: In cases where a child has lost a parent, Hallowitz feels, nurturance may be provided by the therapist. The child may not be able to share the therapist's attention with other family members. Family sessions must also continue in order for relationships to be dealt with appropriately. Hallowitz describes the case of an eight-year-old girl whose father died and who had become negativistic and uncooperative with her mother. In family sessions, they both expressed resentment and unhappiness. Several sessions revealed no sign of any progress, so the girl was seen weekly and every three weeks with her mother. Individual therapy thus provided a type of father substitute, one who liked and accepted her. Her problems were discussed, much progress made, and termination took place.

ADOLESCENT DEVELOPMENT: Rebellious adolescents may refuse to participate in family interviews. Family sessions can be resumed after a period of individual therapy with the adolescent and separate parental therapy. Hallowitz offers an illustrative case concerning a rebellious, angry, destructive boy. In the first session, he was very angry and did not want to be seen together with his parents. Through separate sessions, they learned to appreciate each other's feelings. The boy appeared to enjoy the individual sessions and rapport with the therapist. Hallowitz also discusses the case of another sixteen-year-old boy to illustrate the need for some adolescents to verbalize problems about sex, self-image, peer relations, authority, education, and vocation.

CONFIDENTIALITY AND COMMUNICATION: Hallowitz notes that confidentiality should be discussed with the family. Although confidential material should not be revealed, the therapist should recommend that some information be shared and discussed openly. In individual sessions, the therapist should ask the child specific questions about family problems. The goal is to help the child deal with adjustment problems at home, in school, and in the community. Hallowitz considers it beneficial to spend a brief time with child and parent to discuss problems before the individual sessions. Also, the therapist should praise progress and achievements.

COMMENTARY: Hallowitz writes from the perspective of a family therapist deciding also to do individual therapy. This is different from most of the approaches described in this book, in which either individual therapy or parent counseling are the primary methods. Hallowitz considers the family sessions to be the starting and ending points, with individual therapy when needed. Flexibility is obviously necessary in this system. Note that he developed this approach in response to a perceived lack of progress in the family. A decision on whether the method is indicated might be guided by reviewing the three types of situations in which Hallowitz suggests individual sessions be added to family therapy with defiant, angry youngsters.

SOURCE: Hallowitz, D. "Individual Treatment of the Child in the Context of Family Therapy." *Social Casework,* 1966, *47,* 82–86.

Changing the Behavior of a Defiant Boy's Parents

AUTHORS: Stephen M. Johnson and Richard A. Brown

PRECIS: Modeling effective behavioral methods and a contingency reversal for a mother and her defiant six-year-old son

INTRODUCTION: Johnson and Brown describe a situation involving a learning technique (modeling) to change parental behavior. Changing behavioral contingencies has been demonstrated to alter behavior. This article focuses on how the changes in the parents were produced.

CASE STUDY: A six-year-old boy was referred when he was expelled from school. He was defiant, aggressive, and unpredictable and refused to follow instructions. A long history of poor adjustment and slow development was reported. At home he was disobedient, overly demanding, and manipulative. Johnson and Brown present a detailed excerpt of a behavioral observation. His mother often complied with his demands and his annoying behavior very frequently earned attention from others.

The boy was sent to a day school for boys with severe behavior problems. Contingency management principles used in the classroom led to considerably improved behavior. At home, his poor behavior continued. His mother attended a group, but was resistant to the suggestion of ignoring undesirable behavior. She was concerned that ignoring his behavior would lead to even worse behavior.

Mother and son were observed in a situation designed to lead to problem behaviors. After two minutes of play, she asked him to do arithmetic problems for five minutes. Observers recorded repeated measures. When asked to do arithmetic, the boy made many excuses and distracting comments. The mother responded to these comments and very little work was completed. His unusual behavior (head banging, making noises, and so forth) elicited even stronger diverting responses from his mother. The goal was the termination of her attention and compliance. For eight months, group discussion and weekly counseling did not accomplish this goal.

A modeling procedure was then used to change the mother's behavior. For a brief period, hourly sessions were held twice a week. A therapist performed the play and arithmetic procedure, while the mother observed with another therapist. She was asked to record behavior in order to focus her attention on relevant model behaviors. The therapist rewarded on-task behavior, mildly criticized off-task behavior, and did not respond to other behavior. The mother also observed the dramatic effect of the contingency reversal procedures used by the therapist. When the therapist did not reward on-task behavior but responded to (rather than criticized) off-task behavior, the boy's on-task time decreased from 4.5 minutes to .5 minutes.

Johnson and Brown present data reflecting the mother's behavior change as a result of modeling. Her attention to off-task behavior decreased from 98 percent at baseline to 20 percent in two sessions and critical comments decreased from 12.5 percent to 50 percent. In tracking the results, criticism was found to be ineffective in eliciting compliance, so the mother was instructed to reduce critical comments. She agreed that modeling was the most effective procedure. The boy was returned to a regular school five months after modeling was used. Behavior generalized to the home.

COMMENTARY: Johnson and Brown describe the use of modeling, direct instruction, group discussion, behavioral direction, and reinforcement in the case of a six-year-old who was overly active and uncontrollable. Modeling was considered the crucial factor in the successful treatment. Many children appear to respond more quickly to a therapist's contingency management than to their parents. In the case presented, a striking feature is the mother's observation of contingency reversal. Seeing may well lead to believing, because the parent can observe that his or her old pattern of responding demonstrably leads to the appearance of more problem behavior. Modeling of appropriate child-rearing techniques is a very promising method. Creative uses for this approach are unlimited. Modeling has been successfully used by therapists of many orientations, and modeling nondirective parental behavior has improved parental and child behaviors and attitudes.

SOURCE: Johnson, S. M., and Brown, R. A. "Producing Behaviour Change in Parents of Disturbed Children." *Journal of Child Psychology and Psychiatry,* 1969, *10,* 107–121.

Training Parents to Provide Corrective Social Interaction

AUTHOR: Shirley Sanders

PRECIS: Improving family interaction by training parents to "follow," accept feelings, model and provide positive feedback, set limits and compromise, discuss alternatives, and resolve problems

INTRODUCTION: Sanders considers destructive parent-child interaction to be the cause of behavior disorders in children: Overprotection, domination, and hostility impair development, whereas warmth and acceptance enhance positive psychological growth. This article describes steps in defining warmth and developing a program to teach parents to express warmth and acceptance.

Parents were observed while interacting with their disturbed children. They frequently made demands on their children and rarely modeled, followed (gave neutral feedback) or provided any feedback (positive or negative). Children frequently responded inappropriately and showed little spontaneity. The goal of therapy was to bring warmth into family relations. Warmth on the part of the parents was operationally defined as making minimal demands, acknowledging feelings by following, giving positive feedback, and encouraging spontaneity. The goals were then set for parent training. Parents were to (1) model or set an example, ask fewer questions, and give fewer demands; (2) follow the child's behavior and feelings by giving recognition and acceptance; (3) give positive feedback and fewer but consistent negative responses; and (4) encourage spontaneity.

A program had to be developed for nonverbal parents who often did not recognize feelings. For them, active participation, rather than insight and verbal skills, was stressed. Imitation, role modeling, and mutual role playing were employed. In role playing, the child directly learns about the parent's role. The parent can model appropriate behavior and give the child positive feedback. Also, the parent learns which techniques influence the child positively. Communication is enhanced and corrected interaction is experienced.

METHOD: Ten emotionally disturbed children and their parents participated in the program (seven males and three females, ages five to thirteen years). Family interaction patterns were negative and the children were described as aggressive or immature.

Training consisted of parents and their child practicing the following six exercises until success was attained. Sessions lasted fifteen minutes once a week, but parents practiced daily at home. The therapist explained and demonstrated each exercise, and then observed parent and child. Roles were always reversed, to enhance sensitivity to the needs and feelings of the other person.

1. *Following.* The parent gives neutral feedback. The parent can watch quietly, describe, imitate, or repeat what the child says or does. The child's feelings can be recognized and clarified by the parents.

2. *Accepting Feelings.* Like following, except that rather than following behavior, the parent focuses on feelings.

3. *Modeling and Positive Feedback.* In this exercise, the parent demonstrates and explains (rather than demands). Direction and guidance are provided by positive feedback. The child's success is recognized by the parent and rewarded.

4. *Limit Setting and Compromising.* Rather than being overly demanding or submissive, the child learns to compromise. The child then participates in decision making and the parents listen and accept within realistic limits.

5. *Alternatives.* The parent discusses various alternatives so the child can become aware of consequences of his behavior. The parent is told to accept the child's decision.

6. *Resolving Problems.* The child's specific problems are resolved by role playing. Warmth and acceptance of the child's difficulties are displayed by the parents.

Sanders describes pre- and postassessment procedures. Observers recorded fifteen minutes of structured parent-child interaction. Parent behaviors were significantly modified by the training: Parental demanding and negative feedback decreased, while following and positive feedback increased. A dramatic increase was observed for children's correct and spontaneous behaviors. Sanders notes that role playing is nonthreatening, because the child does not fear negative consequences.

COMMENTARY: Parents can quickly learn to express warmth to their children by practicing Sanders' exercises with their children. In many settings, it has been demonstrated that positive responses to others are rare. In classrooms, for example, teachers too rarely provide positive feedback to students. The technique described by Sanders appears particularly applicable with overly dependent or shy, withdrawn children. Parental provision of more warmth may be appropriate with all children's behavior disorders. Literature on normal child development indicates that appropriate provision of warmth may prevent negative family interaction patterns and behavior problems.

SOURCE: Sanders, S. "Corrective Social Interaction Therapy: Role Modeling." *American Journal of Orthopsychiatry,* 1975, *45,* 875–883.

Additional Readings

Aleksandrowicz, M. K. "The Little Prince: Psychotherapy of a Boy with Borderline Personality Structure." *International Journal of Psychoanalytic Psychotherapy,* 1975, *4,* 410–425.

This article describes in great detail psychotherapy with a nine-year-old boy with autistic features. Problems were numerous, including violent arguments (especially with his mother), enuresis, and being dangerously accident prone. Rage reactions often followed any oedipal interpretations. Aleksandrowicz describes the therapist's physically controlling the boy's rage and directly interpreting the negative transference. In family therapy, which took place monthly, significant progress was made in overcoming the roadblock caused by the boy's rage. The changes in him and his parents broke the vicious cycle of destructive family relationships. Aleksandrowicz suggests that the boy's aggression was caused by narcissistic injury and fear of physical closeness. The decrease of anger was probably caused by a clarification of his sexual identity and his acceptance of masculinity.

Barnard, J. D., Rainey, S. K., Christophersen, E. R., and Sykes, B. W. "The Family Training Program: Short and Long-Term Evaluation." Paper presented at the 84th Annual Convention of the American Psychological Association, Washington, D.C., September 1976.

Parents involved in the family training program described here were given skill-oriented training to apply at home. Behavioral methods included systematic monitoring of child behavior, teaching and maintaining appropriate behavior, and eliminating undesirable actions. The parents' complaints about their children included general noncompliance and backtalk. This program was seen as being more effective than conventional treatment provided by a participating child guidance clinic. An important aspect of the study was the long-term maintenance of improved behavior as assessed in a two-year follow-up. The authors see reprograming the home environment as a key element in the successful intervention.

Bernal, M. E., Duryee, J. S., Pruett, H. L., and Burns, B. J. "Behavior Modification and the Brat Syndrome." *Journal of Consulting and Clinical Psychology*, 1968, *32*, 447–455.

"Brats" are very frequently brought to mental health services. The authors define brat behavior as throwing tantrums, being assaultive, threatening, and showing behavior with which adults cannot cope. A mother was successfully trained to use behavior modification with her eight-and-a-half-year-old emotionally disturbed son. The article presents details regarding the use of learning principles as taught to the mother through instructions and videotape feedback. Instructions to her were phrased in terms of what she could do and correct performance was emphasized (past mistakes were not focused on). The mother was to follow three steps: ignore abusive behavior, express anger or spank after continued abuse, and positively reinforce acceptable behaviors. In three weeks, abusive behavior significantly diminished and a twenty-three-week follow-up revealed that appropriate behavior continued.

Boardman, W. K. "Rusty: A Brief Behavior Disorder." *Journal of Consulting Psychology*, 1962, *26*, 293–297.

Rusty, a six-year-old boy, was extremely defiant, hostile, manipulative, and self-destructive. In order to change his behavior, the parents were told to clearly define unacceptable and acceptable behavior. If he persisted in undesirable behavior, they would punish him severely and continuously. A shift to appropriate behavior, however, resulted in prompt and adequate rewards. Entrance to the house and meals would not be forthcoming if he misbehaved. One episode involving destructive acts and disobedience resulted in a severe spanking and no dinner. Within one week, Rusty learned that rebellion was too costly. For eleven months, he remained spirited but not rebellious. Boardman notes that the effectiveness of this procedure depends on several detailed conditions, including specific and voluntary misbehavior, arrangements for withholding gratification during misbehavior and for rewarding alternative behavior, and continuous application of the procedure.

Bugental, D. B., and Love, L. "Nonassertive Expression of Parental Approval and Disapproval and Its Relationship to Child Disturbance." *Child Development,* 1975, *46,* 747–752.

Bugental and Love studied the voice intonation of mothers in forty cases: twenty normal and twenty disturbed children. Many of the children were uncooperative, hostile, disruptive, defiant, or aggressive. Mothers of normal children showed a more assertive voice quality in expressing approval or disapproval. Mothers of disturbed children showed a less assertive voice quality in expressing approval or disapproval than in neutral statements. The authors suggest that a circular process involving giving weak messages and feelings of impotence in influencing a child can produce child disturbance.

Christophersen, E. R., Arnold, C. M., Hill, D. W., and Quilitch, H. R. "The Home Point System: Token Reinforcement Procedures for Application by Parents of Children with Behavior Problems." *Journal of Applied Behavior Analysis,* 1972, *5,* 485–497.

Two sets of parents were taught to use a token economy with their children. Typical problems were refusal to do chores, bickering, and sassy talk to parents. Appropriate chores and social behaviors were specified, recorded, and rewarded. Rewards used included money and various privileges, such as attending a movie or going on a camping trip. Fines (loss of points) were used for undesirable behavior. Usually, one or two behaviors were selected at first and later the system was expanded. Generally, parents stopped using the system, with somewhat less effective, but still satisfactory results. The parents were pleased with the decrease of a total of twenty-one problem behaviors.

Dreikurs, R. "Counseling a Boy: A Demonstration." *Journal of In-dividual Psychology,* 1972, *28,* 223–231.

Dreikurs presents a verbatim transcript of one interview with a twelve-year-old boy in treatment with an Adlerian therapist. One major problem was his aggravating peers, parents, and other adults. He described becoming involved in parental arguments. An inter-pretation was made that it is easy for him to get attention by dis-turbing others. Also, doing what adults or friends wanted was viewed as giving in. He ate too much and constantly requested things as a means of getting his mother angry. Dreikurs describes the interview as helping the child understand his problems and notes that attention seeking was a key to his difficulties with people.

Ehrlich, F. M. "Family Therapy and Training in Child Psychiatry." *Journal of the American Academy of Child Psychiatry,* 1973, *12,* 482–498.

Ehrlich discusses psychoanalytically oriented family therapy and points out that family interviews are especially useful with disorganized and impoverished families. Also, scapegoating and family pacts of silence regarding a topic are very appropriate sub-jects for family therapy. An illustrative case involved a ten-year-old boy, described as disrespectful, irresponsible, and uncaring about any family members. The father and his two sons avoided complain-ing about the mother, who was disturbed and ineffectual. A key to the interaction was the unspoken agreement to never express hos-tility or dependency toward the mother. During therapy, the family came to see that the pact was depriving them of the mother's sup-port. After eight sessions, treatment was terminated with better and more open communication reported. A two-year follow-up indicated continued progress.

Fraiberg, S. "A Comparison of the Analytic Method in Two Stages of a Child Analysis." *Journal of the American Academy of Child Psychiatry,* 1965, *4,* 387–400.

Fraiberg reports in detail two analytic sessions with a boy— when he was five and when he was six and a half. He was seen for a successful psychoanalysis from age four through age eight. When referred, he was wild and destructive, having experienced much violence at home. This behavior was interpreted as identification with the aggressor. Analysis resulted in a positive transference and revealed his terrors, helplessness, castration anxiety, and bad dreams. His communication through play was often used as the basis for direct interpretations. Fraiberg notes that a child will give the analyst the right to investigate if he believes that the understanding then offered by the analyst will help alleviate painful problems and fears.

Hawkins, R. P., Peterson, R. F., Schweid, E., and Bijou, S. W. "Behavior Therapy in the Home: Amelioration of Problem Parent Child Relations with the Parent in a Therapeutic Role." *Journal of Experimental Child Psychology,* 1966, *4,* 99–107.

An extremely difficult to manage four-year-old boy was treated by his mother at home. The mother had been helpless in dealing with his disobedience, demands for attention, and tantrums. An observer recorded objectionable behavior and the mother was given three different signals, at appropriate times. Signals indicated that the mother should tell him to stop a behavior; put him in his room and lock the door; or give him attention, praise, and affectionate physical contact. The authors feel that home treatment may be more effective than office treatment, especially when undesirable behavior occurs primarily at home. The parent thus becomes more skilled at handling difficulties.

Kifer, R. E., Lewis, M. A., Green, D. R., and Phillips, E. L. "Training Predelinquent Youths and Their Parents to Negotiate Conflict Situations." *Journal of Applied Behavior Analysis,* 1974, *7,* 357–364.

One approach used with conflicts between youths and authority figures has been arbitration of specific conflicts. This study is a modification of the communication process, emphasizing new adaptive behaviors rather than eliminating problem behaviors. The techniques used were educational, rather than therapeutic. Three pairs, of one teen-ager and one parent each, participated for approximately ten hours per pair. During a home observation, a pair was asked to identify three most troublesome problems and to discuss each for five minutes. Hypothetical conflicts were role played in classroom sessions. Each member received a list of related responses and consequences and, through discussion, additional options and consequences were added. Negotiation behaviors—complete communication and identification of issues and suggestions of options—were measured. Training procedures led to significant increases in negotiation behaviors, which generalized to actual conflict situations.

Levy, D. M. "Attitude Therapy." *American Journal of Orthopsychiatry,*
    1937, *7,* 103–113.

When treatment of the child fails because of maternal problems, Levy suggests using attitude therapy. This article describes an illustrative case in which the mother had to be confronted with her own contribution to a pattern of defiant behavior in her daughter. In attitude therapy, the mother elaborated her experience, to bring about an emotional release and to reveal the typical attitude pattern in her relationship with her child. This method was designed for social workers and requires two to three interviews per week for approximately two years.

Martin, B. "Family Interaction Associated with Child Disturbance:
    Assessment and Modification." *Psychotherapy: Theory, Research
    and Practice,* 1967, *4,* 30–35.

Four boys, ages nine through twelve, were each seen with their parents. They were all behavior problems and underachievers in school. Martin believes that responses of family members often elicit a chain of ineffective or angry responses in others. An apparatus with "talk" and "don't talk" signs was used to smooth conversation between two people. During sessions, they were asked to discuss a recent disagreement or incident in which someone was hurt or angry. Interaction was scored, using five categories—indirect blaming, direct blaming, self blaming, description of situation, and description of own feelings. Modification consisted of pointing out stereotyped interaction and encouraging experimentation with new ways of responding. In six sessions, families made less blaming responses and children exhibited better behavior in class. Martin believes that, theoretically, parents thus take the "heat" off their child.

Masters, J. C. "Treatment of 'Adolescent Rebellion' by the Re-Construal of Stimuli." *Journal of Consulting and Clinical Psychology,* 1970, *35,* 213–216.

Discussion and behavioral assignments were used to alter the extent to which a seventeen-year-old boy felt that he controlled his environment. He had a great deal of difficulty with any authorities and was quite jealous of his older brother's freedom (and his being favored by the parents). He frequently disobeyed his parents. Therapy focused on analyzing the "rules of the game," so that by "playing the game" he could become more in control. The boy realized that he could comply and be able to control his parents' behavior. By performing chores without being asked, he eliminated being commanded and his father felt obligated to him. By reinterpreting his family as neutral rather than negative, he engaged in fewer family arguments and offered fewer complaints of overcontrol. Masters feels that stimulus reinterpretation led to a change in perception, a change in behavior (complaints), and a change in family interactions.

Scarboro, M. E., and Forehand, R. "Effects of Two Types of Response—Contingent Time-Out on Compliance and Oppositional Behavior of Children." *Journal of Experimental Child Psychology,* 1975, *19,* 252–264.

A study of the comparative effectiveness of time-out procedures was conducted with twenty-four five-year-olds. Time out is a period of time following a response and is used when a variety of reinforcers are not available. Undesirable behavior has been controlled in many studies using this method. In this study, within-room and out-of-room times out were contrasted as to effectiveness in influencing compliance and oppositional behavior. Mothers were instructed as to responses via a receiver placed in their ears. If within five seconds of a request the child did not comply, the mother would not interact for two minutes (within-room time out). Out-of-room time out involved having the mother leave with the toys for two minutes and then returning. Strikingly, within-room time out was as effective as out-of-room time out—both significantly modified behavior. Within-room time out required more times out to affect behavior. Mothers learned the procedures in a brief time, and posttraining sessions revealed continued low levels of oppositional behavior and high levels of compliance.

Seitz, S., and Terdal, L. "A Modeling Approach to Changing Parent-Child Interactions." *Mental Retardation,* 1972, *10,* 39–43.

A mother learned role-appropriate ways of interacting with her four-year-old son by modeling rather than by instruction. She viewed a nondirective, interpretative therapist treating the boy, who did not obey her, was overactive, and had frequent tantrums. Commands and criticisms by the mother, who viewed him as inadequate, led to noncompliance and reinforced the mother's view of him as being retarded and helpless. Praise and recognition were frequently employed by the therapist. The mother and another therapist watched and discussed the sessions and the mother became aware of her commanding, intrusive, and nonsupportive approach. Instead of being given advice, the mother was supported and encouraged for developing changed attitudes and behavior. Both the mother's and the boy's behavior improved.

Silverman, H. "A Technique of Brief Psychotherapy of a Child Disorder." *Journal of Clinical Child Psychology,* 1974, *3,* 39–40.

One session was held with a mother who engaged in a chronic struggle for autonomy with her eight-year-old daughter. The girl had been openly rebellious and her father often sided with her. Four visits followed, to discuss the effects of the treatment strategy. The mother kept a record of problem behavior, did not attempt to correct the child, and reinforced approved behavior. Use of the strategy by the mother resulted in improved morale and a less tense relationship. The girl became more flexibly adaptive and was no longer dominated by a need to be stubborn and controlling.

Strober, M., and Bellack, A. S. "Multiple-Component Behavioral Treatment for a Child with Behavior Problems." *Journal of Behavior Therapy and Experimental Psychiatry,* 1975, *6,* 250–251.

Parent training, self-control training, positive reinforcement, and punishment were used to modify a boy's behavior at home and at school. At home, the nine-year-old boy refused to do chores, was verbally abusive, and often became highly agitated. In school, he threw tantrums and was provocative. His mother was told to ignore his tantrums and to tell him that he could only make one request for what he wanted. He was told to repeat these instructions aloud and to himself. For provoking his siblings, he was reprimanded or sent to his room and deprived of television. He was also sent to his room until he was willing to do his chores. Adaptive behaviors were reinforced. Daily telephone contact by the mother with the teacher resulted in the use of similar procedures according to school behavior (loss of television, later bedtime, and so on). Strober and Bellack call for more use of strengthening self-regulatory verbal mediation and the use of home contingencies based on school behavior.

Symonds, M. "Therapeutic Approaches to Acting Out." *American Journal of Psychotherapy*, 1974, *28*, 362–368.

Symonds discusses acting-out behavior in detail, dividing it into two categories—behavior unrelated to other people and behavior in which the individual is very aware of others. The condition of unrelatedness is illustrated by Symonds' description of an action-oriented, psychopathic twelve-year-old boy, who had been placed in a residential program because of constant difficulties with foster parents and with any authority figures. Symonds suggests that such children develop their attitudes because of profoundly defective parenting. In therapy, their unrelatedness must be diminished and trust must be developed through a consistent and durable relationship. In order to grow, these youngsters have to go through depression and anxiety. Symonds describes these children as egocentric, unrelated to others and living only in the present. The therapist must be firm and clear in his expressing his attitudes and values.

Wahler, R. G. "Setting Generality: Some Specific and General Effects of Child Behavior Therapy." *Journal of Applied Behavior Analysis*, 1969, *2*, 239–246.

Wahler discusses two cases in which changing behavioral contingencies at home did not affect the same behavior at school. The two boys, five and six years old, showed oppositional and disruptive behaviors. Selective parent attention and time out were employed when desirable or undesirable behavior occurred. Only when the school employed similar contingencies did behavioral changes occur in the school setting. Wahler feels that contingencies must be changed in the setting in which undesirable behavior occurs. For example, when problem behavior occurs with peers after school, change agents are not present in that setting.

Wahler, R. G. "Oppositional Children: A Quest for Parental Reinforcement Control." *Journal of Applied Behavior Analysis,* 1969, *2,* 159–170.

Two boys of elementary school age were referred for oppositional behavior; they were described as disobedient, stubborn, negativistic, and headstrong. All observations and procedures took place at home. Parental differential attention and time out resulted in dramatic and stable improvement in the two boys' behavior. They were isolated in their bedrooms for approximately five minutes following oppositional behavior. If undesirable behavior occurred, such as screaming or crying, they had to remain in their rooms until the behavior ceased. Cooperative behavior was immediately followed by parental approval, expressed in any manner that the parents desired. One set of parents required four training sessions; the other required seven longer sessions. Wahler feels that oppositional behavior is best defined as the absence of cooperative behavior and is therefore a behavioral deficit rather than an excessive amount of particular behaviors. Informal observations to evaluate the effect of treatment showed more smiling and positive contacts by the parents. Time out appeared to produce a change in parents' behavior that in turn was reinforcing to their child.

Wiltz, N. A. "Behavioral Therapy Techniques in Treatment of Emotionally Disturbed Children and Their Families." *Child Welfare,* 1973, *52,* 483–492.

Wiltz describes procedures for assessing interaction patterns between child and parent and for using the information for retraining them to develop better interactions. Stimulus control (clearer cues), consequation (appropriate behavioral consequences), and shaping of responses (step by step learning) are discussed. Wiltz also discusses various kinds of disturbances, including negativistic and aggressive behavior by children. Observations are done in naturalistic settings (home and school), not in an office. Coding systems permit recording of positive and negative interactions, which makes dramatic changes possible. For example, one mother berated, nagged, or spanked her nine-year-old boy twenty times more than she offered positive responses. In the approach described by Wiltz, the parents learn better child-rearing skills based on the observations in natural settings and the application of behavioral techniques.

Wiltz, N. A., and Patterson, G. R. "An Evaluation of Parent Training Procedures Designed to Alter Inappropriate Aggressive Behavior of Boys." *Behavior Therapy,* 1974, *5,* 215–221.

Six boys, average age nine, were referred for aggressive behavior. Behaviors of concern to parents included noncompliance, destructiveness, teasing, and other aggressive behaviors. In five weeks, the parents were taught the theories and skills necessary to carry out a behavior modification program. A control group of comparable boys' parents received no instructions. Observations in the home revealed an increase in inappropriate behaviors for the control group boys, while a significant decrease of deviant behavior was recorded for the treatment group. Graphs of target behavior were reviewed each week and discussed by therapists and parents and all participants offered suggestions. Contingency management programs were employed as outlined in a programmed text, *Living with Children: New Methods for Parents and Teachers,* by G. R. Patterson and M. E. Gullion (Champaign, Ill.: Research Press, 1968). Wiltz and Patterson recommend that families be trained to alter the deviant behavior of their aggressive boys. Family training produces effective results, which do not occur by placing families on a waiting list for therapy.

Zeilberger, J., Sampen, S. E., and Sloane, H. N. "Modification of a Child's Problem Behaviors in the Home with the Mother as Therapist." *Journal of Applied Behavior Analysis,* 1968, *1,* 47–53.

Differential reinforcement contingencies were successfully used by a mother to modify the behavior of her four-and-a-half-year-old boy, who was disobedient, screamed, bossed others, and fought frequently. Observation demonstrated that the mother reinforced undesirable behavior with excessive attention, provided inconsistent consequences, and gave long, ineffective verbal explanations. Zeilberger did not use parental explorations and discussions with their son. The parents were encouraged to speak in a matter-of-fact tone. Arrangements were made for the mother to watch the boy play with neighborhood children. Disobedience with his mother or aggression with children resulted in immediate, brief times out. Mildly undesirable behavior was ignored and desirable cooperative play was reinforced at least once every five minutes without interrupting the play. Reinforcing comments included saying that they were all having a good time or direct praise of the boy. Special treats or toys were brought out after periods of desirable play (but were not used to interrupt undesirable play). The authors believe that behavior should be modified in the environment in which it occurs—school, home, backyard, and so forth. Both of the boys' undesirable behaviors were vastly decreased—especially disobedience.

Overdependent Relationship with Parents

Dependency problems arise when a child becomes overly reliant on parents for support. At different ages, varying degrees of independence are expected of children. Although norms may differ widely, enough consensus exists so that adults and other children can reliably identify a child as being overly dependent on adults. The child may lack self-direction, insist on continuous care and affection, and be unable to engage in give-and-take interactions with peers.

471

Treating the "Mama's Boy"

AUTHOR: Aman U. Khan

PRECIS: Promoting independence by separating (hospitalizing) overly dependent children from their parents and using parent counseling, individual therapy, and behavioral methods

INTRODUCTION: Khan describes "Mama's boys" as immature, passive, unable to handle peer aggression, lacking initiative, having difficulty in developing friendships, and, often, as being poor achievers. Referral for therapy often occurs early in their school career and they are frequently called "sissy" or "baby" by peers. Helping mother or watching television are their most frequent activities. Khan theorizes that the problem stems from a prolonged mutually dependent relationship with mother and from a lack of appropriate socialization and competition with peers. The mother is seen as deriving too much of her satisfaction from her child. Often, a dependency relationship begun during a child's illness is continued after the child is well. Other contributing causes are separation of the parents, the mother's difficulty in setting limits, or the mother's guilt regarding real or imagined rejection of her child.

TREATMENT: Khan reports that outpatient treatment, including individual, family, and group psychotherapy and parent counseling, is often unsuccessful because one of the pair counteracts progress. The therapist encounters great difficulty in motivating the child to take a greater interest in his environment. The crisis of physical separation, however, may lead to personality change. Both parties can thus be helped to examine their relationship and to view the world more independently. Over a two-year period, thirteen children were selected, one after the other, to fill one bed on a general ward in a hospital. All children, ages five to thirteen years, had a history of a prolonged mutually dependent relationship. Selection was based on the completion of at least six months of unsuccessful outpatient treatment. Hospitalization ranged from four to twelve weeks, with a six-week median length of stay.

Khan presents the case of a twelve-year-old boy in detail. The mother had a very difficult time in promoting independence in her diabetic son, who had slept with her until age seven. In school, he was described as immature and overly demanding. After seven months of individual therapy and family conferences, several sessions were spent preparing for hospital admission. When he was admitted, the mother could not leave for several hours. It took three weeks before his mother was allowed to visit, since the therapist had stipulated the achievement of self-management of diabetes and of many other specified activities in the hospital. The mother was encouraged to develop her own interests and especially to get a job. One weekend was spent at home, after the relationship had improved. After discharge, a brief period of dependency was resolved by provision of psychological support to both mother and child. Follow-up for the boy revealed good friendships, satisfactory school work, and involvement in activities, while the mother was now employed full time.

Other families showed similar successful courses. Three mothers who were described as functioning in a marginal manner withdrew their children within two weeks of hospitalization. Under separation, they became paranoid, one being convinced that her child was going to be taken away from her.

In the hospital, each child was told that he was too immature, dependent, and unable to take care of himself. Tokens were awarded for completion of chores; the number earned was indicated on a chart in the nurses' station. Tokens were necessary to buy privileges and visits by parents. All tasks were explained to the child as being designed to promote self-care and independence. Psychotherapy often focused on separation, anger, and depression. At the end of each day, the child's appropriate and inappropriate behavior were discussed with him. Parents were also seen in therapy and urged to find more personal satisfaction. Often, some type of job was suggested for the mother.

Khan describes problems encountered in detail. Several sessions were seen as necessary, in order to cope with parental anxiety over separation. Often, mothers began to overprotect one of the other children at home. Many mothers began to realize that they had been neglecting their families and their own interests.

In the hospital, the child usually was quiet and withdrawn at first, then became more hostile and aggressive toward adults, and finally went through a readjustment period. Structure and token rewards were important in handling aggression. Khan characterizes the readjustment period as growing up and giving up infantile gratification. The child needed help in developing new socialization and recreation skills. At home, the child was encouraged to spend time outside the home, join groups, and meet new friends. The parents were warned about the initial regression that occurred on return to home. Khan considers that the hospital situation, unlike camp or other away situations, provides the necessary pressure to reduce the dependency.

COMMENTARY: The technique of separation appears very promising in breaking the destructive effects of child-parent over-dependency. The method described by Khan combines many elements—physical separation, parent counseling, individual therapy, behavioral reinforcement system, and environmental manipulation. One wonders if the same forceful techniques might have been successfully employed by parents and teachers while the child remained at home. Other reports indicate the feasibility of this approach as used by therapists in this book using an eclectic or behavioral approach. Khan clearly states the position that physical separation in a controlled, therapeutic environment (here, a general hospital) is maximally effective. It is a provocative idea to consider a small group living situation, where the parents might live (or periodically live) with the child while all receive intensive, prolonged involvement with experienced staff. Rapid improvement of any of the behavior disorders covered in this book might occur under such conditions.

SOURCE: Khan, A. U. "'Mama's Boy' Syndrome." *American Journal of Psychiatry*, 1971, *128*, 712–717.

Child Psychoanalysis and Dependency on Parents

AUTHORS: Selma Kramer and Calvin F. Settlage

PRECIS: A psychoanalytic approach to helping children become more independent and avoid conflicts with parents

INTRODUCTION: Kramer and Settlage present an extensive review and discussion of child psychoanalysis. Some issues and cases presented here are related to dependency in children. The authors stress that children can be effectively analyzed without treating the parents, even though the child is dependent on the parents. The family's impact on the child's developing, vulnerable personality need not necessarily impair effective treatment. Also, transference neurosis—neurosis developed by the strong emotions felt toward the analyst—can be worked through although the child has an ongoing dependent relationship with the parents. It is pointed out, however, that treatment of the parents may be necessary and is suggested when feasible.

Theoretically, the child's gradual psychological development is formed by the interaction of mother and child. In psychoanalytic terms, object relations progress from need-satisfying objects (normal symbiotic phase) to object constancy and then to actual object relationships. This last stage of mutuality occurs when separation and individuation occur.

ILLUSTRATIVE CASES: An eleven-year-old boy was successfully analyzed, although no attempt was made to change the parents (nor did they change). This happens especially when the conflicts center on one specific phase of development. The conflicts are analyzed and worked through in the treatment of the child. When difficulties arise, the child who truly understands his problems avoids provoking parents or others and avoids becoming enmeshed with the parents' psychological difficulties. The boy in this case was referred because of his constant battles with his father, depression, stammering, and poor school performance. He was physically or verbally abused daily by his father, who had very serious psychological problems. The pattern developed when the boy provoked violent outbursts. Kramer and Settlage considered the relationship to be passive, homoerotic and masochistic. Analysis aided the boy's maturation and enabled him to avoid completely the pathological involvement with his father.

Kramer and Settlage use another case to illustrate that parental involvement is very significant in the analysis of young children. Because dependency on parents is greatest in these years of development, unless the parents accept treatment, the very young child cannot tolerate deviation from the parental ego ideal or, indeed, accept change in himself. A five-and-a-half-year-old girl was referred for her inability to separate from her mother, compulsive and ritualistic behavior, and other problems. At the beginning of treatment, the girl required the mother to sit in the office and give the girl permission to play. After many sessions, she allowed her mother to leave. When positive feelings toward analysis and the analyst arose, the girl again refused to leave her mother. A session was held with the mother to discuss the situation and she was asked to aid in the separation process. The mother said to the child in the office that she was glad the girl liked going to the doctor and that she wanted her to be friends with the doctor. This enabled the girl to explore the loyalty conflict in analysis.

COMMENTARY: Kramer and Settlage present a general discussion of child psychoanalysis. The issues related to dependency are discussed here to give the reader an idea of the psychoanalytic view of dependency in child development. Although the two cases presented are quite different, both may be seen as types of overdependency on parents. Both children are seen as having to become more independent and able to separate (psychologically and/or physically from parents). The analyst requests the girl's mother to state verbal approval and support of the relationship between child and analyst. This indicates the mother's approval of physical separation for analysis and implies approval of psychological separation (independence). In the first case, the boy learned to avoid provoking his disturbed father, which eliminated paternal abuse. It is also possible to directly teach the child methods of avoiding interpersonal conflicts.

SOURCE: Kramer, S., and Settlage, C. F. "On the Concepts and Techniques of Child Analysis." *Journal of the American Academy of Child Psychiatry,* 1962, *1,* 509–535.

Desensitizing a Child to a Tense, Inhibiting Relationship with Her Mother

AUTHOR: James H. Straughan

PRECIS: Parent counseling and counterconditioning after a mother observes her eight-year-old daughter in play therapy

INTRODUCTION: An eight-year-old girl's mother placed demands on her daughter that elicited inhibition, tension, and anxiety. Since the father's relationship with the girl was seen as appropriate, he was not involved in treatment. The child was described as often lying, having no friends at school, and unhappy. She showed overconcern with adult approval, accuracy, and neatness. Straughan made the interpretation that, rather than produce any emotional disturbance, she had learned to inhibit spontaneous emotional expression. A friend had told the mother that the girl was under too much pressure at home. Free choices were not offered to her and she was told to do too many things.

Straughan hypothesized that gradual participation in the playroom by the mother would lead to a more comfortable relationship between mother and child and saw counterconditioning as the cause of changed responses of both parties. The child was encouraged to be free and spontaneous in the playroom. At the beginning, the mother observed through a one-way mirror and discussed events with another therapist. When appropriate, the mother entered the playroom for brief periods and prompted the child's spontaneous play.

TREATMENT: In the playroom, the girl quickly relaxed and could play boisterously. Five play sessions took place. The mother had been told that it would be beneficial if she observed some of the therapist's behavior. Observation had been explained to the girl and she did not appear to be inhibited when being observed. The mother was told how important simple rules and honest explanations were. With the second therapist, the mother entered the playroom when her daughter was playing in a happy, enthusiastic manner. After the first brief period, the mother reported being impressed by the girl's enthusiasm and liveliness. Reasons for the child's spontaneity were discussed with the mother. The mother was made aware that when she was in the room, the behavior of the girl was relatively subdued. During the fourth session, as the mother observed, the girl gradually became more relaxed. The mother was encouraged to play with, and follow the leads of, her daughter. When the mother tried to get her daughter to do better, the child was frustrated and changed her activity. Discussion with the mother focused on building a positive relationship with her daughter.

Generally improved behavior was reported, including better relationships with peers. An eight-month follow-up revealed continued progress. The mother reported that she remembered how much freer the girl was at the clinic than she was at home. She now perceived that she put an inordinate amount of pressure and control on the girl at home and did not express pleasure with any of her daughter's behavior.

Although he recognizes that other variables were also operating, Straughan believes that conditioning was a significant factor in leading the girl to show relaxed and exuberant behavior in the mother's presence. The mother was also influenced by being taught better methods and by imitation learning of the therapist's behavior. Straughan feels that merely inhibiting the mother's inappropriate behavior would be insufficient.

COMMENTARY: The procedure described combines counterconditioning with parent counseling. The parent's presence in the playroom (or office with an older child) is a direct way of changing any pattern that has developed between parent and child. It appears particularly useful when the child is dependent or inhibited in the parent's presence. Having the parent present when the child is happy or successful is a provocative way of changing the child's usual dependent, tense, or unhappy relationship with the parent. Observation of the child's play and discussion with parents are also widely applicable methods. It would be an exciting venture to have parents watch older children talking to therapists, using the procedures presented in Straughan's article. Observation and parent counseling have also been used to teach parents nondirective play with their child. (See B. G. Guerney, *Journal of Consulting Psychology,* 1964, *28,* 304–310.)

SOURCE: Straughan, J. H. "Treatment with Child and Mother in the Playroom." *Behaviour Research and Therapy,* 1964, *2,* 37–41.

Mother as Behavior Therapist for Her Overdependent Child

AUTHORS: Robert G. Wahler, Gary H. Winkel, Robert G. Peterson, and Delmont C. Morrison

PRECIS: Using a signal light as a cue to teach mothers when to extinguish dependent behavior and reinforce independent behavior

INTRODUCTION: The authors of this article note that deviant behavior of children and adults has been modified in the office through reinforcement, punishment, or extinction. If the natural environment is not changed, however, the deviant behavior may be strengthened and the new appropriate behavior weakened. To change the child's natural environment, a change should be made in the parents' behavior, which presumably has reinforced and maintained the deviant behavior. Parents should be trained to replace old contingencies with new contingencies that produce and maintain appropriate behavior. The authors undertook a study to discover how parents maintain deviant behavior and how changes may take place.

METHOD: A playroom with two observation rooms, with six channel recorders each, was used. A signal light in the playroom could be turned on by a switch in either observation room. Parents were interviewed to report their child's problem behavior and their usual reactions when such behavior occurred. The authors describe an analysis of mother and child play, in which behavior incompatible with deviant behavior and possible reinforcers were identified. Observers kept detailed written records. Microswitches were pressed to give cue signals for deviant and incompatible child behavior and for appropriate reactions by the mother.

Behavior Modification. Instructions were given to the mother before and after play sessions. The signal light was used to cue her according to an arranged plan. Later, the light was used to reinforce the mother's appropriate behavior. She was trained to use extinction of deviant behavior and reinforcement of the incompatible appropriate behavior. She was to respond only when the light was turned on (following incompatible behavior). In one difficult case, a punishment technique was also used.

CASE STUDY: A four-year-old boy was referred because of his very dependent behavior. In school, he hit peers or the teacher when they were not attentive to him. He displayed aggressive behavior in showing dependency on others for support or direction. At home he was not aggressive but followed his mother around, asking questions and often requesting help. She responded to this behavior and appeared to interrupt lone or peer play because she was afraid he would get into trouble and she felt better when he was within her view.

In the formal analysis, the boy's deviant actions were defined as dependent behavior, including questions and nonverbal requests for help. Independent behavior (incompatible with dependency) was defined as any lone behavior not accompanied by comments to his mother. The mother was told to ignore dependency behavior and be approving of independent behavior. Significantly improved behavior occurred as a result of such contingencies. When the mother was told to resume her old behavior for a period of time, the boy's behavior reverted to his previous pattern.

COMMENTARY: Training parents as behavior therapists would logically have applicability to the wide range of problems that behavior therapists work with. This article also reports that two other mothers successfully modified their children's behavior. A six-year-old boy was referred because he forced his parents to comply with his wishes (commanding, as opposed to cooperative, behavior). A four-year-old boy was seen for extreme stubbornness with his mother (oppositional, as opposed to cooperative, behavior). Training parents contrasts with any therapeutic approach where only the child is seen. One might speculate that home visits might be even more effective, as therapists would participate in the situations in which problematic behavior occurred.

SOURCE: Wahler, R. G., Winkel, G. H., Peterson, R. G., and Morrison, D. C. "Mothers as Behavior Therapists for Their Own Children." *Behavior Research and Therapy*, 1965, *3*, 113–124.

Additional Readings

Fisher, L., and Warren, R. C. "The Concept of Role Assignment in Family Therapy." *International Journal of Group Psychotherapy,* 1972, *22,* 60–76.

Fisher and Warren explain an approach in which the family therapist is assigned a role that represents a family conflict or "role failure." This role reflects the family's faulty communications regarding role expectations. The authors describe in detail the family dynamics affecting a thirteen-year-old girl with somatic complaints. She often acted in a helpless, needful, and demanding manner. The cotherapists were placed in the role of good, strong, understanding parents. The therapists accepted the role and used it to understand the conflicts and to clearly present the significant problems of the family (inability to trust, fear of closeness, and feelings of helplessness) to them.

Gottsegen, M. G., and Grasso, M. "Group Treatment of the Mother-Daughter Relationship." *International Journal of Group Psychotherapy,* 1973, *23,* 69–81.

Four pairs of mothers and their daughters (ages thirteen to fourteen) were seen in group therapy for eight months, once a week. Two pairs clung to each other, the girls being overly dependent, shy, and fearful. The other two pairs battled, the girls being disobedient and verbally abusive. Initial resistance was followed by formation of dyadic pairing and then by appropriate functioning of members as a cohesive group. The mothers' own fears and sexual concerns were seen as directly related to their daughters' difficulties. Three of the pairs benefited significantly. One pair (abusive girl) gained little and dropped out after dramatically expressing their problems. One conclusion was that many daughters find becoming independent impossible unless their mothers allow them to do so. A group experience allows for the treatment of the problematic patterns. Other pairs gain courage for growth as they see one pair face their conflicts.

Author Index

485

Subject Index

Achievement Place, 265
Actometer, 339
Adaptive behavior, 322
Aggressive behavior, 263–266, 291–299; and behavior contracting, 296; and fantasy therapy, 294; and group therapy, 296; ignoring of, 410; and peer therapy groups, 415; and play therapy, 292; and psychoanalytic interpretation, 292; and sexual impulses, 292; tolerance of, 279. *See also* Fighting
Agoraphobia, 44
Amenorrhea, 158
Amitriptyline, 184
Amobarbital, 120
Amphetamine, 200, 326, 389
Anal fixation, 107
Anger: and death of sibling, 74; and humor, 282; inhibition of ex-

pression of, 38, 39; and relaxation, 282, 283; and school phobia, 96; and self-instruction, 282; and shyness, 81
Animals, 83, 84, 120. *See also* Dogs
Anorexia, 157–176; behavioral therapy for, 170–173; and burned children, 135; family therapy for, 166–169; and hyperactive children treated with drugs, 346; and operant conditioning, 174, 175; outpatient treatment of, 158–160; and rewards, 171, 174, 175; and vomiting, 161, 162
Anxiety dreams. *See* Nightmares
Anxiety-inhibiting responses, 16
Applied behavior analysis, 175, 401
Art therapy, 68–70; and hair pulling, 248, 249; and hysterical blindness, 51; and obscene lan-